NORTHEAST HOME LANDSCAPING

Fourth Edition

Other titles available in the *Home Landscaping* series:

CALIFORNIA

MID-ATLANTIC

MIDWEST
including South-Central Canada

NORTHWEST
including Western British Columbia

SOUTHEAST

SOUTHERN COASTAL

TEXAS

WESTERN

NORTHEAST HOME LANDSCAPING

54 Landscape Designs with 200+ Plants & Flowers for Your Region

Fourth Edition

Roger Holmes and Rita Buchanan

Technical Editor for Current Edition: Ruth Rogers Clausen

CREATIVE
HOMEOWNER®

FOURTH EDITION

MANAGING EDITOR Gretchen Bacon
EDITOR Christa Oestreich
TECHNICAL EDITOR Ruth Rogers Clausen
DESIGNER Freire Disseny*Comunicació

Northeast Home Landscaping, 4th Edition
ISBN 978-1-58011-587-2

Library of Congress Control Number: 2023904607

We are always looking for talented authors. To submit an idea, please send a brief inquiry to acquisitions@foxchapelpublishing.com.

Printed in China

Current Printing (last digit)
10 9 8 7 6 5 4 3 2 1

Creative Homeowner®, *www.creativehomeowner.com*, is an imprint of New Design Originals Corporation and distributed exclusively in North America by Fox Chapel Publishing Company, Inc., 800-457-9112, 903 Square Street, Mount Joy, PA 17552, and in the United Kingdom by Grantham Book Service, Trent Road, Grantham, Lincolnshire, NG31 7XQ.

About the Authors

Roger Holmes is the founding editor of *Fine Gardening* magazine. He co-edited the monumental Taylor's *Master Guide to Gardening* and other highly regarded gardening books, and produced the landscaping series of which this book is part. He also co-wrote Creative Homeowner's *Creating Good Gardens*.

Rita Buchanan is a lifelong gardener with degrees in botany and an encyclopedic knowledge of plants. She worked with Roger Holmes to edit *Fine Gardening* magazine and co-edit several books, including Taylor's *Master Guide to Gardening*. She is the author of numerous award-winning books and is a contributor to many gardening magazines.

About the Technical Editor

Ruth Rogers Clausen is the co-author of *50 Beautiful Deer-Resistant Plants*, and other highly regarded gardening books. She was horticulture editor for *Country Living Garden* magazine and long-time contributor to *Country Gardens*. Ruth lectures widely to garden societies and clubs. In 2017, she was awarded the Garden Media Award by the Perennial Plant Association.

Safety First

Though all concepts and methods in this book have been reviewed for safety, it is not possible to overstate the importance of using the safest working methods possible. What follows are reminders—do's and don'ts for yard work and landscaping. They are not substitutes for your own common sense.

- *Always* use caution, care, and good judgment when following the procedures described in this book.
- *Always* determine locations of underground utility lines before you dig, and then avoid them by a safe distance. Buried lines may be for gas, electricity, communications, or water. Start research by contacting your local building officials. Also contact local utility companies; they will often send a representative free of charge to help you map their lines. In addition, there are private utility locator firms that may be listed in your Yellow Pages. Note: previous owners may have installed underground drainage, sprinkler, and lighting lines without mapping them.
- *Always* read and heed the manufacturer's instructions for using a tool, especially the warnings.
- *Always* ensure that the electrical setup is safe; be sure that no circuit is overloaded and that all power tools and electrical outlets are properly grounded and protected by a ground-fault circuit interrupter (GFCI). Do not use power tools in wet locations.
- *Always* wear eye protection when using chemicals, sawing wood, pruning trees and shrubs, using power tools, and striking metal onto metal or concrete.
- *Always* read labels on chemicals, solvents, and other products; provide ventilation; heed warnings.
- *Always* wear heavy rubber gloves rated for chemicals, not mere household rubber gloves, when handling toxins.
- *Always* wear appropriate gloves in situations in which your hands could be injured by rough surfaces, sharp edges, thorns, or poisonous plants.
- *Always* wear a disposable face mask or a special filtering respirator when creating sawdust or working with toxic gardening substances.
- *Always* keep your hands and other body parts away from the business ends of blades, cutters, and bits.
- *Always* obtain approval from local building officials before undertaking construction of permanent structures.
- *Never* work with power tools when you are tired or under the influence of alcohol or drugs.
- *Never* carry sharp or pointed tools, such as knives or saws, in your pockets. If you carry such tools, use special-purpose tool scabbards.

The Landscape Designers

Carter Lee Clapsadle is a horticulturist with the College of St. Catherine, St Paul, MN. Trained at the University of Minnesota, he maintains 110 acres of college land, including managing the greenhouse and designing garden displays. His design appears on pp. 34–35.

Walter Cudnohufsky is a Harvard School of Design graduate and the founding director of Conway School of Landscape Design in MA. He is also the owner of Walter Cudnohufsky Associates, Inc. in Ashfield, MA. His firm were first place winners in "Sustainable, Equitable, SMART: An Ideas Competition for the Pioneer Valley" in 2010. His designs appear on pp. 52–55, 106–109, and 114–117.

Sydney Eddison has transformed her two-acre property in Newtown, CT, into one of the region's finest gardens. She is the author of *Gardening for a Lifetime: How to Garden Wiser as You Grow Older, The Gardener's Palette, Gardens to Go, The Self-Taught Gardener, A Patchwork Garden, The Unsung Season: Gardens and Gardeners in Winter,* and *A Passion for Daylilies: The Flowers and the People*. Her designs appear on pp. 30–33, 40–43, 102–105, and 110–113.

Larry Giblock helped to form the Native Plant Society of Ohio. In 1988 the Cleveland Botanical Garden hired him to develop their Wildflower Garden, and in 1993 they added care of the Japanese Garden to his responsibilities. His design appears on pp. 60–61.

Jan Johnsen operates a landscape design/build firm in Westchester County, NY. Trained as a landscape architect with a master's degree in planning, Ms. Johnsen has worked in landscape and planning offices around the world. She is the author of *Floratopia: 110 Flower Garden Ideas for Your Yard, Patio, or Balcony* and *Gardentopia: Design Basics for Creating Beautiful Outdoor Spaces*. Her designs appear on pp. 26–29, 62–65, 80–83, 88–91, and 120–123.

Jan Little is the manager of horticultural education at the Morton Arboretum in Lisle, IL. A registered landscape architect, she has worked on a wide range of projects and has received several landscape design awards. Her designs appear on pp. 70–73, 92–93, and 118–119.

Cathy Plumer of Monroe, CT, has worked on a wide range of landscape projects. She has taught continuing education courses in residential landscape design for homeowners. Her designs appear on pp. 20–23, 56–59, and 74–77.

Michael Schroeder is a University of Minnesota graduate and has practiced landscape architecture and urban design in the region since 1985. He currently works as the Assistant Superintendent for Planning for the Minneapolis Park and Recreation Board. He has received several awards and recognitions for his professional work. His designs appear on pp. 24–25 and 78–79.

Sara Jane von Trapp lives in New York City and writes extensively on residential landscape problem solving. Her books include *The Landscape Makeover Book: How to Bring New Life to An Old Yard, Landscape Doctor,* and *Landscaping from the Ground Up*. Her designs appear on pp. 36–39, 44–47, 48–51, 66–69, 84–87, 94–97, 98–101, and 124–127.

Contents

About This Book

Of all the home-improvement projects homeowners tackle, few offer greater rewards than landscaping. Paths, patios, fences, arbors, and most of all, plantings can enhance home life in countless ways, large and small, functional and pleasurable, every day of the year. At the main entrance, an attractive brick walkway flanked by eye-catching shrubs and perennials provides a cheerful send-off in the morning and welcomes you home from work in the evening. A carefully placed grouping of small trees, shrubs, and fence panels creates privacy on the patio or screens a nearby eyesore from view. An island bed showcases your favorite plants, while dividing the backyard into areas for several different activities.

Unlike some other home improvements, the rewards of landscaping can be as much in the activity as in the result. Planting and caring for lovely shrubs, perennials, and other plants can afford years of enjoyment. And for those who like to build things, outdoor construction projects can be especially satisfying.

While the installation and maintenance of plants and outdoor structures are within the means and abilities of most people, few of us are as comfortable determining exactly which plants or structures to use and how best to combine them. It's one thing to decide to dress up the front entrance or patio, another to come up with a design for doing so.

That's where this book comes in. Here, in the Portfolio of designs, you'll find 54 designs for common home-landscaping situations, created by landscape professionals who live and work in the Northeast. Drawing on years of experience, these designers balance functional requirements and aesthetic possibilities, choosing the right plant or structure for the task, confident of its proven performance in similar situations.

Complementing the Portfolio of designs is the second section, Plant Profiles, which gives information on all the plants used in the book. The book's third section, the Guide to Installation, will help you install and maintain the plants and structures called for in the designs. The discussions that follow take a closer look at each section; we've also printed representative pages of the sections on pp. 9 and 10 and pointed out their features.

Portfolio of Designs

This section is the heart of the book, providing examples of landscaping situations and solutions that are at once inspiring and accessible. Some are simple, others more complex, but each one can be installed in a few weekends by homeowners with no special training or experience.

For most situations, we present two designs, the second a variation of the first. As the sample pages on the facing page show, the first design is displayed on a two-page spread. A perspective illustration (called a "rendering") depicts what the design will look like several years after installation, when the perennials and many of the shrubs have reached mature size. (For more on how plantings change as they age, see "As Your Landscape Grows," pp. 16–17.) The rendering also shows the planting as it will appear at a particular time of year. A site plan indicates the positions of the plants and structures on a scaled grid. Text introduces the situation and the design and describes the plants and projects used.

The second design, presented on the second two-page spread, addresses the same situation as the first but differs in one or more important aspects. It might show a planting suited for a shady rather than a sunny site, or it might incorporate different structures or kinds of plants to create a different look. As with the first design, we present a rendering, site plan, and written information, but in briefer form. The second spread also includes photographs of a selection of the plants featured in the two designs. The photos showcase noteworthy qualities—lovely flowers, handsome foliage, or striking forms—that these plants contribute to the designs.

Installed exactly as shown here, the designs will provide years of enjoyment. But individual needs and properties will differ, and we encourage you to alter the designs to suit your site and desires. Many types of alterations are easy to make. You can add or remove plants and adjust the sizes of paths, patios, and arbors to accommodate larger or smaller sites. You can rearrange groupings and substitute favorite plants to suit your taste. Or you can integrate the design with your existing landscaping. If you are uncertain about how to solve specific problems or about the effects of changes you'd like to make, consult with staff at a local nursery or with a landscape designer in your area.

PORTFOLIO OF DESIGNS

FIRST DESIGN OPTION

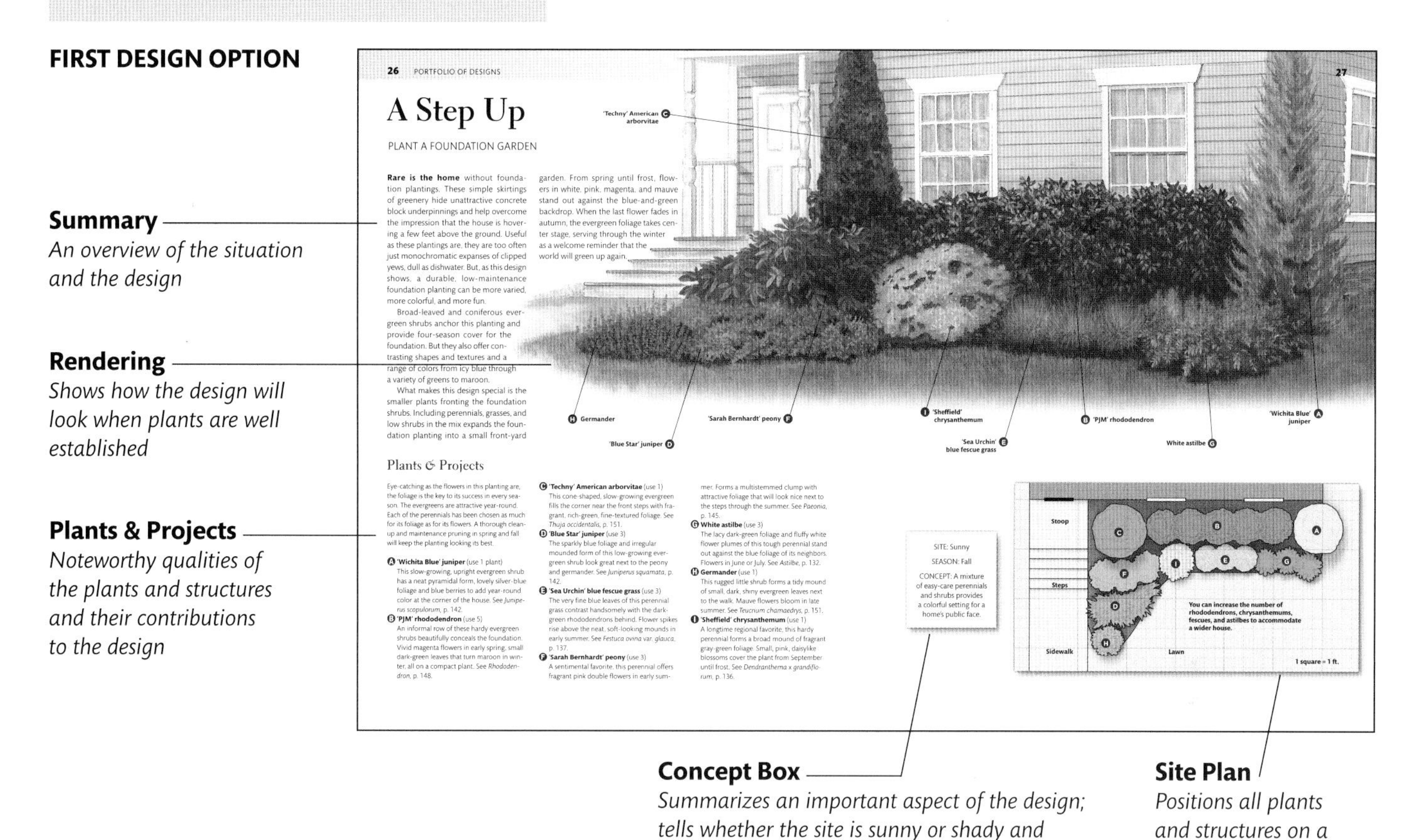
26 PORTFOLIO OF DESIGNS

A Step Up

PLANT A FOUNDATION GARDEN

Rare is the home without foundation plantings. These simple skirtings of greenery hide unattractive concrete block underpinnings and help overcome the impression that the house is hovering a few feet above the ground. Useful as these plantings are, they are too often just monochromatic expanses of clipped yews, dull as dishwater. But, as this design shows, a durable, low-maintenance foundation planting can be more varied, more colorful, and more fun.

Broad-leaved and coniferous evergreen shrubs anchor this planting and provide four-season cover for the foundation. But they also offer contrasting shapes and textures and a range of colors from icy blue through a variety of greens to maroon.

What makes this design special is the smaller plants fronting the foundation shrubs. Including perennials, grasses, and low shrubs in the mix expands the foundation planting into a small front-yard garden. From spring until frost, flowers in white, pink, magenta, and mauve stand out against the blue-and-green backdrop. When the last flower fades in autumn, the evergreen foliage takes center stage, serving through the winter as a welcome reminder that the world will green up again.

Summary
An overview of the situation and the design

Rendering
Shows how the design will look when plants are well established

Plants & Projects
Noteworthy qualities of the plants and structures and their contributions to the design

Concept Box
Summarizes an important aspect of the design; tells whether the site is sunny or shady and what season is depicted in the rendering

Site Plan
Positions all plants and structures on a scaled grid

SECOND DESIGN OPTION

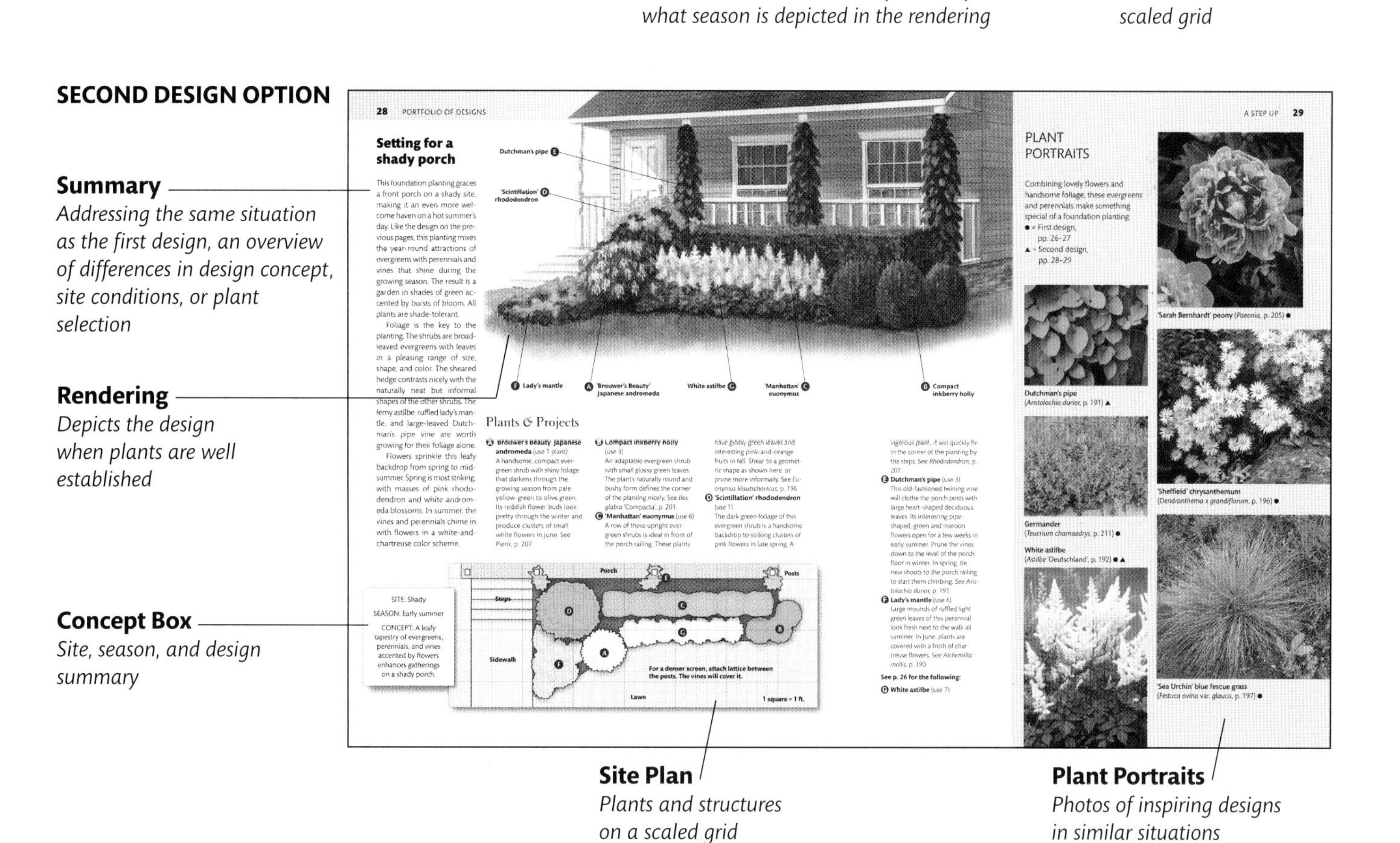
28 PORTFOLIO OF DESIGNS

Setting for a shady porch

This foundation planting graces a front porch on a shady site, making it an even more welcome haven on a hot summer's day. Like the design on the previous pages, this planting mixes the year-round attractions of evergreens with perennials and vines that shine during the growing season. The result is a garden in shades of green accented by bursts of bloom. All plants are shade-tolerant.

Foliage is the key to the planting. The shrubs are broad-leaved evergreens with leaves in a pleasing range of size, shape, and color. The sheared hedge contrasts nicely with the naturally neat but informal shapes of the other shrubs. The ferny astilbe, ruffled lady's mantle, and large-leaved Dutchman's pipe vine are worth growing for their foliage alone.

Flowers sprinkle this leafy backdrop from spring to midsummer. Spring is most striking, with masses of pink rhododendron and white andromeda blossoms. In summer, the vines and perennials chime in with flowers in a white-and-chartreuse color scheme.

Summary
Addressing the same situation as the first design, an overview of differences in design concept, site conditions, or plant selection

Rendering
Depicts the design when plants are well established

Concept Box
Site, season, and design summary

Site Plan
Plants and structures on a scaled grid

Plant Portraits
Photos of inspiring designs in similar situations

PLANT PROFILES

Choices
Selections here help you choose from the many varieties of certain popular plants.

Plant Portraits
Photos of selected plants

Detailed Plant Information
Descriptions of each plant's noteworthy qualities and requirements for planting and care

Bergenia cordifolia 'Bressingham White'

Astilbe chinensis var. *pumila*

Asclepias tuberosa
Butterfly weed. A perennial wildflower with flat heads of bright orange flowers in early summer and attractive pods in fall. Forms a clump up to 2 ft. tall and wide, with more stems each year. Needs full sun. Carefree. Pages: 90, **91**.

'Purple Dome' New England aster. A compact form of the popular perennial wildflower, this aster forms a dense mound of dark green foliage all summer, then bears thousands of dark purple flowers for a month or so in early fall. Grows about 2 ft. tall and wide. Needs full sun and good air circulation because it is subject to mildew in shady or too-sheltered sites. Grows best in rich, moist soil but adapts to garden soil. Divide every year or two in early spring. Pages: 38, 53, **55**, 74.

Astilbe
Astilbe. Among the best perennials for shady or partly shady sites, astilbes have fluffy plumes of tiny flowers in June or July and healthy, glossy, compound leaves all season. There are many kinds of hybrid astilbes, sold by cultivar name, that grow from 18 to 42 in. tall and have white, pale pink, rose, or red flowers. Choose whatever size and color you prefer (pp. 26, 29, **29**, 73). A related plant, the dwarf Chinese astilbe, *A. chinensis* var. *pumila* (pp. 100, 123, **124**), grows only 1 ft. tall and has mauve flowers in August. All astilbes prefer rich, moist, well-drained soil and need shade from midday sun. Cut foliage to the ground in late fall or early spring. Divide every three to five years in spring or late summer, using a sharp spade, ax, or old pruning saw to cut the tough woody rootstock into a few large chunks.

Aurinia saxatilis
Basket-of-gold. One of the first perennials to bloom in spring, it needs full sun and well-drained soil. Cut stems back halfway after it blooms and again in summer if the leaves get diseased during a spell of hot, humid weather. This is a fast-growing but short-lived plant, so buy replacements every few years. Grows about 6 to 8 in. tall, spreads 2 to 3 ft. wide. Pages: 25, 61.

Baptisia australis
False indigo. A perennial prairie wildflower that's unusually carefree and long-lived. Forms a mushroom-shaped mound of blue-green foliage, topped in early summer with showy spikes of indigo blue flowers, followed by clusters of decorative seedpods that last through the fall. Adapts to full sun or partial shade. Grows about 3 ft. tall and 3 to 6 ft. wide. Pages: 90, 119, **121**.

***Berberis thunbergii* 'Crimson Pygmy'**
'Crimson Pygmy' Japanese barberry. A deciduous shrub that grows naturally into a broad, low, cushionlike mound. Valued for its shape and its foliage, which is dark maroon all summer, turning crimson in fall. Needs full sun and well-drained soil. Grows about 2 ft. tall, spreads 3 to 5 ft. wide. Pages: 31, 31, **31**, 77, 80.

***Bergenia cordifolia* 'Bressingham White'**
'Bressingham White' bergenia. A perennial with unusually large, thick, glossy leaves that are fresh green in summer and turn garnet in winter. Clusters of white flowers are held above the foliage for a few weeks in late spring. Forms a clump about 1 ft. tall and 2 ft. wide. Prefers partial shade and moist soil but tolerates sun and garden soil. Divide every few years in spring or fall. Pages: 51, 77, 82, 100, 103.

Betula nigra
River birch. A deciduous tree with very attractive beige, tan, or coppery bark that peels off in curly

Recommended bulbs

***Colchicum autumnale*, Meadow saffron**
A fall-blooming bulb with rosy pink or lilac flowers like giant crocuses on 6-in. stalks in October. Plant bulbs 4 in. ... Thick straplike leaves develop in early spring and die down in July. Page: 119.

***Crocus*, Crocus**
Cup-shaped flowers on 4-in. stalks in March. Available in white, yellow, lilac, and purple. Plant bulbs 4 in. deep, 4 in. apart. Forms large clumps after a few years. Slender grassy leaves die down in June. Page: 41, 119.

***Endymion hispanica*, Spanish bluebell**
Bell-shaped blue flowers dangle from 18-in. stalks in April. Plant bulbs 5 in. deep, 5 in. apart. Forms large clumps after a few years and also spreads by seed. Flat grassy leaves die down in June, or you can pull them out earlier. Pages: 37, **39**.

***Galanthus nivalis*, Snowdrop**
Bright white flowers droop from 6-in. stems in March or April. Plant 3 in. deep, 3in. apart. Page: 41.

***Muscari armeniacum*, Grape hyacinth**
Grapelike clusters of sweet-scented purple flowers on 6-in. stalks last for several weeks in April and May. Plant bulbs 3 ... until spring, and dies down in June. Page: 37, 41.

***Narcissus*, Daffodils, jonquils, and narcissus**
Bright yellow, white, or bicolor flowers, often fragrant, on stalks 6 to 18 in. tall. Different kinds bloom in sequence from early February through early May. Leaves die down in July. Plant bulbs 4 to 6 in. deep, 4 to 6 in. apart, depending on their size. Very reliable, carefree, and long-lived. Use dwarf daffodils such as 'Baby Moon', 'February Gold', and 'Tête 'a Tête' close to the house, because after they bloom, their short leaves are less conspicuous. Use larger daffodils such as 'King Alfred' or 'Mt. Hood' for plantings viewed from a distance. Pages: 37, **39**, 41.

***Tulipa*, Tulip**
Cup- or bell-shaped flowers on short or tall stalks in April or May. Plant the bulbs 3 to 4 in. deep, 3 to 4 in. apart. Page: 41.

strips. The leaves are an attractive glossy green all summer and turn tan or gold in fall. Grows 1 to 2 ft. a year, reaching 60 ft. tall and almost that wide when mature. Needs full sun, prefers moist soil but adapts to garden soil. Subject to various diseases and insects, but usually the damage is minor. Train young trees as described on p. 181 to eliminate narrow crotches, which break apart in ice storms. Pages: 88, 91, **91**.

***Betula platyphylla* 'White Spire'**
'White Spire' birch. A deciduous tree with bright white bark and fresh green leaves that turn yellow in fall. Grows about 40 ft. tall, 25 ft. wide, with a narrow profile. Needs full sun and well-drained garden soil. Train young trees to eliminate narrow crotches (p. 181), which often break apart in ice storms. Pages: 22, 44, **46**.

***Boltonia asteroides* 'Snowbank'**
'Snowbank' boltonia. A perennial wildflower that blooms for many weeks in fall, bearing thousands of small white asterlike blossoms. Forms an erect clump of many stems. Foliage is pale green and stays healthy all summer. Takes full or partial sun, garden or moist soil. Grows 3 to 4 ft. tall, 2 to 4 ft. wide. Cut stems back partway in late spring to reduce height of clump, if desired. Pages: 119, **121**.

Bulbs
The bulbs recommended in this book are all perennials that come up year after year and bloom in late winter, spring, or early summer. After they flower, their leaves keep growing and stay growing until sometime in summer, when they gradually turn yellow and die down to the ground. To get started, you must buy bulbs from a garden center or catalog sometime in the fall. Plant them promptly in a sunny or partly sunny bed with well-prepared soil, burying them two to three times as deep as the bulb is high. In subsequent years, all you have to do is pick off the faded flowers in spring and remove (or ignore, if you choose) the old leaves after they turn brown in summer. For more information on bulbs, see box above.

GUIDE TO INSTALLATION

Sidebars
Detailed information on special topics, set within ruled boxes

Step-by-Step
Process illustrations; steps keyed by number to discussion in the main text

Laying the surface
Whether you're laying a loose or hard material, take time to plan your work. Provide access for delivery trucks, and have material deposited as close to the worksite as possible.

Loose materials
Install water-permeable landscape fabric over the gravel base to prevent gravel from mixing with the surface material. Spread bark or wood chips 2 to 4 in. deep. For a pine-needle surface, spread 2 in. of needles on top of several inches of bark or chips. Spread loose pea gravel about 2 in. deep. For a harder, more uniform surface, add ½ in. of fine crushed stone on top of the gravel. You can let traffic compact crushed-rock surfaces, or compact them by hand or with a machine.

Bricks and precast pavers
Take time to figure out the pattern and spacing of the bricks or pavers by laying them out on the lawn or driveway, rather than disturbing your carefully prepared sand base. When you're satisfied, begin in a corner, laying the bricks or pavers gently on the sand so the base remains even ❶. Lay full bricks first; then cut bricks to fit as needed along the edges of the patio. To produce uniform joints, space bricks with a piece of wood cut to the joint width. You can also maintain alignment with either a straightedge or a string stretched across the path between nails or stakes. Move the string along the path as you proceed with the work.

As you complete a row or section, bed the bricks or pavers into the sand base with several firm raps of a rubber mallet or a hammer on a scrap 2x4. Check with a level or straightedge to make sure the surface is even ❷. (You'll have to do this by feel or eye across the width of a crowned path.) Lift low bricks or pavers carefully and fill beneath them with sand; then reset them. Don't stand on the walk until you've filled the joints.

When you've finished a section, sweep fine, dry mason's sand into the joints, working across the surface of the path in all directions ❸. Wet thoroughly with a fine spray and let dry; then sweep in more sand if necessary. If you want a "living" walk, sweep a loam-sand mixture into the joints and plant small, tough, ground-hugging plants, such as thyme, in them.

Rare is the brick walk that can be laid without cutting something to fit. To cut brick, mark the line of the cut with a dark pencil all around the brick. With the brick resting firmly on sand or soil, score the entire line by rapping a wide mason's chisel called a "brickset" with a heavy wooden mallet or a soft-headed steel hammer as shown on the facing page. Place the brickset in the scored line across one face and give it a sharp blow with the hammer to cut the brick.

If you have a lot of bricks to cut, or if you want greater accuracy, consider renting a masonry saw. Whether you work by hand or machine, always wear safety glasses.

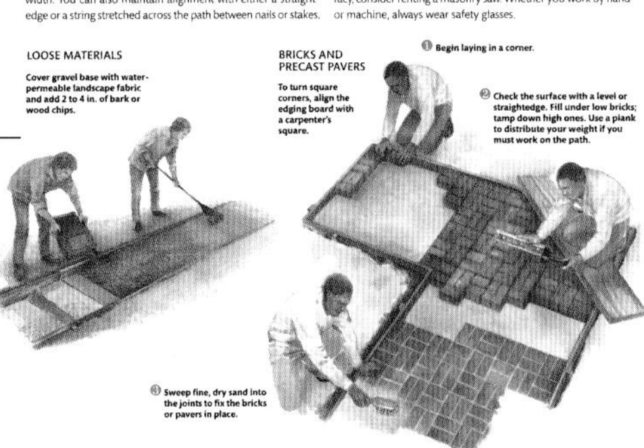

Steppingstones

A steppingstone walk set in turf creates a charming effect and is very simple to lay. You can use cut or irregular flagstones or fieldstone, which is irregular in thickness as well as in outline. Arrange the stones on the turf; then set them one by one. Cut into the turf around the stone with a sharp flat shovel or trowel, and remove the stone; then dig out the sod with the shovel. Placing stones at or below grade will keep them away from mower blades. Fill low spots beneath the stone with earth or sand so the stone doesn't move when stepped on.

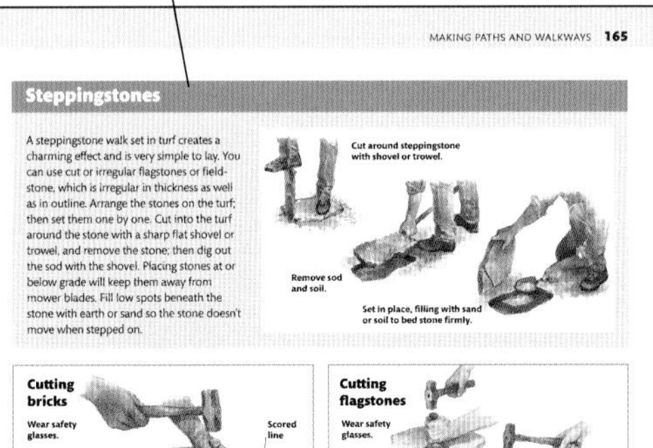

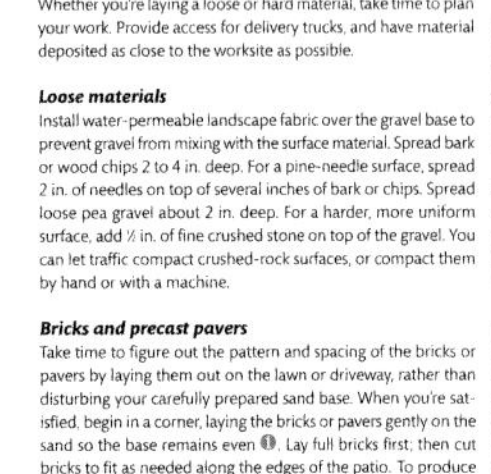

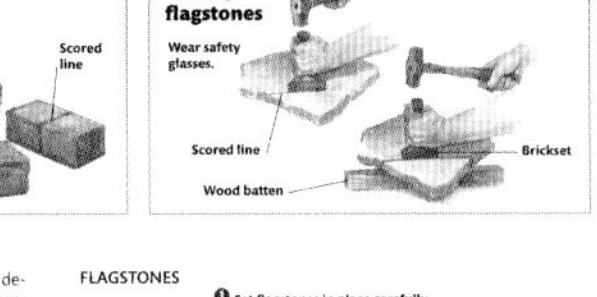

Flagstones
Install cut stones of uniform thickness as described for bricks and pavers. Working out patterns beforehand is particularly important—stones are too heavy to move around more than necessary. To produce a level surface with cut or irregular stones of varying thickness, you'll need to add or remove sand for each stone. Set the stone carefully on sand; then move it back and forth to work it into place ❶. Lay a level or straightedge over three or four stones to check the surface's evenness ❷. When a section is complete, fill the joints with sand or with sand and loam as described for bricks and pavers.

You can cut flagstone with a technique similar to that used for bricks. Score the line of the cut on the top surface with a brickset and hammer. Prop the stone on a piece of scrap wood, positioning the line of cut slightly beyond the edge of the wood. Securing the bottom edge of the stone with your foot, place the brickset on the scored line and strike sharply to make the cut.

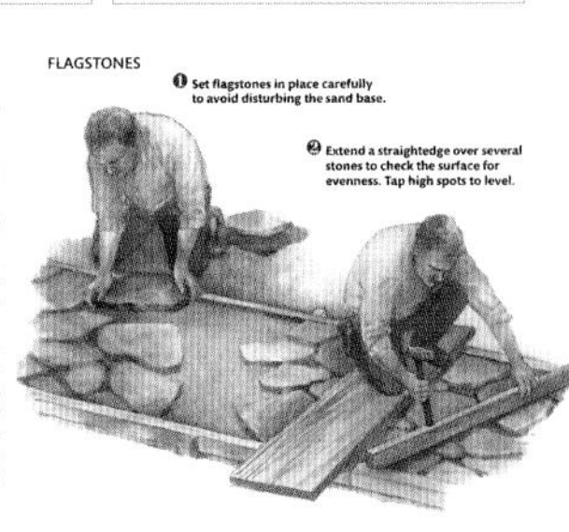

Plant Profiles

The second section of the book includes a description of each of the plants featured in the Portfolio. These profiles outline the plants' basic preferences for environmental conditions—such as soil, moisture, and sun or shade—and provide advice about planting and ongoing care.

Working with the book's landscape designers, we selected plants carefully, following a few simple guidelines. Every plant should be a proven performer in the region; once established, it should thrive without pampering. All plants should be available from a major local nursery or garden center. If they're not in stock, they could be ordered, or you could ask the nursery staff to recommend suitable substitutes for them.

In the Portfolio section, you'll note that plants are referred to by their common name but are cross-referenced to the Plant Profiles section by their Latinized scientific name. While common names are familiar to many people, they can be confusing. Distinctly different plants can share the same common name, or one plant can have several different common names. Scientific names, therefore, ensure greatest accuracy and are more appropriate for a reference section such as this. Although you can confidently purchase most of the plants in this book from local nurseries using the common name, knowing the scientific name allows you to ensure that the plant you're ordering is the same one shown in our design.

Guide to Installation

In this section you'll find detailed instructions and illustrations covering all the techniques you'll need to install any design from start to finish. Here we explain how to think your way through a landscaping project and anticipate the various steps. Then you'll learn how to do each part of the job: readying the site; laying out the design; choosing materials; addressing basic irrigation needs; building paths, trellises, or other structures; preparing the soil for planting; buying the recommended plants and putting them in place; and caring for the plants to keep them healthy and attractive year after year.

We've taken care to make installation of built elements simple and straightforward. The paths, trellises, and arbors all use basic, readily available materials, and they can be assembled by people who have no special skills or tools beyond those commonly used for home maintenance. The designs can easily be adapted to meet specific needs or to fit in with the style of your house or other landscaping features.

Installing different designs requires different techniques. You can find the techniques that you need by following the cross-references in the Portfolio to pages in the Guide to Installation or by skimming the Guide. You'll find that many basic techniques are reused from one project to the next. You might want to start with one of the smaller, simpler designs. Gradually you'll develop the skills and confidence to do any project you choose.

Most of the designs in this book can be installed in several weekends; some will take a little longer. Digging planting beds and erecting fences and arbors can be strenuous work. If you lack the energy for such tasks, consider hiring a neighborhood teenager to help out; local landscaping services can provide more comprehensive help.

NORTHEAST HARDINESS ZONES

This map is based on one developed by the U.S. Department of Agriculture. It divides the region into "hardiness zones" based on minimum winter temperatures. While most of the plants in this book will survive the lowest temperatures in the region, a few may not. These few are noted in the Plant Profiles descriptions, where we have usually suggested alternatives. When you buy plants, most will have "hardiness" designations, which correspond to a USDA hardiness zone on the map. A Zone 5 plant, for example, can be expected to survive winter temperatures as low as –20°F, and it can be used with confidence in Zones 5 and 6 but not in the colder Zone 4. It is useful to know your zone and the zone designation of plants you wish to add to those in this book.

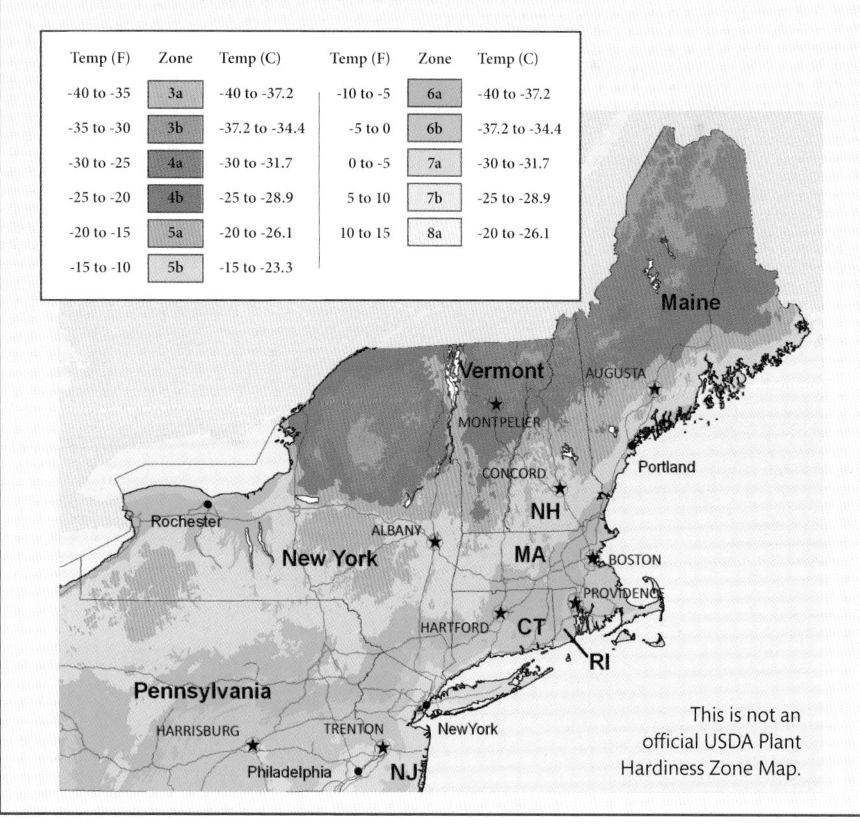

Temp (F)	Zone	Temp (C)	Temp (F)	Zone	Temp (C)
-40 to -35	3a	-40 to -37.2	-10 to -5	6a	-40 to -37.2
-35 to -30	3b	-37.2 to -34.4	-5 to 0	6b	-37.2 to -34.4
-30 to -25	4a	-30 to -31.7	0 to -5	7a	-30 to -31.7
-25 to -20	4b	-25 to -28.9	5 to 10	7b	-25 to -28.9
-20 to -15	5a	-20 to -26.1	10 to 15	8a	-20 to -26.1
-15 to -10	5b	-15 to -23.3			

This is not an official USDA Plant Hardiness Zone Map.

Seasons in Your Landscape

One of the rewards of landscaping is watching how plants change through the seasons. During the dark winter months, you look forward to the bright, fresh flowers of spring. Then the lush green foliage of summer is transformed into the blazing colors of fall. Perennials that rest underground (go dormant) in winter can grow head-high by midsummer, and hence a flower bed that looks flat and bare in December becomes a jungle in July.

To illustrate typical seasonal changes, we've chosen one of the designs from this book and shown here how it would look in spring, summer, fall, and winter. (See p. 98.) As you can see, this planting looks quite different from one season to the next, but it always remains interesting. Try to remember this example of transformation as you look at the other designs in this book. There we show how the planting will appear in one season and indicate which plants will stand out at other times.

The task of tending a landscape also changes with the seasons. Below we've noted the most important seasonal jobs in the annual work cycle.

Spring

Daffodils, forsythia, and other early-spring flowers start blooming in April in the Northeast. That's the time to do a thorough garden cleanup. Remove last year's perennial flower stalks and tattered foliage, prune late-blooming shrubs and trees, renew the mulch, and neaten the edges between lawn and beds. By the end of April, it's time to start mowing the lawn.

Many trees and shrubs, such as the Amur maple and 'Carol Mackie' daphne shown here, bloom in May. Others, such as 'Midnight Wine,' have less showy flowers, but their new leaves are conspicuously bright-colored. Meanwhile, perennials are also sending up clumps of fresh foliage. Bloody cranesbill, shown here, starts blooming in late spring, along with peonies, irises, and other popular perennials.

Summer

In summer, flowering perennials such as blazing star, false sunflower, lavender, daylily, and lady's mantle shown here add spots of color to the otherwise green landscape. To coax as many flowers as possible from these plants and to keep the garden tidy, cut or shear off spent blossoms as they fade. Summer weather is typically humid throughout the Northeast region, but droughts are not uncommon. Water new plantings at least once a week during dry spells, and water older plants, too, if the soil gets so dry that they wilt. Pull any weeds that sprout up through the mulch. This is easiest when the soil is moist from rain or watering.

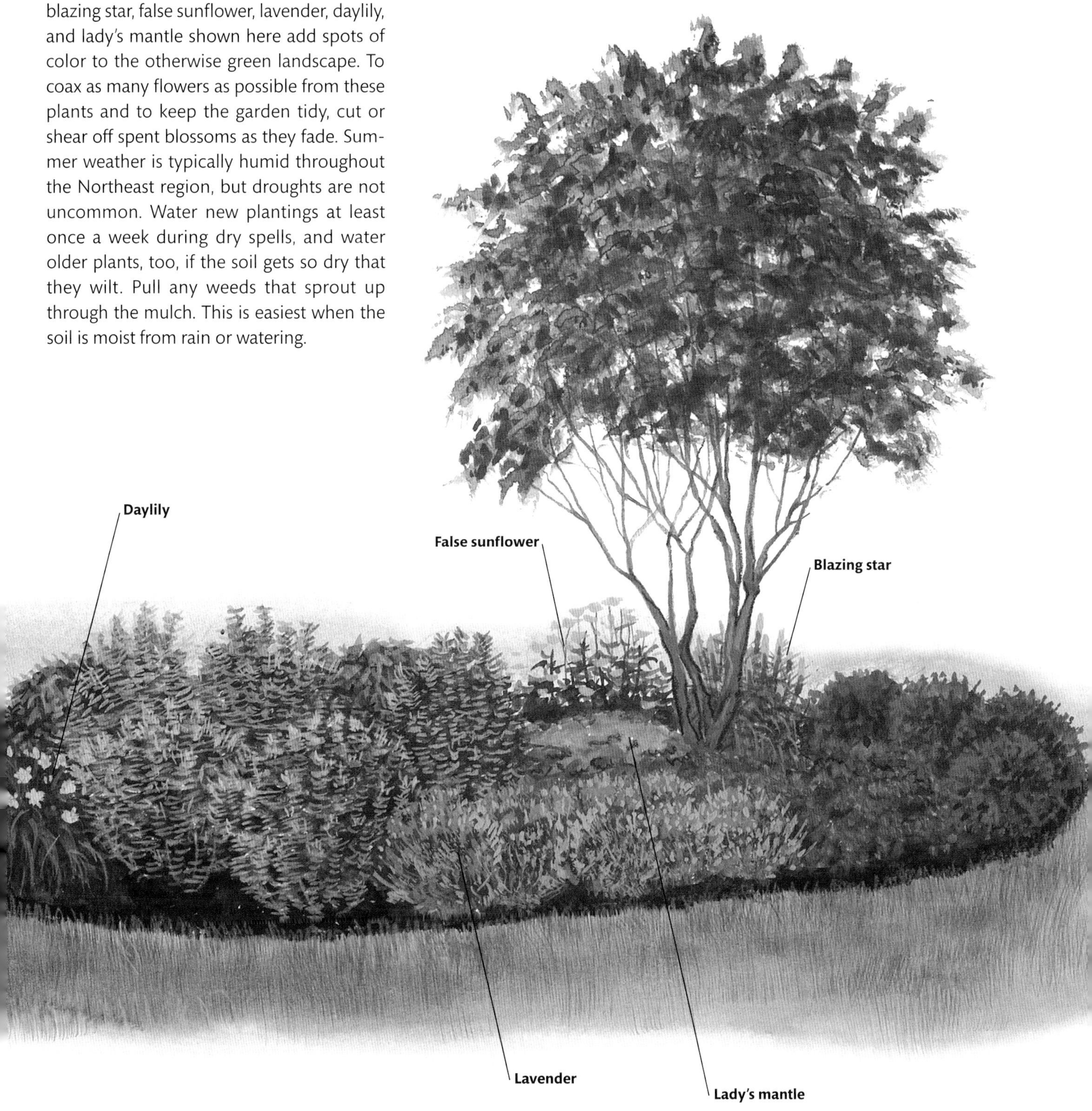

Fall

A few bright-colored leaves appear here and there in September, and fall foliage season peaks in early to mid-October in the Northeast region. While trees turn red, orange, and yellow overhead and roadside [illegible] dry to shades of russet and tan, perennials such as daylilies shown here bloom into the fall. The foliage of lavender, lady's mantle, and bloody cranesbill is still handsome, while the false sunflower and blazing star have been cut back.

Sometime in September or October, the first hard frost will kill tender plants to the ground, signaling the time for fall cleanup. Toss frosted plants on the compost pile. Rake leaves into a pile or bin, and save them to use as mulch in the spring.

Climate Change

Climate change seems to be on the tip of everyone's tongues. Indeed, it is a seriously critical problem manifested by such climate conditions as widespread heat waves, droughts, floods, gale force winds, and high waves, to name a few. This is crucially serious not only for mankind but also for plant life, especially food crops. Rising temperatures and carbon dioxide levels affect plant growth, causing earlier or later crops and reproduction often because insect pollinators have yet to migrate to a particular location as is "normal." Forest fires abound over huge areas due to lack of rain and frequent lightning strikes. The removal of forests causes air quality to be reduced and erosion of soils to occur. Plant breeders are working to breed earlier- or later-blooming plants as well as crops less reliant on dependable rainfall. It beneficial to research how these changes might affect your area and to plan ways to combat them.

Winter

In winter, when deciduous trees and shrubs are leafless and many perennials die down to the ground, you'll appreciate evergreen plants such as the dwarf bird's-nest Norway spruce and variegated 'Carol Mackie' daphne shown here. Also welcome in winter are clumps of rustling grass, as well as shrubs and trees with colorful twigs, interesting bark, or bright berries.

Normally, garden plants don't need any care in winter. If heavy snow or an ice storm snaps or crushes some plants, you can trim away the broken parts as soon as it's convenient. But if plants get frozen during a severe cold spell, wait until spring to assess the damage before deciding how far to cut them back.

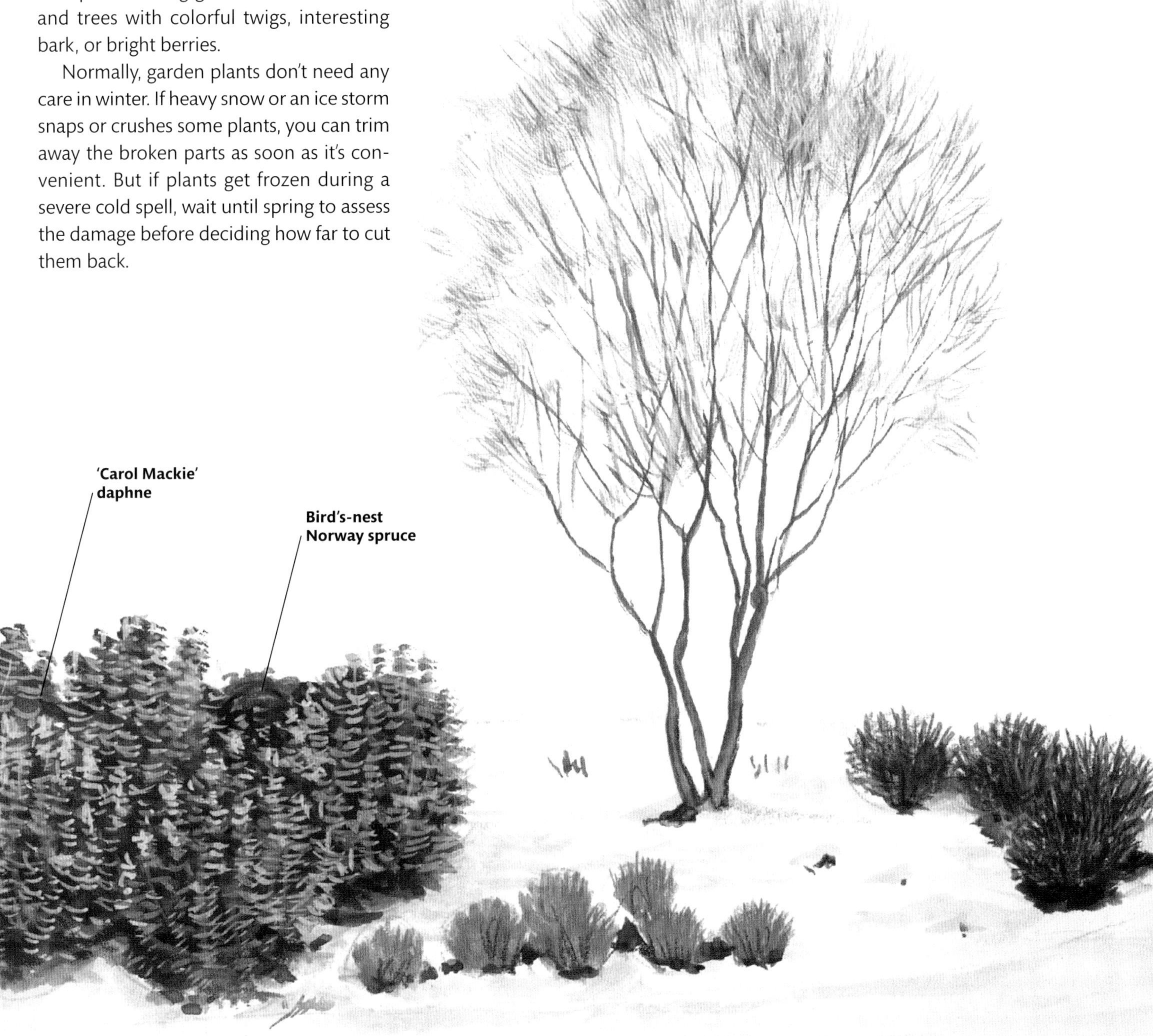

As Your Landscape Grows

Landscapes change over the years. As plants grow, the [illegible] from sparse to lush. Trees cast cool shade where the sun used to shine. Shrubs and hedges grow tall and dense enough to provide privacy. Perennials and ground covers spread to form colorful patches of foliage and flowers. Meanwhile, paths, arbors, fences, and other structures gain the patina of age.

Constant change over the years—sometimes rapid and dramatic, sometimes slow and subtle—is one of the joys of landscaping. It is also one of the challenges. Anticipating how fast plants will grow and how big they will eventually get is difficult, even for professional designers, and was a major concern in formulating the designs for this book.

To illustrate the kinds of changes to expect in a planting, these pages show one of the designs at three different "ages." (See p. 40.) Even though a new planting may look sparse at first, it will soon fill in. With careful spacing, the planting will look as good in ten to fifteen years as it does after three to five. It will, of course, look different, but that's part of the fun.

AT PLANTING

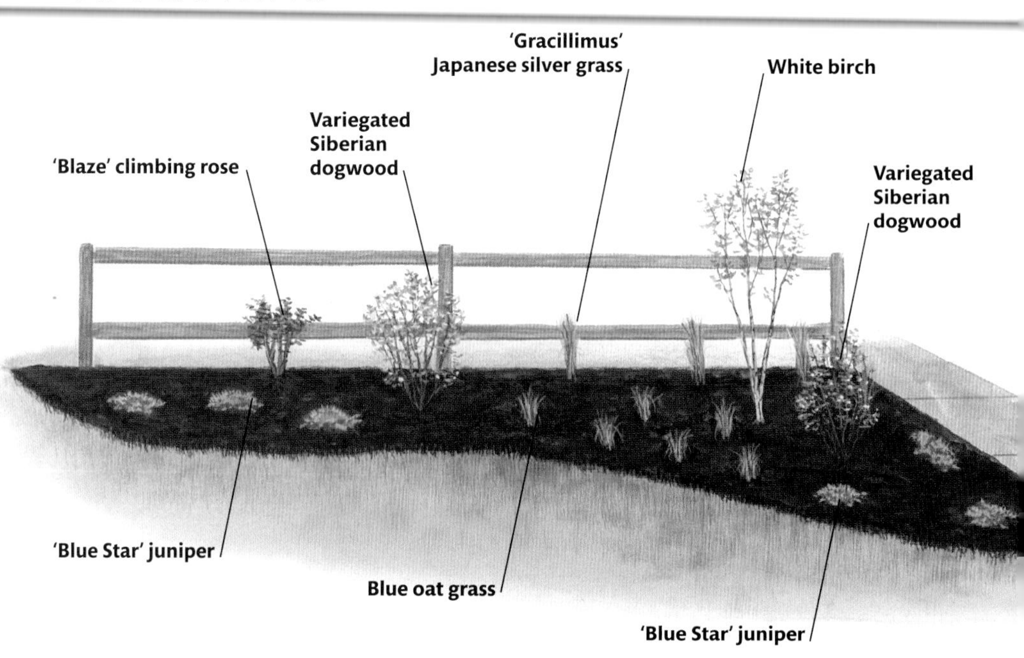

THREE TO FIVE YEARS

At Planting—Here's how the corner might appear in early summer immediately after planting. The white birch tree is only 5 to 6 ft. tall, with trunks no thicker than broomsticks. The variegated Siberian dogwoods have a few main stems, each about 3 to 4 ft. tall. The 'Blaze' rose has just short stubs where the nursery cut back the old stems, but it will grow fast and may bloom the first year. The 'Blue Star' junipers are low mounds about 6 to 10 in. wide. The blue oat grass forms small, thin clumps of sparse foliage. The 'Gracillimus' Japanese silver grass may still be dormant, or it may have a short tuft of new foliage. Both grasses will grow vigorously the first year.

Three to Five Years—The birch tree has grown 1 to 2 ft. taller every year but is still quite slender. Near the base, it's starting to show the white bark typical of maturity. The variegated Siberian dogwoods are well established now. If you cut them to the ground every year or two in spring, they grow back 4 to 6 ft. tall by midsummer, with strong, straight stems. The 'Blaze' rose covers the fence, and you need to remove a few of its older stems every spring. The slow-growing 'Blue Star' junipers make a series of low mounds; you still see them as individuals, not a continuous patch. The grasses have reached maturity and form lush, robust clumps. It would be a good idea to divide and replant them now, to keep them vigorous.

Ten to Fifteen Years—The birch tree is becoming a fine specimen, 20 to 30 ft. tall, with gleaming white bark on its trunks. Prune away the lower limbs up to 6 to 8 ft. above ground level to expose its trunks and to keep it from crowding and shading the other plants. The variegated dogwoods and 'Blaze' rose continue to thrive and respond well to regular pruning. The 'Blue Star' junipers have finally merged into a continuous mass of glossy foliage. The blue oat grass and Japanese silver grass will still look good if they have been divided and replanted over the years. If you get tired of the grasses, you could replace them with shade-loving cinnamon fern and astilbe, as shown here, or other perennials or shrubs.

Portfolio *of* Designs

This section presents 54 designs for situations that are common in home landscapes. You'll find designs to enhance entrances, decks, and patios. There are gardens of colorful perennials and shrubs, as well as structures and plantings, to create shady hideaways, dress up nondescript walls, and even make a centerpiece of a lowly mailbox. Large color illustrations show what the designs will look like, and site plans delineate the layout and planting scheme. Texts explain the designs and describe the plants and projects appearing in them. Installed as shown or adapted to meet your site and personal preferences, these designs can make your property more attractive, more useful, and—most important—more enjoyable for you, your family, and your friends.

Up Front and Formal

GREET VISITORS WITH CLASSIC SYMMETRY

Formal gardens have a special appeal. Their simple geometry can be soothing in a hectic world, and the look is timeless, never going out of style. The front yard of a classical house, such as the one shown here, invites a formal makeover. (A house with a symmetrical facade in any style has similar potential.)

In this design, a paved courtyard and a planting of handsome trees, shrubs, and ground covers have transformed a site typically given over to lawn and a concrete walkway. The result is a more dramatic entry, but also one where you can happily linger with guests on a fine day.

Tall hedges on the borders of the design and the centrally placed redbud provide a modicum of privacy in this otherwise public space. Lower hedges along the sidewalk and front of the driveway allow a view of the street and make these approaches more welcoming.

A matched pair of viburnums makes a lovely setting for the front door. To each side, layered groups of shrubs give depth and interest to the house's facade. From spring through fall, the planting's flowers and foliage make the courtyard a comfortable spot, and there is ample evergreen foliage to keep up appearances in winter. Completing the scene is an ornamental focal point and a bench for enjoying the results of your landscaping labors.

SITE: Sunny

SEASON: Early summer

CONCEPT: Wide paving, hedges, trees, and shrubs create an appealing entry courtyard.

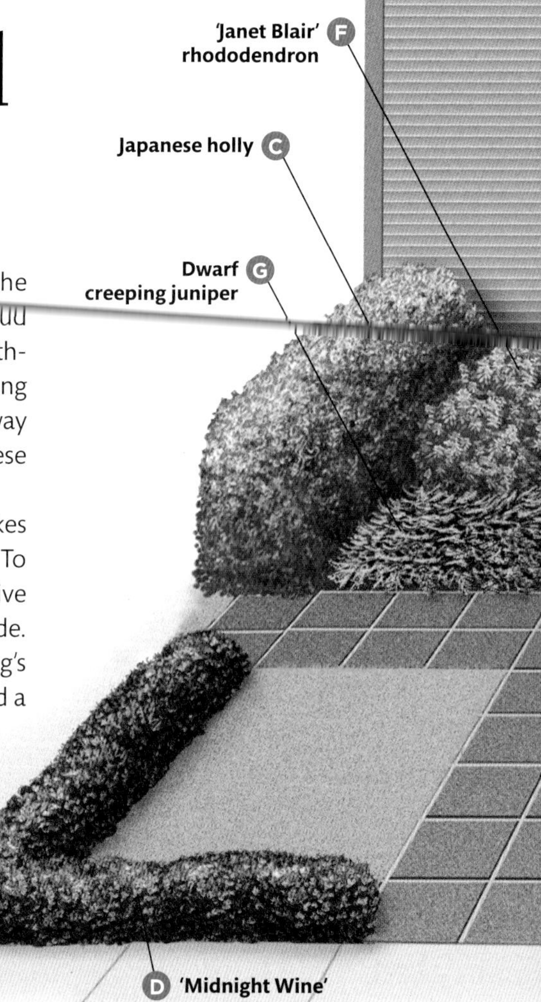

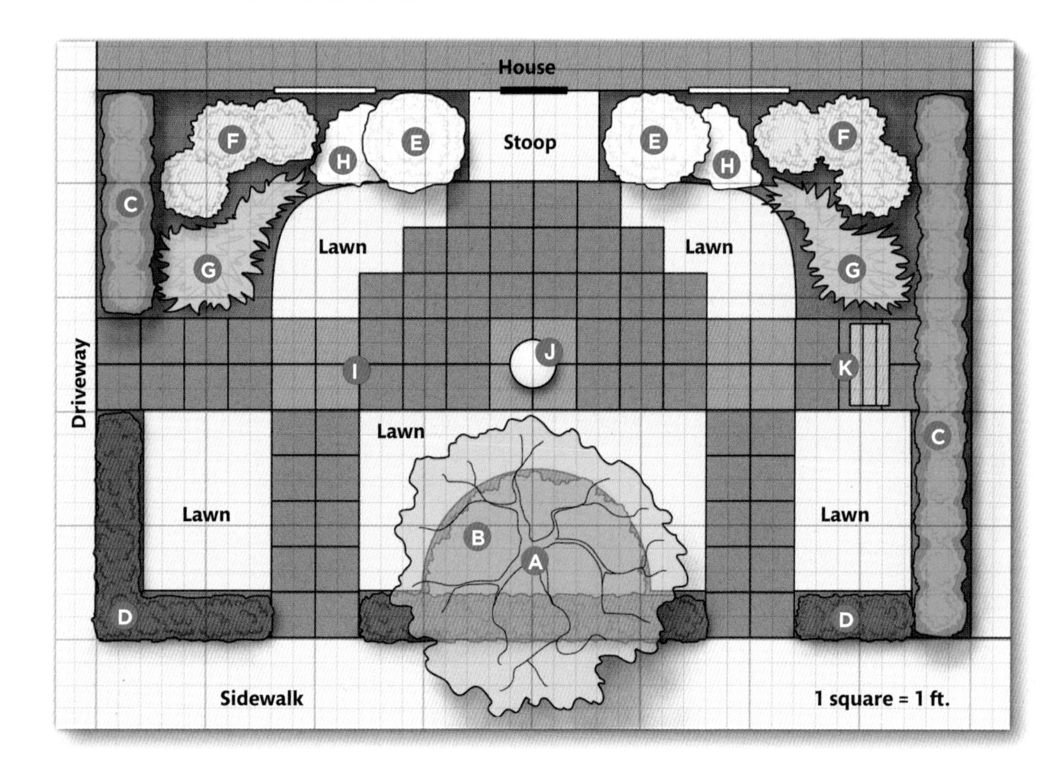

Plants & Projects

Spring is the season for flowers in this planting, with redbud, rhododendron, and candytuft blossoms in shades of pink and white. The colorful leaves and berries of viburnum, redbud, and barberry brighten the fall. While the hedge plants are dependable and problem-free, you'll need to shear them at least once a year to maintain the formal shapes.

A Redbud (use 1 plant)
Small pink flowers line the branches of this deciduous tree in early spring before the foliage appears. The heart-shaped leaves emerge reddish, mature to a lustrous green, and turn gold in fall. Bare branches form an attractive silhouette in winter, especially as the tree ages. See *Cercis canadensis*, p. 153.

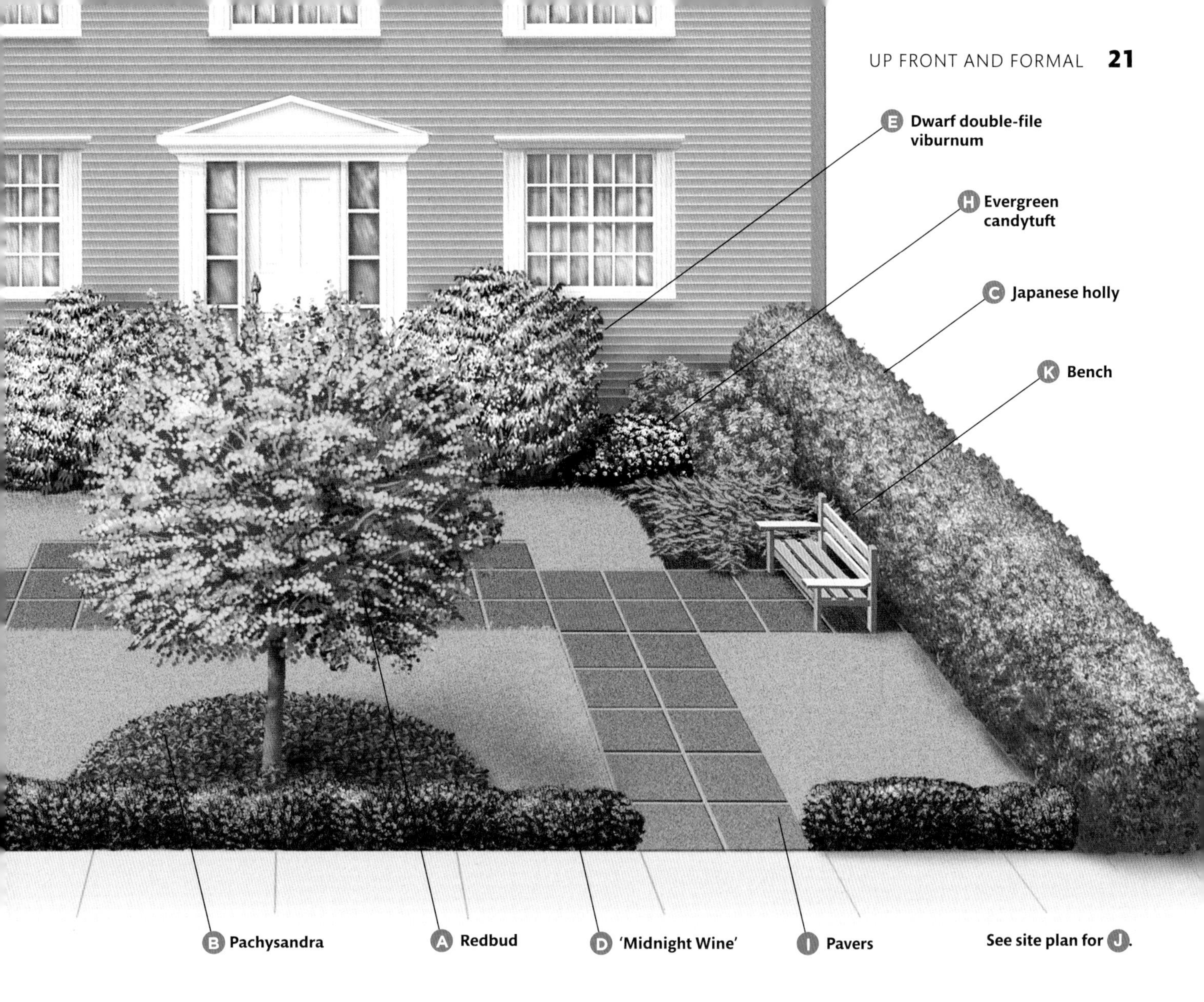

B Pachysandra (use 250)
Hardy, adaptable evergreen ground cover that will spread in the shade of the redbud, forming an attractive, weed-smothering, glossy green carpet. See *Pachysandra terminalis*, p. 145.

C Japanese holly (use 19)
Choose an upright cultivar of this evergreen shrub to form a hedge of dark-green leaves. See *Ilex crenata*, p. 140. In Zones 4 and 5 substitute the hardier compact burning bush, *Euonymus alatus* 'Compactus', p. 136.

D 'Midnight Wine' (use 34)
This deciduous shrub bears dark burgundy wine leaves and only reaches about 10 to 12 in. tall. Its light pink blooms appear in late spring. Best foliage color appears in full or partial sun; in shade it may become greenish. See *Weigela florida*, p. 153.

E Dwarf double-file viburnum (use 2)
A pair of these deciduous shrubs make an elegant frame for the door. Tiers of horizontal branches are smothered with small clusters of pure-white flowers from May through fall. Large, crinkled leaves are medium green. See *Viburnum plicatum* var. *tomentosum*, p. 152.

F 'Janet Blair' rhododendron (use 6)
The wonderful evergreen foliage and light pink flowers of this compact shrub anchor the planting at the corners of the house. Blooms in late spring. 'Mist Maiden' and 'Anna Hall' rhododendrons are good substitutes. See *Rhododendron*, p. 148.

G Dwarf creeping juniper (use 10)
Layered sprays of this evergreen shrub's prickly bright-green foliage lay like thick rugs on the edge of the lawn. A lovely contrast to the dark-green rhododendrons behind. For extra color in spring, plant handfuls of crocuses, snowdrops, or grape hyacinths next to the junipers. See *Juniperus procumbens* 'Nana', p. 142.

H Evergreen candytuft (use 12)
An evergreen perennial ground cover, it forms a low, sprawling mound of glossy foliage. Bears small white flowers for weeks in the spring. See *Iberis sempervirens*, p. 140.

I Pavers
The courtyard is surfaced with 2-ft.-square precast pavers. Use two complementary colors to create patterns if you choose. Substitute flagstones or bricks if they would look better with your house. See p. 161.

J Ornament
An ornament centered in the courtyard paving provides a focal point. Choose a sculpture, sundial, reflecting ball, birdbath, or large potted plant to suit your taste.

K Bench
Enjoy the courtyard garden from a comfortable bench in a style that complements the garden and the house.

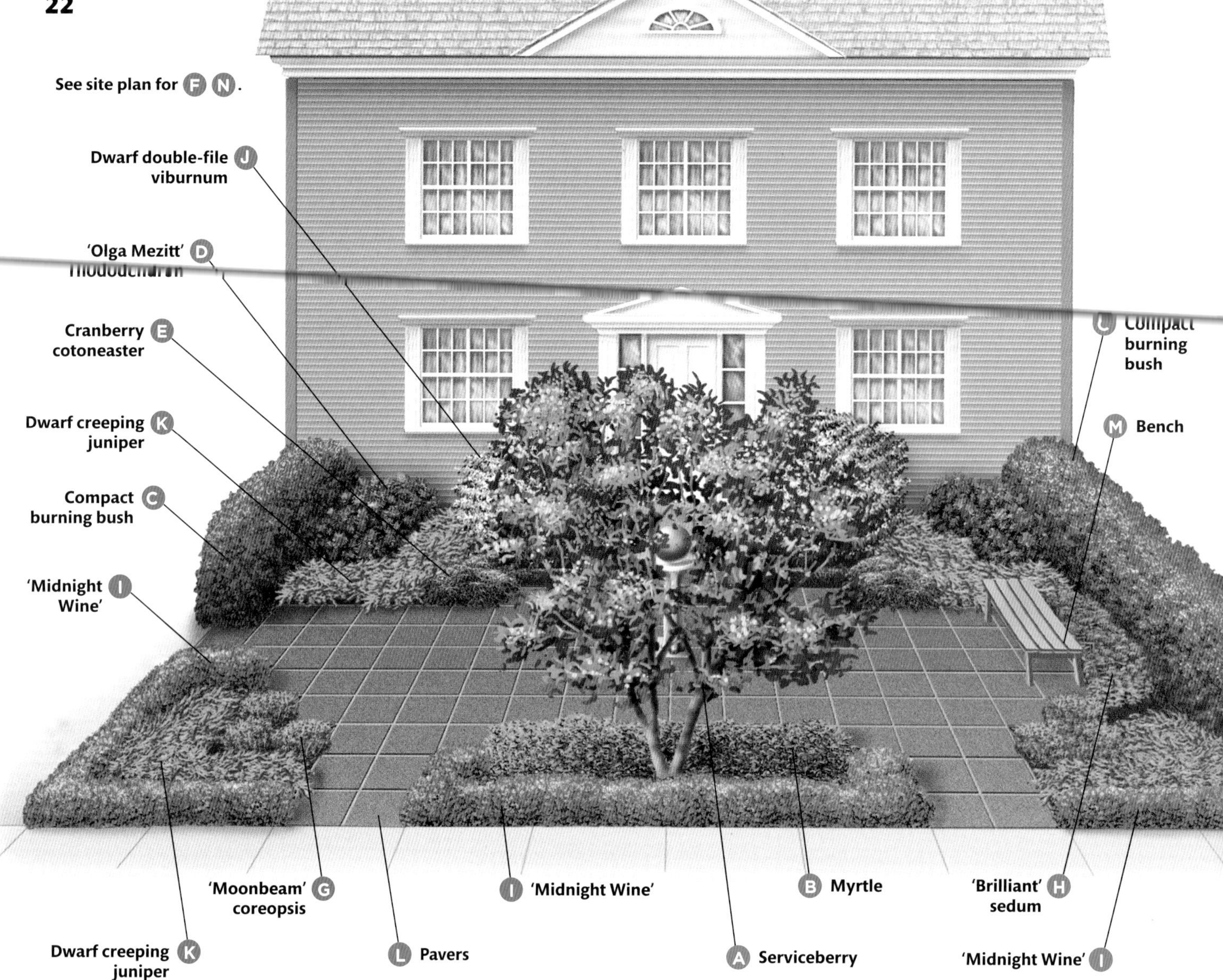

Expanded courtyard

If the paved courtyard on the previous pages struck your fancy, there's even more here. The basic design idea remains the same, but by extending the paving and adding more shrubs, ground covers, and perennials, the lawn is eliminated altogether.

Spring still features colorful flowers, but the most striking time of year for this planting is fall. The blazing red foliage of the tall burning bush hedge, serviceberry tree, and low-growing cotoneasters makes autumn a fiery season.

Summer and winter are more subdued. Lush foliage in a variety of hues and textures and a sprinkling of delightful yellow flowers in the front corners give character to the summer garden. In winter, evergreen leaves and a tracery of bare branches are particularly appealing when dusted with fresh snow.

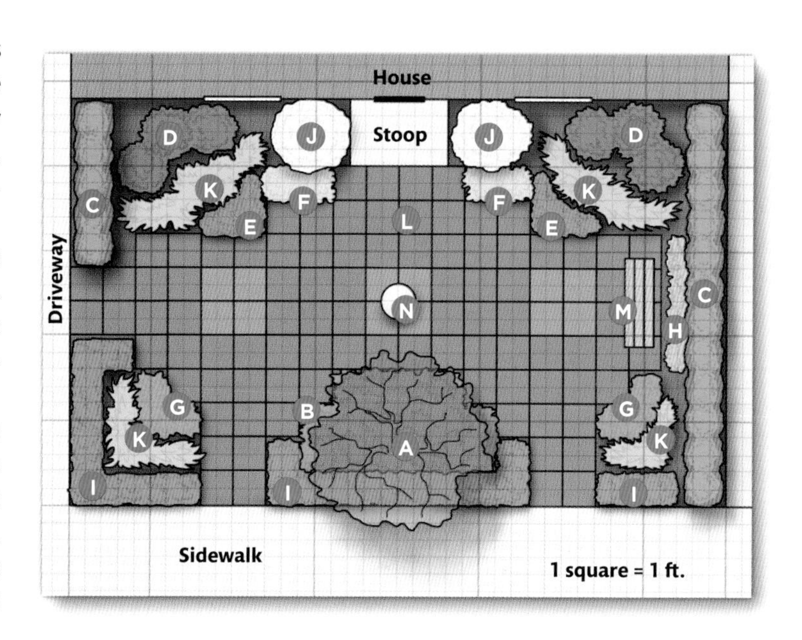

SITE: Sunny

SEASON: Fall

CONCEPT: Plantings and paving replace lawn to create a formal courtyard entry.

Plants & Projects

- **A** **Serviceberry** (use 1 plant)
  A deciduous tree with white early-spring flowers and bright-red fall color. See *Amelanchier* x *grandiflora*, p. 131.
- **B** **Myrtle** (use 450)
  An evergreen ground cover with shiny leaves and pretty blue spring flowers. See *Vinca minor*, p. 153.
- **C** **Compact burning bush** (use 19)
  Dark-green leaves and horizontal branches form a fine deciduous hedge. Flaming red fall color. See *Euonymus alatus* 'Compactus', p. 136.
- **D** **'Olga Mezitt' rhododendron** (use 6)
  The small evergreen leaves of this shrub turn maroon in winter. Pretty clusters of pink flowers in midspring. See *Rhododendron*, p. 148.
- **E** **Cranberry cotoneaster** (use2)
  Low-growing deciduous shrub with lustrous dark-green leaves, red fruits, and red fall foliage. See *Cotoneaster apiculatus*, p. 135.
- **F** **Bigroot geranium** (use 10)
  A perennial with large fragrant leaves. Bears magenta flowers in June. See *Geranium macrorrhizum*, p. 138.
- **G** **'Moonbeam' coreopsis** (use 6)
  Perennial with dark fine-textured foliage and tiny lemon-yellow flowers. Blooms for several weeks in late summer. See *Coreopsis verticillata*, p. 135.
- **H** **'Brilliant' sedum** (use 7)
  Perennial with fleshy leaves and rosy flowers makes a colorful backdrop behind the bench. See *Sedum*, p. 150.

See p. 21 for the following:

- **I** **'Midnight Wine'** (use 40)
- **J** **Dwarf double-file viburnum** (use 2)
- **K** **Dwarf creeping juniper** (use 18)
- **L** **Pavers**
- **M** **Bench**
- **N** **Ornament**

PLANT PORTRAITS

These trouble-free plants need little more than regular pruning or shearing to maintain their clean lines and well-defined shapes.

● = First design, pp. 20–21

▲ = Second design, pp. 22–23

Redbud (*Cercis canadensis*, p. 134) ●

Dwarf double-file viburnum (*Viburnum plicatum* var. *tomentosum*, p. 152) ● ▲

'Midnight Wine' (*Weigela florida*, p. 153) ● ▲

Bigroot geranium (*Geranium macrorrhizum*, p. 138) ▲

Dwarf creeping juniper (*Juniperus procumbens* 'Nana', p. 142) ● ▲

First Impressions

THIS PLANTING LETS YOU PUT YOUR BEST FOOT FORWARD

SITE: Sunny

SEASON: Summer

CONCEPT: A distinctive walkway and colorful plantings make an enticing entry to your home.

Well-chosen plants and a revamped walkway not only make the short journey to your front door a pleasant one, they can also enhance your home's most public face and help settle it comfortably in its surroundings.

The curved walk in this design offers visitors a friendly welcome and a helpful "Please come this way." The first stage of the journey passes between two clipped shrub roses into a handsome garden "room" with larger shrubs near the house and smaller, colorful perennials by the walk. An opening in a hedge of long-blooming shrub roses then leads to a wider paved area that functions as an outdoor foyer. There you can greet guests or relax on the bench and enjoy the plantings that open out onto the lawn. A double course of pavers intersects the walk and an adjacent planting bed, and the circle it describes contrasts nicely with the rectilinear lines of the house and hedge.

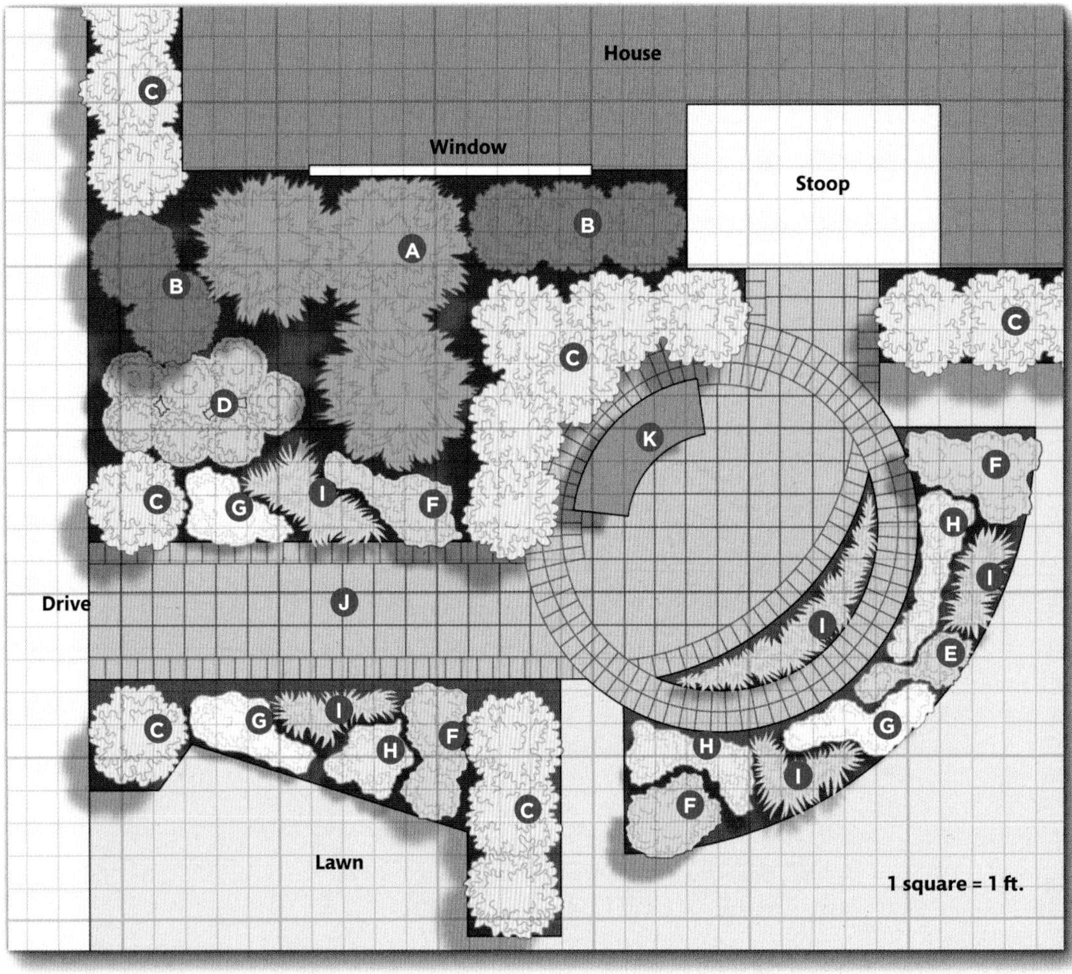

Plants & Projects

Mixing shrubs and perennials, this planting offers colorful flowers and attractive foliage from spring through fall. The shrubs provide structure through the winter and are handsome when covered with new snow. The perennials are dormant in winter; cut them to the ground to make room for snow shoveled off the walk. Maintenance involves pruning the shrubs and clipping spent flowers (deadheading) to keep everything tidy.

A 'Sea Green' juniper (use 3 plants)
This rugged evergreen shrub anchors a corner of the first garden "room" with arching branches that provide year-

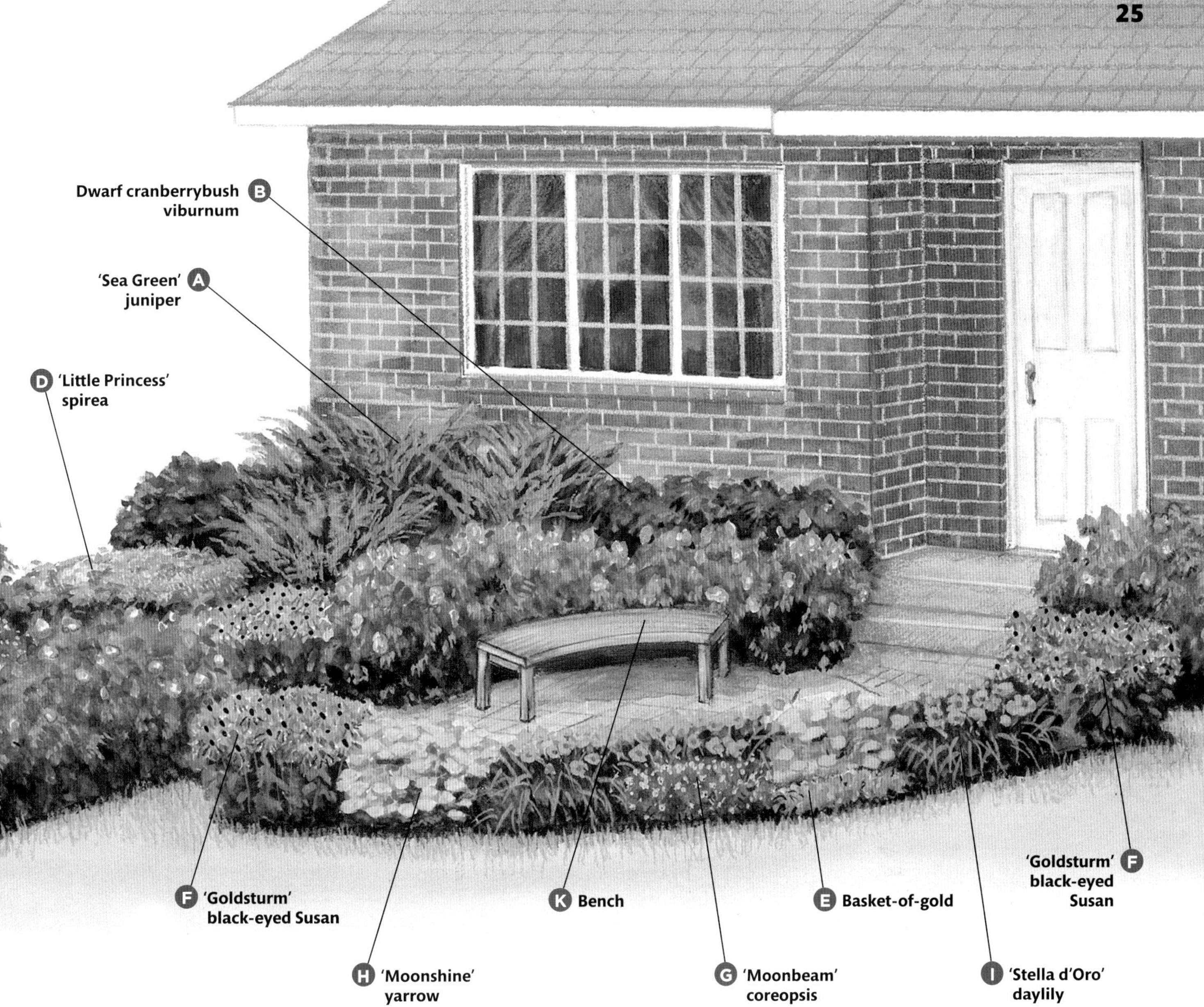

round pale-green color. See *Juniperus chinensis*, p. 142.

B Dwarf cranberry bush viburnum (use 5)
This small deciduous shrub has a dense, bushy habit and dark- green, maplelike leaves that turn shades of red in fall. It won't outgrow its place beneath the windows. See *Viburnum opulus* 'Nanum', p. 152.

C 'Frau Dagmar Hartop' rose (use 18 or more)
With its crinkly bright-green leaves, fragrant single pink flowers, and colorful red hips from autumn into winter, this easy-to-grow deciduous shrub puts on quite a show. Flowers all summer; forms a dense natural-looking hedge. Extend the planting along the house as needed. See *Rosa*, p. 149.

D 'Little Princess' spirea (use 7)
Another compact deciduous shrub, with dainty twigs and leaves. Bears clusters of pink flowers in June and July. See *Spiraea japonica*, p. 150.

E Basket-of-gold (use 4)
The planting's first flowers appear on this perennial in spring. After the fragrant yellow blooms fade, the low mounds of gray leaves look attractive through late fall. See *Aurinia saxatilis*, p. 132.

F 'Goldsturm' black-eyed Susan (use 20)
A popular prairie perennial, this bears large golden yellow flowers (each with a dark "eye" in the center) that are a cheerful sight in late summer. See *Rudbeckia fulgida*, p. 149.

G 'Moonbeam' coreopsis (use 22)
For months during the summer, this perennial features masses of tiny pale-yellow flowers on neat mounds of lacy dark-green foliage. See *Coreopsis verticillata*, p. 135.

H 'Moonshine' yarrow (use 17)
A perennial offering flat heads of sulphur yellow flowers for much of the summer. The fine gray-green leaves contrast nicely with surrounding foliage. See *Achillea*, p. 130.

I 'Stella d'Oro' daylily (use 30)
Distinctive golden yellow flowers hover over this perennial's attractive grassy foliage from mid-June until fall. See *Hemerocallis*, p. 139.

J Walk
Made of precast concrete pavers, the walk and decorative edgings require careful layout and installation. Consider renting a mason's saw to ensure accuracy when cutting pavers. See p. 160.

K Bench
A nursery or garden center can usually order a simple curved bench like the one shown here, although a straight bench will do, too.

A Step Up

PLANT A FOUNDATION GARDEN

Rare is the home without foundation plantings. These simple skirtings of greenery hide unattractive concrete block underpinnings and help overcome the impression that the house is hovering a few feet above the ground. Useful as these plantings are, they are too often just monochromatic expanses of clipped yews, dull as dishwater. But, as this design shows, a durable, low-maintenance foundation planting can be more varied, more colorful, and more fun.

Broad-leaved and coniferous evergreen shrubs anchor this planting and provide four-season cover for the foundation. But they also offer contrasting shapes and textures and a range of colors from icy blue through a variety of greens to maroon.

What makes this design special is the smaller plants fronting the foundation shrubs. Including perennials, grasses, and low shrubs in the mix expands the foundation planting into a small front-yard garden. From spring until frost, flowers in white, pink, magenta, and mauve stand out against the blue-and-green backdrop. When the last flower fades in autumn, the evergreen foliage takes center stage, serving through the winter as a welcome reminder that the world will green up again.

Plants & Projects

Eye-catching as the flowers in this planting are, the foliage is the key to its success in every season. The evergreens are attractive year-round. Each of the perennials has been chosen as much for its foliage as for its flowers. A thorough cleanup and maintenance pruning in spring and fall will keep the planting looking its best.

A 'Wichita Blue' juniper (use 1 plant)
This slow-growing, upright evergreen shrub has a neat pyramidal form, lovely silver-blue foliage and blue berries to add year-round color at the corner of the house. See *Juniperus scopulorum*, p. 142.

B 'PJM' rhododendron (use 5)
An informal row of these hardy evergreen shrubs beautifully conceals the foundation. Vivid magenta flowers in early spring, small dark-green leaves that turn maroon in winter, all on a compact plant. See *Rhododendron*, p. 148.

C 'Techny' American arborvitae (use 1)
This cone-shaped, slow-growing evergreen fills the corner near the front steps with fragrant, rich-green, fine-textured foliage. See *Thuja occidentalis*, p. 151.

D 'Blue Star' juniper (use 3)
The sparkly blue foliage and irregular mounded form of this low-growing evergreen shrub look great next to the peony and germander. See *Juniperus squamata*, p. 142.

E 'Sea Urchin' blue fescue grass (use 3)
The very fine blue leaves of this perennial grass contrast handsomely with the dark-green rhododendrons behind. Flower spikes rise above the neat, soft-looking mounds in early summer. See *Festuca ovina* var. *glauca*, p. 137.

F 'Sarah Bernhardt' peony (use 3)
A sentimental favorite, this perennial offers fragrant pink double flowers in early summer. Forms a multistemmed clump with attractive foliage that will look nice next to the steps through the summer. See *Paeonia*, p. 145.

G White astilbe (use 3)
The lacy dark-green foliage and fluffy white flower plumes of this tough perennial stand out against the blue foliage of its neighbors. Flowers in June or July. See *Astilbe*, p. 132.

H Germander (use 1)
This rugged little shrub forms a tidy mound of small, dark, shiny evergreen leaves next to the walk. Mauve flowers bloom in late summer. See *Teucrium chamaedrys*, p. 151.

I 'Sheffield' chrysanthemum (use 1)
A longtime regional favorite, this hardy perennial forms a broad mound of fragrant gray-green foliage. Small, pink, daisylike blossoms cover the plant from September until frost. See *Dendranthema* x *grandiflorum*, p. 136.

SITE: Sunny

SEASON: Fall

CONCEPT: A mixture of easy-care perennials and shrubs provides a colorful setting for a home's public face.

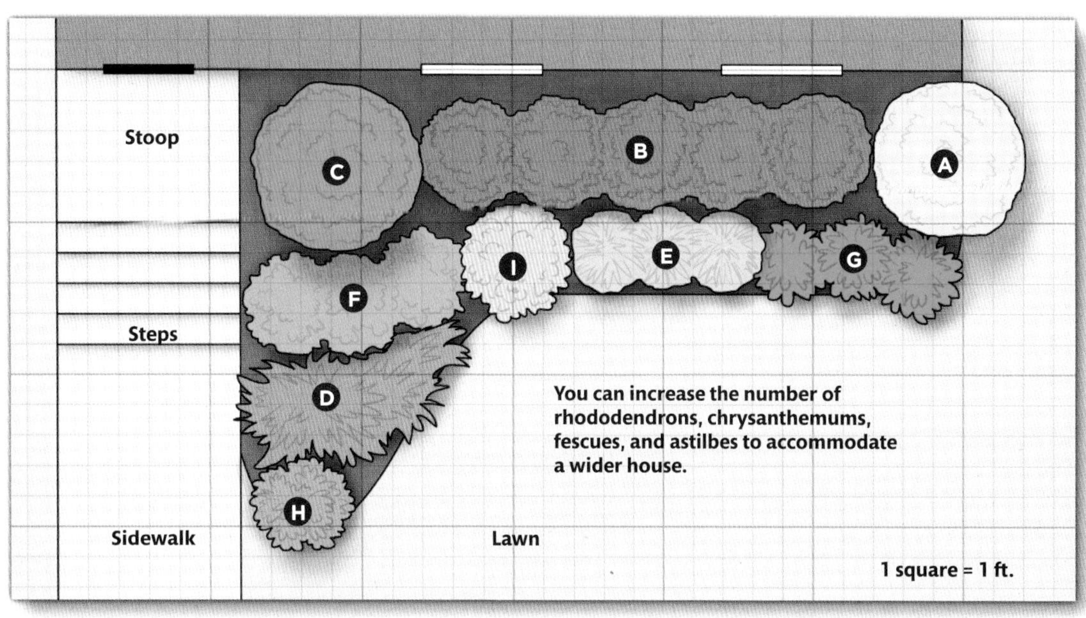

Setting for a shady porch

This foundation planting graces a front porch on a shady site, making it an even more welcome haven on a hot summer's day. Like the design on the previous pages, this planting mixes the year-round attractions of evergreens with perennials and vines that shine during the growing season. The result is a garden in shades of green accented by bursts of bloom. All plants are shade tolerant.

Foliage is the key to the planting. The shrubs are broad-leaved evergreens with leaves in a pleasing range of size, shape, and color. The sheared hedge contrasts nicely with the naturally neat but informal shapes of the other shrubs. The ferny astilbe, ruffled lady's mantle, and large-leaved Dutchman's pipe vine are worth growing for their foliage alone.

Flowers sprinkle this leafy backdrop from spring to midsummer. Spring is most striking, with masses of pink rhododendron and white andromeda blossoms. In summer, the vines and perennials chime in with flowers in a white-and-chartreuse color scheme.

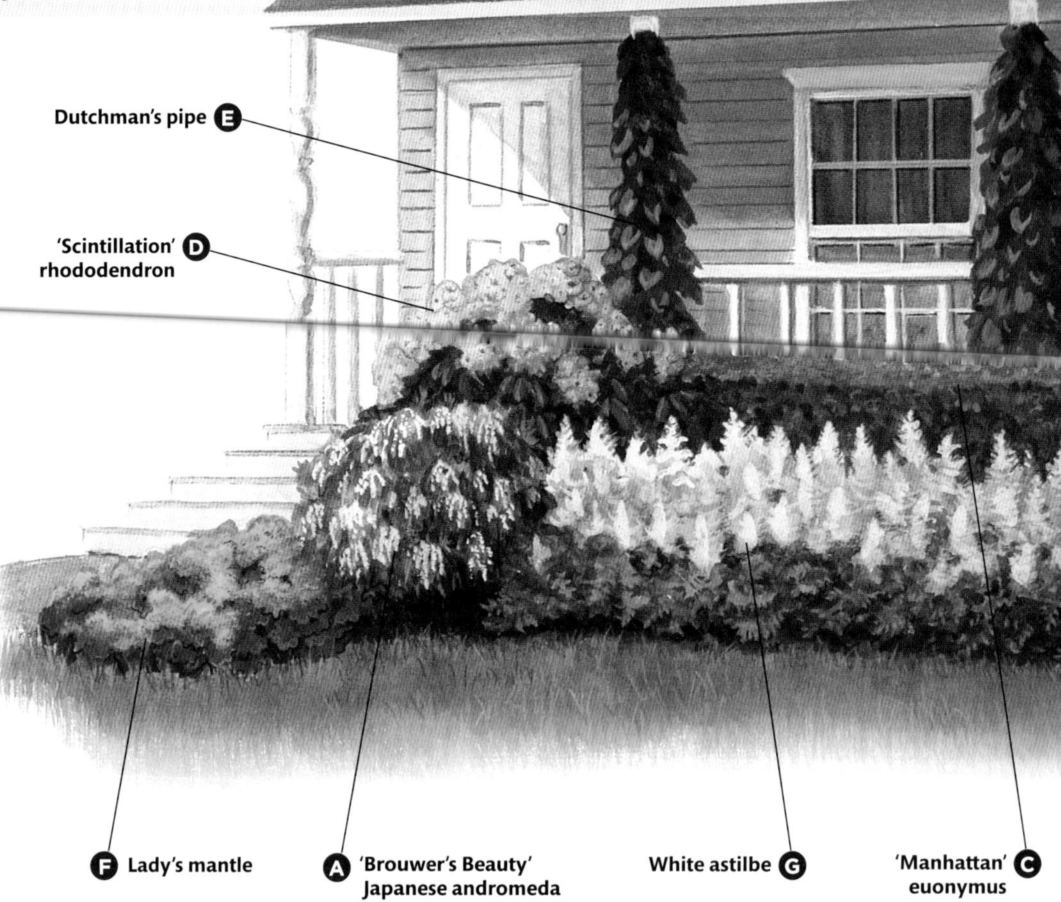

Plants & Projects

A 'Brouwer's Beauty' Japanese andromeda (use 1 plant)
A handsome, compact evergreen shrub with shiny foliage that darkens through the growing season from pale yellow-green to olive green. Its reddish flower buds look pretty through the winter and produce clusters of small white flowers in June. See *Pieris*, p. 146.

B Compact inkberry holly (use 3)
An adaptable evergreen shrub with small glossy green leaves. The plant's naturally round and bushy form defines the corner of the planting nicely. See *Ilex glabra* 'Compacta', p. 141.

C 'Manhattan' euonymus (use 6)
A row of these upright evergreen shrubs is ideal in front of the porch railing. These plants have glossy green leaves and interesting pink-and-orange fruits in fall. Shear to a geometric shape as shown here, or prune more informally. See *Euonymus kiautschovicus*, p. 137.

D 'Scintillation' rhododendron (use 1)
The dark-green foliage of this evergreen shrub is a handsome backdrop to striking clusters of pink flowers in late spring. A

SITE: Shady

SEASON: Early summer

CONCEPT: A leafy tapestry of evergreens, perennials, and vines accented by flowers enhances gatherings on a shady porch.

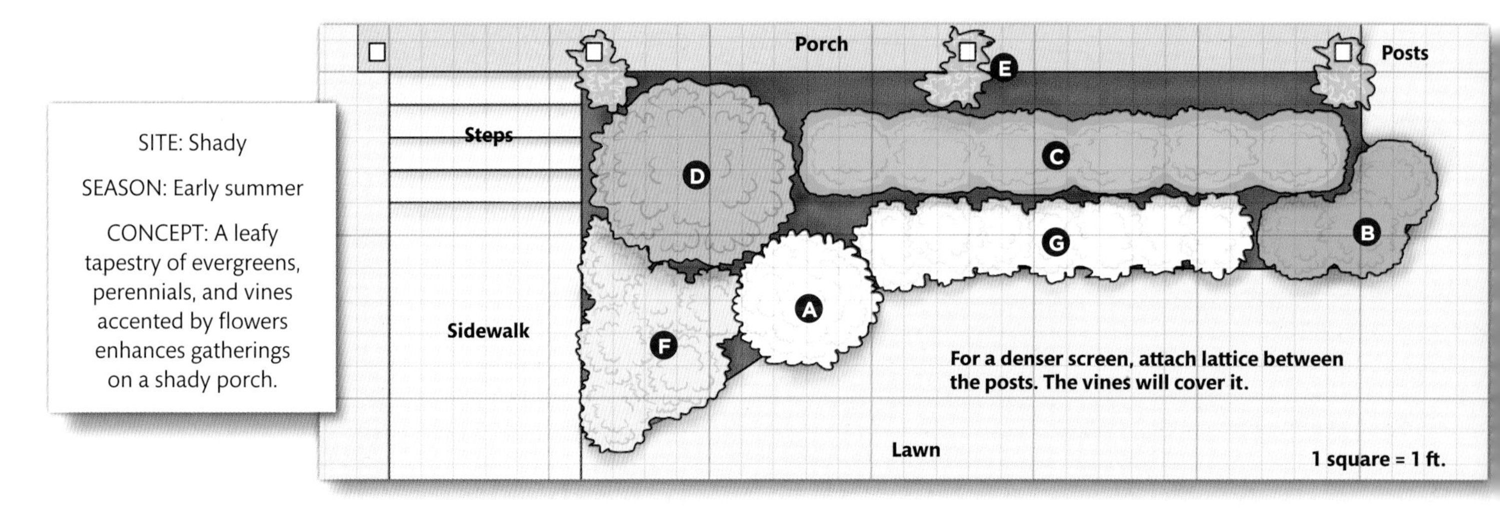

vigorous plant, it will quickly fill in the corner of the planting by the steps. See *Rhododendron*, p. 148.

E **Dutchman's pipe** (use 3)
This old-fashioned twining vine will clothe the porch posts with large heart-shaped deciduous leaves. Its interesting pipe-shaped green-and-maroon flowers open for a few weeks in early summer. Prune the vines down to the level of the porch floor in winter. In spring, tie new shoots to the porch railing to start them climbing. See *Aristolochia durior*, p. 131.

F **Lady's mantle** (use 6)
Large mounds of ruffled light-green leaves of this perennial look fresh next to the walk all summer. In June, plants are covered with a froth of chartreuse flowers. See *Alchemilla mollis*, p. 130

See p. 26 for the following:

G **White astilbe** (use 7)

PLANT PORTRAITS

Combining lovely flowers and handsome foliage, these evergreens and perennials make something special of a foundation planting.

● = First design, pp. 26–27

▲ = Second design, pp. 28–29

'Sarah Bernhardt' peony (*Paeonia*, p. 145) ●

Dutchman's pipe
(*Aristolochia durior*, p. 131) ▲

'Sheffield' chrysanthemum
(*Dendranthema* x *grandiflorum*, p. 136) ●

Germander
(*Teucrium chamaedrys*, p. 151) ●

White astilbe
(*Astilbe* 'Deutschland', p. 132) ● ▲

'Sea Urchin' blue fescue grass
(*Festuca ovina* var. *glauca*, p. 137) ●

A Warm Welcome

MAKE A PLEASANT PASSAGE TO YOUR FRONT DOOR

Why wait until a visitor reaches the front door to extend a cordial greeting? Have your landscape offer a friendly welcome and a helpful "Please come this way." Well-chosen plants and a revamped walkway not only make a visitor's short journey a pleasant one, they can also enhance your home's most public face.

This simple arrangement of plants and paving produces an elegant entrance that deftly mixes formal and informal elements. A wide walk of neatly fitted flagstones and a rectangular bed of roses have the feel of a small formal courtyard, complete with a pair of standard roses in planters, each displaying a mound of flowers atop a single stem. Clumps of ornamental grass rise from the paving like leafy fountains.

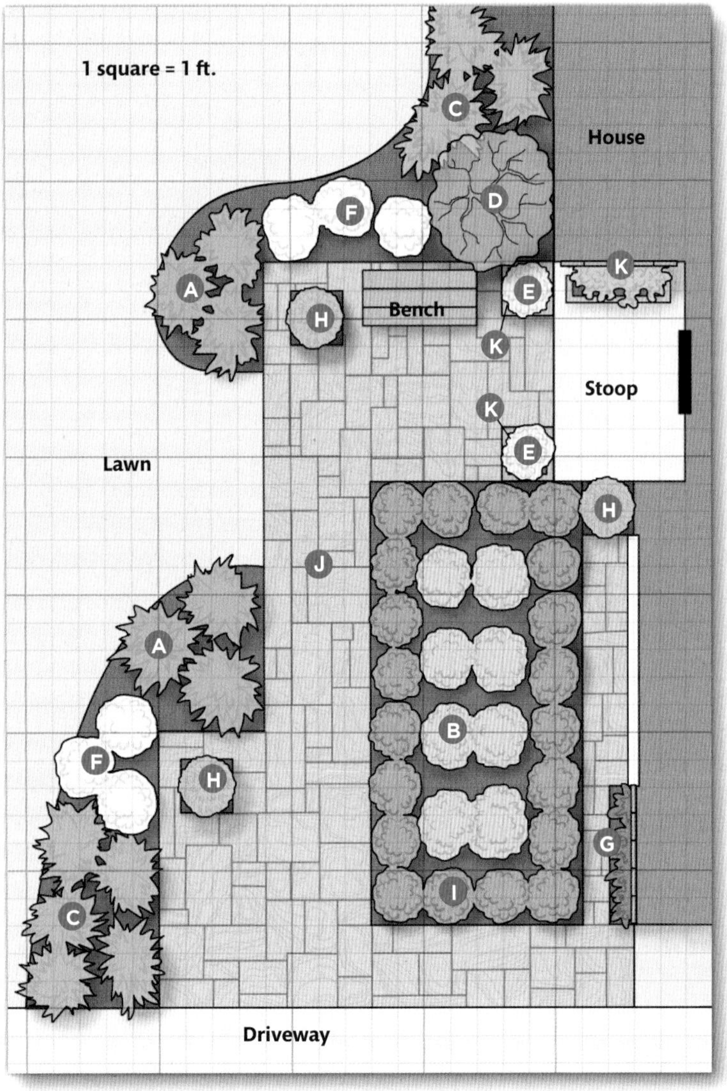

Gently curving beds of low-growing evergreens and shrub roses edge the flagstones, softening the formality and providing a comfortable transition to the lawn. Morning glories and clematis climb simple trellises to brighten the walls of the house.

Flowers in pink, white, purple, and violet are abundant from early summer until frost. They are set off by the rich green foliage of the junipers and roses and the gray leaves of the catmint edging.

Add a bench, as shown here, so you can linger and enjoy the scene; in later years, the lovely star magnolia behind it will provide comfortable dappled shade.

Plants & Projects

Once established, these shrubs and perennials require little care beyond deadheading and an annual pruning. (See p. 206 for rose care.) Ask the nursery where you buy the standard roses for advice on how to protect the plants in winter. (See p. 184 for a method of attaching lattice to the house for the planters and clematis.)

A 'Blue Star' juniper (use 6 plants)
The sparkly blue foliage of this low-growing evergreen shrub neatly edges the opening onto the lawn. See *Juniperus squamata*, p. 142.

B 'Bonica' rose (use 8)
This deciduous shrub blooms from June until frost, producing clusters of double, soft-pink flowers. See *Rosa*, p. 149.

C Dwarf creeping juniper (use 8)
This low, spreading evergreen with prickly green foliage makes a tough, handsome ground cover. See *Juniperus procumbens* 'Nana', p. 142.

D Star magnolia (use 1)
This small multitrunked deciduous tree graces the entry with lightly scented white flowers in early spring. See *Magnolia stellata*, p. 144.

E 'The Fairy' rose (use 2)
Clusters of small, double, pale-pink roses appear in abundance from early summer to frost. Buy plants trained as standards at a nursery. Underplant with impatiens. See *Rosa*, p. 149.

F 'White Meidiland' rose (use 6)
A low, spreading shrub, it is covered with clusters of lovely single white flowers all summer. See *Rosa*, p. 149.

G Jackman clematis (use 2)
Trained to a simple lattice, this deciduous vine produces large, showy, dark-purple flowers for weeks in summer. See *Clematis* x *jackmanii*, p. 134.

H 'Gracillimus' Japanese silver grass (use 3)
The arching leaves of this perennial grass are topped by fluffy seed heads from late summer through winter. See *Miscanthus*, p. 144.

I 'Six Hills Giant' catmint (use 20)
A perennial with violet-blue flowers and aromatic gray-green foliage edges the roses. See *Nepeta* x *faassenii*, p. 144.

J Flagstone paving
Rectangular flagstones in random sizes. See p. 161.

K Planters
Simple wooden boxes contain blue-flowered annual morning glories (on the stoop, trained to a wooden lattice) and standard roses (in front of the stoop). See p. 182.

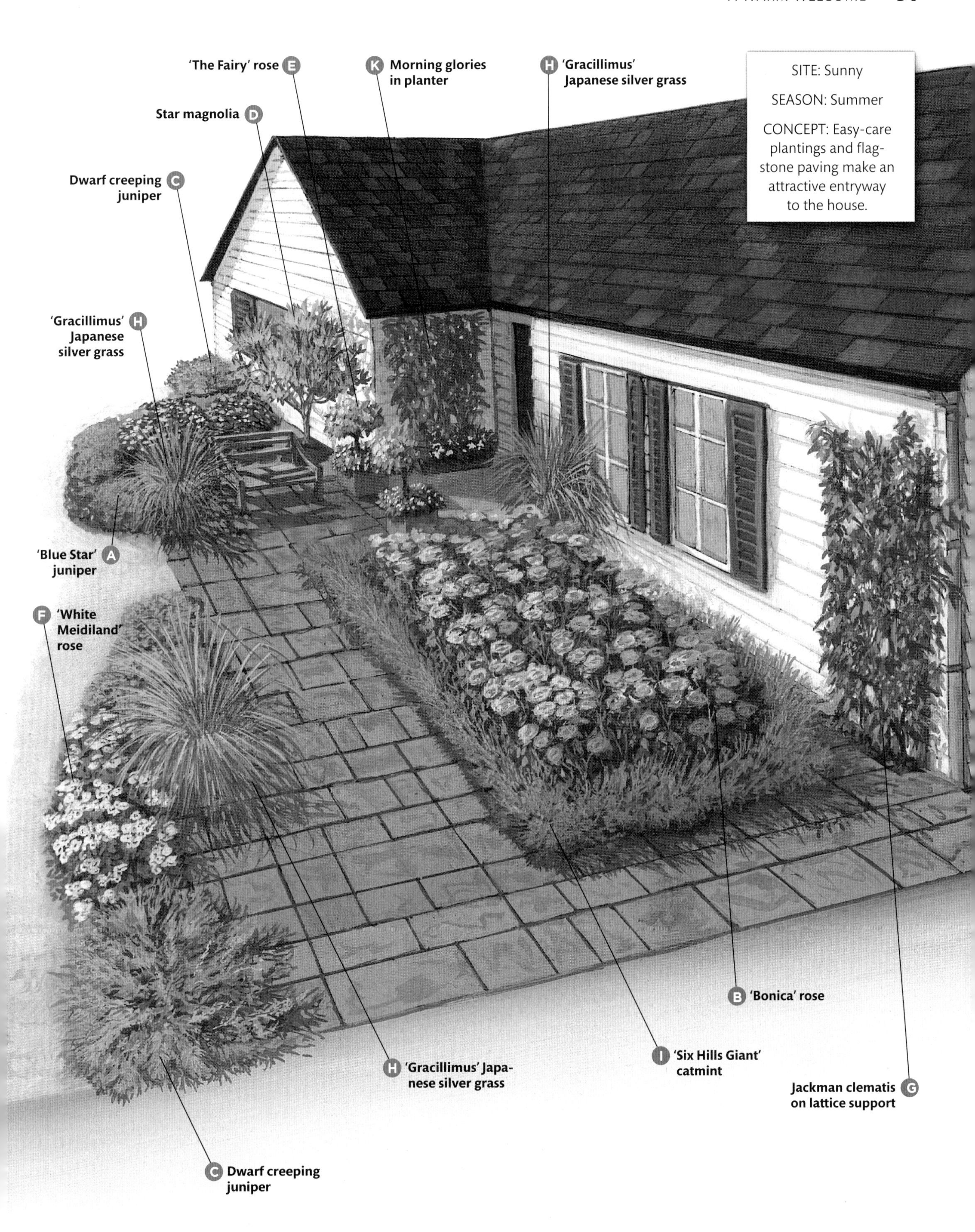

SITE: Sunny

SEASON: Summer

CONCEPT: Easy-care plantings and flagstone paving make an attractive entryway to the house.

PLANT PORTRAITS

With colorful flowers, textured foliage, bright berries, and attractive bark, these trees, shrubs, perennials, and vines welcome you throughout the year.

● = First design, pp. 30–31

▲ = Second design, pp. 32–33

Jackman clematis (*Clematis x jackmanii*, p. 134) ●

Pachysandra
(*Pachysandra terminalis*, p. 145) ▲

'The Fairy' rose (*Rosa*, p. 149) ●

'China Boy' holly or 'China Girl' holly
(*Ilex x meserveae*, p. 141) ▲

'Wintergreen' boxwood
(*Buxus microphylla*, p. 133) ▲

A shady welcome

If your entry is shady, receiving less than six hours of sunlight a day, try this planting scheme, which replaces the sun-loving plants from the previous design with shade-loving plants. Overall, the emphasis is still on year-round good looks.

Small trees and shrubs give the entry a woodland air. They provide lovely flowers in spring, green foliage dotted with berries in summer, and handsome fall color. Evergreen foliage and striking bark keep up appearances in winter.

Near the house is a small outdoor "room," complete with a lush green carpet of pachysandra and a place to sit and enjoy the surroundings in the company of birds flitting among branches and berries.

Plants & Projects

Ⓐ **'Golden Glory' cornelian cherry dogwood** (use 2 plants)
This small deciduous tree offers something to visitors in every season: yellow flowers in early spring, showy red berries in summer, colorful foliage in fall, and flaky bark in winter. See *Cornus mas*, p. 135.

Ⓑ **White birch** (use 1)
A lovely deciduous tree with striking white bark and glossy dark-green leaves that turn yellow in fall. See *Betula platyphylla* 'White Spire', p. 132.

Ⓒ **Azalea** (use 12)
Choose one of the Northern Lights varieties of hardy deciduous azaleas, shrubs that will brighten the garden with large clusters of fragrant flowers in midspring. See *Rhododendron*, p. 147.

Ⓓ **'Boule de Neige' rhododendron** (use 3)
A hardy rhododendron with glossy dark-evergreen leaves and big clusters of showy white flowers in June. Has a neat, rounded habit

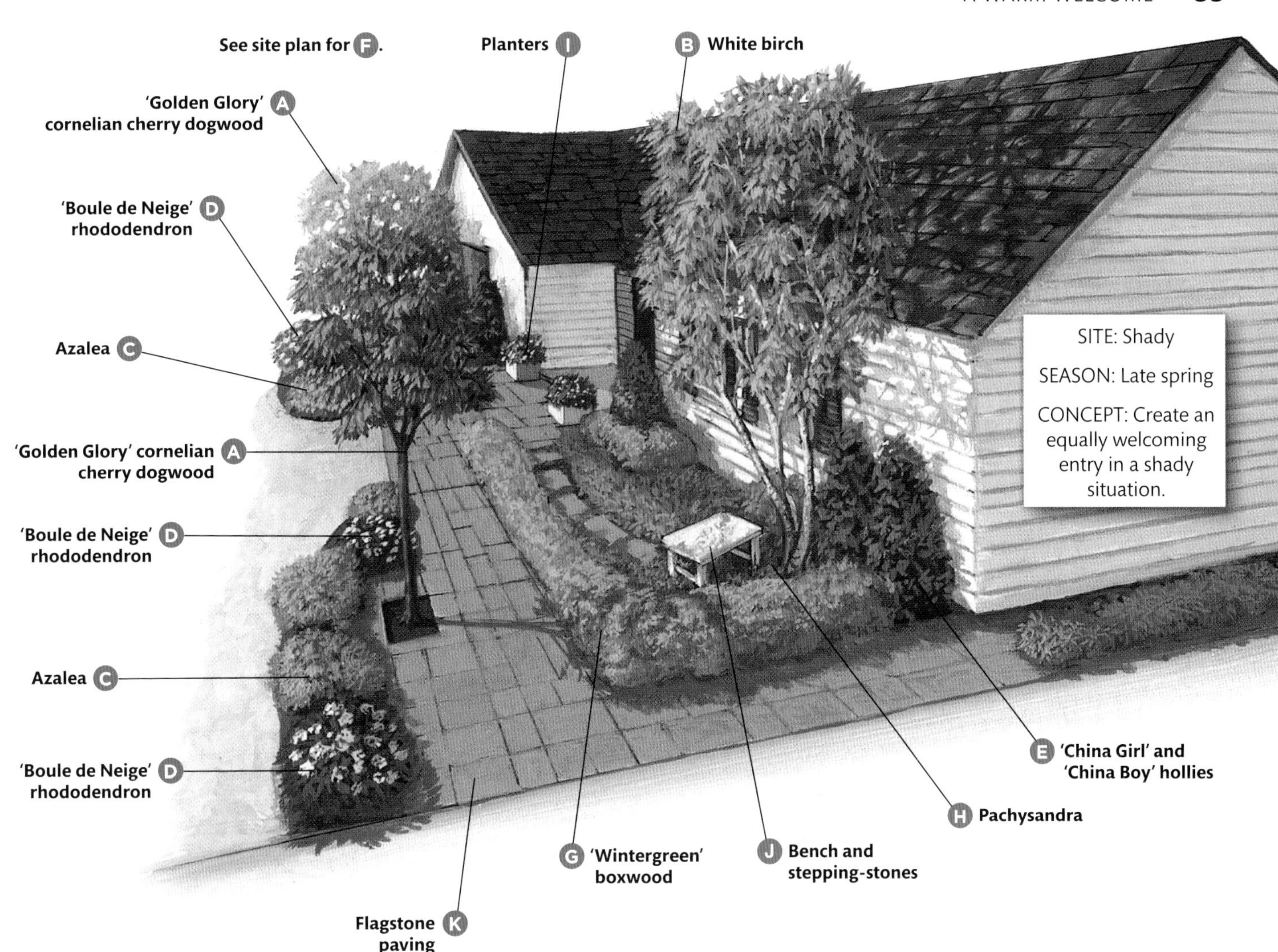

and doesn't grow too large. See *Rhododendron*, p. 148.

E 'China Girl' and 'China Boy' hollies (use 4)
The dense dark-green foliage of these evergreen shrubs is a striking backdrop for the white birch. Plant one 'China Boy' to ensure an abundant crop of red berries on the three female 'China Girl' plants. Berries last all winter. See *Ilex* x *meserveae*, p. 141.

F Variegated Siberian dogwood (use 3)
A clump-forming deciduous shrub with green-and-white foliage that looks fresh and bright in the shade. Glossy red twigs are eye-catching in winter. Prune hard every spring to keep it vigorous and compact. See *Cornus alba* 'Elegantissima', p. 135.

G 'Wintergreen' boxwood (use 16)
An evergreen shrub with small bright-green leaves and a tidy low-growing form that makes it perfect for edging the little garden bed next to the house. See *Buxus microphylla*, p. 133.

H Pachysandra (use 250)
This hardy evergreen ground cover makes a dense carpet of dark-green leaves and chokes out weeds. See *Pachysandra terminalis*, p. 145.

I Planters
Paint the planter boxes white and fill them with white-flowered impatiens for unending summer bloom. See p. 182.

J Bench and steppingstones
An iron or wooden bench painted white fits well here. Set flagstone stepping-stones to provide access. See p. 161.

See p. 30 for the following:

K Flagstone paving

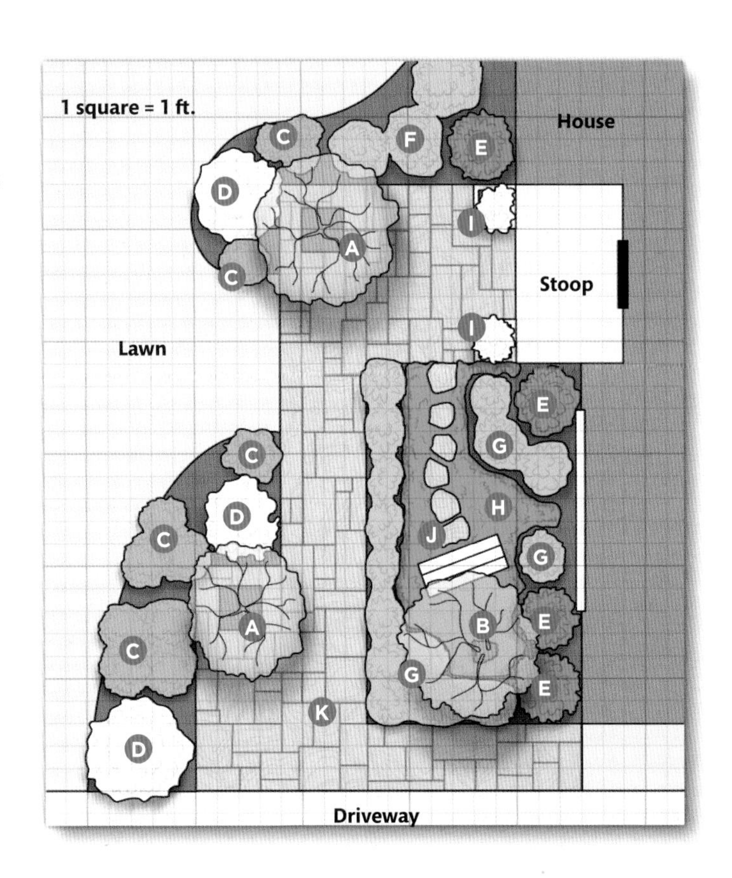

Formal and Fresh

GARDEN GEOMETRY TRANSFORMS A SMALL FRONT YARD

This design creates a small courtyard at the center of four rectangular beds defined by evergreen hedges and flagstone walkways. Inside the hedges, carefree perennial catmint makes a colorful floral carpet during the summer. The flagstone paving reinforces the design's geometry, while providing access to the front door from the sidewalk. (If a driveway runs along one side of the property, the crosswalk could extend to it through an opening in the hedge.) At the center of the compositon, the paving widens to accommodate a planter filled with annuals, a pleasant setting for greetings or good-byes. A bench at one end of the crosswalk provides a spot for longer chats or restful moments enjoying the plantings or, perhaps, contemplating a garden ornament at the other end, which provides balance for the bench.

Loose, informal hedges soften the rigid geometry. Deciduous shrubs change with the seasons, offering flowers in the spring and brilliant fall foliage, while the evergreens are a dependably colorful presence year-round.

arborvitae B

ornament I

'Blue Wonder' catmint F

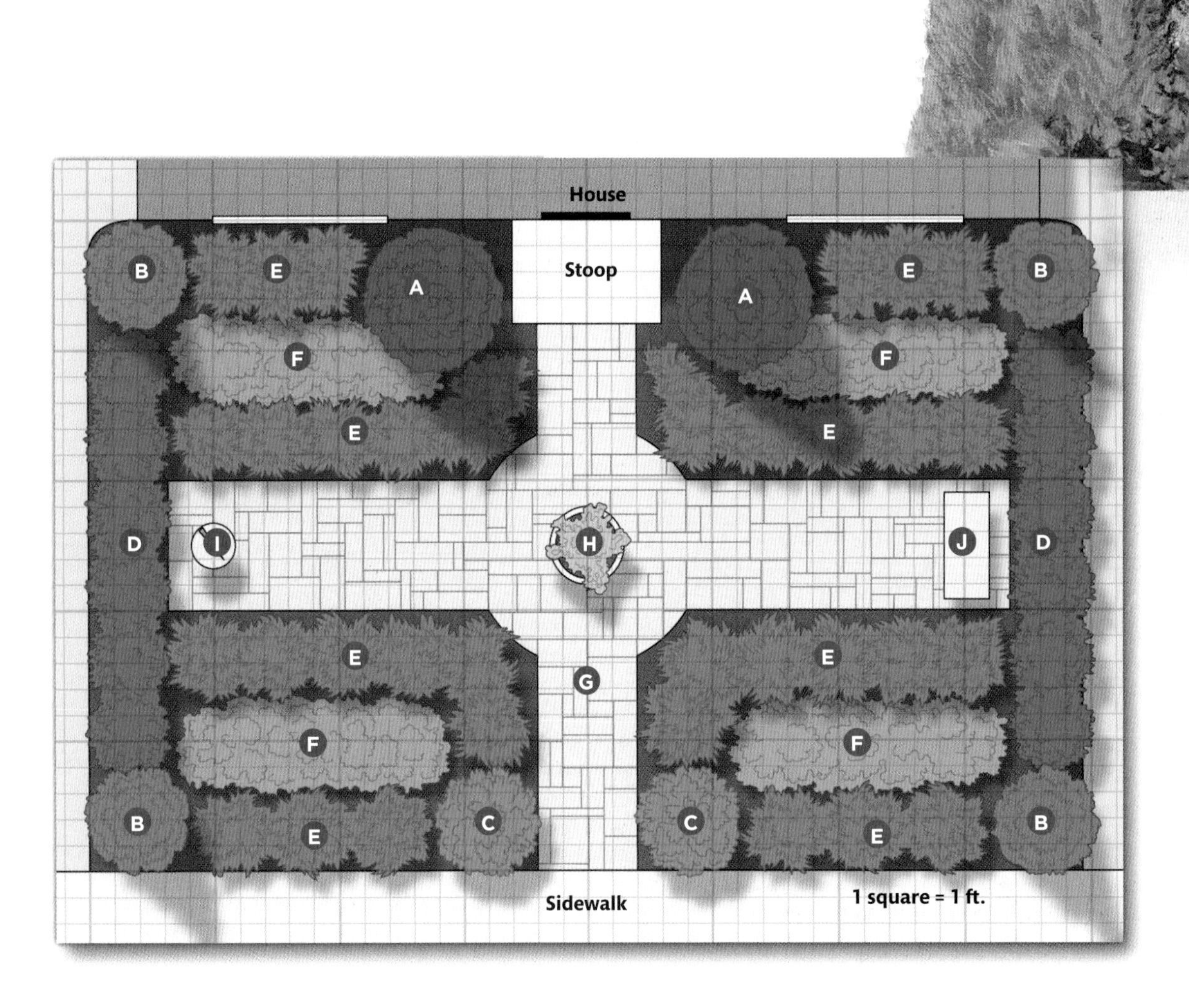

SITE: Sunny

SEASON: Summer

CONCEPT: A courtyard garden of elegant simplicity complements a home's formal facade.

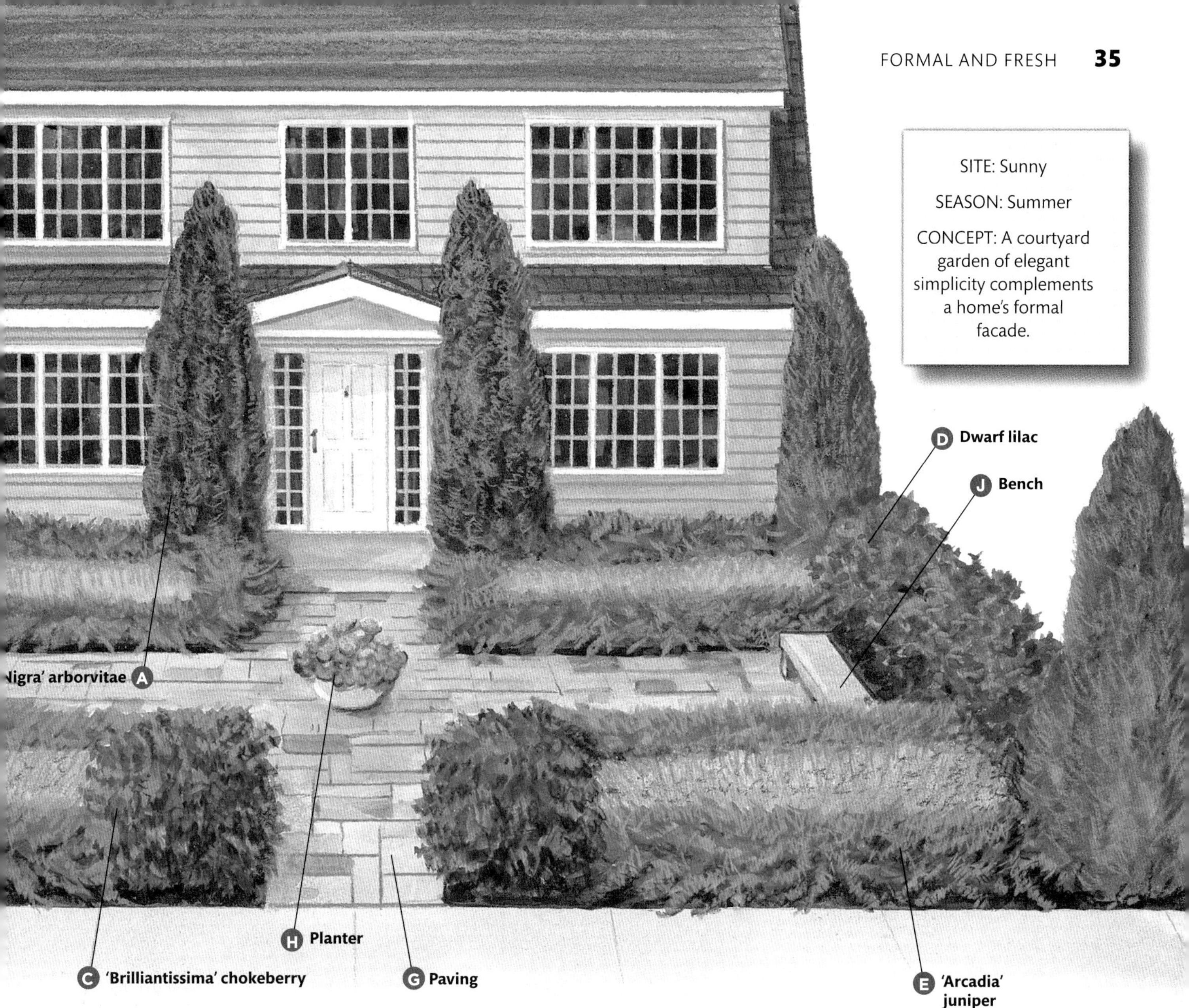

Plants & Projects

Precise layout is important in a simple design such as this. Start with the flagstone walks; they aren't difficult to build but require some time and muscle. The hedge shrubs are chosen for their compact forms. You'll need to clip the lilacs annually to maintain their shape, but the junipers will require little pruning over the years.

A 'Nigra' arborvitae (use 2 plants)
These upright, pyramidal evergreen trees stand like sentinels at the front door, where their scented foliage greets visitors. Prune to keep their height in scale with the house. See *Thuja occidentalis*, p. 151.

B 'Techny' arborvitae (use 4)
Marking the corners of the design, this evergreen tree forms a shorter, broader cone than its cousin by the door. See *Thuja occidentalis*, p. 151.

C 'Brilliantissima' chokeberry (use 2)
A deciduous native shrub that grows erect, up to about 10 ft. tall and 8 ft. wide, with white flowers in late spring, crimson fall foliage, and small red berries that last all winter. See *Aronia arbutifolia*, p. 131.

D Dwarf lilac (use 12)
This compact deciduous shrub makes an attractive loose hedge offering fragrant springtime flowers and glossy green foliage that has a purplish cast in fall. See *Syringa meyeri* 'Palibin', p. 150.

E 'Arcadia' juniper (use 36)
The arching branches of this spreading evergreen shrub line the walks with bright-green color through four seasons. See *Juniperus sabina*, p. 142.

F 'Blue Wonder' catmint (use 40)
Loose spikes of misty-blue flowers rise above the silvery, aromatic foliage of this perennial in June, filling the beds with color. Blooms continue or repeat through the summer. See *Nepeta* x *faassenii*, p. 144.

G Paving
Rectangular flagstones in random sizes suit the style of this house; brick or precast pavers work with other house styles. See p. 160.

H Planter
Nurseries and garden centers offer a range of planters that are suitable for formal settings. Choose one that complements the style of your house, and fill it with colorful annuals such as the geraniums in the round stone planter shown here. If you're ambitious, change the plantings with the seasons.

I Garden ornament
Place a sundial (shown here), reflecting ball, statue, or other ornament as a focal point at the end of the crosswalk.

J Bench
A stone bench is a nice companion for the planter and sundial here, but wood or metal benches can also work well in formal settings.

Make a No-Mow Slope

A TERRACED PLANTING TRANSFORMS A STEEP SITE

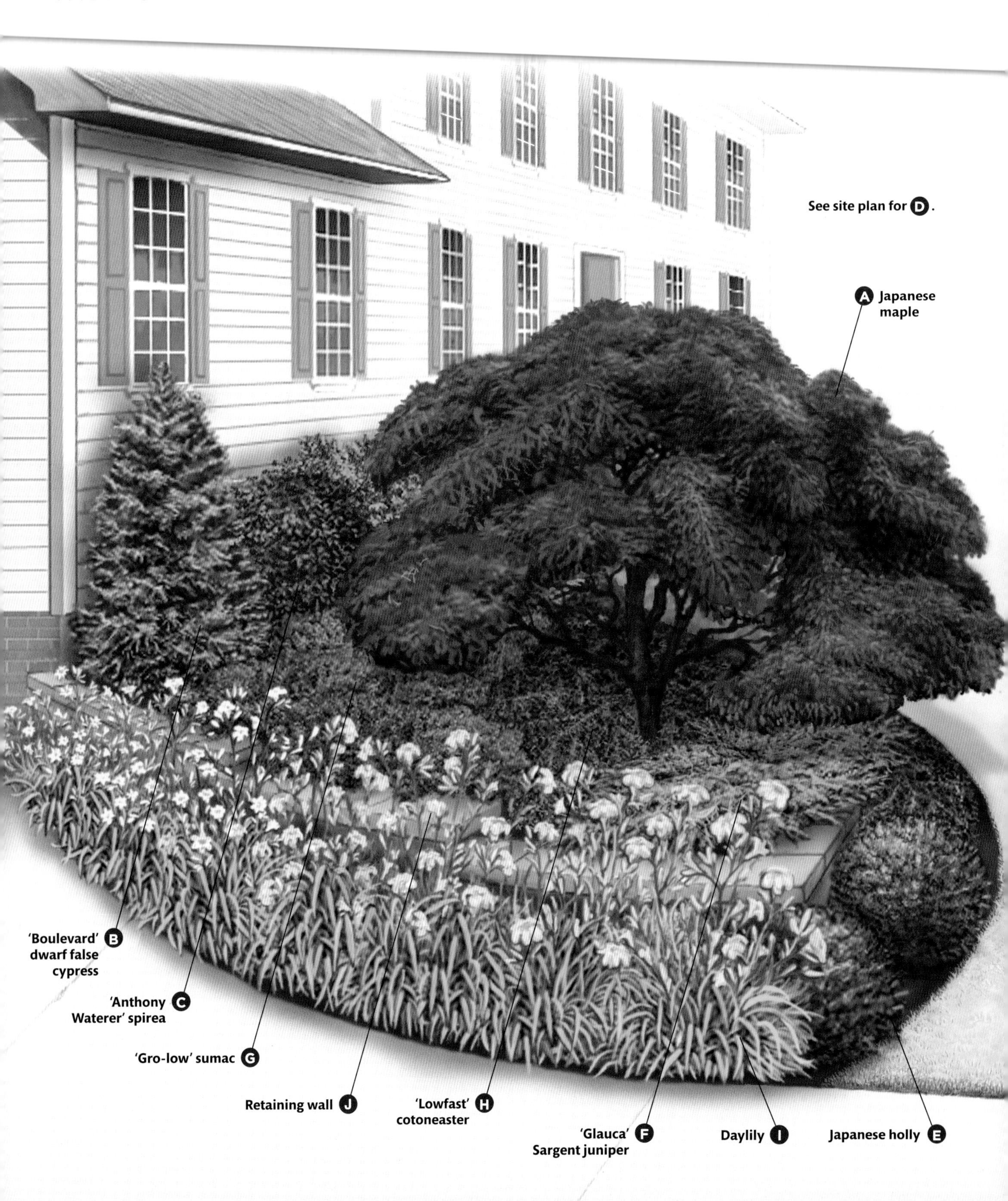

Loved by children with sleds, steep slopes can be a landscape headache for adults. They are a chore to mow and can present erosion and maintenance problems if you try to establish other plantings. One solution to this dilemma is shown here—tame the slope with a retaining wall and plant the resulting beds with low-care trees, shrubs, and perennials.

Steep slopes near the house are common on properties with walk-out basements or lower-level garages. Here, a low retaining wall echoes the curve of the driveway and a swath of colorful daylilies carpets the lower bed. Above the wall, a small multistemmed tree anchors an informal planting of shrubs that mixes deciduous and evergreen foliage for year-round interest.

When viewed from the sidewalk, the planting frames the house and directs attention to the front entrance. It also screens the semiprivate area of drive and garage from the more public entrance, while looking good from each of these vantage points. The planting can be easily extended along the house with the addition of more shrubs.

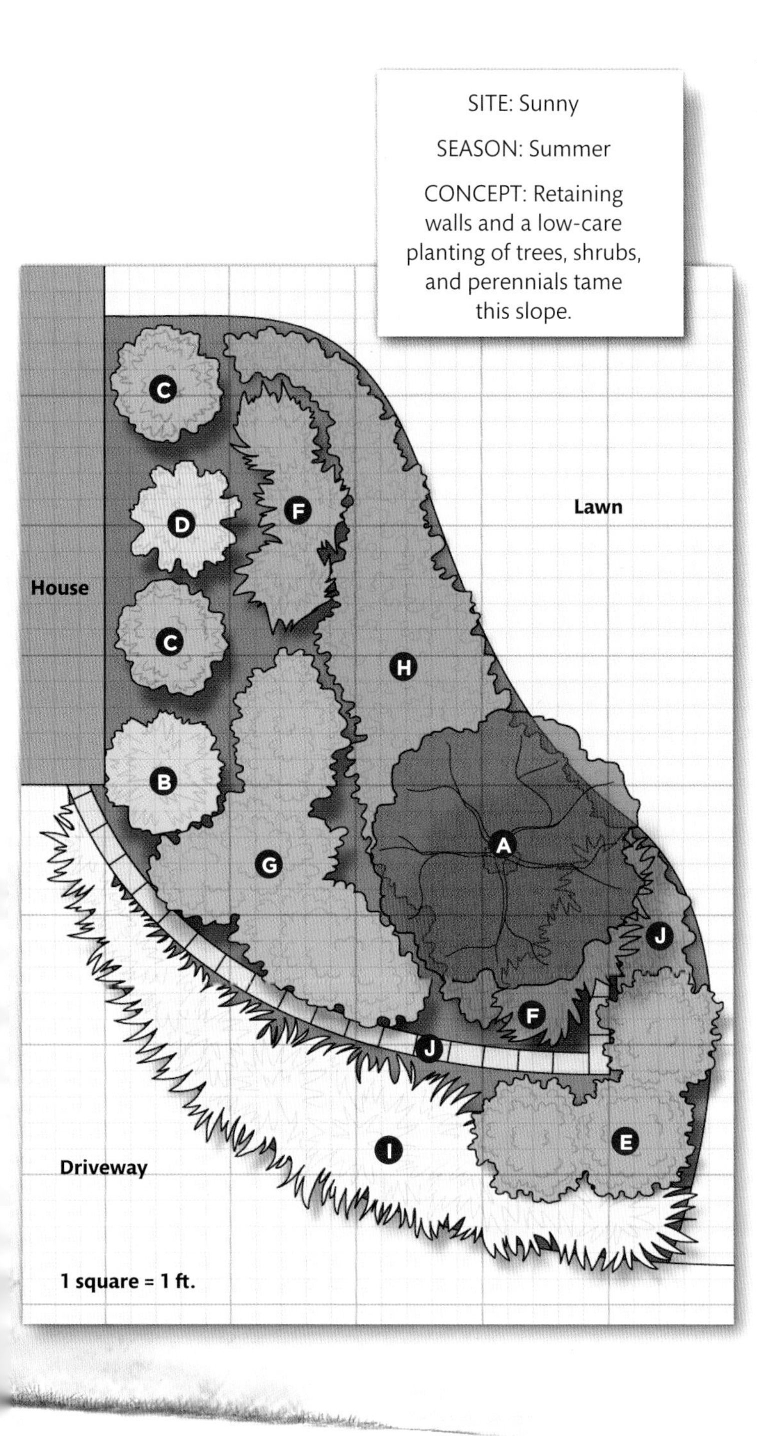

Plants & Projects

A 3 to 4 in. thick bark mulch will keep weeds down between small, young plants and help retain moisture as the planting matures. Tidy up the woody plants with annual pruning, and clear off spent daylily foliage in early winter. A spade-cut edge will keep the lawn from creeping into the planting bed.

A Japanese maple (use 1 plant)
This handsome deciduous tree is small and often multitrunked and has finely divided leaves. Choose a dwarf cultivar that has red to purple leaves during the summer. Prune to maintain it at a height of 6 to 8 ft. See *Acer palmatum*, p. 130. In a Zone 4 garden, substitute the hardier compact Amur maple (*Acer ginnala* 'Compactum').

B 'Boulevard' dwarf false cypress (use 1)
This slow-growing evergreen accents the corner of the house with slender sprays of feathery blue foliage that naturally form an irregular cone. See *Chamaecyparis pisifera*, p. 134.

C 'Anthony Waterer' spirea (use 2)
A deciduous shrub worth growing for its compact habit and small, fine leaves alone. The dark-pink flowers that appear in July and early August are a bonus. Will thrive in the dry-soil spot beneath the eaves. See *Spiraea* x *bumalda*, p. 150.

D 'Minuet' weigela (use 1)
This tidy deciduous shrub won't outgrow its place as a foundation planting. The purple-tinted leaves set off the dark-red flowers perfectly. It blooms in summer. See *Weigela florida*, p. 153.

E Japanese holly (use 3)
This evergreen shrub rounds out and hides the end of the wall with its dense mass of dark-green leathery leaves. See *Ilex crenata*, p. 140. In Zone 4, substitute the hardier compact inkberry, *Ilex glabra* 'Compacta'.

F 'Glauca' Sargent juniper (use 6)
A low-growing evergreen shrub, used as a ground cover under the Japanese maple. It has soft blue-green foliage. See *Juniperus chinensis* var. *sargentii*, p. 142.

G 'Gro-low' sumac (use 3)
The glossy green leaves of this low, spreading deciduous shrub blaze scarlet in early autumn. They add interesting texture as they spill over the wall. See *Rhus aromatica*, p. 147.

H 'Lowfast' cotoneaster (use 9)
Glossy dark-green leaves of this spreading semievergreen shrub are the perfect background for small white May flowers and the red fruits that follow in late summer and fall. See *Cotoneaster dammeri*, p. 136.

I Daylily (use 30)
These durable perennials put on an eye-popping summer display, then die back in winter when there's snow to shovel off the drive. Flowers come in a vast range of colors; plant a cheerful mixture, or use bold swaths of one or two colors. Select plants with different bloom times. See *Hemerocallis*, p. 139.

J Retaining wall
Built from a prefabricated wall system, the wall diminishes in height from the corner of the house to the return corner bordering the lawn. Adapt heights to your site. See p. 172.

Planting for a shady slope

The challenge here is the same as before—to make a steep slope from the house to the driveway attractive and easy to maintain—but here the slope is shaded (perhaps by the house or a large tree). While the design is similar, this time shade-tolerant plants are on display.

Once again, handsome varied foliage sets the tone. These shrubs also offer lovely flowers, several deliciously fragrant. Blooms of the rhododendrons, the andromeda, and the two ground covers brighten the spring, while summersweet lives up to its name with aromatic August blossoms. Fall is a mix of green, red, and gold foliage. Broad- and needle-leaved evergreens provide a substantial presence through the winter.

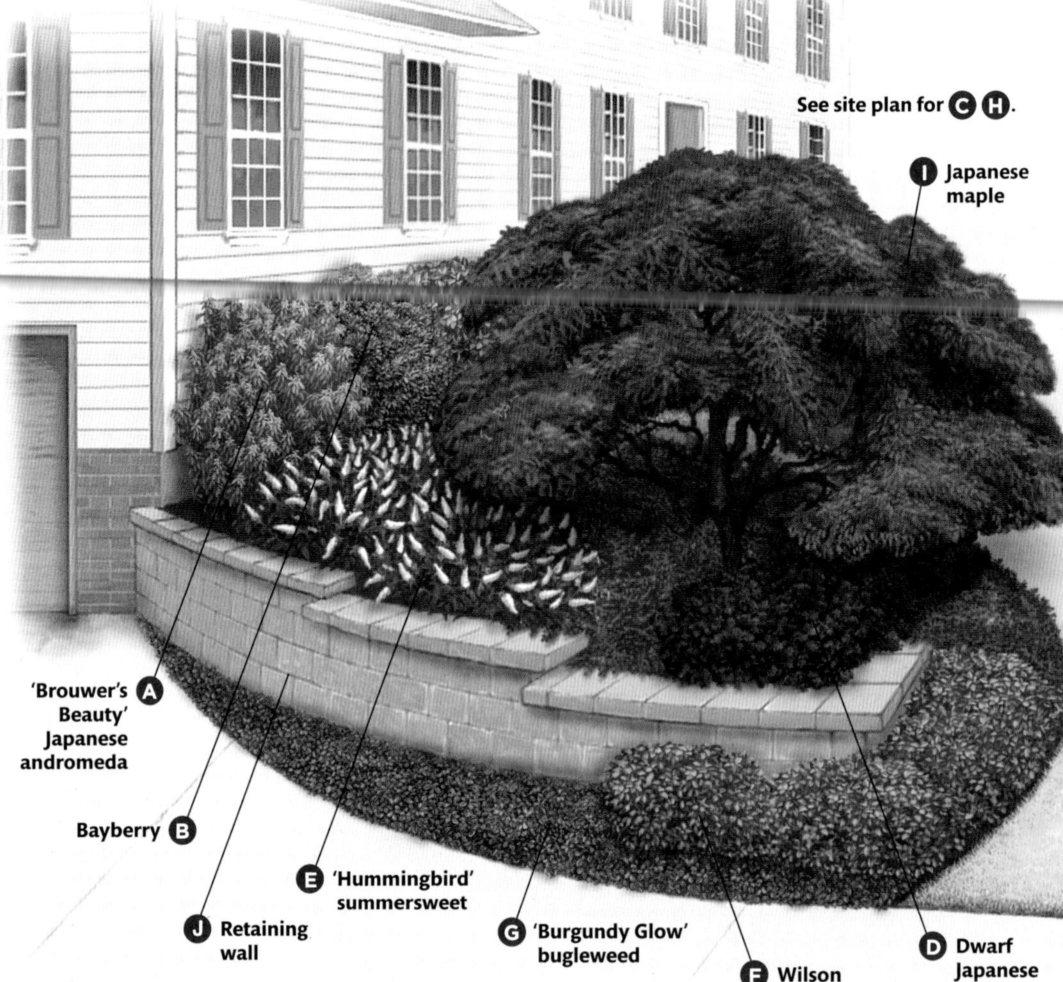

SITE: Shady

SEASON: Summer

CONCEPT: Shade-tolerant trees, shrubs, and perennials adapt the design to a site with little sun.

House

Lawn

Driveway

1 square = 1 ft.

Plants & Projects

A 'Brouwer's Beauty' Japanese andromeda (use 1 plant)
This is a handsome evergreen shrub with shiny green leaves and reddish buds that form in fall and open in spring as fragrant white flowers. See *Pieris*, p. 146.

B Bayberry (use 2)
The aromatic leaves of this deciduous shrub are glossy green in summer, turning purple in fall. Waxy silver-gray berries last into winter. See *Myrica pensylvanica*, p. 144.

C 'Olga Mezitt' rhododendron (use 1)
In spring, the evergreen foliage of this shrub sparkles against striking pink flowers. The leaves turn maroon in winter. See *Rhododendron*, p. 148.

D Dwarf Japanese yew (use 6)
The spreading dark-green branches of this tough, slow-growing evergreen shrub reach over the wall. Prune to a 2-ft. height. See *Taxus cuspidata* 'Nana', p. 151.

E 'Hummingbird' summersweet (use 5)
Deciduous shrub with sweet-scented white flowers in August and gold fall foliage. See *Clethra alnifolia*, p. 134.

F Wilson rhododendron (use 3)
Neat evergreen shrub with small rose-pink flowers in spring. See *Rhododendron laetivirens*, p. 148.

G 'Burgundy Glow' bugleweed (use 45)
A tough, vigorous perennial ground cover with variegated leaves and bright-blue flowers in early summer. See *Ajuga reptans*, p. 130.

H Myrtle (use 50)
Glossy leaves of this evergreen ground cover are carpeted with lilac flowers in late spring. See *Vinca minor*, p. 153.

See p. 37 for the following:

I Japanese maple (use 1)

J Retaining wall

PLANT PORTRAITS

These plants drape the slope with a lovely selection of foliage colors and textures accented from spring through fall by flowers.

● = First design, pp. 36–37

▲ = Second design, p. 38

'Burgundy Glow' bugleweed (*Ajuga reptans*, p. 130) ▲

Dwarf Japanese yew (*Taxus cuspidata* 'Nana', p. 151) ▲

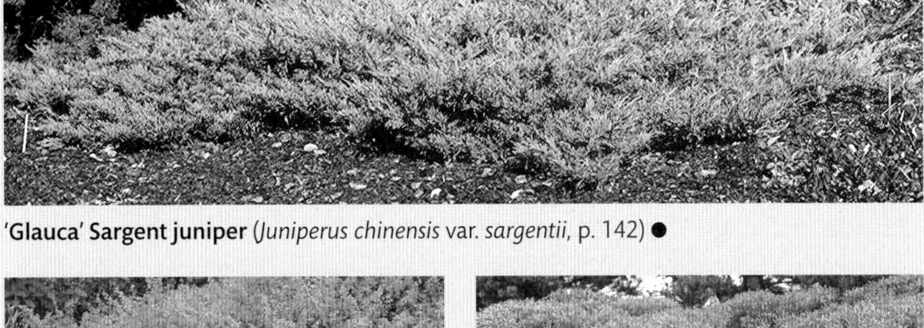

'Glauca' Sargent juniper (*Juniperus chinensis* var. *sargentii*, p. 142) ●

'Hummingbird' summersweet (*Clethra alnifolia*, p. 134) ▲

'Gro-low' sumac (*Rhus aromatica*, p. 147) ●

Bayberry (*Myrica pensylvanica*, p. 144) ▲

'Anthony Waterer' spirea (*Spiraea* x *bumalda*, p. 150) ●

Japanese maple (*Acer palmatum*, p. 130) ● ▲

A Neighborly Corner

BEAUTIFY A BOUNDARY WITH EASY-CARE PLANTS

The corner where your property meets your neighbor's and the sidewalk can be a kind of grassy no-man's-land. This design defines the boundary with a planting that can be enjoyed by the property owners as well as by people passing by.

Because of its exposed location, remote from the house and close to the street, this is a less personal planting than those in other more private parts of your property. It is meant to be appreciated from a distance. Anchored by a multitrunked birch tree, attractive grasses and shrubs are arrayed in large masses at several heights. An existing split-rail fence on the property line now serves as a scaffold for a rose trained around its rails. While not intended as a barrier, the planting also provides a modest physical and psychological screen from activity on the street.

Variegated Siberian dogwood **C**

'Blaze' climbing rose **B**

'Blue Star' juniper **D**

SITE: Sunny

SEASON: Summer

CONCEPT: Enhance the property line with a low-care, neighbor-friendly planting of trees and shrubs.

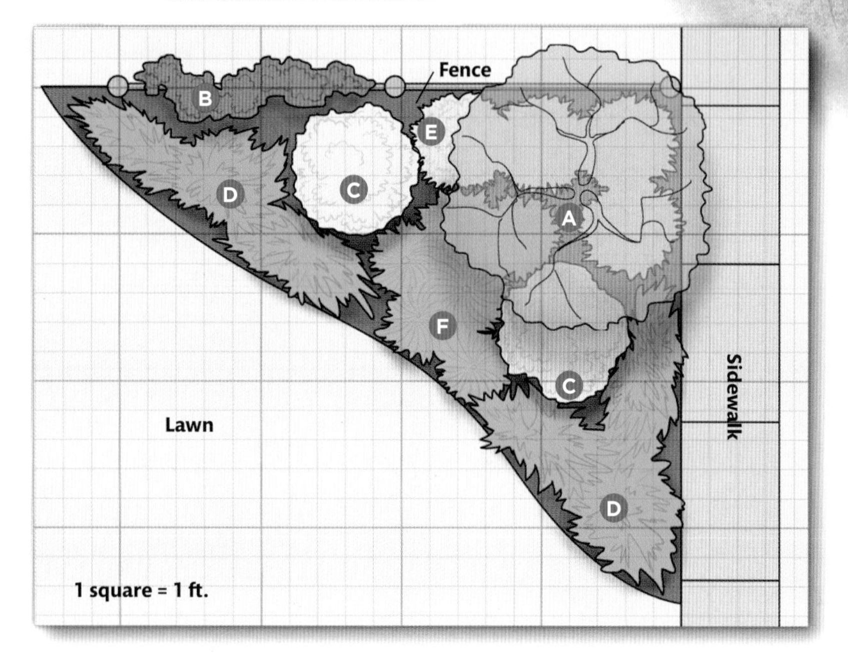

Plants & Projects

These plants all have a four-season presence, including the grasses, whose foliage stands up as well as many shrubs to the rigors of winter. Good gardens make good neighbors, so we've used well-behaved plants that won't make extra work for the person next door—or for you. The rose will need training throughout the summer, there will be some birch leaves to rake in fall, and the grasses must be trimmed back in late winter or early spring.

A **White birch** (use 1 plant)
A deciduous tree grown for its graceful upright form and striking white bark. Green

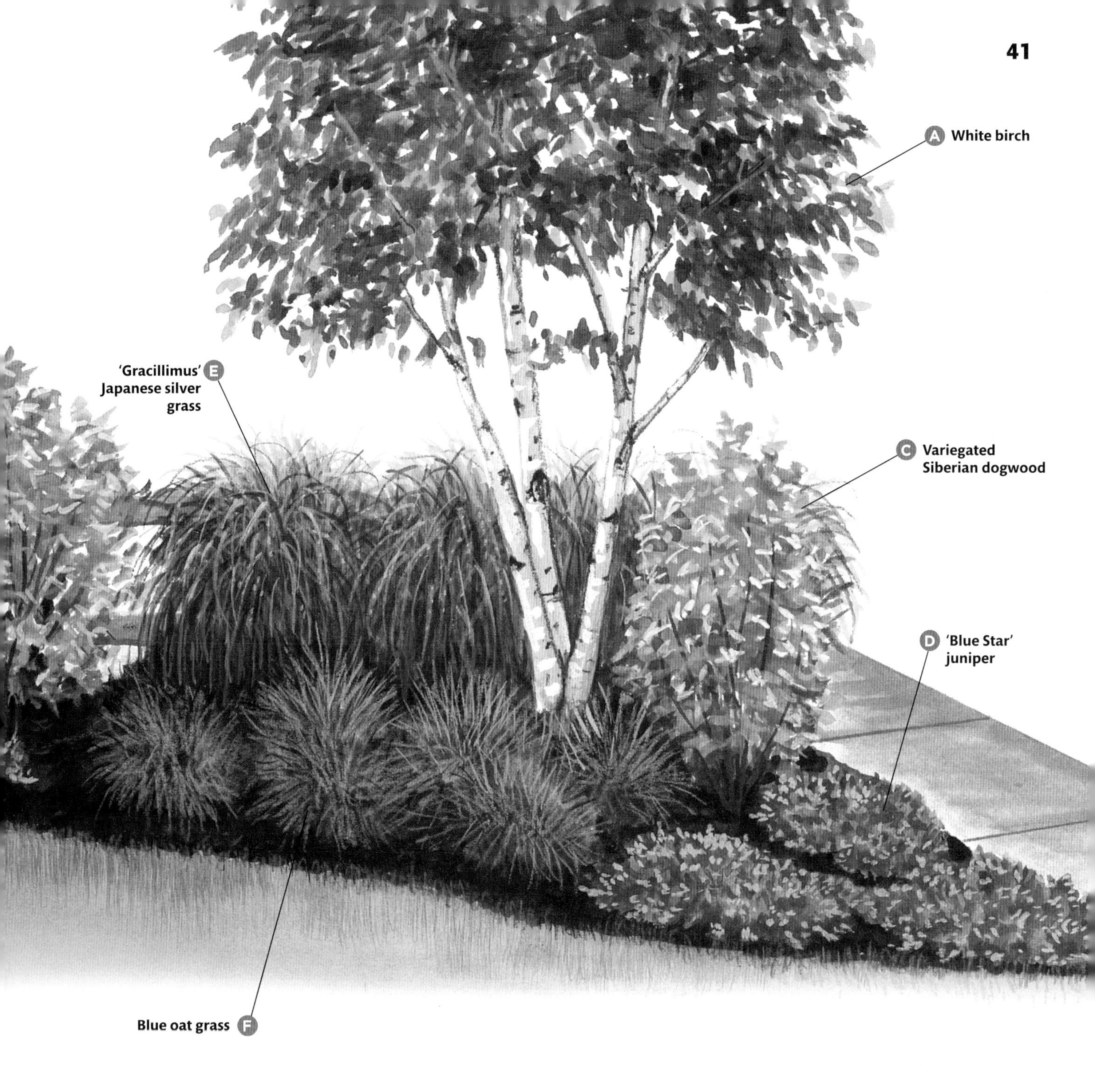

leaves dance in the summer breezes and turn a pretty yellow in fall. Buy a multitrunked specimen, and keep the lower limbs pruned so it won't cast too much shade on the shrubs and grasses underneath. See *Betula platyphylla* 'White Spire', p. 132.

B 'Blaze' climbing rose (use 1)
This vigorous climbing rose has long flexible canes that can be trained horizontally. Tied to or wrapped around the rails, they'll cover the fence quickly. They bear lots of red semidouble flowers in June and blooms off and on until frost. The flowers are only mildly fragrant. See *Rosa*, p. 149.

C Variegated Siberian dogwood (use 2)
This deciduous shrub has eye-catching features year-round: white flowers in spring, white-and-green leaves in summer, and pale blue berries in fall. In winter, dark-red stems provide a lovely contrast to the blue foliage of the juniper. See *Cornus alba* 'Elegantissima', p. 135.

D 'Blue Star' juniper (use 6)
This evergreen shrub forms an irregular sparkling blue mass. It grows slowly and never needs pruning. An excellent ground cover, it is a nice counterpoint to the flowing grasses. See *Juniperus squamata*, p. 142.

E 'Gracillimus' Japanese silver grass (use 4)
This perennial grass is always beautiful, but never more so than in fall and winter, when silvery plumes of tiny seeds wave above an arching clump of tan foliage. Earlier, the narrow leaves are green striped with white. See *Miscanthus*, p. 144.

F Blue oat grass (use 6)
Less than half as tall as the silver grass, this perennial is just as lovely. Dense compact mounds bristle with wiry blue leaves, which often live through the winter. Thin stalks carry slender seed heads that turn tan in winter. See *Helictotrichon sempervirens*, p. 138.

PLANT PORTRAITS

For these two designs, woody plants provide a smorgasbord of texture, color, and form, while perennials offer months of cheerful flowers.

● = First design, pp. 40–41

▲ = Second design, pp. 42–43

Variegated Siberian dogwood (*Cornus alba* 'Elegantissima', p. 135) ● ▲

'Blaze' climbing rose (*Rosa*, p. 149) ●

White birch (*Betula platyphylla* 'White Spire', p. 132) ●

Blue oat grass (*Helictotrichon sempervirens*, p. 138) ● ▲

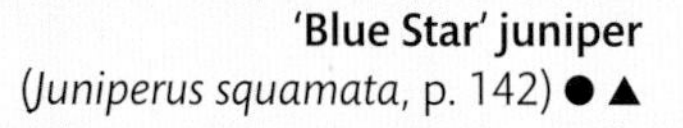

'Blue Star' juniper (*Juniperus squamata*, p. 142) ● ▲

Summer flowers

Retaining the year-round good looks of the shrubs and grasses, this design adds flowering perennials to make the planting more colorful in summer.

To make room for the new plants and to afford the sunny conditions they prefer, we've removed the birch tree. A rose still covers the fence with flowers for months, but here the blossoms are pink and fragrant. Catmint and daylilies provide flowers in a range of cheerful colors from early summer to frost. The sedum adds its distinctive flat flower clusters in late summer, and they carry through the fall. Dogwood, juniper, and tawny grasses enliven the winter months.

Plants & Projects

A 'Autumn Joy' sedum (use 6)
One of the best year-round perennials, it forms a low mound of attractive blue-green fleshy foliage, topped by distinctive flat flower heads that turn from pink in late summer to dark red in fall. Seed heads are tough enough to stand through the winter. See *Sedum*, p. 150.

B Daylily (use 7)
The large blooms and grassy foliage of these perennials look wonderful against the foliage of the variegated dogwood. There are hundreds of cultivars available in a wide range of colors, sizes, and bloom times. Taller daylilies will look best here; mix several kinds to extend the blooming season through much of the summer. For a fuller look the first year or two, you can plant up to 14 in this space, but you'll need to divide them sooner. See *Hemerocallis*, p. 139.

C 'Six Hills Giant' catmint (use 3)
Large mounds of soft gray foliage complement colors and textures of surrounding plants. This perennial produces masses of little violet-blue flowers starting in June and continuing throughout the season, encouraged by midsummer pruning. See *Nepeta* x *faassenii*, p. 144.

D 'Frau Dagmar Hartop' rose (use 1)
A carefree rose with handsome foliage and large fragrant pink flowers from June through September. Plant one in the middle of each 8-ft. section of fence and tie the canes along rails in both directions as they grow. See *Rosa*, p. 149.

See p. 41 for the following:

E Variegated Siberian dogwood (use 2)

F 'Gracillimus' Japanese silver grass (use 4)

G 'Blue Star' juniper (use 4)

H Blue oat grass (use 2)

Fence on property line

Lawn

Sidewalk

Plant crocuses, grape hyacinths, or other small bulbs under the dogwoods if you'd like some flowers in early spring.

1 square = 1 ft.

SITE: Sunny

SEASON: Late summer

CONCEPT: Durable flowering perennials enliven a setting of handsome shrubs.

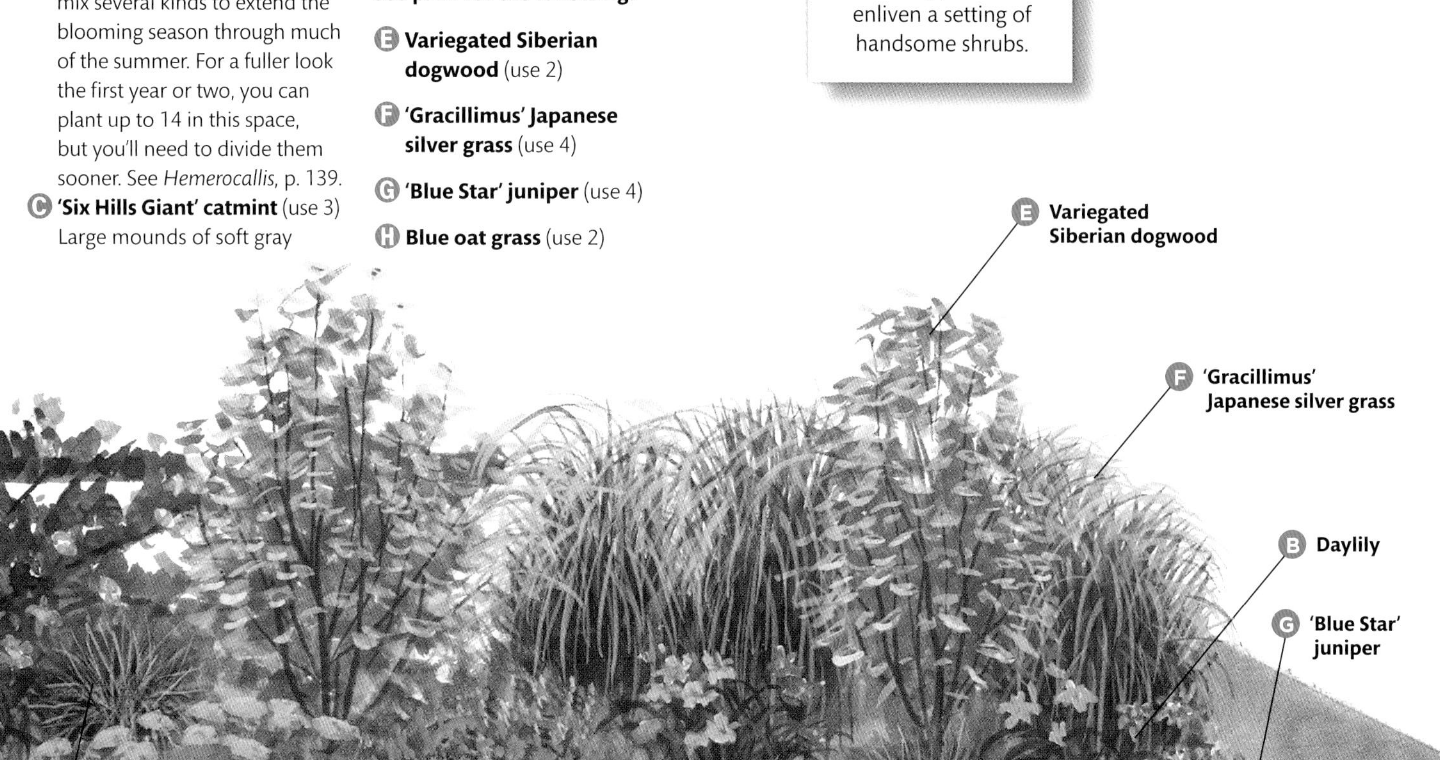

Streetwise and Stylish

GIVE YOUR CURBSIDE STRIP A NEW LOOK

Homeowners seldom think much about the area that runs between the sidewalk and street. At best it is a tidy patch of lawn; at worst, a weed-choked eyesore. But it is one of the most public parts of your property. The colorful planting shown here and a weekend's work can transform the area, warmly welcoming visitors and adding a touch of beauty to your yard and the entire neighborhood.

A handsome cobblestone path splits the planting, allowing visitors who park on the street easy access to the sidewalk. On each side lie plants tough enough to stand up to life on the street, where masses of concrete keep things hot in summer and snow and road salt can make winter brutal.

Attractive evergreen shrubs form the backbone of the design, surrounded by perennials chosen for their bold, long-blooming flowers or striking foliage. All of these plants are short, and the overall effect is like laying a bright carpet at the foot of your property.

Curbside strips are often city-owned, so check local ordinances for restrictions before you begin to dig. It is easy to extend the planting to fill a larger space by repeating plants shown here or adding other tough, low-growing favorites.

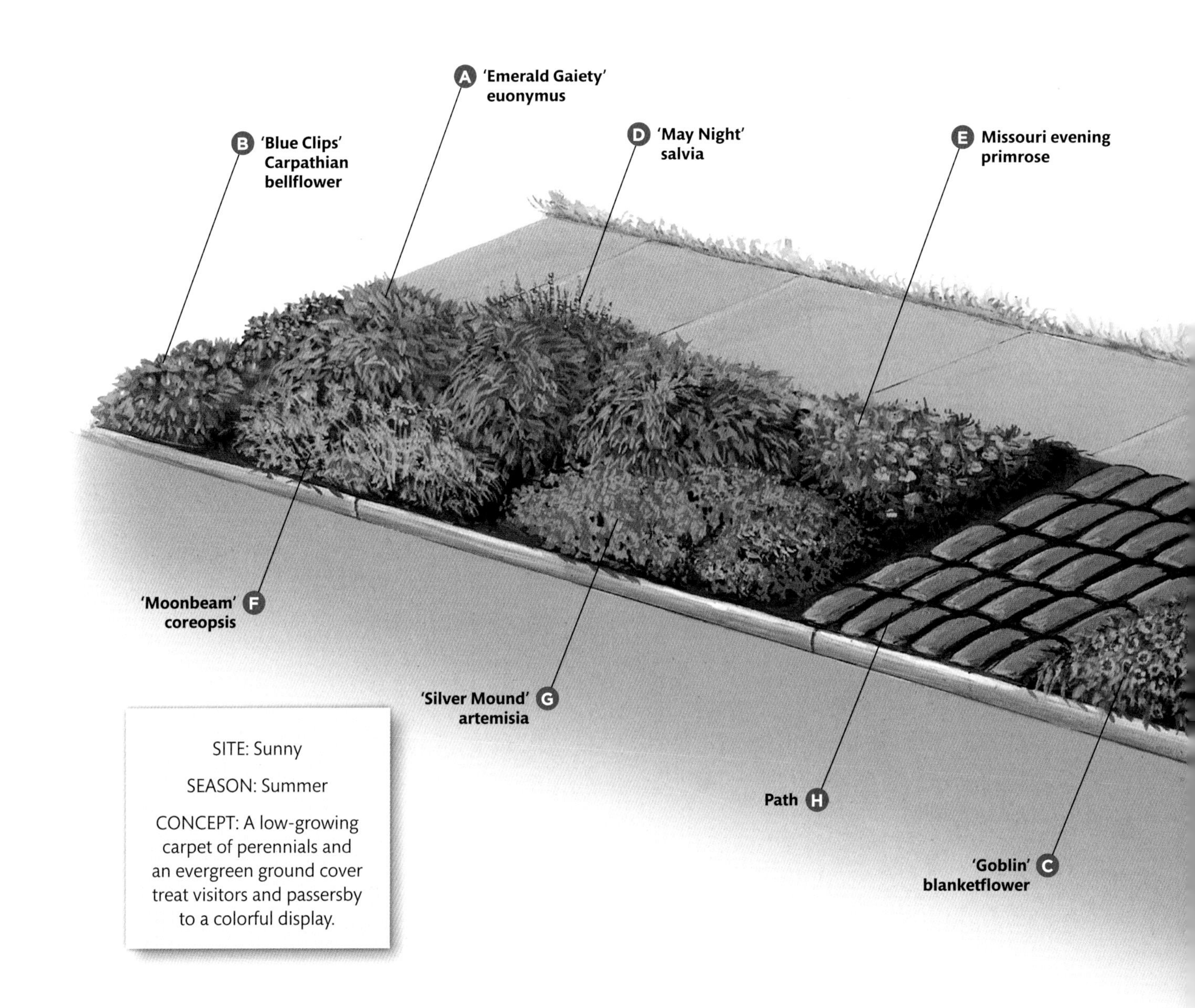

SITE: Sunny

SEASON: Summer

CONCEPT: A low-growing carpet of perennials and an evergreen ground cover treat visitors and passersby to a colorful display.

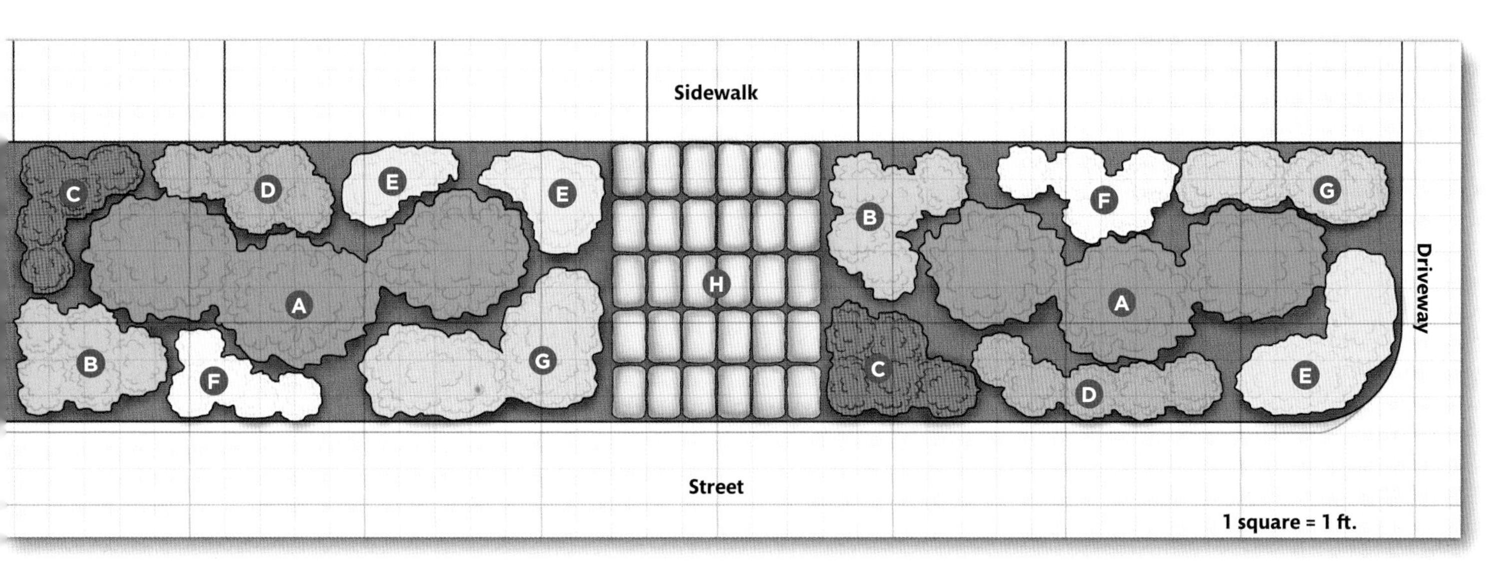

Plants & Projects

Mound the soil in the beds so the center is about a foot higher than the edges. The euonymus cascades down this little hill, providing a backdrop for the flowering plants at its feet. Use a layer of bark mulch to conserve soil moisture, inhibit weeds, and make the bed look neat in this highly visible location. Cut all the perennials to the ground in early spring and rake or renew the mulch at the same time.

A 'Emerald Gaiety' euonymus (use 6 plants)
A small evergreen shrub with trailing stems that won't be harmed by a heavy load of snow. The small leathery leaves are dark green edged with white and frequently turn pinkish purple in winter. See *Euonymus fortunei*, p. 136.

B 'Blue Clips' Carpathian bellflower (use 10)
Small spreading mounds of delicate glossy green leaves look pretty beneath this perennial's summer-long display of blue cuplike flowers. See *Campanula carpatica*, p. 134.

C 'Goblin' blanketflower (use 10)
The cheerful red-and-yellow daisylike flowers of this native perennial keep coming from June until frost, and it thrives in the heat radiating from the pavement. See *Gaillardia* x *grandiflora*, p. 138.

D 'May Night' salvia (use 10)
These dark indigo-purple flower spikes rise like exclamation points between brightly colored blanketflowers and cup-shaped primroses. This hardy perennial blooms from late spring to frost if spent flowers are deadheaded. See *Salvia* x *superba*, p. 150.

E Missouri evening primrose (use 4)
This perennial spreads a mat of glossy deep-green leaves that is covered with large, glowing yellow flowers from mid- to late summer. See *Oenothera missouriensis*, p. 145.

F 'Moonbeam' coreopsis (use 10)
Clouds of tiny lemon-yellow flowers float above this perennial's dark-green foliage from July into September. See *Coreopsis verticillata*, p. 135.

G 'Silver Mound' artemisia (use 4)
The mounded soft silvery foliage of this perennial contrasts with and sets off the foliage and flowers of nearby plants. See *Artemisia schmidtiana*, p. 131.

H Path
A combination landing and path, it is wide enough to accommodate open car doors and disembarking visitors. The surface shown here is precast pavers made to resemble cobblestones. See p. 160.

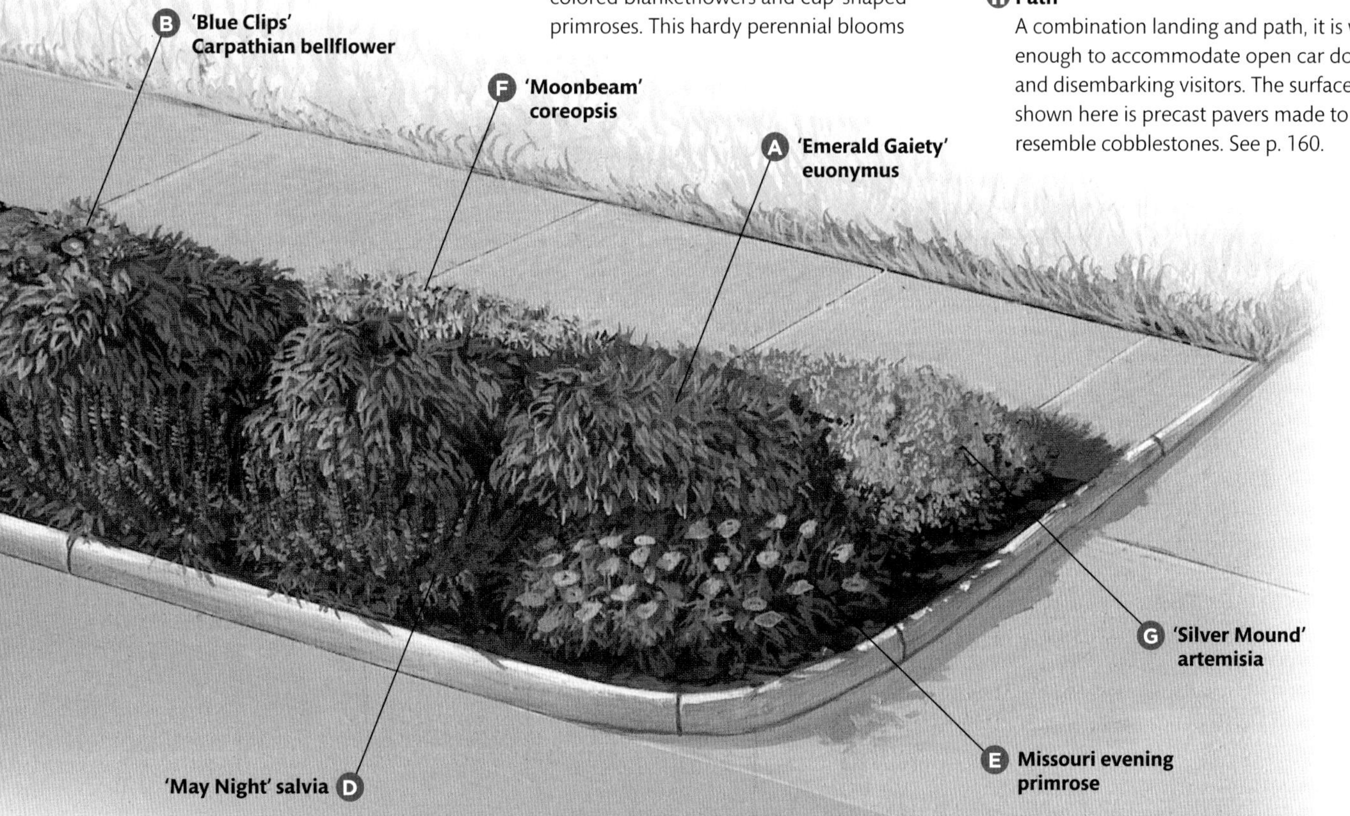

PLANT PORTRAITS

Rugged shrubs, perennials, and ground covers combine attractive foliage and pretty flowers while withstanding the rigors of curbside life.

● = First design, pp. 44–45

▲ = Second design, p. 47

'White Nancy' lamium
(*Lamium maculatum*, p. 143) ▲

'Blue Clips' Carpathian bellflower
(*Campanula carpatica*, p. 134) ●

'Emerald Gaiety' euonymus
(*Euonymus fortunei*, p. 136) ●

'Goblin' blanketflower
(*Gaillardia* x *grandiflora*, p. 138) ●

'Silver Mound' artemisia
(*Artemisia schmidtiana*, p. 131) ●

'Luxuriant' bleeding heart (*Dicentra*, p. 136) ▲

'Mrs. Moon' lungwort (*Pulmonaria saccharata*, p. 147) ▲

Enliven a shady curb

If mature trees shade the streets in your neighborhood, try this combination of plants selected to thrive in dry shade. As in the previous design, low-growing plants make a loosely symmetrical composition around a cobblestone path. Here, colorful foliage of contrasting textures provides long-term interest, dappled from spring to fall with a procession of the delicate flowers characteristic of many shade-loving plants. Most of the perennials die back in winter, helping them to survive snow, gravel, and salt thrown from the sidewalk and street.

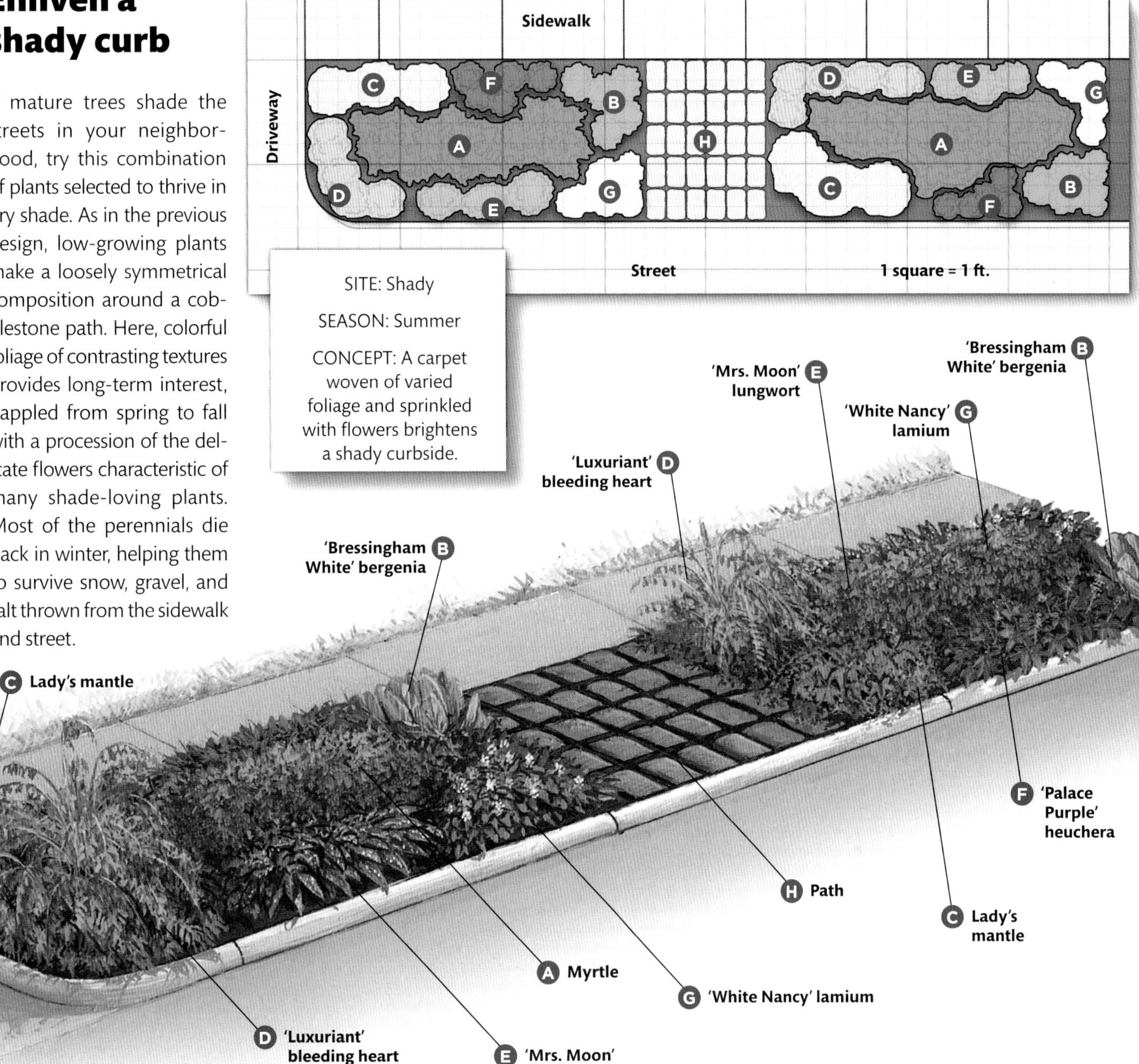

Plants & Projects

A Myrtle (use 50 plants)
Planted along the raised spine of the bed, this low-care evergreen ground cover soon forms a thick carpet of glossy, leathery dark-green leaves. See *Vinca minor*, p. 153.

B 'Bressingham White' bergenia (use 10)
Large, glossy dark-green leaves turn red in cool fall weather. Clusters of white flowers appear barely above foliage in spring. See *Bergenia cordifolia*, p. 132.

C Lady's mantle (use 6)
This perennial favorite features large mounds of ruffled light-green leaves that look fresh all summer. In June, clusters of small yellow-green flowers stand out nicely against the foliage of surrounding plants. See *Alchemilla mollis*, p. 130.

D 'Luxuriant' bleeding heart (use 10)
The small heart-shaped rose-red flowers of this perennial dangle on slim stems from June until frost above clumps of soft lacy foliage. See *Dicentra*, p. 136.

E 'Mrs. Moon' lungwort (use 6)
In April, this perennial's pink buds mature to rich pink-and-blue flowers that last for weeks. Large leaves spotted with white flecks make a handsome ground cover the rest of the season. See *Pulmonaria saccharata*, p. 147.

F 'Palace Purple' heuchera (use 10)
A perennial forming tidy mounds of striking purple foliage that adds color all season. Small white flowers in summer aren't showy. See *Heuchera micrantha*, p. 139.

G 'White Nancy' lamium (use 10)
Small silver leaves with green edges lighten the shady site. Pure white flowers increase this perennial ground cover's appeal in early summer. See *Lamium maculatum*, p. 143.

See p. 45 for the following:

H Path

Landscaping a Low Wall

TWO-TIER GARDEN REPLACES A SHORT SLOPE

Some things may not love a wall, but plants and gardeners do. For plants, walls offer warmth for an early start in spring and good drainage for roots. Gardeners appreciate the rich visual potential of composing a garden on two levels, as well as the practical advantage of working on two relatively flat surfaces instead of a single sloping one. If you have a wall, or have a place to put one, grasp the opportunity for some handsome landscaping.

This design places two complementary perennial borders above and below a wall bounded at one end by a set of stairs. While each bed is narrow enough for easy maintenance, when viewed from the lower level they combine to form a border almost 8 ft. deep, with plants rising to eye level. The planting can be easily extended on both sides of the steps.

Building the wall that makes this impressive sight possible doesn't require the time or skill it once did. Nor is it necessary to scour the countryside for tons of fieldstone or to hire an expensive contractor. Thanks to precast retaining-wall systems, a knee-high do-it-yourself wall can be installed in as little as a weekend. More experienced or ambitious wall builders may want to tackle a natural stone wall, but anyone with a healthy back (or access to energetic teenagers) can succeed with a prefabricated system.

> SITE: Sunny
>
> SEASON: Summer
>
> CONCEPT: Low retaining wall creates easy-to-maintain beds for a distinctive two-level planting.

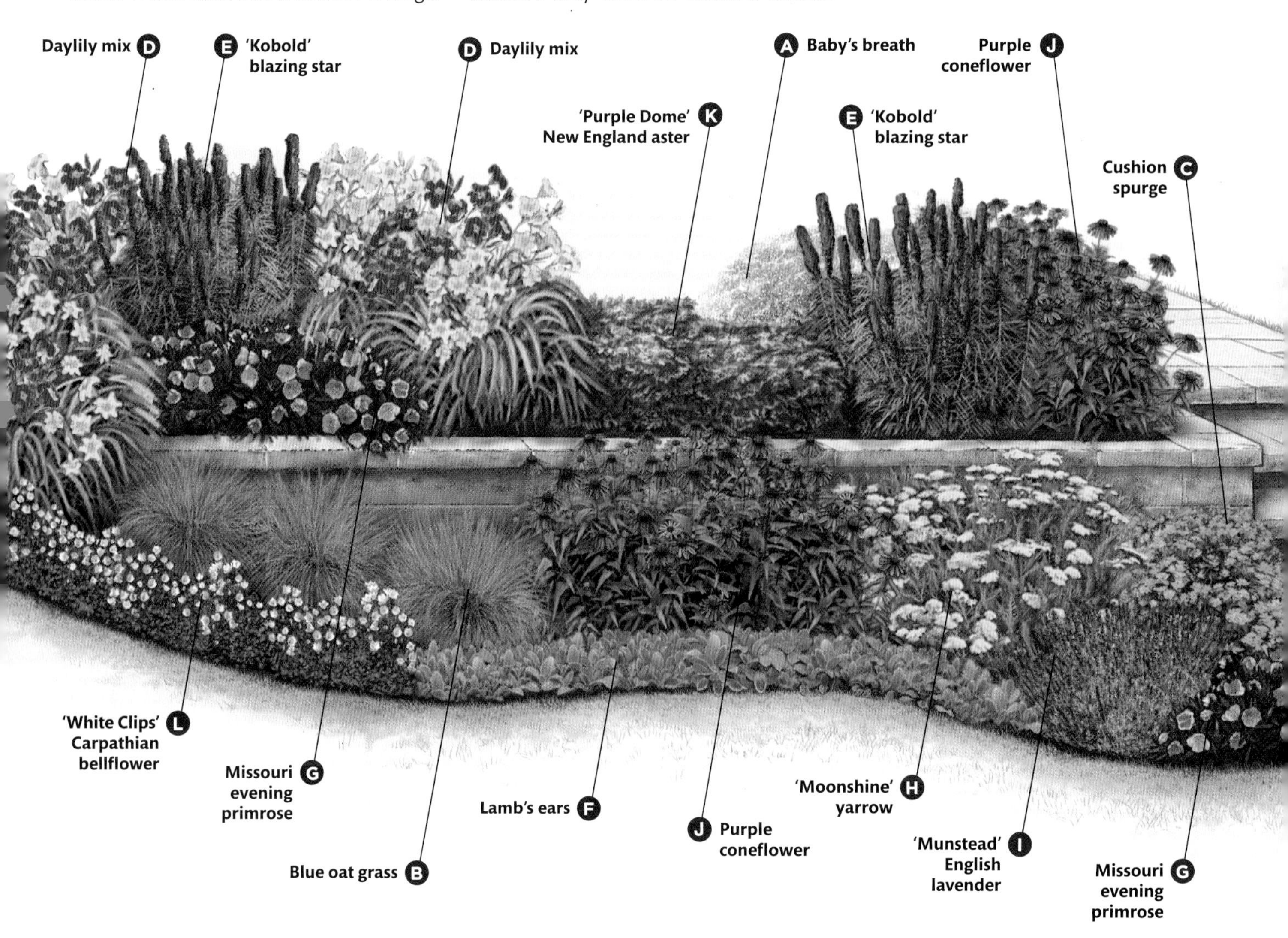

Plants & Projects

These plants provide color from spring until frost with little care from you. All are perennials that need minimal maintenance beyond clipping of spent blooms and a fall or spring cleanup. Several offer excellent flowers for cutting or drying.

A Baby's breath (use 3 plants)
This popular perennial produces a cloud of tiny white flowers in June and July that add an airy texture to the garden and are excellent for cutting. A good foil to the stronger colors and textures of the adjacent plants. See *Gypsophila paniculata*, p. 138.

B Blue oat grass (use 3)
A carefree grass, it forms a neat, dense clump of thin blue leaves that maintain their color through winter. *See Helictotrichon sempervirens*, p. 138.

C Cushion spurge (use 1)
The electric-yellow spring color of this showy perennial is produced by long-lasting flower bracts, not petals, so it serves as a garden focal point for weeks. Its mound of foliage neatly fills the corner by the steps and turns red in fall. See *Euphorbia polychroma*, p. 137.

D Daylily mix (use 6)
For an extended show of lovely lilylike flowers, combine early- and late-blooming cultivars in a selection of your favorite colors. The grassy foliage of this perennial covers the end of the wall. See *Hemerocallis*, p. 139.

E 'Kobold' blazing star (use 6)
Magenta flower spikes of this durable perennial rise from a clump of dark-green foliage from late July through August. A good mate for its prairie companion, purple coneflower. Flowers are great for cutting and drying, and butterflies love them. See *Liatris spicata*, p. 143.

F Lamb's ears (use 6)
The large soft leaves of this spreading perennial ground cover are a season-long presence; their silvery color is a nice foil to the blues and yellows nearby. It bears small purple flowers in early summer. See *Stachys byzantina*, p. 150.

G Missouri evening primrose (use 6)
Large, glowing yellow flowers cover the glossy foliage of this low spreading perennial, which will cascade over the wall. Blooms from late June through August. See *Oenothera missouriensis*, p. 145.

H 'Moonshine' yarrow (use 3)
This perennial's flat heads of lemon yellow flowers light up the center of the garden much of the summer. Grayish foliage is fragrant, surprisingly tough despite its lacy looks. Flowers are good for drying. See *Achillea*, p. 130.

I 'Munstead' English lavender (use 3)
The gray foliage of this classic bushy herb seems to deepen the greens nearby. It bears a profusion of fragrant pale lavender flower spikes in July, a pretty combination with the yellow yarrow and primroses. See *Lavandula angustifolia*, p. 143.

J Purple coneflower (use 6)
In July and August, stiff stalks carrying large daisylike pink flowers with dark-brown cone-shaped centers rise above this native perennial's basal clump of rich green leaves. Leave some flower stalks standing for winter interest and to provide seeds for songbirds. See *Echinacea purpurea*, p. 136.

K 'Purple Dome' New England aster (use 2)
This native perennial makes a mound of foliage and is covered with purple flowers in the fall, when the garden needs a shot of color. See *Aster novae-angliae*, p. 132.

L 'White Clips' Carpathian bellflower (use 6)
A hardy little perennial with tufts of glossy green leaves and white cuplike flowers that stand out beside the blue oat grass from July until frost. See *Campanula carpatica*, p. 134.

M Wall and steps
This wall and steps are built from a readily available prefabricated wall system. It is 15 ft. long and 24 in. high. Select a system to match the colors and style of your home. See p. 172.

N Walkway
This is built from flagstone dressed to random rectangular sizes. Precast concrete pavers or gravel would also go well with a prefabricated wall. See p. 160.

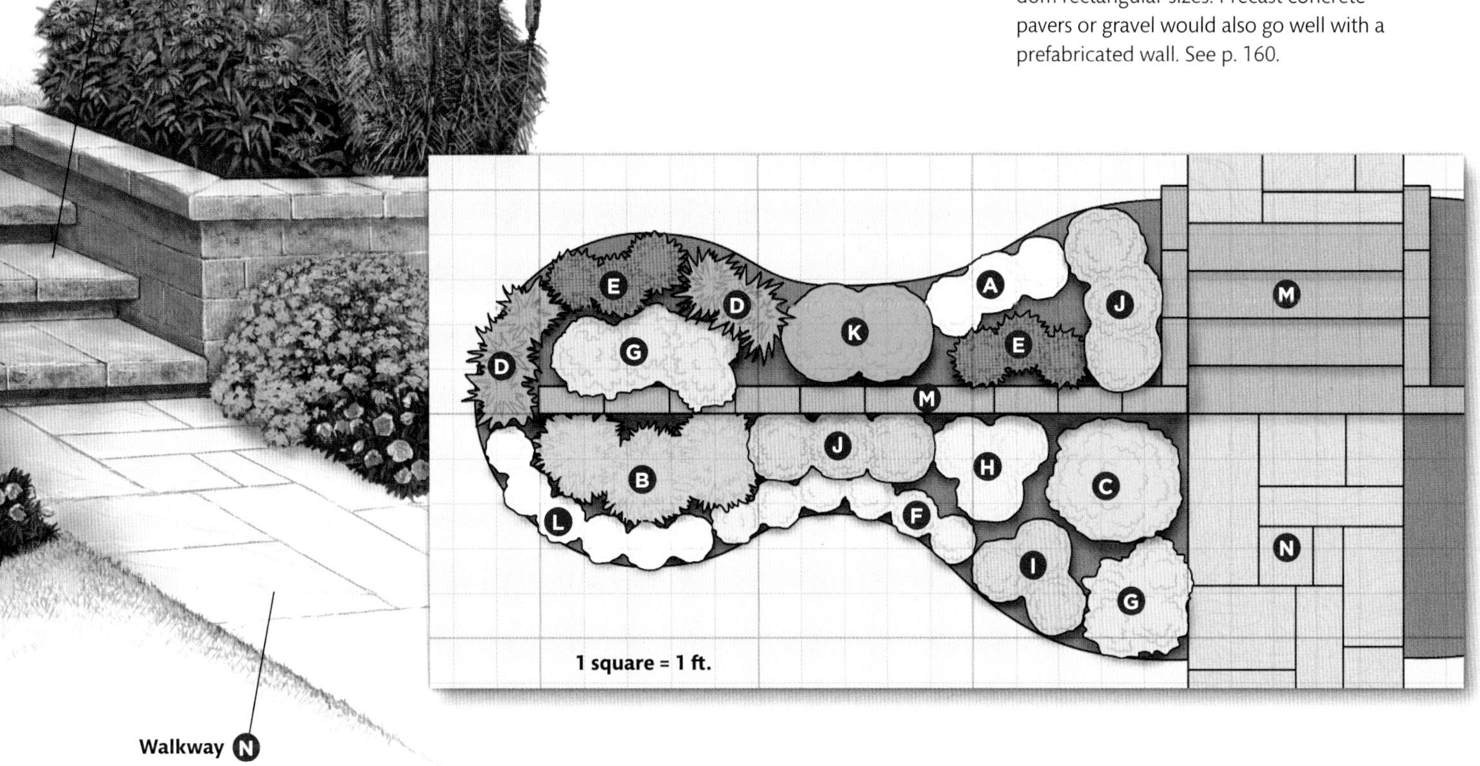

Shrubs change the scene

Carefree roses and cheerful daylilies look lovely along a wall, perhaps because they're reminiscent of plants seen along walls bordering old fields or meadows. The combination of shrubs and perennials gives this planting a look distinctly different from that of the perennial border of the previous design.

The spreading sumac on the upper tier creates a wide, low mound of handsome foliage; green in summer, red in fall. In winter, its bare stems contrast nicely with the prickly evergreen foliage of the spruce on the level below. Near the walk is another contrasting pair of shrubs. From spring to frost, the rose, covered with pretty pink flowers, grabs the attention of strollers. In winter, the blue foliage of the juniper stands out against a snowy carpet. Care is limited to snipping spent flowers, pruning the rose, and cutting back the perennials during spring and fall cleanup.

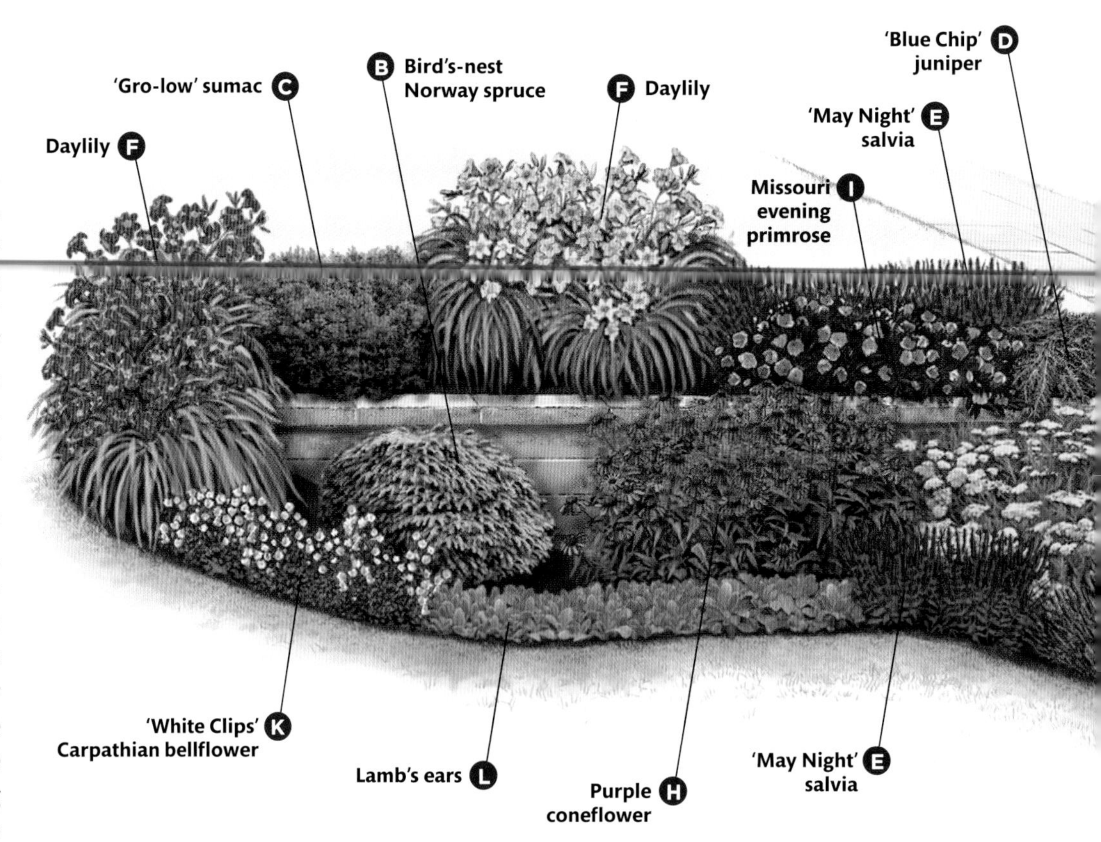

SITE: Sunny

SEASON: Summer

CONCEPT: Addition of shrubs and another palette of perennials create a different look.

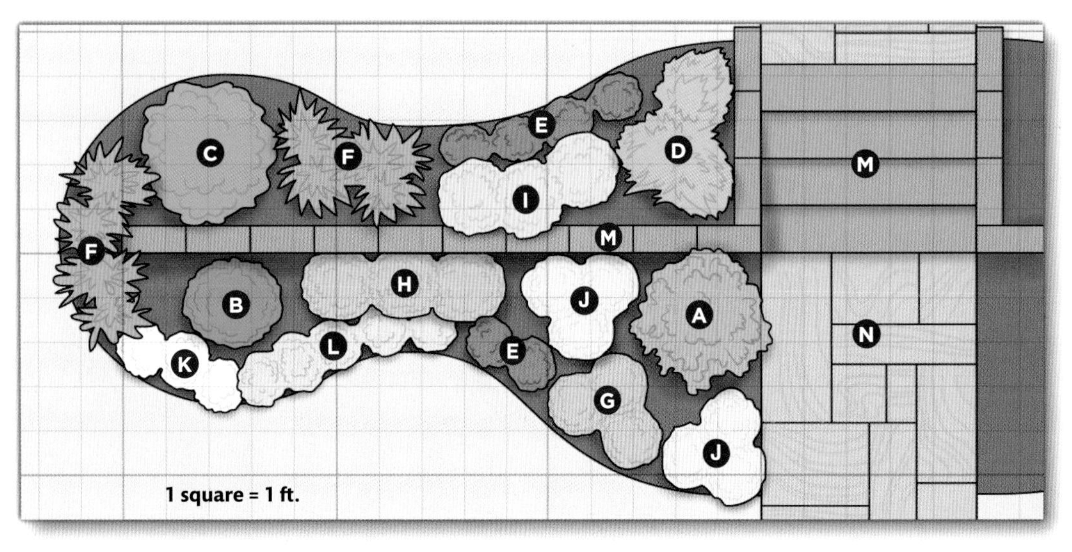

Plants & Projects

A 'Bonica' rose (use 1 plant)
Roses can be easy to grow, and this shrub proves it. It blooms happily from June until frost with little encouragement, producing clusters of double, soft pink flowers. See *Rosa*, p. 149.

B Bird's-nest Norway spruce (use 1)
This dwarf evergreen won't outgrow its spot on the lower level of the garden. The dark-green cushion of foliage is interesting in every season and makes a good backdrop for the perennials. See *Picea abies* 'Nidiformis', p. 146.

C 'Gro-low' sumac (use 1)
This tough deciduous native shrub with glossy green leaves adds texture to the upper tier of the garden. A good ground cover, it stays short and spreads sideways. Small red fruits ripen in late summer. Leaves turn a striking orange-red in autumn. See *Rhus aromatica*, p. 147.

D 'Blue Chip' juniper (use 3)
The fine-textured foliage of this handsome low-growing evergreen edges the walk and trails over the wall, adding year-round color to the upper tier. In winter the blue foliage is tinged

A 'Bonica' rose
M Wall and steps
J 'Moonshine' yarrow
G 'Munstead' English lavender
Walkway N

with burgundy. See *Juniperus horizontalis*, p. 142.

E 'May Night' salvia (use 6)
The blue-violet flower spikes and dark-green foliage of this long-blooming perennial stand out against the surrounding gray-foliaged plants. See *Salvia x superba*, p. 150.

See p. 49 for the following:

- **F Daylily** (use 8)
- **G 'Munstead' English lavender** (use 3)
- **H Purple coneflower** (use 3)
- **I Missouri evening primrose** (use 3)
- **J 'Moonshine' yarrow** (use 6)
- **K 'White Clips' Carpathian bellflower** (use 3)
- **L Lamb's ears** (use 5)
- **M Wall and steps**
- **N Walkway**

PLANT PORTRAITS

These shrubs and perennials thrive in the sunny warmth of this two-tiered garden..

● = First design, pp. 48–49

▲ = Second design, pp. 50–51

'Moonshine' yarrow (*Achillea*, p. 130) ● ▲

Purple coneflower (*Echinacea purpurea*, p. 136) ● ▲

'Purple Dome' New England aster (*Aster novae-angliae*, p. 132) ●

Lamb's ears (*Stachys byzantina*, p. 150) ● ▲

'White Clips' Carpathian bellflower (*Campanula carpatica*, p. 134) ● ▲

A Postal Planting

PROVIDE A PERENNIAL SETTING FOR THE DAILY MAIL

For some, the lowly mailbox may seem a surprising candidate for landscaping. But posted like a sentry by the driveway entrance, it is highly visible to visitors and passersby. And it is one of the few places on your property that you visit every day. A pretty planting like the one shown here pleases the passing public and rewards your daily journey (and that of your friendly letter carrier).

The design here provides months of lovely flowers and handsome foliage on tough perennials that can thrive in the often hot, dry conditions found at the curbside. Crocuses bloom in early spring, followed by false indigo in June. Summer brings pastel yarrow blossoms in a range of colors. Fall, the season shown here, is the most colorful, with lavender, meadow saffron, and white boltonia joining the long-blooming yarrow.

Plants & Projects

These are all tough plants that can survive under a pile of plowed snow and need little watering if you add a 3-in.-deep bark mulch to the bed. Maintenance is minimal. In early spring, before the crocuses are up, cut the old stems of the perennials back near the ground, sweep or gently rake away winter road sand and grit, and renew the mulch. Then enjoy your trips to the mailbox.

A False indigo (use 3 plants)
This hardy perennial gradually forms a large mound of attractive blue-green foliage. In early summer it bears showy indigo-blue flower spikes, which are followed by interesting black seedpods through the fall. See *Baptisia australis*, p. 132.

B 'Summer Pastels' yarrow (use 1)
These tough perennials thrive in hot, dry conditions. Feathery aromatic green foliage is topped by flat clusters of tiny pastel flowers in pink, yellow, and creamy white. Will bloom all summer and into fall if you keep cutting off spent flowers. See *Achillea*, p. 130.

C 'Snowbank' boltonia (use 1)
A perennial forming a large upright clump of finely cut pale-green foliage that looks good all season. In autumn, it becomes a cloud of small white asterlike flowers. See *Boltonia asteroides*, p. 133

D 'Silver Brocade' beach wormwood (use 30)
The large silvery leaves of this perennial ground cover contrast with the fine-textured leaves of the other perennials and have the virtue of not showing road dust. Winter road salt won't harm it, either. See *Artemisia stelleriana*, p. 131.

E Crocus (use 24 or more)
Plant generous clumps (6 or 8 per square foot) of these early-spring corms under the beach wormwood, which will hide the spent foliage after bloom. See Bulbs: *Crocus*, p. 133.

F Meadow saffron (use 24 or more)
Large, lavender-pink, crocuslike flowers in fall peek up above the beach wormwood. Plant 2 or 3 of these corms per square foot. See Bulbs: *Colchicum autumnale*, p. 133.

G Edging
Set off the bed from the lawn with edging. Here we show precast "cobblestones" installed on sand like a brick mowing strip. See p. 162.

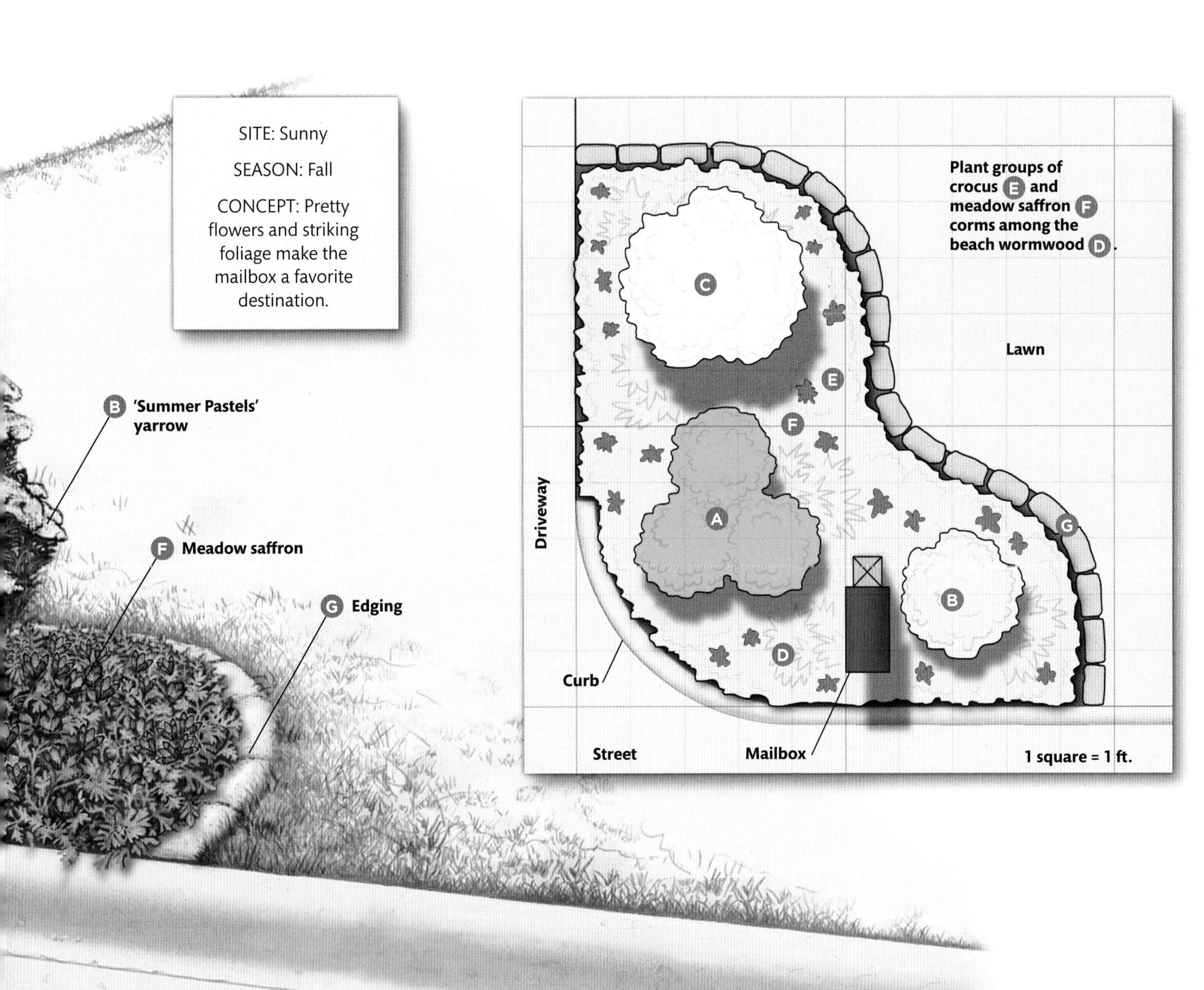

Delivering simple pleasures

This design would fit right into a landscape of mature shrubs and trees. It has the simplicity and something of the feel of a Japanese garden, with its slightly mounded bed, dense ground cover, partially revealed "boulders," and small spring-flowering tree.

The myrtle and daylily provide attractive foliage, accented in spring and summer with colorful flowers. The star of the planting is the hawthorn, which performs admirably in all four seasons. Small white flowers line the branches in late spring, giving way to glossy green leaves that turn red in fall. Winter finds the tree alive with birds flitting among the wonderful glistening twigs and thorns, harvesting the tree's crop of red berries.

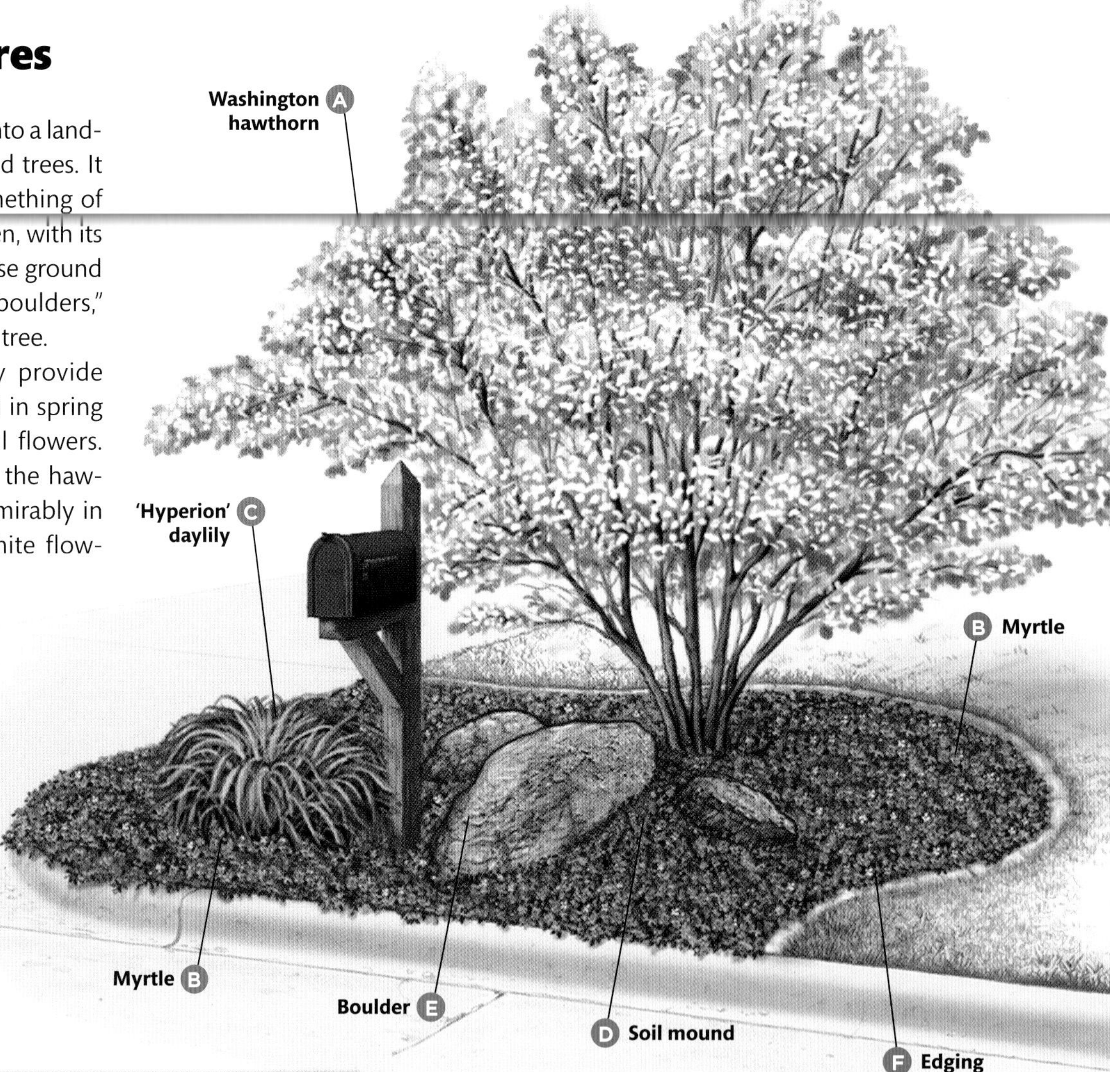

1 square = 1 ft.
Lawn
Driveway
Curb
Mailbox

Plants & Projects

A Washington hawthorn (use 1 plant)
This small deciduous tree pleases in every season: spring flowers, good summer and fall foliage, and winter berries. Combine mail chores with bird-watching; birds nest in the thorny crown, feeding on the berries later in the year. See *Crataegus phaenopyrum*, p. 136.

B Myrtle (use 300)
An evergreen ground cover, it forms a thick-textured shiny green carpet. Bears small lilac flowers in late spring. See *Vinca minor*, p. 153.

C 'Hyperion' daylily (use 1)
A perennial with graceful leaves and a fresh display of scented yellow flowers every day in late July. See *Hemerocallis*, p. 139.

D Soil mound
Raise the bed's center 15 in. above grade and taper it gently to the lawn.

E Boulders
Bury these large stones so only about one-third shows above the ground.

See p. 53 for the following:

F Edging

SITE: Sunny

SEASON: Spring

CONCEPT: A simple design showcases the many charms of the tree at its center.

PLANT PORTRAITS

Send a cheerful message with this selection of rugged flowering plants and ground covers.

● = First design, pp. 52–53

▲ = Second design, pp. 54

'Hyperion' daylily (*Hemerocallis*, p. 139) ▲

False indigo (*Baptisia australis*, p. 132) ●

Myrtle (*Vinca minor*, p. 153) ▲

'Silver Brocade' beach wormwood (*Artemisia stelleriana*, p. 131) ●

Washington hawthorn (*Crataegus phaenopyrum*, p. 136) ▲

'Snowbank' boltonia (*Boltonia asteroides*, p. 133) ●

A Pleasant Passage

RECLAIM A NARROW SIDE YARD FOR A SHADE GARDEN

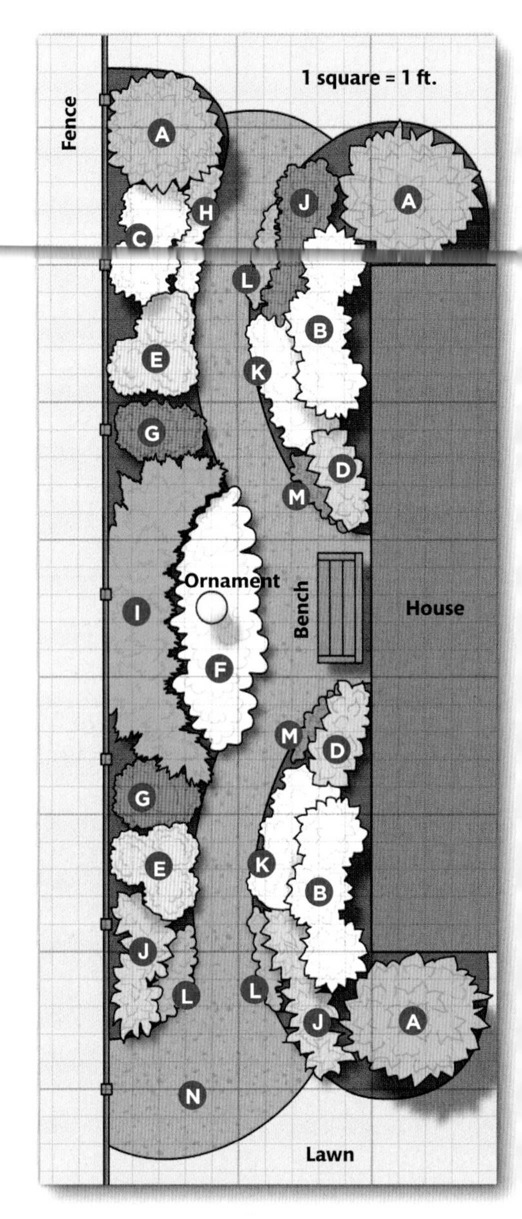

Many residential lots include a slender strip of land between the house and a property line. Usually overlooked by everyone except children and dogs racing between the front yard and the back, this often shady corridor can become a valued addition to the landscape.

In the design shown here, a wood-chip path meanders through a garden of shade-loving shrubs and perennials. The wall of the house and a tall fence on the property line shade the space for most of the day and give it a closed-in feeling, like a narrow room. The design uses plants to enlarge these confines in the same way that furniture, rugs, and pictures on the walls seem to enlarge a small room in a house.

Although this planting supplies plenty of lovely flowers, particularly in spring, foliage is its main attraction. From glossy evergreen shrubs to lush colorful hostas and ferns, nearly every plant offers leaves of noteworthy texture or color. At the center of the planting, a small garden "room," complete with a bench, an ornament, and a carpet of low-growing perennials, provides a quiet spot to pause and enjoy the cool, colorful surroundings.

Plants & Projects

Take your time laying out the curves that define the beds and path; they're instrumental in making the space seem larger than it really is. Upkeep is minimal: just spring and fall cleanup, pruning shrubs to size and shape, and renewing the wood chips.

A Mountain laurel (use 3 plants)
Lovely broad-leaved evergreen shrubs announce the entrance. White, pink, or rosy cuplike flowers brighten the planting in June. See *Kalmia latifolia*, p. 142.

B 'Dora Amateis' rhododendron (use 6)
A compact, upright evergreen shrub with clusters of creamy white flowers in late spring. In northern areas, substitute a cultivar of the hardier Northern Lights azaleas. See *Rhododendron*, p. 148.

C Compact Korean spice viburnum (use 2)
The fragrant white flowers of this deciduous shrub invite you down the path in May. See *Viburnum carlesii* 'Compactum', p. 152.

D 'Elegans' hosta (use 6)
This perennial's huge blue-gray, textured leaves add color to the shade from spring until frost. It forms broad clumps. See *Hosta sieboldiana*, p. 140.

E Lenten rose (use 6)
Some of the very first flowers to appear in spring are this evergreen perennial's nodding cuplike blooms in pink, rose, white, and green. See *Helleborus orientalis*, p. 139.

F 'Bressingham White' bergenia (use 21)
Foliage is this perennial's main contribution. Large glossy leaves turn deep red in winter. Clusters of white flowers in late spring. See *Bergenia cordifolia*, p. 132.

G 'Luxuriant' bleeding heart (use 2)
Heart-shaped rose-red flowers dangle on thin stalks above sprays of this perennial's handsome lacy foliage. Clip off faded flowers to the base to extend bloom from late spring until fall. See *Dicentra*, p. 136.

H Coralbells (use 5)
A low-growing perennial with large, leathery semievergreen leaves. Tiny flowers float well above the foliage for most of the summer. Choose a white cultivar here. See *Heuchera* x *brizoides*, p. 139.

I Dwarf Chinese astilbe (use 21)
The ground beneath the ornament springs to life when the pink fluffy spires of this low-growing perennial bloom in late summer. Lacy foliage is a pleasing contrast to the bergenia during the rest of the season. See *Astilbe chinensis* var. *pumila*, p. 132.

J Japanese painted fern (use 15)
Perhaps the loveliest fern; its delicately painted fronds blend silver, green, and maroon. Combines beautifully with the wild ginger nearby. See Ferns: *Athyrium goeringianum* 'Pictum', p. 137.

K Foamflower (use 20)
The fleecy white flower spikes of this native woodland perennial rise like fluffy bottlebrushes above the evergreen leaves in late spring. Quickly forms a thick patch. See *Tiarella cordifolia*, p. 152.

L Wild ginger (use 21)
Plantings by the path afford a close-up view of this mature perennial's large, elegant heart-shaped leaves. Though slow-spreading, it is an excellent ground cover. See *Asarum canadense*, p. 131.

M Sweet violet (use 9)
The small purple flowers waft their fragrance over the bench when they bloom in early spring and again during the cool fall days. This spreading perennial quickly fills a space with its dark green leaves. See *Viola odorata*, p. 153.

N Path
A wood-chip path blends with the mulch on the beds and suits the woodsy look of this planting. It is easy and inexpensive to install. See p. 160.

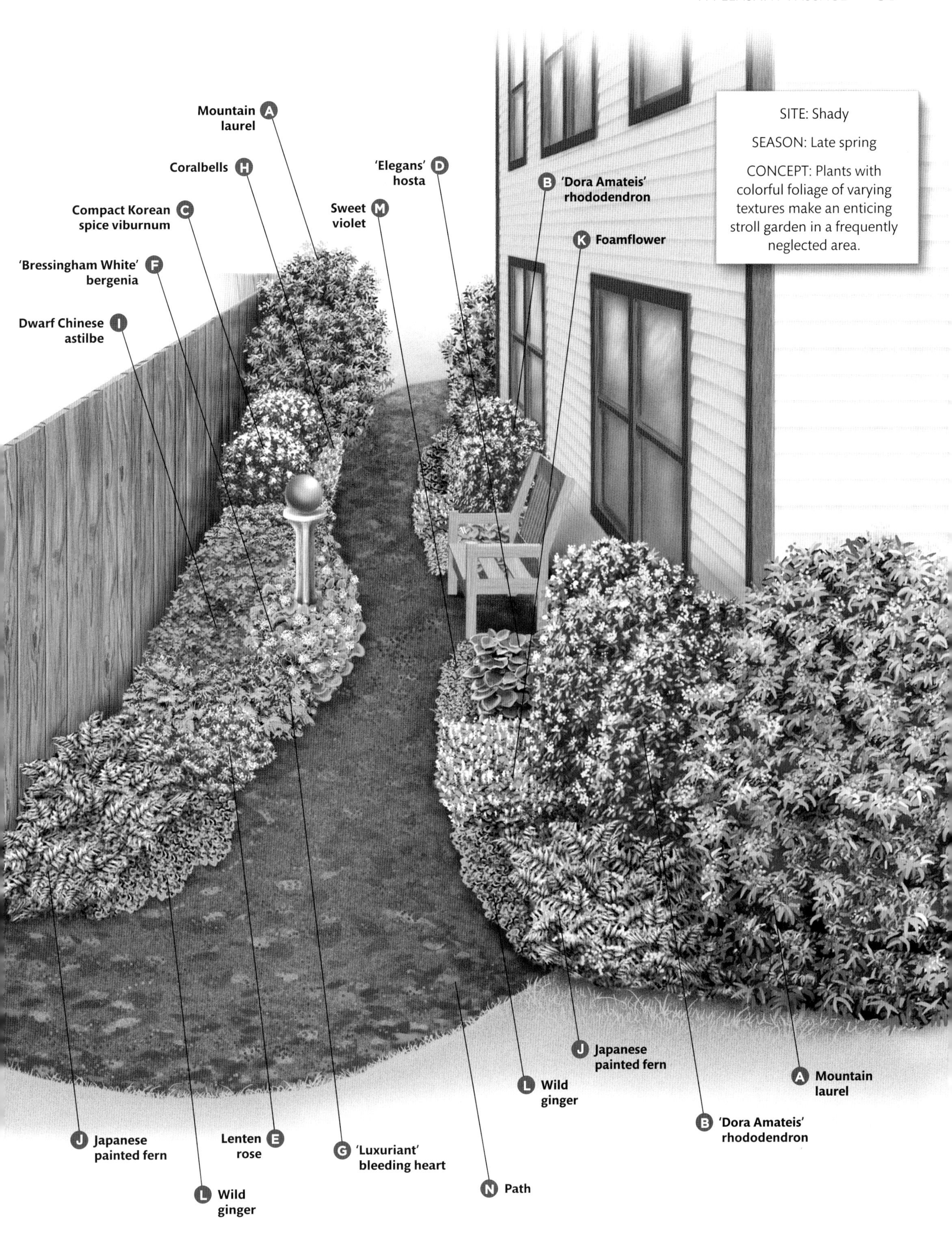
Mountain laurel A
Coralbells H
Compact Korean spice viburnum C
'Bressingham White' bergenia F
Dwarf Chinese astilbe I
'Elegans' hosta D
Sweet violet M
B 'Dora Amateis' rhododendron
K Foamflower
SITE: Shady
SEASON: Late spring
CONCEPT: Plants with colorful foliage of varying textures make an enticing stroll garden in a frequently neglected area.
J Japanese painted fern
L Wild ginger
A Mountain laurel
B 'Dora Amateis' rhododendron
J Japanese painted fern
Lenten rose E
G 'Luxuriant' bleeding heart
N Path
L Wild ginger

PLANT PORTRAITS

Combining flowers, foliage, and fragrance, these plants join to make passage from the front yard to the back a pleasant stroll.

● = First design, pp. 56–57

▲ = Second design, pp. 58–59

Wild ginger (*Asarum canadense*, p. 131) ● ▲

Sweet woodruff (*Galium odoratum*, p. 138) ▲

Lenten rose (*Helleborus orientalis*, p. 139) ● ▲

Japanese painted fern (Ferns: *Athyrium goeringianum* 'Pictum', p. 137) ● ▲

Coralbells (*Heuchera x brizoides*, p. 139) ●

Compact European cranberry bush (*Viburnum opulus* 'Compactum', p. 152) ▲

On the sunny side

In this design, a low picket fence opens up the space and lets in more sunlight, calling for some plants that prefer bright light. Lining the fence are colorful deciduous shrubs and an evergreen hedge that screens the sitting area.

There are changes on the shady side of the path, too. Fragrant azaleas greet visitors near both entrances. Dwarf firs flank the bench, where the fresh scent of their evergreen foliage mingles with the heady aroma of the sweet violets tucked at the base of the little trees.

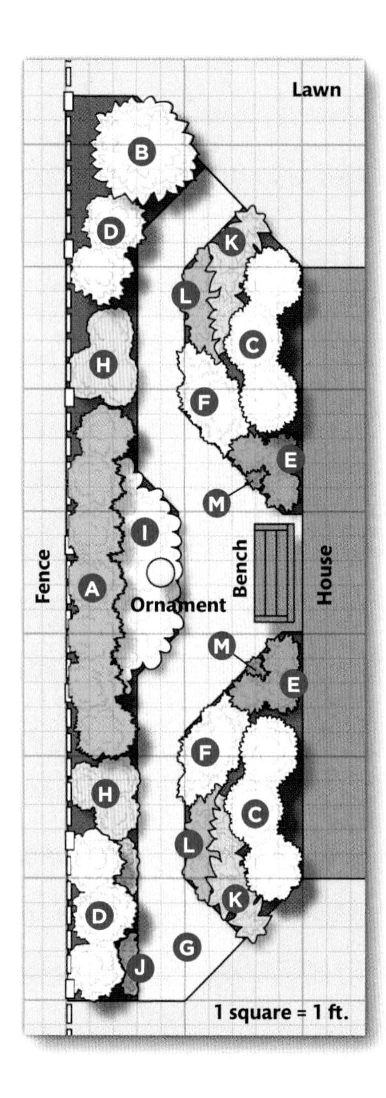

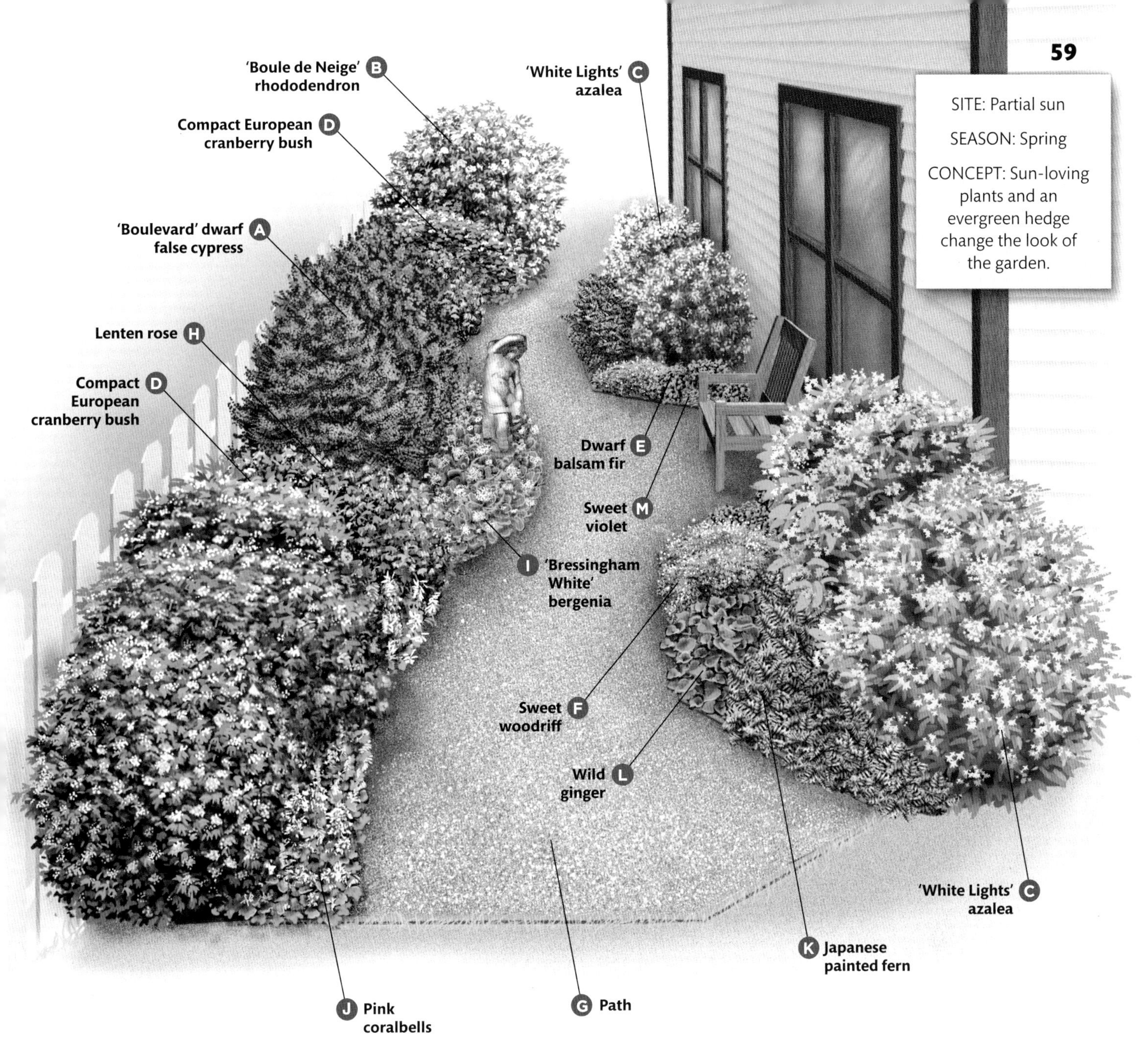

SITE: Partial sun

SEASON: Spring

CONCEPT: Sun-loving plants and an evergreen hedge change the look of the garden.

Plants & Projects

A 'Boulevard' dwarf false cypress
(use 7 plants) A fine choice for an informal hedge, this evergreen shrub has a neat upright habit and foliage like rough blue fur. See *Chamaecyparis pisifera*, p. 134.

B 'Boule de Neige' rhododendron (use 1)
A rounded evergreen shrub. In late spring, showy white flowers gleam against glossy dark-green leaves. See *Rhododendron*, p. 148.

C 'White Lights' azalea (use 6)
This hardy deciduous shrub brightens the bed next to the house wall with large white fragrant flowers in late spring. Foliage is a good backdrop for the ferns and ground covers arrayed at its feet. See *Rhododendron:* Northern Lights azaleas, p. 148.

D Compact European cranberry bush
(use 5)
This compact shrub has lacy clusters of beautiful white flowers in June, lovely maplelike leaves that turn yellow-red in the fall, and shiny red fruits lasting the winter. See *Viburnum opulus* 'Compactum', p. 152.

E Dwarf balsam fir (use 6)
Sitting on the bench, you can enjoy the fragrance of the dark-green foliage on this small mounded evergreen. See *Abies balsamea* 'Nana', p. 130.

F Sweet woodruff (use 14)
A perennial ground cover with whorled leaves that are green in summer and dry to beige in winter. Tiny white flowers appear in spring. See *Galium odoratum*, p. 138.

G Path
This path meanders through the planting, but its straight edges make it more formal than the previous design. Pressure-treated 1x4 edging contains the crushed stone surface. (Wood chips would work here, too.) See p. 160.

See p. 56 for the following:

H Lenten rose (use 10)

I 'Bressingham White' bergenia (use 21)

J Pink coralbells (use 9)

K Japanese painted fern (use 10)

L Wild ginger (use 10)

M Sweet violet (use 6)

Side-Yard Walkway

CREATE BEAUTIFUL ACCESS TO THE FRONT AND REAR YARDS

In this design for a narrow side yard similar to the one on p. 56, a selection of shrubs bordering a comfortable flagstone path makes a garden that invites adults, and even children, to linger as they stroll from one part of the property to another.

The wall of the house and a tall, opaque fence on the property line shade the space most of the day and give it a closed-in feeling, like a long empty hallway or a narrow room. The path and plantings create a cozy passage, and like the furnishings of a room, they make a small space seem bigger than it is. A rose-covered arch flanked by tall, narrow junipers marks one entrance, while a pair of junipers alone frame the entrance at the other end. In between, evergreen and deciduous shrubs, vines, and ground covers delight the eye in all seasons with a mixture of foliage textures and colors, as well as weeks of flowers and bright berries. Lily-of-the-valley lines the path, and in spring its sweet-scented flowers perfume the entire passageway. In fall, the starry flowers of the sweet autumn clematis covering the fence perform the same service.

SITE: Shady

SEASON: Early fall

CONCEPT: Plants with colorful foliage of varying textures make an enticing stroll garden in a frequently neglected area.

Plants & Projects

Flowers brighten the shade for many weeks of the growing season, but foliage is this planting's main attraction. To keep the foliage looking its best, keep pruning shears handy and snip off damaged or diseased growth as soon as you see it. In spring or fall, prune to control the size and shape of the clematis, rose, and Japanese holly. Every few years, cut the weigela to the ground; the new growth will look better than ever.

A Sweet autumn clematis (use 2 plants)
This vigorous deciduous vine will cover the fence with small light-green leaves on twining stems. In autumn the sweet fragrance of its starry white flowers wafts over the path. Attach lengths of polypropylene cord horizontally to the fence at 1-ft. intervals for the vines to climb on. Self-seed freely. See *Clematis terniflora*, p. 134.

B 'Zéphirine Drouhin' rose (use 1)
An unusually shade-tolerant rose, ideal for a trellis in a partially shaded spot. Long, nearly thornless canes carry fragrant pink blooms from early summer to frost. See *Rosa*, p. 149.

C 'Skyrocket' juniper (use 4)
The blue-green foliage of these tall and very narrow evergreen shrubs handsomely frames the entrances at each end of the planting. See *Juniperus scopulorum*, p. 142.

D 'Hetzii' Japanese holly (use 4)
A compact evergreen shrub whose dense mass of small dark-green leaves contrasts in form and texture with the nearby junipers. See *Ilex crenata*, p. 140.

E Compact cranberry bush viburnum (use 2)
A four-season performer, this deciduous shrub anchors the center of the planting with beautiful white flowers in May, lovely maplelike leaves that turn red in fall, and shiny red fruits that last through winter. See *Viburnum trilobum* 'Compactum', p. 152.

F Variegated weigela (use 4)
With cream-colored edges, the leaves of this deciduous shrub add a subtle touch to the passageway. Bears light-pink flowers in early summer. See *Weigela florida*, p. 153.

G Lily-of-the-valley (use 100)
This perennial ground cover that forms a carpet of upright leaves. In spring, tiny white, bell-shaped, fragrant flowers dangle from slender stalks. Leaves turn a rich golden yellow mingled with green in fall. See *Convallaria majalis*, p. 135.

H Arched trellis
Well-made free-standing arched trellises of wrought iron, wire, or wood are available at most garden centers or through mail-order catalogs. Buy one wide enough to accommodate people walking side by side or pushing wheelbarrows.

I Flagstone path
Irregular flagstones set in a random pattern make a pleasantly informal path. Unobtrusive wooden edging contains the sand filling gaps between the flags. See p. 161.

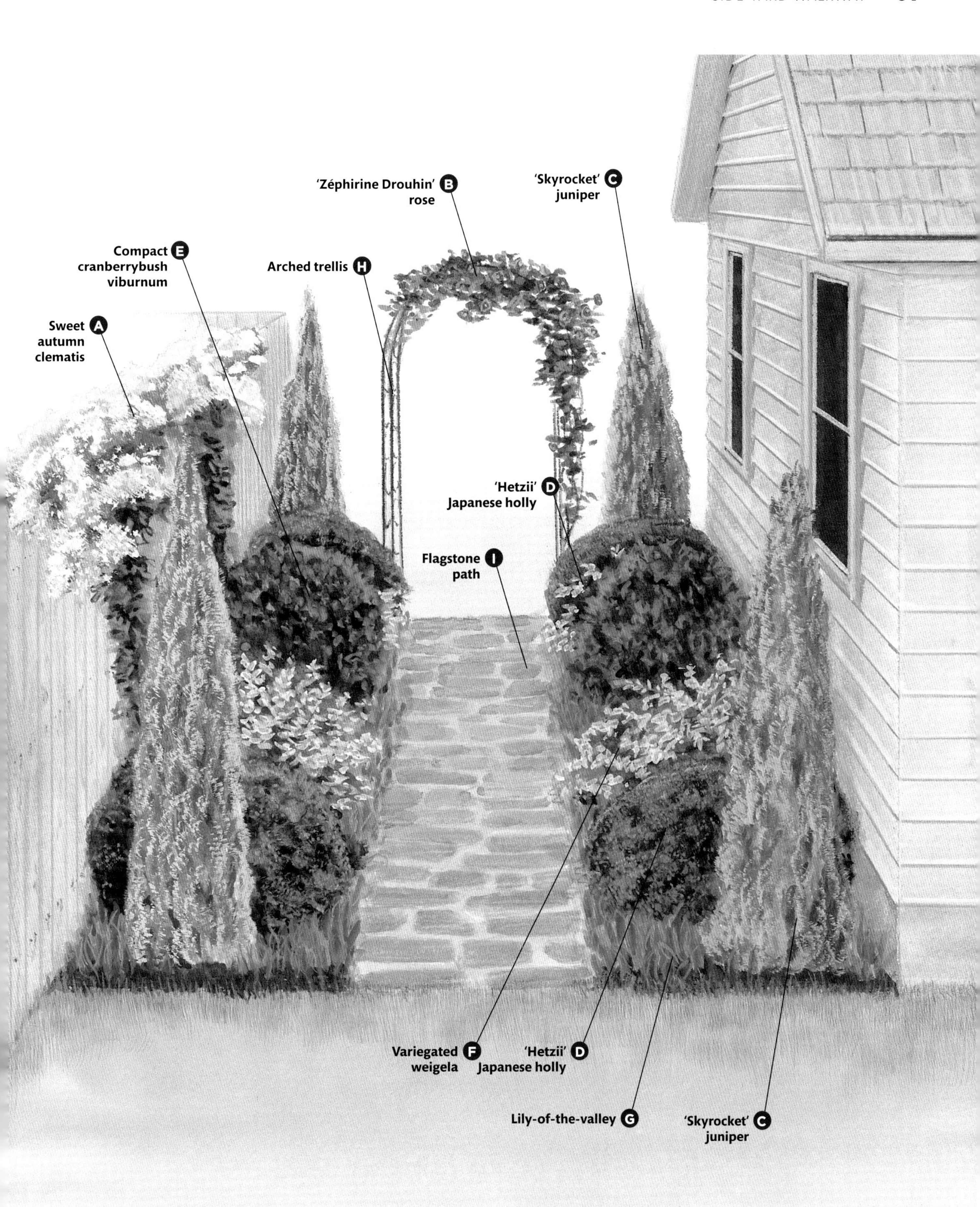
'Zéphirine Drouhin' B rose
'Skyrocket' C juniper
Compact E cranberrybush viburnum
Arched trellis H
Sweet A autumn clematis
'Hetzii' D Japanese holly
Flagstone I path
Variegated F weigela
'Hetzii' D Japanese holly
Lily-of-the-valley G
'Skyrocket' C juniper

Gateway Garden

SIMPLE STRUCTURE AND PLANTING MAKE A HANDSOME ENTRY

Entrances are an important part of any landscape. They can welcome visitors onto your property; highlight a special feature, such as a rose garden; or mark passage between two areas with different character or function. The design shown here can serve in any of these situations. A low fence and plantings create a friendly attractive barrier, just enough to signal the confines of the front yard or to contain the family dog. The simple vine-covered arbor provides welcoming access.

The design combines basic elements imaginatively, creating a romantic, cottage-garden feel. An attractive shrub and lacy vine surround the arbor with flowers and fragrance in spring and late summer. Cheerful perennials along the picket fence and annuals in large containers provide additional bloom and scent throughout the growing season.

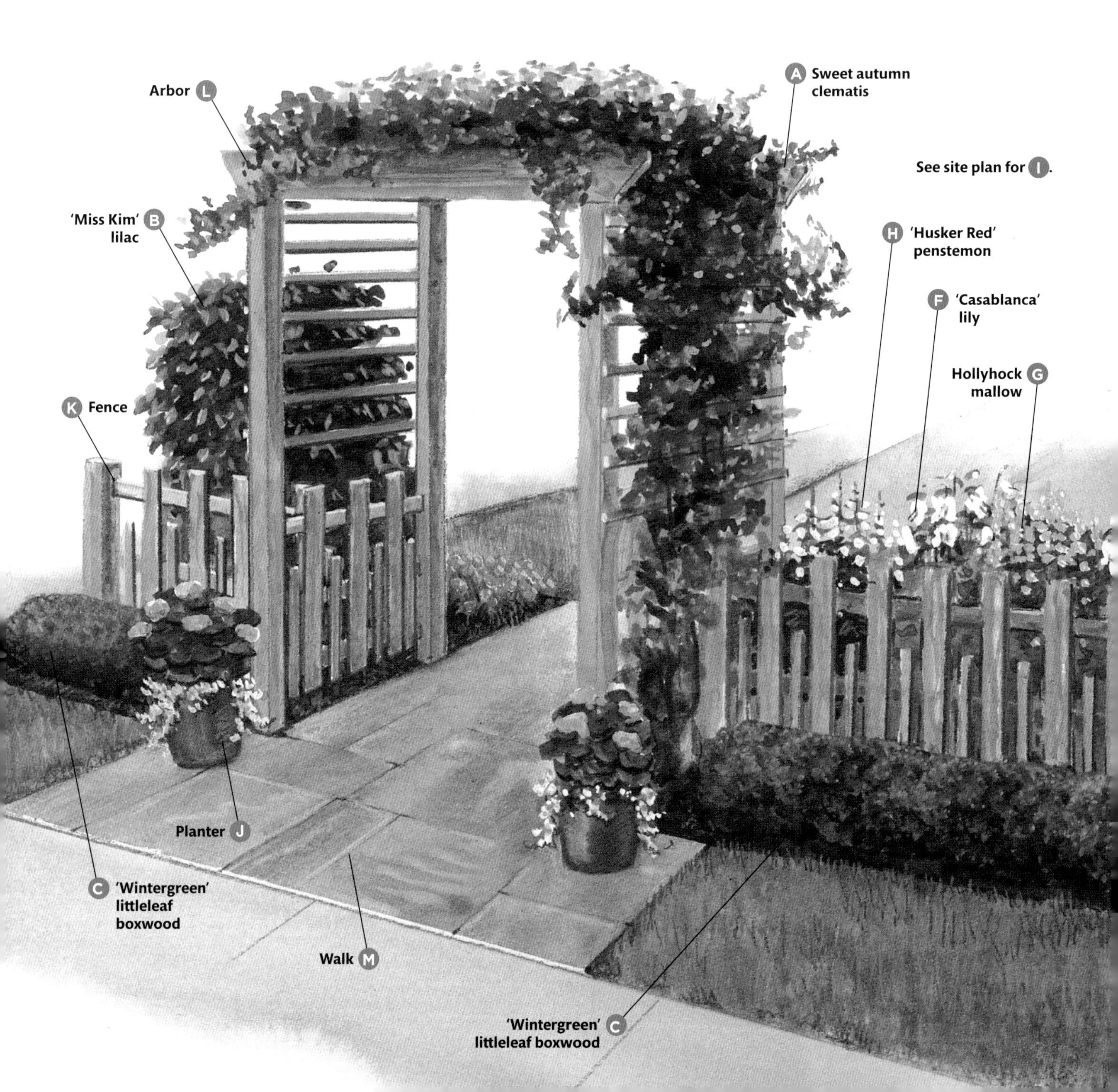

Plants & Projects

SITE: Sunny

SEASON: Summer

CONCEPT: Arbor, fence, flowers, and fragrance make an enticing little entry garden.

For many people, a picket fence and vine-covered arbor represent old-fashioned neighborly virtues. The structures and plantings are easy to install and care for. Other than routine spring and fall clean-up, you just need to train the vine to the arbor (see p. 209), clip spent flowers off the perennials, and cut older branches from the lilac every few years. You can extend the fence and plantings as needed.

A Sweet autumn clematis (use 1 plant)
This deciduous vine quickly covers the arbor with lacy light-green leaves. In September, clusters of starry white flowers fill the air with sweet fragrance. See *Clematis terniflora*, p. 134.

B 'Miss Kim' lilac (use 1)
The lilac-blue spring flowers of this compact deciduous shrub are deliciously fragrant. Leaves turn purple in fall. See *Syringa patula*, p. 150.

C 'Wintergreen' littleleaf boxwood (use 8)
This compact evergreen shrub is perfect for this sheared hedge, with small glossy leaves. See *Buxus microphylla*, p. 134.

D 'Alaska' Shasta daisy (use 3)
A perennial that bears large white daisies above dark-green, shiny foliage in July. Fill a vase with the flowers. See *Chrysanthemum* x *superbum*, p. 134.

E 'Bright Eyes' phlox (use 3)
Fragrant clusters of light-pink flowers with a crimson eye rise on strong stems above dark-green foliage. Blooms in August and September. See *Phlox paniculata*, p. 146.

F 'Casablanca' lily (use 9 to 15 bulbs)
Lovely white fragrant flowers rise just above the fence on strong leafy stalks in August. Plant in groups of 3 to 5 bulbs. See *Lilium*, p. 143.

G Hollyhock mallow (use 3)
In midsummer, this bushy perennial sends up dozens of flower stems, each covered with lovely soft-pink flowers. See *Malva alcea* 'Fastigiata', p. 144.

H 'Husker Red' penstemon (use 1)
A perennial with striking red-purple foliage. Tubular white flowers line upright stalks in midsummer. See *Penstemon digitalis*, p. 145.

I Thrift (use 12)
Spherical flower heads in shades of rose, pink, and white bloom for weeks above this perennial's grassy foliage. See *Armeria maritima*, p. 131.

J Planters
The 12-in. terra-cotta pots shown here are filled with red, pink, or coral geraniums and variegated vinca vine, all readily available at local nurseries.

K Fence
Alternating narrow and wide slats of different heights makes an interesting variation on the traditional picket fence. Made of standard dimension material, the 3-ft.-high fence is easy to build. See p. 190.

L Arbor
Short panels of picket fence join the arbor posts on each side. A simple ladder trellis runs up the sides and over the top of the arbor to support the vines. See p. 190.

M Walk
The flagstone walk shown here is ideal for a high-traffic entry. In a less traveled spot, gravel or even stepping-stones would be appropriate. See p. 160.

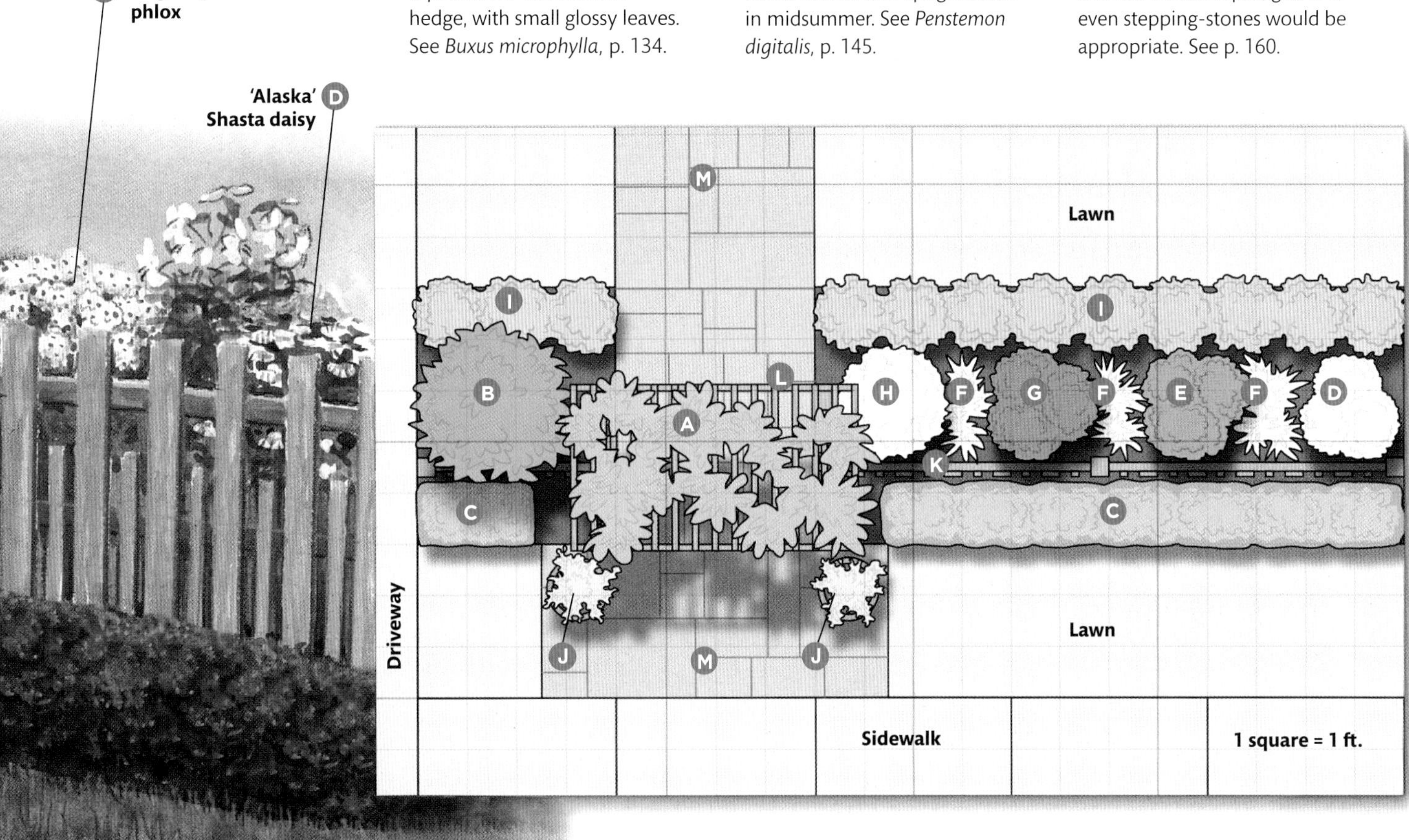

PLANT PORTRAITS

These vines, shrubs, and perennials clothe the arbor and adorn the fence line and hedge with lovely flowers and foliage.

● = First design, pp. 62–63

▲ = Second design, pp. 65

'Diana' rose-of-Sharon
(*Hibiscus syriacus*, p. 139) ▲

'Marshall's Delight' bee balm
(*Monarda*, p. 144) ▲

Hollyhock mallow
(*Malva alcea* 'Fastigiata', p. 144) ●

'Husker Red' penstemon
(*Penstemon digitalis*, p. 145) ●

Goldflame honeysuckle
(*Lonicera* x *heckrottii*, p. 143) ▲

Thrift (*Armeria maritima*, p. 131) ●

'Alaska' Shasta daisy (*Chrysanthemum* x *superbum*, p. 134) ●

Flowers everywhere

Not every situation calls for a fenced enclosure. In this simpler design, shrub roses make an informal hedge. In summer it is covered with foliage and pink flowers, in winter the hedge is a barrier of bare thorny stems.

This planting bursts with flowers, many of which are fragrant, from spring until fall. On the arbor, honeysuckle and the neighboring rose-of-Sharon bloom week after week, as does the rose. Perennials and annuals add accents to the color scheme of blue, pink, and white. A background of handsome healthy foliage makes the colors even more vibrant.

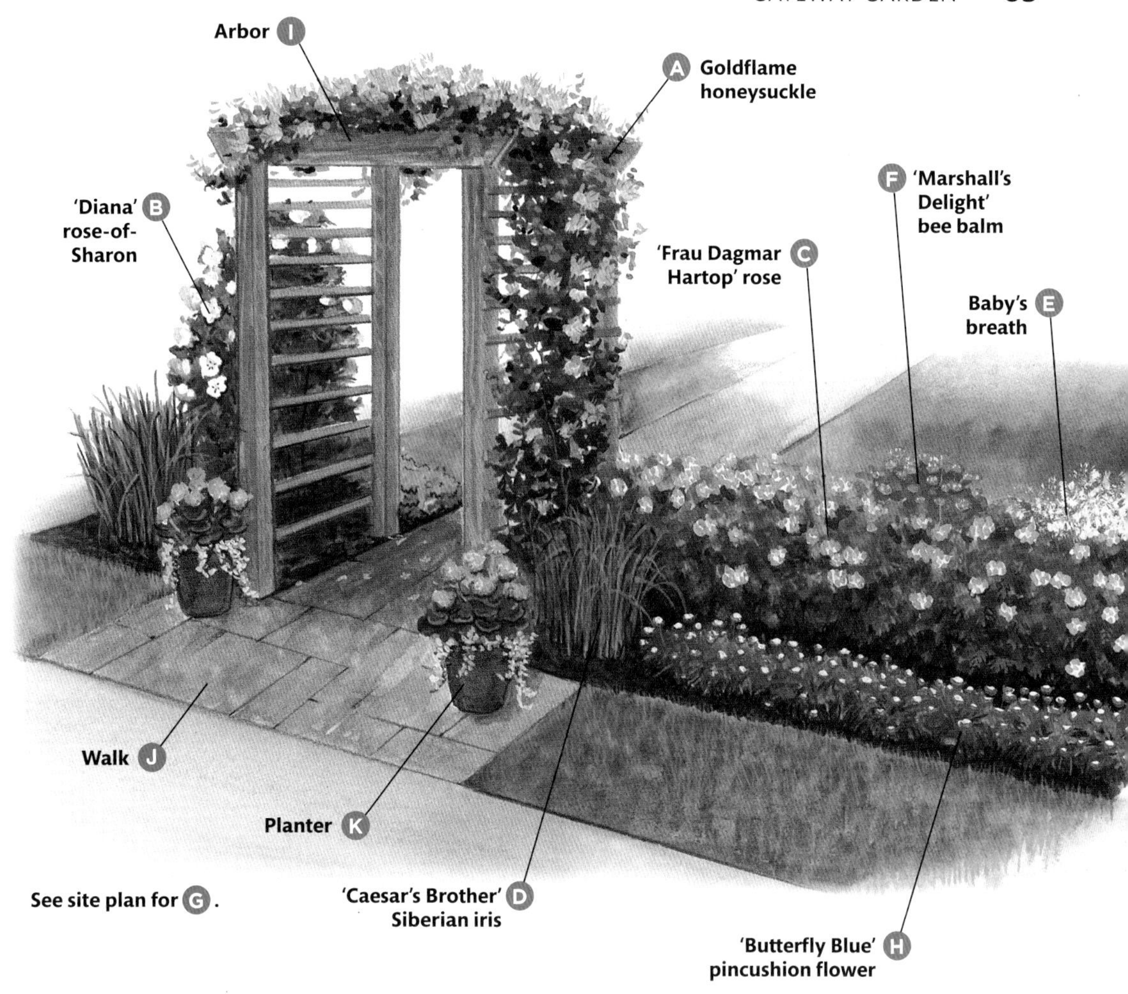

Plants & Projects

A Goldflame honeysuckle (use 1 plant)
A fragrant favorite, this vine will cover the arbor quickly with blue-green leaves and distinctive pink-and-yellow flowers. Blooms all season, heaviest in spring and fall. See *Lonicera* x *heckrottii*, p. 143.

B 'Diana' rose-of-Sharon (use 1)
Next to the arbor, this erect deciduous shrub bears large, pure-white, hollyhock-like flowers from midsummer into fall. See *Hibiscus syriacus*, p. 139.

C 'Frau Dagmar Hartop' rose (use 5)
This deciduous shrub rose makes a beautiful hedge, covered all season with glossy dark-green leaves and fragrant single pink flowers. See *Rosa*, p. 149.

D 'Caesar's Brother' Siberian iris (use 2)
A perennial that forms an attractive clump of slender arching leaves. Elegant blue-purple flowers add brilliant June color. See *Iris sibirica*, p. 142.

E Baby's breath (use 3)
A white cloud of tiny flowers covers this perennial's airy mound of gray-green foliage for weeks in early summer. Use 'Pink Fairy' if you prefer pink flowers. See *Gypsophila paniculata*, p. 138.

F 'Marshall's Delight' bee balm (use 1)
Big, globe-shaped, pink flowers perch on stiff leafy stalks above a mass of green aromatic foliage. This perennial blooms for weeks from the end of June. See *Monarda didyma*, p. 144.

G Lady's mantle (use 6)
A perennial grown as much for its mound of pretty, ruffled light-green leaves as for the clusters of small yellow flowers that hover over it in June. See *Alchemilla mollis*, p. 130.

H 'Butterfly Blue' pincushion flower (use 10)
A perennial with round, frilly sky blue flowers and a bright-green rosette of leaves. They bloom all season, attract butterflies, and are good cut flowers. For a pretty blue-and-pink mix, combine with 'Pink Mist'. See *Scabiosa columbaria*, p. 150.

See p. 63 for the following:

I Arbor

J Walk

K Planters

SITE: Sunny

SEASON: Summer

CONCEPT: Perennials and a flowering hedge make an attractive barrier next to a vine-covered arbor.

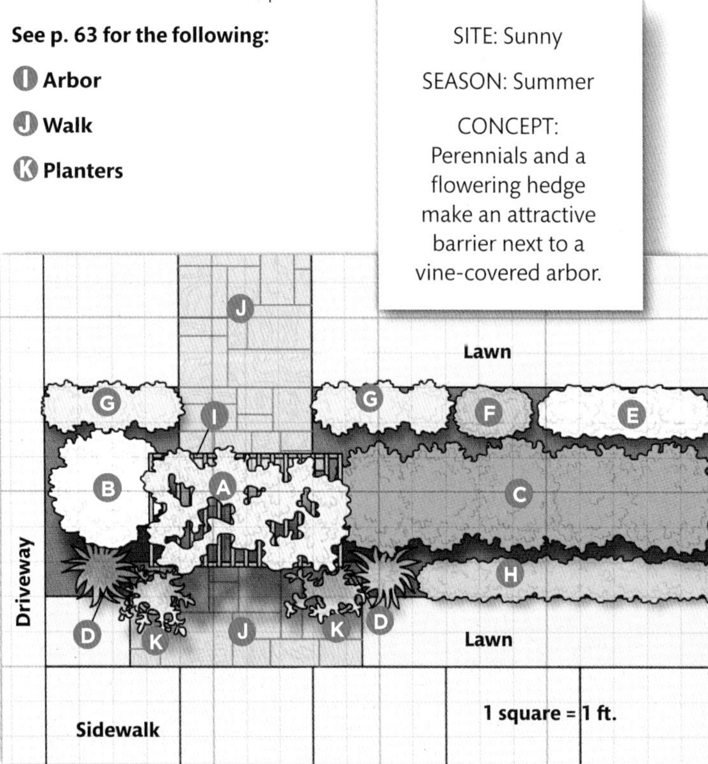

Angle of Repose

MAKE A BACK-DOOR GARDEN FOR A SHELTERED NICHE

Many homes offer the opportunity to tuck a garden into a protected corner. In the front yard, such spots are ideal for an entry garden or a landscaping display that showcases your house when viewed from the sidewalk or the street. If the planting is in the backyard, like the site shown here, it can be more intimate, part of a comfortable outdoor room you can enjoy from a nearby patio or window.

The curved bed wraps around the small patio, increasingly shaded by the neighboring crab apple as the years pass. The planting has been designed with spring especially in mind, so we're showing that season here. (For a look at the planting later on, when perennials take over the show, see pp. 68–69.) Dozens of bulbs light up the corner in April and May, assisted by several early-blooming trees and shrubs. Flowers in white, pink, yellow, purple, and blue carpet the ground or twinkle on bare branches above. Several impart a delicious scent to the fresh spring air.

Early flowers aren't the only pleasures of spring in the garden. Watch buds fatten and burst into leaf on the deciduous trees and shrubs, and mark the progress of the season as new, succulent shoots of summer perennials emerge.

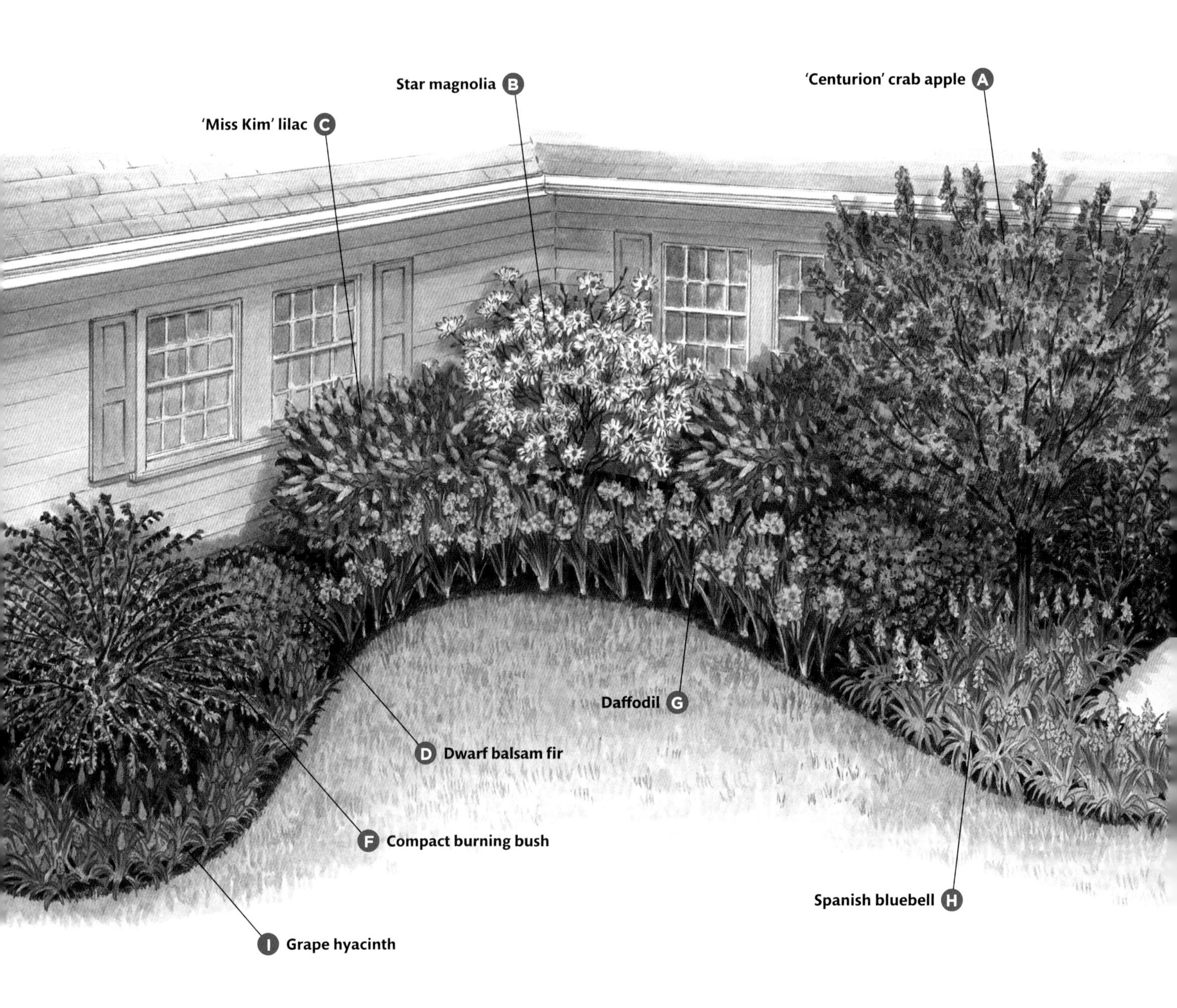

Plants & Projects

Once established, these plants require little maintenance. The shrubs won't overgrow nearby windows, and the trees will need little pruning. Every few years you will have to divide the bulbs.

A 'Centurion' crab apple (use 1 plant)
This small deciduous tree offers cheerful rosy pink flowers in May, attractive summer foliage, and glossy little fruits that last into winter. Will broaden to shade the terrace as it ages. See *Malus*, p. 144.

B Star magnolia (use 1)
This small, rounded, multitrunked deciduous tree won't outgrow the corner. Delightful white flowers bloom in early spring, before leaves appear. See *Magnolia stellata*, p. 144.

C 'Miss Kim' lilac (use 2)
This well-behaved, compact deciduous shrub has clusters of purple flowers in May. Open nearby windows to enjoy their wonderful scent. See *Syringa patula*, p. 150.

D Dwarf balsam fir (use 1)
Lustrous dark-green needles and a compact rounded form make this low-growing evergreen shrub an ideal companion for the taller deciduous shrubs and a good backdrop for spring bulbs. See *Abies balsamea* 'Nana', p. 130.

E 'Rhumba' weigela (use 1)
With dark-red flowers in summer and dark green-and-purple leaves, this compact deciduous shrub is eye-catching throughout the growing season. See *Weigela florida*, p. 153.

F Compact burning bush (use 1)
This deciduous shrub lights up the end of the planting with its dependable fall color: the dark-green leaves turn pale copper and then bright crimson red. See *Euonymus alatus* 'Compactus', p. 136.

G Daffodil (use 35)
One of the cheeriest sights in spring is the butter yellow trumpets of this prince of flowering bulbs. To keep the flowers coming each year, allow the foliage die down naturally, but the daylilies (see p. 139) will hide it as they grow. See Bulbs: *Narcissus*, p. 133.

H Spanish bluebell (use 24)
Dangling above attractive grassy foliage, the pretty blue bell-like flowers of this spring bulb dapple the ground beneath the crab apple. When its foliage gets ragged, you can pull or trim it. See Bulbs: *Endymion hispanica*, p. 133.

I Grape hyacinth (use 35 or more)
These little bulbs will spread happily beneath the burning bush, making a carpet of grassy foliage and fragrant dark blue-purple flowers arranged in grapelike clusters. See Bulbs: *Muscari armeniacum*, p. 133.

J Planter
Extend springtime color onto the patio with Darwin tulips and pansies in the large planter next to the door. Plant tulip bulbs in fall; replace them every year. Add a few dozen pansy plants in early spring. See p. 182.

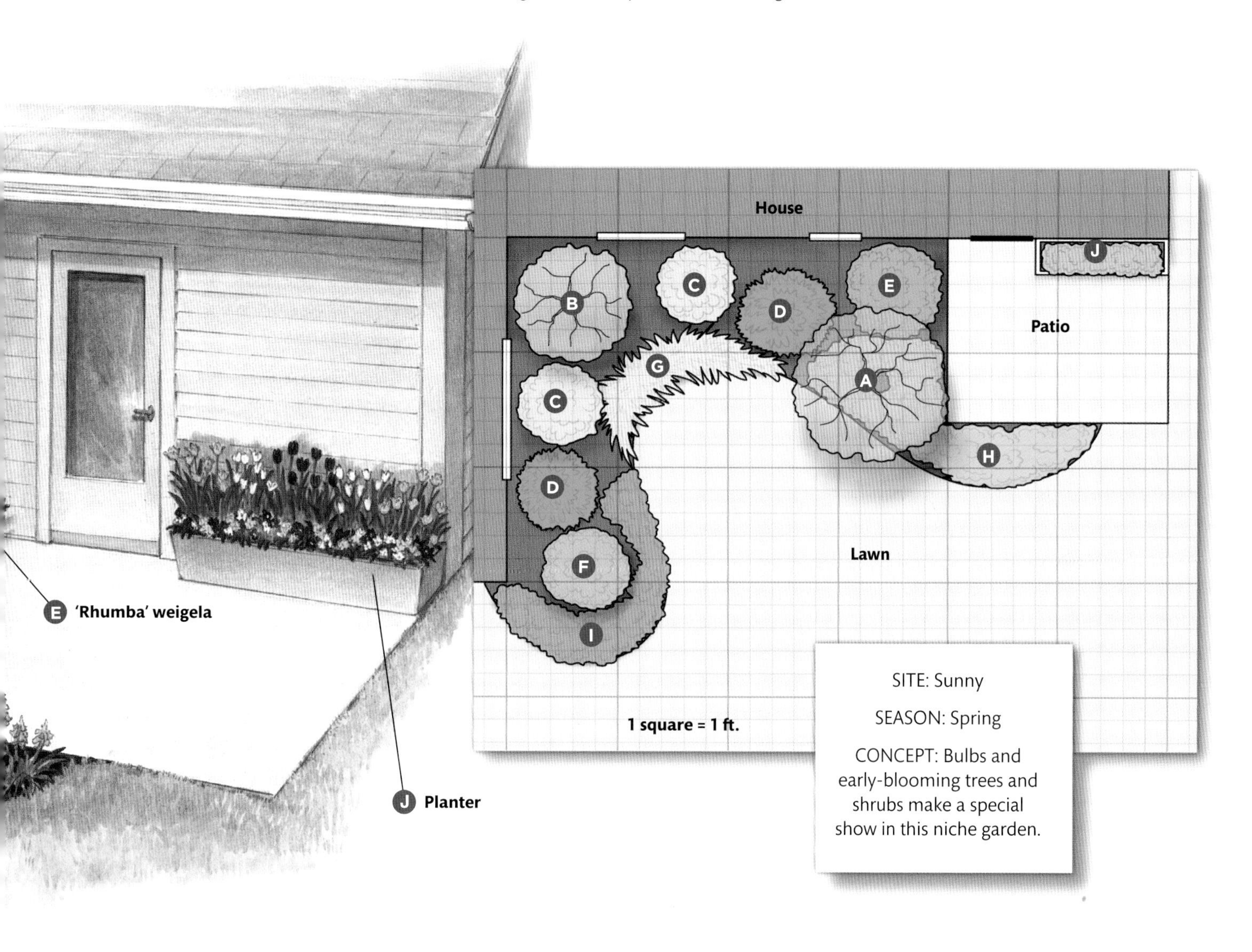

The scene in summer

There's no drop-off in interest or enjoyment as this planting moves from spring (shown on the previous pages) to summer and fall. Against a background of leafy shrubs, perennials at the front of the bed offer months of flowers in blue, yellow, pink, and purple as bright annuals spill over the sides of the planter. In fall, purple asters join the bright-red foliage of the burning bush and the purple leaves of the lilac.

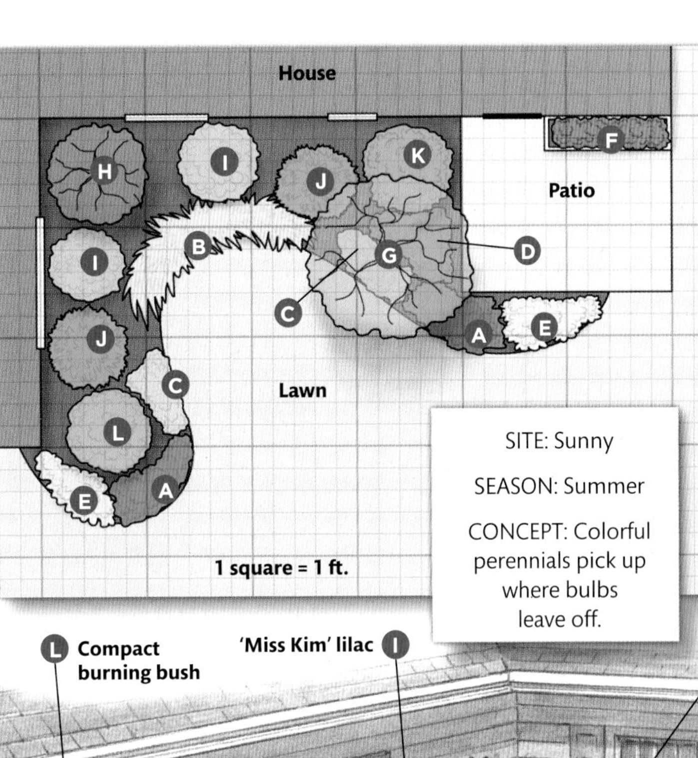

SITE: Sunny

SEASON: Summer

CONCEPT: Colorful perennials pick up where bulbs leave off.

Plants & Projects

A 'May Night' salvia (use 8 plants)
This long-blooming perennial is covered with numerous dark indigo-purple flower spikes from May to fall if you remove spent flowers. A great edging plant for the patio. See *Salvia* x *superba*, p. 150.

B 'Stella d'Oro' daylily (use 12)
Golden-yellow flowers sparkle on this perennial all summer, and the grasslike foliage makes a nice informal ground cover beneath the lilacs and magnolia. See *Hemerocallis*, p. 139.

C 'Brilliant' sedum (use 9)
Flat clusters of pink flowers form above light-green succulent leaves in late summer. The rust-colored seed heads are attractive well into the winter. See *Sedum*, p. 150.

D 'Purple Dome' New England aster (use 4)
In summer, this dwarf perennial is an attractive mound of dark foliage. In fall, it bursts into bloom with countless small dark-purple flowers that last for a month or so. See *Aster novae-angliae*, p. 132.

E Lamb's ears (use 14)
Long, velvety silver-gray leaves really do look like furry ears and are soft enough to stroke as you sit on the patio. A perennial, it bears small purple flowers in early summer, but the foliage provides the main attraction, lasting from spring until frost and sometimes into the winter. See *Stachys byzantina*, p. 150.

F Planter
For a summer display, you can cut back the tulip foliage, pull out the pansies, and fill the planter with pink geraniums, blue lobelia, and white petunias, colors that go well with the perennials. See p. 182.

See p. 67 for the following:

G 'Centurion' crab apple

H Star magnolia

I 'Miss Kim' lilac

J Dwarf balsam fir

K 'Rhumba' weigela

L Compact burning bush

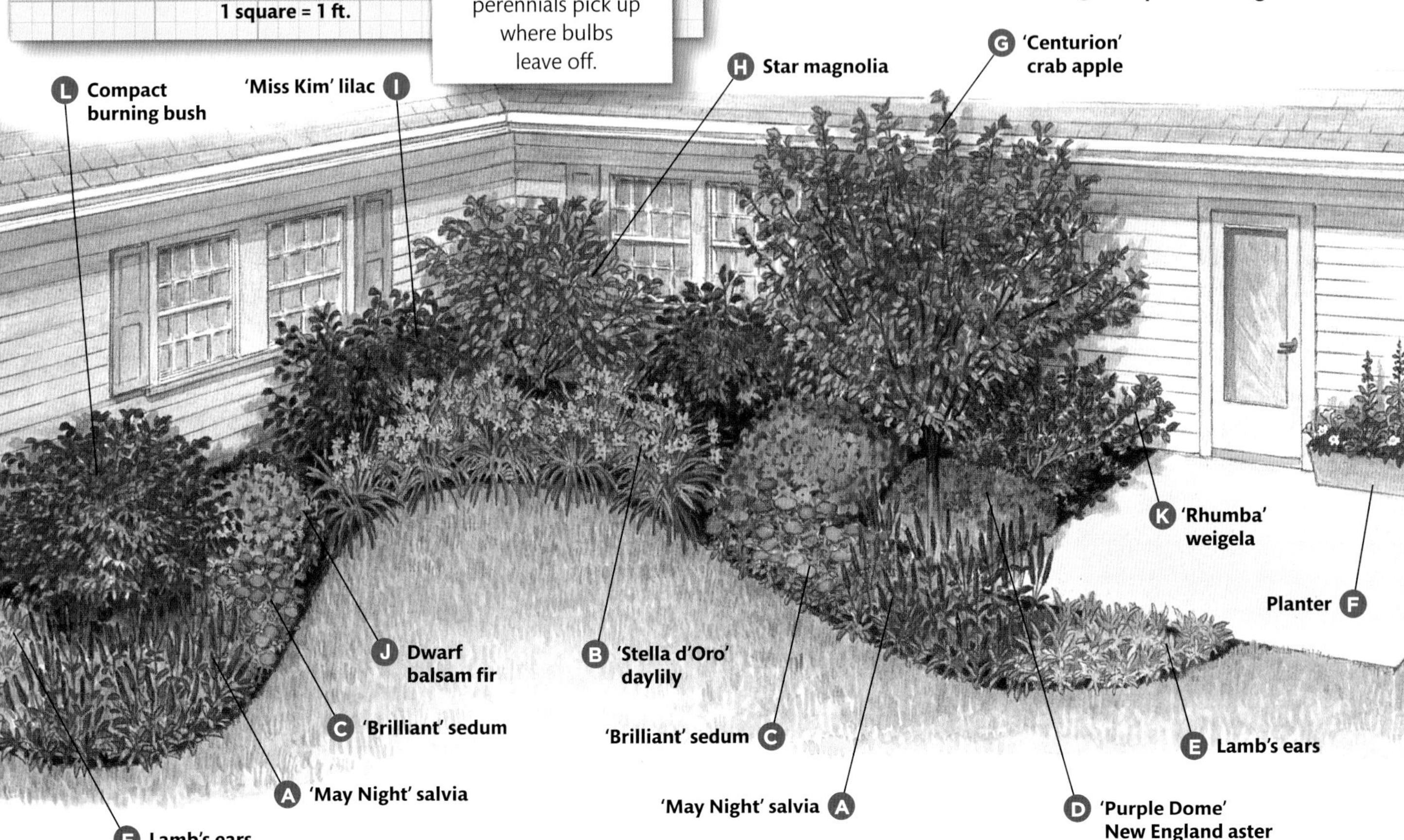

PLANT PORTRAITS

Compact shrubs and small trees combine with bulbs and perennials to fill this corner garden with colorful flowers and foliage from spring through fall.

● = First design, pp. 66–67

▲ = Second design, pp. 68

Dwarf balsam fir
(*Abies balsamea* 'Nana', p. 130) ● ▲

Star magnolia
(*Magnolia stellata*, p. 144) ● ▲

Spanish bluebell
(Bulbs: *Endymion hispanica*, p. 133) ●

Daffodil (Bulbs: *Narcissus*, p. 133) ●

'Centurion' crab apple
(*Malus*, p. 144) ● ▲

'Miss Kim' lilac (*Syringa patula*, p. 150) ● ▲

Compact burning bush (*Euonymus alatus* 'Compactus', p. 136) ● ▲

Another Back-Door Corner

THIS RETREAT IS MOSTLY FOR YOUR OWN ENJOYMENT

This planting has been specially designed with spring in mind, so we're showing that season here. (For a look at the planting later on, when perennials and shrubs take over the show, see p. 72.) Dozens of spring bulbs light up the corner from February through May, assisted by the spring blossoms on the rhododendrons and Korean spice viburnum.

Early flowers aren't the only pleasures of spring, though. Step along the path to appreciate the magic of spring at closer range. Watch buds burst into leaf on the burning bush and cotoneaster, and mark the progress of the season as new, succulent shoots of summer perennials emerge.

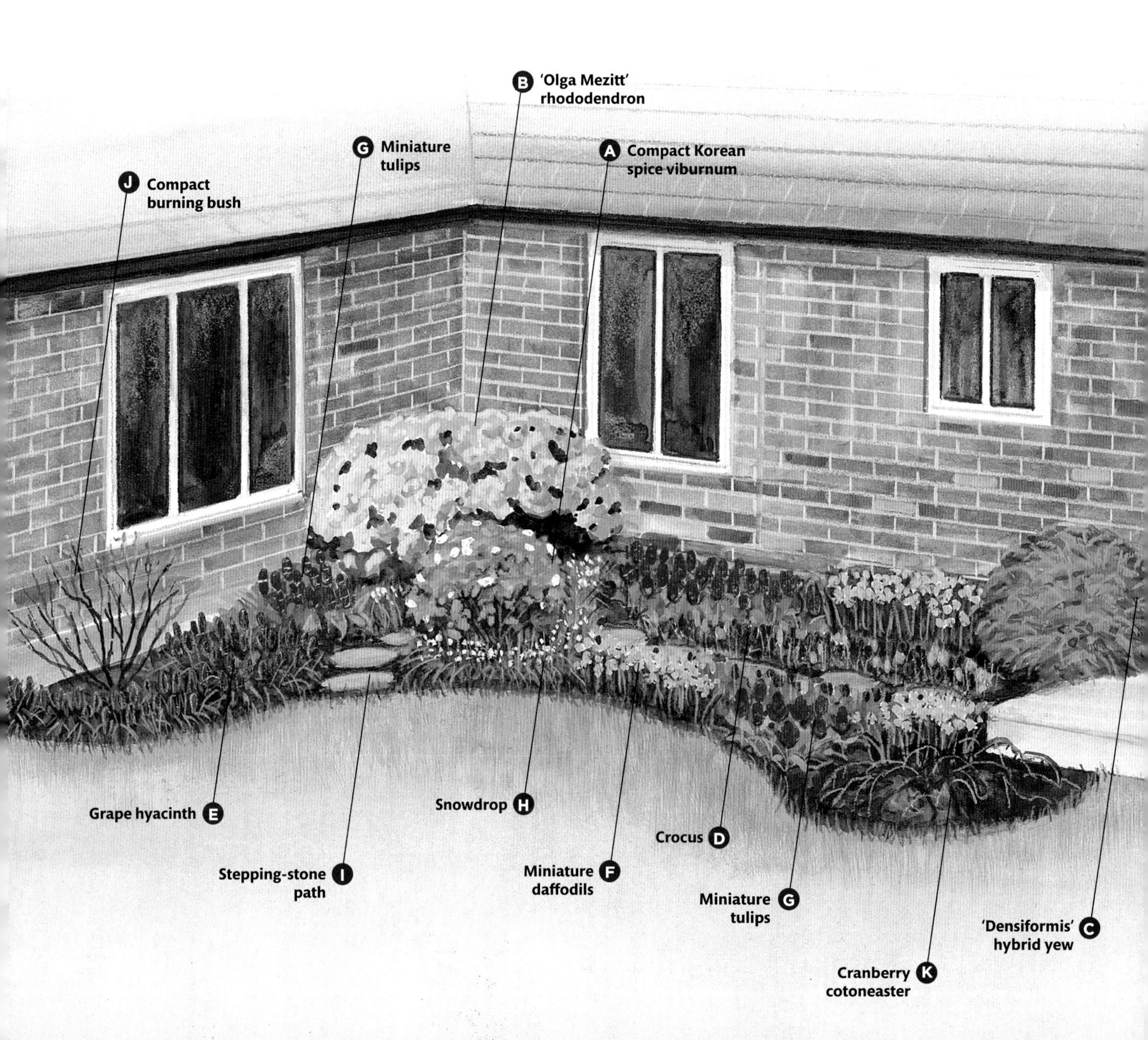

Plants & Projects

Interplant generous drifts and clumps of bulbs among the perennials. Once planted, bulbs require little care beyond clipping off spent flowers. After they bloom, their foliage is hidden by the emerging perennials. Divide the bulbs every few years if the patches become crowded or if you want to plant some elsewhere.

A Compact Korean spice viburnum (use 1 plant)
The fragrant white flower clusters of this spring-blooming deciduous shrub invite you down the path. Foliage is attractive summer and fall. See *Viburnum carlesii* 'Compactum', p. 152.

B 'Olga Mezitt' rhododendron (use 3)
This evergreen shrub is covered with pink flowers for weeks from early spring. The small dark-green leaves (which turn maroon in fall) make a fine backdrop for the perennials. See *Rhododendron*, p. 148.

C 'Densiformis' hybrid yew (use 1)
An evergreen shrub, it makes a low, spreading mound of fine-textured dark-green foliage. See *Taxus* x *media*, p. 151.

D Crocus (use 50)
Cup-shaped flowers on short stalks in early spring. Plant 6 or 8 per square foot along the path. A mix of purple- and gold-flowered types will go well with the other bulbs. See Bulbs: *Crocus*, p. 133.

E Grape hyacinth (use 25)
Grassy foliage and fragrant purple flowers resembling grape clusters make a pretty spring carpet beneath the burning bush. See Bulbs: *Muscari armeniacum*, p. 133.

F Miniature daffodils (use 25)
A spring planting isn't complete without these cheerful favorites. 'February Gold', 'Baby Moon', and 'Tête-à-Tête' offer small, early yellow flowers and low foliage that is easily covered by the perennials. See Bulbs: *Narcissus*, p. 133.

G Miniature tulips (use 20)
Shorter than "ordinary" tulips, but just as colorful, 'Red Riding Hood' and 'Lilac Wonder' are good choices here. See Bulbs: *Tulipa*, p. 133.

H Snowdrop (use 25)
One of the first flowers of spring, the nodding, snowy white blooms beckon above slender, grassy foliage at the bend in the path. See Bulbs: *Galanthus nivalis*, p. 133.

I Stepping-stone path
Precast pavers, 2 ft. in diameter, can be installed after you've prepared the planting bed. Tamp down the soil along the path, set the pavers in place, and spread mulch between them. See p. 160.

See p. 72 for the following:

J Compact burning bush (use 1)

K Cranberry cotoneaster (use 1)

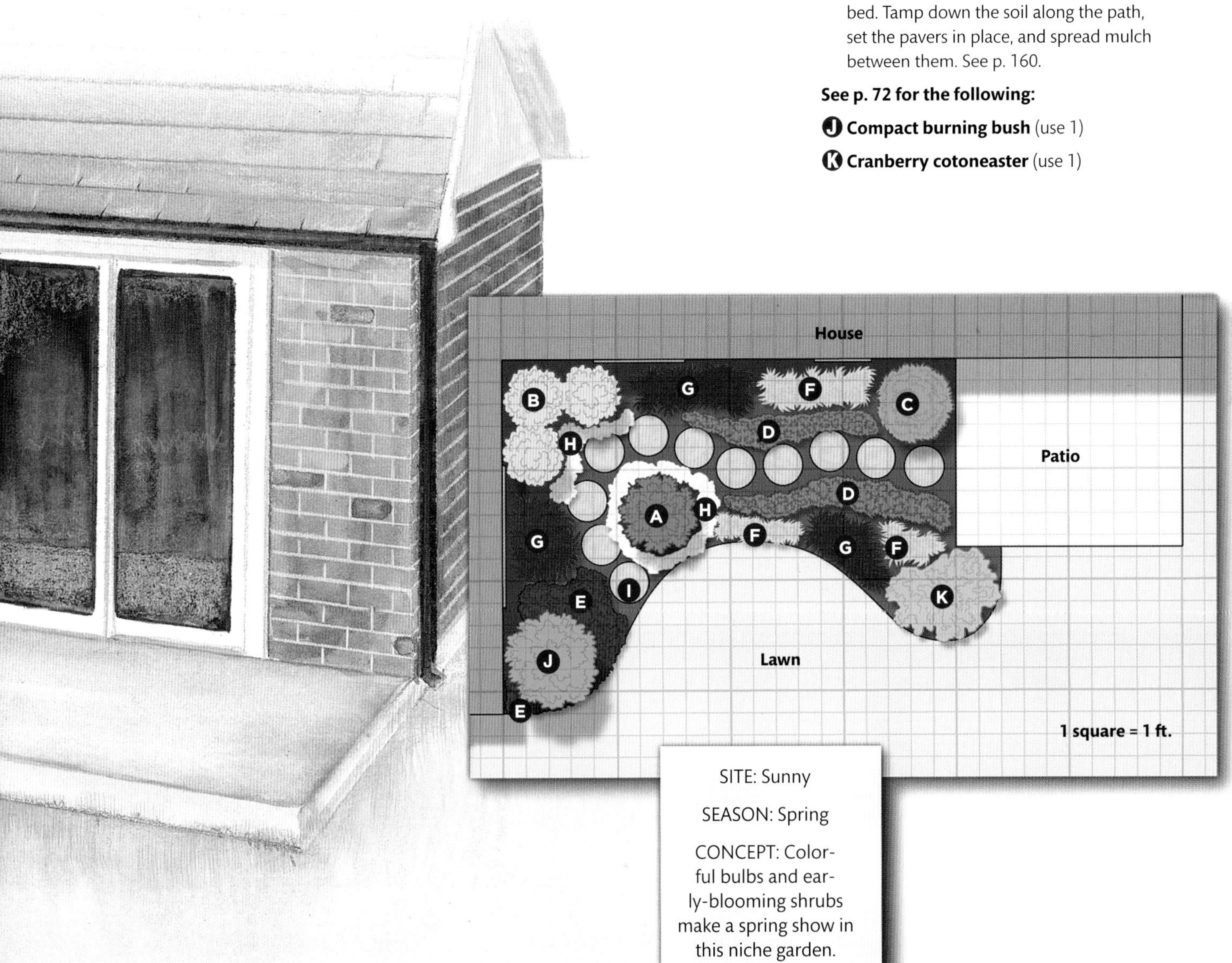

SITE: Sunny

SEASON: Spring

CONCEPT: Colorful bulbs and early-blooming shrubs make a spring show in this niche garden.

Summertime color

As the weather warms, there is no drop-off in interest or enjoyment as this planting moves into summer and fall. During the summer months, perennials join shrubs in a tapestry of colorful foliage and flowers.

Summer flowers come in shades of red, pink, and blue, with mounds of yellow coreopsis as accents. The foliage is equally attractive. Defining the back corners are contrasting evergreens, one broad-leaved, one coniferous. At the front corners, two deciduous shrubs provide a fiery fall display. Tall arching grasses add height; in fall and winter, their dry leaves and seed heads rustle and sway in the breeze.

Plants & Projects

A Compact burning bush (use 1 plant)
Green in summer, this deciduous shrub turns first copper and then an eye-popping crimson in fall. See *Euonymus alatus* 'Compactus', p. 136.

B Cranberry cotoneaster (use 1)
A deciduous shrub whose glossy green leaves turn bright red in fall. Bears small pink flowers in spring and cranberry red fruits in fall. See *Cotoneaster apiculatus*, p. 135.

C Maiden grass (use 2)
Arching clumps of this perennial's silvery green leaves are topped in fall by fluffy seed heads, which are attractive in winter. See *Miscanthus* 'Gracillimus', p. 144.

D 'Stargazer' lily (use 3)
The fragrance of this perennial's lovely pink flowers will entice you down the path in August. See *Lilium*, p. 143.

E Purple coneflower (use 5)
In July and August, this perennial bears large daisylike flowers on stiff stalks above coarse green leaves. Mix pink- and white-flowered cultivars here. See *Echinacea purpurea*, p. 136.

F 'Kobold' blazing star (use 3)
This perennial produces spikes of magenta flowers on leafy stalks in July and August. See *Liatris spicata*, p. 143.

G 'Sunny Border Blue' veronica (use 3)
Spikes of bright-blue flowers top mats of lustrous green leaves. This perennial blooms all summer if you keep clipping off spent flower spikes. See *Veronica*, p. 152.

H 'Blue Clips' Carpathian bellflower (use 6)
This perennial also blooms most of the summer, displaying cuplike blue flowers above clumps of delicate leaves. See *Campanula carpatica*, p. 134.

I 'Moonbeam' coreopsis (use 3)
Masses of small yellow flowers cover this perennial's mounds of lacy green foliage from midsummer into fall. See *Coreopsis verticillata*, p. 135.

See p. 71 for the following:

J Compact Korean spice viburnum

K 'Olga Mezitt' rhododendron

L 'Densiformis' hybrid yew

M Stepping-stone path

SITE: Sunny

SEASON: Summer

CONCEPT: Eye-catching perennials and shrubs pick up where spring bulbs leave off.

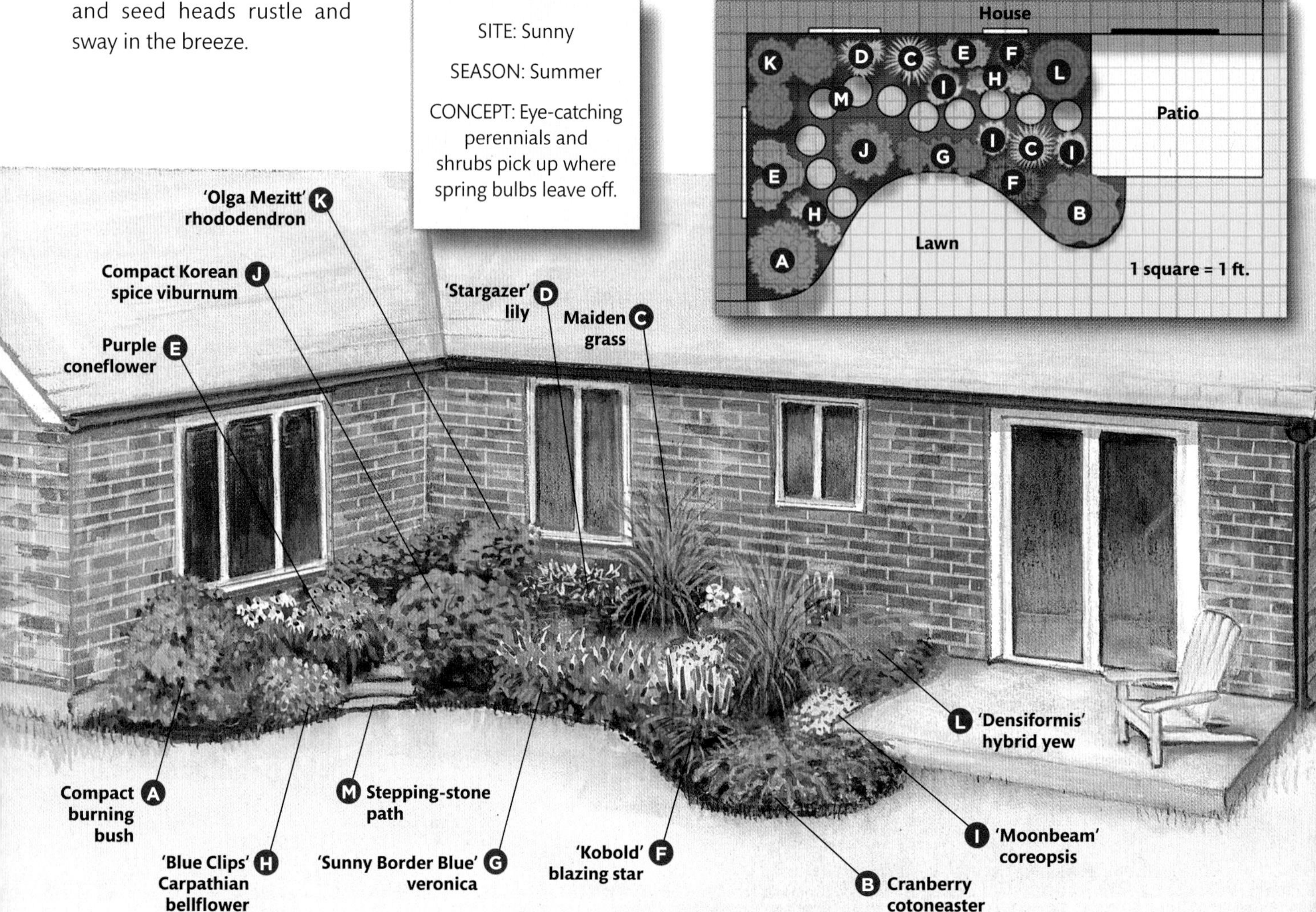

PLANT PORTRAITS

Distinctive shrubs combine with spring-flowering bulbs and summer-flowering perennials to provide months of enjoyment.

● = First design, pp. 70–71

▲ = Second design, pp. 72

'Densiformis' hybrid yew
(*Taxus* x *media*, p. 151) ● ▲

'Kobold' blazing star
(*Liatris spicata*, p. 143) ▲

Purple coneflower
(*Echinacea purpurea*, p. 136) ▲

Cranberry cotoneaster
(*Cotoneaster apiculatus*, p. 136) ● ▲

'Olga Mezitt' rhododendron
(*Rhododendron*, p. 148) ● ▲

"Around Back"

DRESS UP THE FAMILY'S DAY-TO-DAY ENTRANCE

When it comes to landscaping, the most-used parts of a property are often the most neglected. The walk from the garage or driveway to the back door of the house is just such a spot. You make the journey numerous times each day, so why not make it as pleasant a trip as possible? A simple design like the one shown here can transform this space, making it at once more inviting and more functional.

Beginning at the drive, the walkway flares out to accommodate the unloading of a carful of children or groceries. Attractive lattice fences screen the backyard and form a backdrop for evergreen shrubs and groups of colorful perennials.

In a high-traffic area frequented by ball-bouncing, bicycle-riding children as well as busy adults, delicate, fussy plants have no place. The tough, easy-care plants here provide a pleasing mix of foliage and flowers throughout the growing season. In spring, the rhododendron's lovely pink flowers are joined by the deliciously fragrant lily-of-the-valley. Summer and fall present a tapestry of varied colorful foliage embroidered with flowers. While the perennials rest in winter, evergreen shrubs and the handsome bark of the Japanese tree lilac keep up appearances.

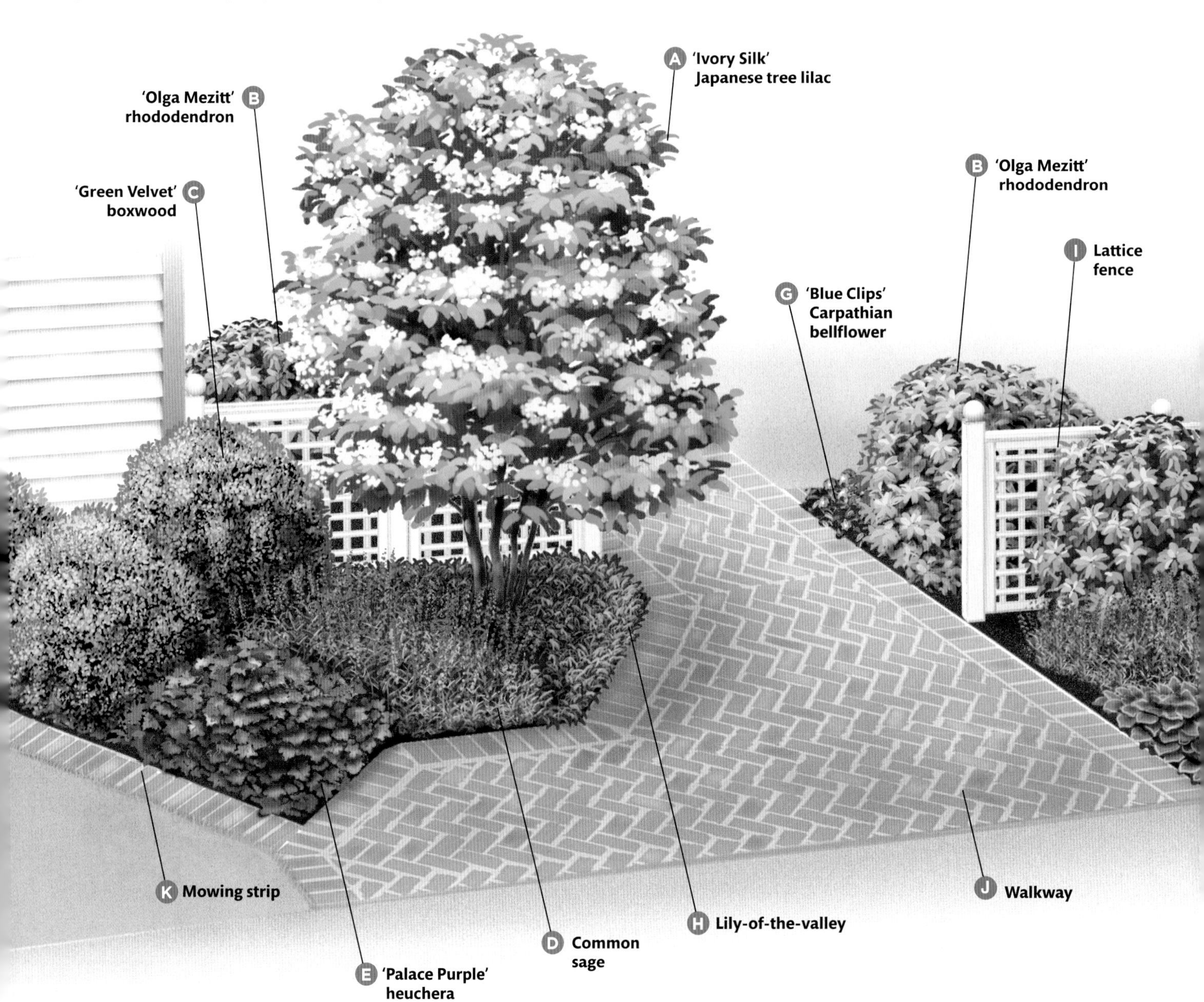

Plants & Projects

Installing the walk, fence, and plantings will take a few weekends, but you'll spend less time than that each year on maintenance. Just clean up the spent perennial foliage in late fall or early spring and add new mulch in spring.

A 'Ivory Silk' Japanese tree lilac (use 1 plant) Fragrant, creamy white flowers stand out against the lush green leaves of this small tough deciduous tree in early summer. Reddish brown peeling bark also looks good. See *Syringa reticulata*, p. 151.

B 'Olga Mezitt' rhododendron (use 5) An evergreen shrub with an attractive upright form, small dark-green leaves that turn maroon in winter, and pink flowers in early spring. See *Rhododendron*, p. 148.

C 'Green Velvet' boxwood (use 3) The small evergreen leaves of this compact shrub hold their green color through winter. Naturally round, tidy shape needs no pruning to keep it in its place along the foundation. 'Wintergreen' is a good substitute. See *Buxus*, p. 134.

D Common sage (use 13) A bushy perennial herb with fragrant gray foliage and very showy blue-purple flowers in June. Its foliage and flower colors nicely complement those of the neighboring rhododendrons and heucheras. See *Salvia officinalis*, p. 150.

E 'Palace Purple' heuchera (use 10) A tough perennial, it forms mounds of large bronzy purple foliage that looks good from early spring to frost. See *Heuchera micrantha*, p. 139.

F Variegated small-leaved hosta (use 3) Popular perennials that are grown primarily for their striking foliage. 'Ginko Craig' is one good cultivar with green-and-white leaves; if it is unavailable, ask your nursery to recommend a substitute. Underplant with crocuses or other small bulbs for flowers in early spring. See *Hosta*, p. 140.

G 'Blue Clips' Carpathian bellflower (use 8) Cheerful blue cuplike flowers bloom for weeks starting in midsummer atop mounds of small dark-green leaves that make a pretty edging along the backyard lawn. You could substitute 'White Clips' for white flowers. See *Campanula carpatica*, p. 134.

H Lily-of-the-valley (use 75) For a few weeks in May, enjoy one of the finest fragrances in nature from this perennial's tiny white bell-shaped flowers. The rest of the summer it's a durable ground cover. For evergreen foliage, substitute sweet violet (*Viola odorata*). See *Convallaria majalis*, p. 135.

I Lattice fence Made with prefabricated lattice, this waist-high fence keeps backyard and driveway activities separate. See p. 183.

J Walkway Build a new walk or expand an existing one. We've shown bricklike precast pavers here. See p. 160.

K Mowing strip Brick edging helps keep beds tidy and makes mowing near them easier. See p. 162.

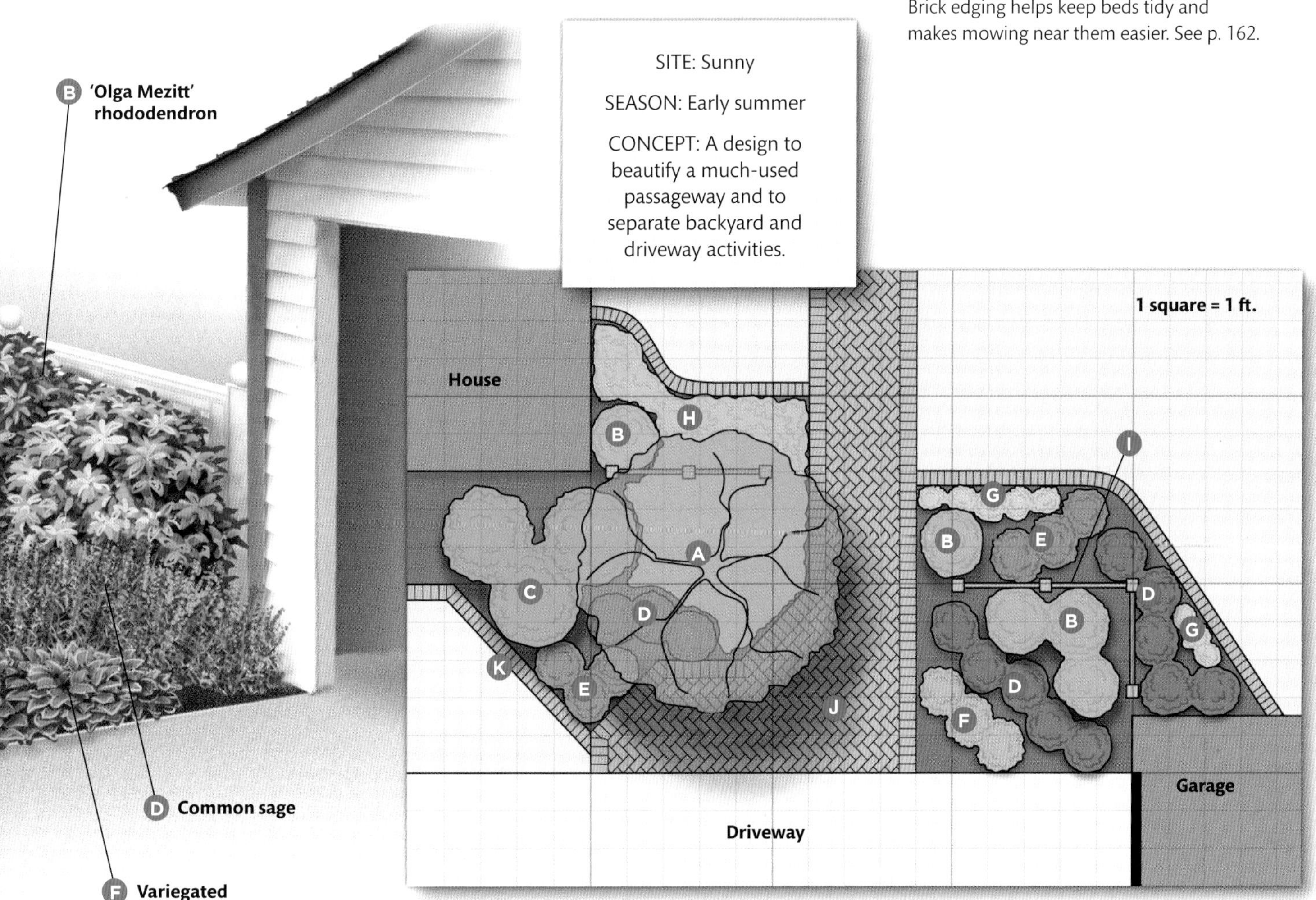

Plants and paving only

If fence building isn't your forte, or if you prefer a simpler, more open look, consider this design. It retains the conveniently wide walkway (shown in dressed flagstones here). Plantings separate driveway and backyard activities less emphatically than a fence. The hedge signals the beginning of private space without blocking the view to or from the street.

Bulbs, perennials, and deciduous shrubs give the planting a pleasing presence from early spring through fall. Fragrant flowers are a special treat in spring and late summer. Evergreen foliage and the silhouettes of branches look attractive through the winter.

The design can be easily altered to suit circumstances and taste. Make a foundation planting of viburnums along the back wall, or extend the bed of hostas farther down the walk.

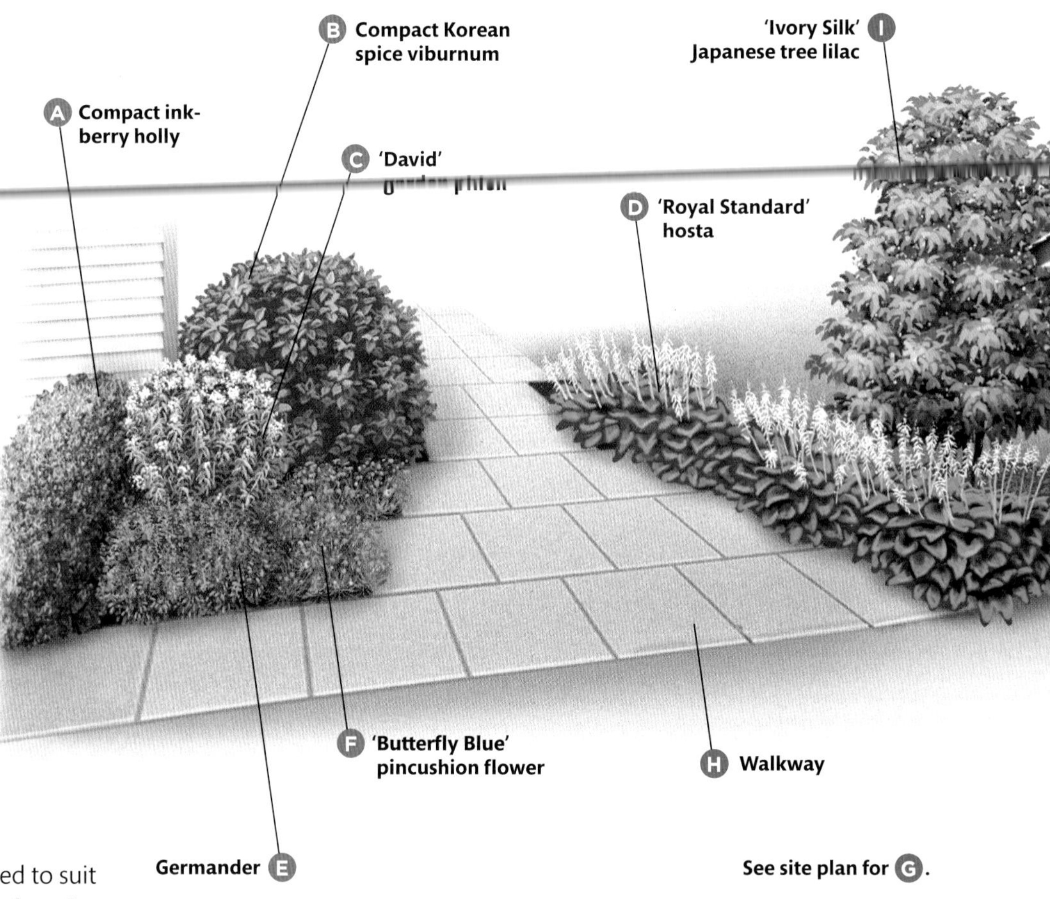

SITE: Sunny

SEASON: Summer

CONCEPT: A more open feeling here; woody plants and perennials frame the wide paving near the drive.

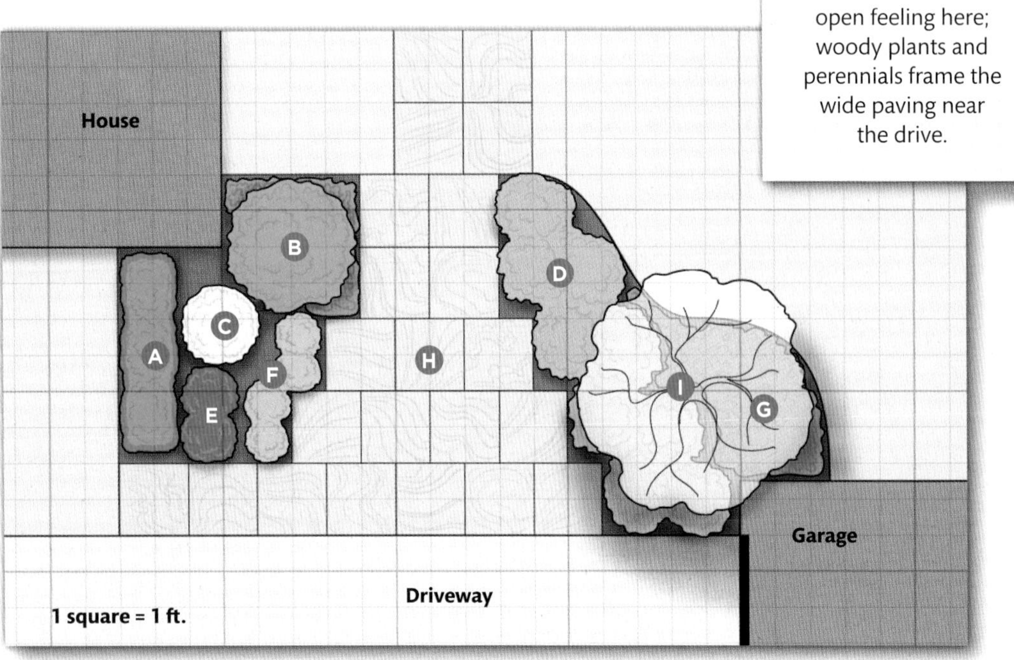

Plants & Projects

A Compact inkberry holly (use 3 plants)
A compact form of a native evergreen shrub. Its small glossy leaves and dense habit make it ideal for the little sheared hedge here. In Zone 6, you can substitute Japanese holly (*Ilex crenata*), another good hedge plant. See *Ilex glabra* 'Compacta', p. 141.

B Compact Korean spice viburnum (use 1)
A delicious spring scent wafts into the backyard in May from the spicy white flower clusters of this deciduous shrub. There is handsome green foliage the rest of the growing season. It won't outgrow its spot in the corner, though you may need to trim stems that encroach on the house or the walk. See *Viburnum carlesii* 'Compactum', p. 152.

C 'David' garden phlox (use 1)
A sturdy upright perennial that will brighten the walk with good green leaves and dense clusters of small, white, fragrant flowers in August and September. See *Phlox paniculata*, p. 146.

D 'Royal Standard' hosta (use 9)
Like most hostas, this one forms a handsome mound of foliage throughout the growing season. This cultivar also bears large fragrant white flowers from August into September that are appealing enough to cut and bring into the house. For an early-spring lift, plant generous clumps (6 or 8 per square foot) of crocuses among the hostas. After bloom, the dying crocus leaves will be hidden by the emerging hosta foliage. See *Hosta*, p. 140.

E Germander (use 2)
This tough little perennial forms a neat mound of small, shiny, fragrant dark-green leaves next to the walk. In late summer and early fall, it bears small clusters of pinkish purple flowers. Shear every spring to keep it compact. See *Teucrium chamaedrys*, p. 151.

F 'Butterfly Blue' pincushion flower (use 4)
For lots of misty blue color near the walk, you can't beat this little perennial. Bloom begins in May and goes right on until frost atop a compact clump of bright-green leaves. Flowers attract butterflies and are good for cutting. See *Scabiosa columbaria*, p. 150.

G Moss phlox (use 21)
This little evergreen perennial makes a mossy-textured carpet beneath the viburnum and tree lilac. Blooms in early spring; a white- or pale-pink-flowered variety will look nice here. See *Phlox subulata*, p. 146.

H Walkway
Carefully laid 2-ft.-square flagstones or concrete pavers are safe for walking and make a surface that's easy to shovel in winter. See p. 160.

See p. 75 for the following:

I 'Ivory Silk' Japanese tree lilac (use 1)

PLANT PORTRAITS

These back-door plants have front-door style: attractive form and foliage, and pretty, often fragrant flowers.

● = First design, pp. 74–75

▲ = Second design, pp. 76–77

Lily-of-the-valley (*Convallaria majalis*, p. 135) ●

'David' garden phlox (*Phlox paniculata*, p. 146) ▲

'Palace Purple' heuchera (*Heuchera micrantha*, p. 139) ●

'Ivory Silk' Japanese tree lila (*Syringa reticulata*, p. 151) ● ▲

Common sage (*Salvia officinalis*, p. 150) ●

'Royal Standard' hosta (*Hosta*, p. 140) ▲

Beautify a Blank Wall

PAINT A PICTURE WITH PLANTS

Just as you enhance your living room by hanging paintings on the walls, you can decorate blank walls in your outdoor "living rooms" with a vertical trellis garden. The design shown here goes a step further, filling an undulating bed with a tree, shrubs, and perennials to create a three-dimensional composition. The result gives pleasure when viewed from a window or when you're strolling by to take a closer look.

Every season has its eye-catching attraction. Spireas and junipers give the design a solid foundation of year-round color and texture against the garage wall. The flowering crab apple holds center stage in spring. Roses, bee balm, and hollyhock mallow provide flowers in shades of pink for months in summer and fall, while other perennials form a low edging of attractive foliage at the front of the bed.

Angling out from the garage wall, its twin "peaks" echoing the gable ends of the garage or house, the homemade trellis adds both height and depth to the planting. Covered with blossoms from early summer, the trellis makes a wonderful focal point.

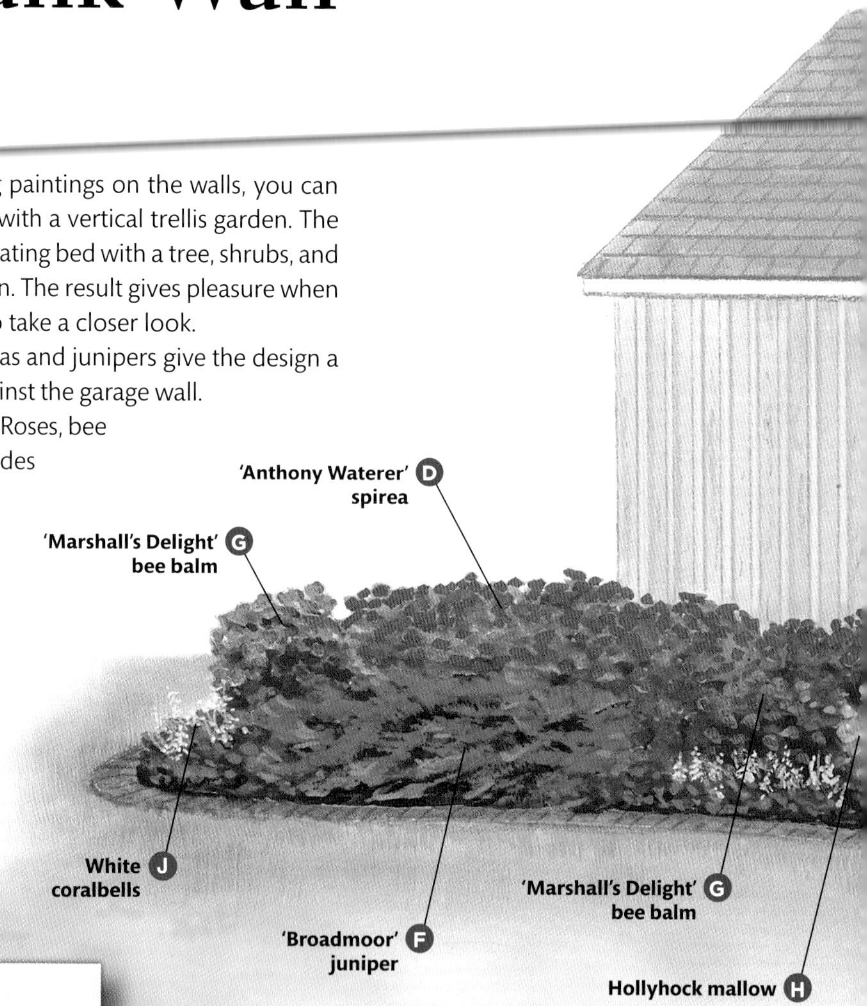

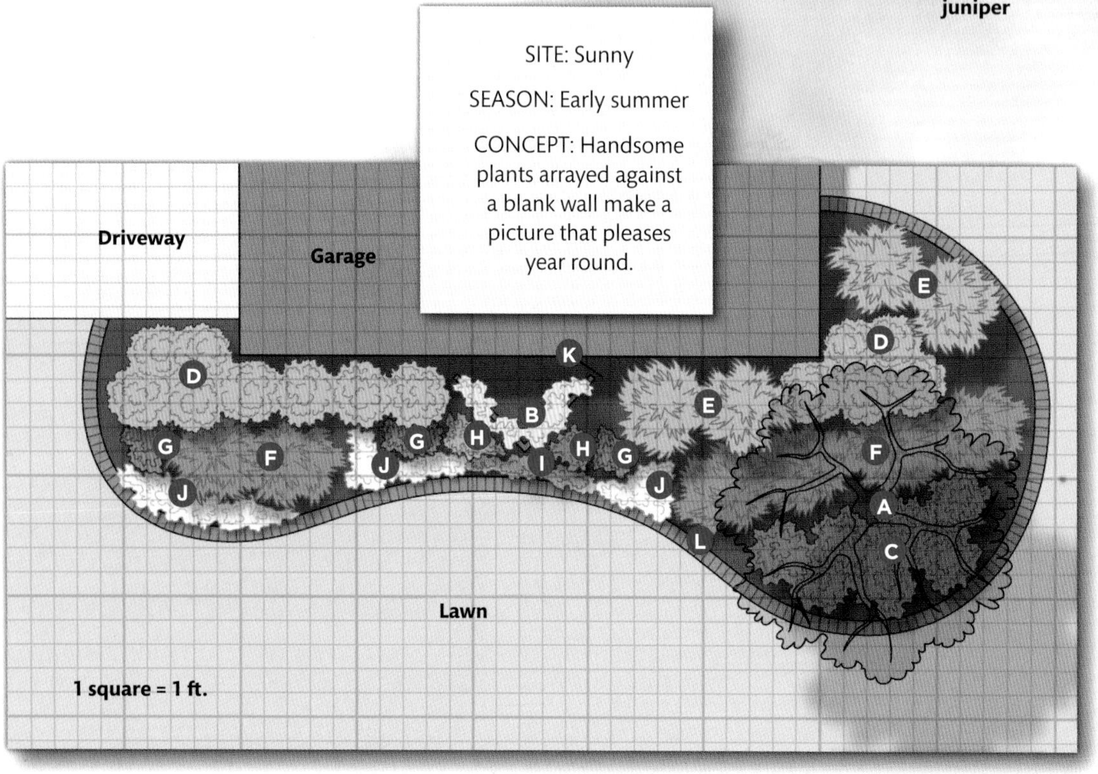

'Anthony Waterer' spirea (D)
'Marshall's Delight' bee balm (G)
White coralbells (J)
'Broadmoor' juniper (F)
'Marshall's Delight' bee balm (G)
Hollyhock mallow (H)

SITE: Sunny

SEASON: Early summer

CONCEPT: Handsome plants arrayed against a blank wall make a picture that pleases year round.

Driveway
Garage
Lawn
1 square = 1 ft.

Plants & Projects

These plants will allow you to sit back and enjoy the view in exchange for performing just a few chores on their behalf. Prune all the roses in spring and tie the climbing roses to the trellis as they grow. (See p. 206 for more on rose care.) Shear the spireas after they've bloomed, clip off spent perennial flowers in summer, and cut their foliage back to the ground in fall.

A 'Pink Spires' crab apple (use 1 plant)
This small deciduous tree brings color to the planting in all seasons: reddish new leaves and lavender flowers in spring; copper-colored fall leaves; and purplish fruits that persist into winter. See *Malus*, p. 144.

B Climbing rose (use 2)
A profusion of pink flowers and shiny green leaves engulfs the trellis from early summer to fall. Plant 'John Cabot' or 'William Baffin'; both produce fragrant flowers throughout the summer. See *Rosa*, p. 149.

C 'Frau Dagmar Hartop' rose (use 7)
This shrub rose offers fragrant single pink flowers, bright-green crinkly leaves, and large red hips that last from fall into winter. See *Rosa*, p. 149.

D 'Anthony Waterer' spirea (use 13)
A compact deciduous shrub with small fine leaves, rosy pink flowers, and a tough constitution ideal for hot, dry conditions beneath the garage eaves. Blooms in midsummer. See *Spiraea* x *bumalda*, p. 150.

E 'Maney' juniper (use 4)
A rugged, bushy evergreen shrub that adds height and winter color at the far end of the planting. Silver-blue foliage makes a nice backdrop for the smaller shrubs and perennials. See *Juniperus chinensis*, p. 142.

F 'Broadmoor' juniper (use 6)
A spreading evergreen shrub whose low mass of soft gray-green color complements the planting's many pink flowers. See *Juniperus sabina*, p. 142.

G 'Marshall's Delight' bee balm (use 6)
This perennial forms a patch of slender leafy stalks topped with clusters of pink flowers in midsummer. See *Monarda*, p. 144.

H Hollyhock mallow (use 8)
Pink flowers are borne in profusion on tall stalks above this perennial's wide mounds of attractive bright-green leaves. Blooms in midsummer. See *Malva alcea* 'Fastigiata', p. 144.

I Basket-of-gold (use 5)
Begin the spring growing season with the bright-yellow, fragrant blooms of this perennial. Low mounds of gray leaves make an attractive edging at the center of the bed. See *Aurinia saxatilis*, p. 132.

J White coralbells (use 22)
Clouds of tiny flowers float above this perennial's neat mounds of semievergreen foliage for most of the summer. White-flowered 'June Bride' works well in this planting. See *Heuchera* x *brizoides*, p. 139.

K Trellis
This easy-to-build grid of 1x2s makes a handsome and functional support for the climbing roses. See p. 184.

L Mowing strip
A neat edging of bricks crisply defines the bed's shape and makes mowing the adjacent lawn easier. See p. 162.

Make a Fresco of Flowers

A VERTICAL GARDEN BEAUTIFIES A BLANK WALL

The design shown here transforms a nondescript garage wall into a living fresco, showcasing a colorful collection of lovely plants. Instead of a view of a plain wall, imagine gazing at this scene from a nearby patio or kitchen window.

This is a tall, narrow garden, ideal for a small lot or restricted space on a larger lot. It is meant to be viewed rather like a painting. A climbing rose is the centerpiece of the planting, bearing large double multicolored flowers all summer long. A vigorous plant, it will quickly cover the trellis. The plants at its feet are just as prolific. 'Stella d'Oro', one of the most popular daylilies, produces a fresh bouquet of gold trumpet-shaped flowers every day from early June into September. At the front of the bed, cushion spurge makes a tidy edging of foliage and spring flowers.

At each end of the symmetrical planting, clumps of green pincushion flower foliage are covered with sky-blue flowers for months—which as a bonus attract butterflies. Behind the pincushion flowers, yuccas stand like well-armed sentinels. You'd hardly suspect these rather forbidding-looking plants to produce beautiful flowers, so when tall flower stalks appear in midsummer, they are as surprising as they are striking.

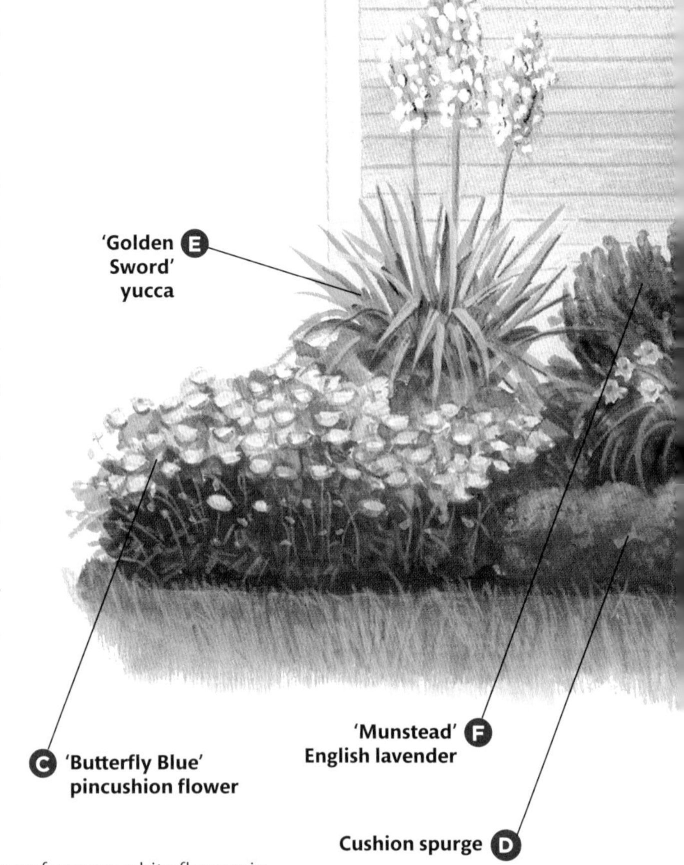

Plants & Projects

This little garden richly repays the small amount of maintenance it requires. Tie the rose canes to the trellis as they grow, and prune them in the spring. Deadhead perennials throughout the summer, and give them an annual spring cleanup.

A 'Climbing Joseph's Coat' rose (use 1 plant)
The cardinal-red buds of this climbing rose open a gold color, turning orange and then red as they mature. Glossy green deciduous leaves are a good background for the summer-long display of flowers. In Zone 4, substitute 'William Baffin', a hardier rose with pink flowers. See *Rosa*, p. 149.

B 'Stella d'Oro' daylily (use 12)
The cheery gold flowers of this popular perennial keep coming all summer long. Grassy foliage looks good, too. See *Hemerocallis*, p. 139.

C 'Butterfly Blue' pincushion flower (use 14)
For lots of misty blue color at each corner of the bed, you can't beat this tough perennial. Bloom begins in May atop tidy clumps of green leaves and goes right on until frost. See *Scabiosa columbaria*, p. 150.

D Cushion spurge (use 12)
In early spring, this showy perennial bears bright-yellow blossoms that last for weeks. After bloom, it is a neat mound of dark-green foliage that turns red in autumn. See *Euphorbia polychroma*, p. 137.

E 'Golden Sword' yucca (use 2)
Bristling with sword-shaped leaves, this shrub produces tall stalks draped with showy clusters of creamy white flowers in midsummer. The dried seedpods are attractive, too. The leaves, striped with yellow and gold, are evergreen. See *Yucca filamentosa*, p. 153.

F 'Munstead' English lavender (use 6)
This shrubby herb would be worth growing just for its handsome bushy mound of silver-gray foliage. It also bears countless spikes of fragrant pale-lavender flowers in July and makes a lovely companion for the nearby daylilies. See *Lavandula angustifolia*, p. 143.

G Trellis
A wooden trellis, which is built in 32-in.-wide modules, supports the climbing rose. It is hung on the garage and can be easily removed when the siding needs painting. See p. 184.

SITE: Sunny

SEASON: Summer

CONCEPT: A rose-covered trellis and narrow flower bed make a focal point of an uninteresting wall.

G Trellis
A 'Climbing Joseph's Coat' rose
B 'Stella d'Oro' daylily
Cushion spurge D
F 'Munstead' English lavender
'Golden Sword' E yucca
C 'Butterfly Blue' pincushion flower

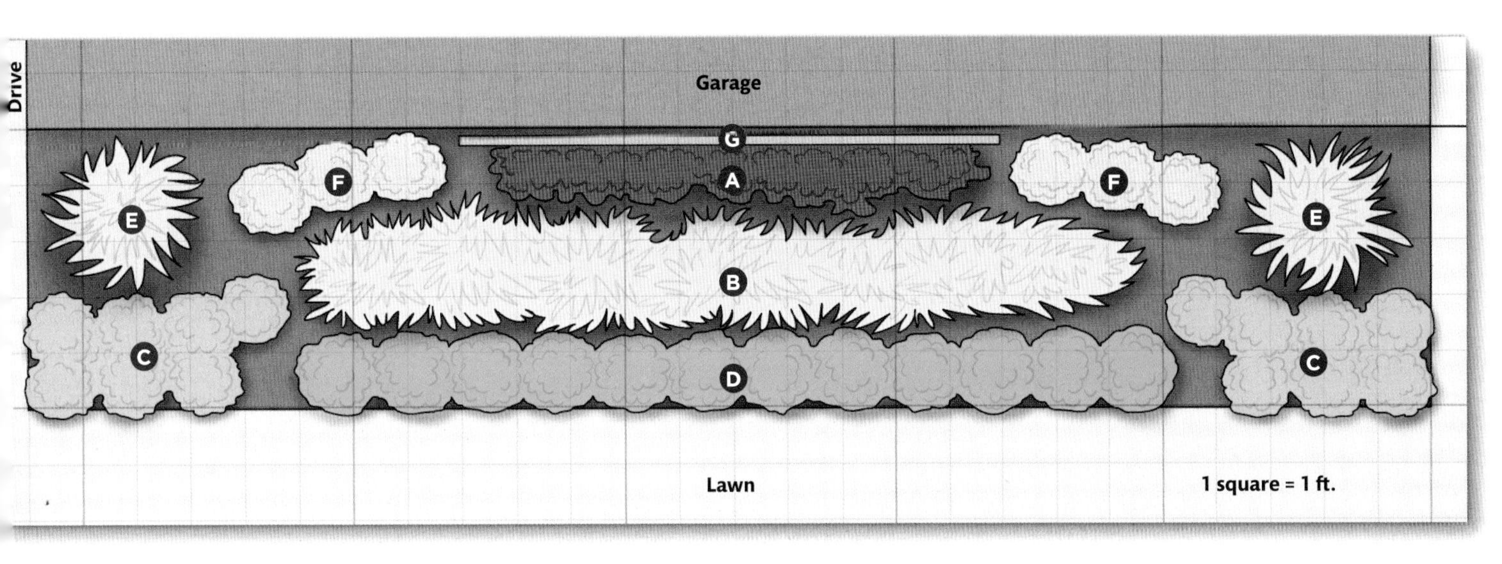
Drive
Garage
G
A
F
F
E
E
B
C
C
D
Lawn
1 square = 1 ft.

A shady wall garden

Shade is a blessing on a hot summer day but can be a challenge for a gardener. This design makes the most of a garage wall that is north-facing or shaded by a tree. The layout is similar to that of the previous design, but the shady conditions call for a different set of plants.

It will take several years for the shade-tolerant hydrangea vine to cover the trellis, but its lush foliage and pretty early-summer flowers make the wait worthwhile. The long narrow bed is filled with perennials chosen mainly for the distinctive textures and colors of their foliage. Deeply cut fern fronds arch over the broad leaves of the hostas and the pretty speckled foliage of the lungwort. All but the ferns offer flowers, too. The brightly colored poppies and the sweet-scented hosta flowers are a special treat.

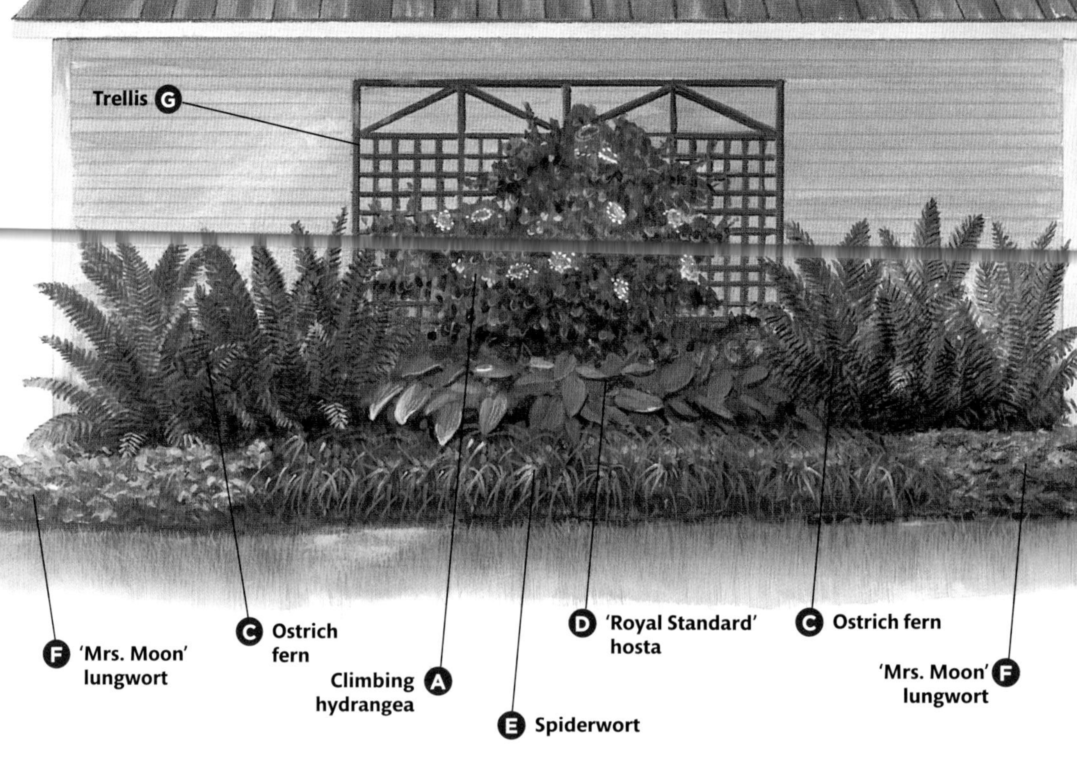

B Oriental poppies are interplanted with ferns and are dormant in summer.

SITE: Shady

SEASON: Summer

CONCEPT: Lush and varied foliage are sprinkled with flowers for a shady site.

Plants & Projects

A Climbing hydrangea (use 1 plant)
This deciduous vine drapes the trellis with glossy leaves from spring through late fall. In June it bears lacy clusters of white flowers. Papery rust-brown bark is revealed in winter. See *Hydrangea petiolaris*, p. 140.

B Oriental poppy (use 10)
Large orange, red, pink, or white flowers with papery petals rise high above the furry divided leaves of this perennial in late spring or summer. Interplant with ferns, whose fronds will hide the poppy foliage when it dies back in summer. If your site is very shady, substitute Lenten rose (*Helleborus orientalis*) for the poppies. See *Papaver orientale*, p. 145.

C Ostrich fern (use 6)
The bright-green fronds of this deciduous fern resemble ostrich plumes and make a lush backdrop for the lungwort. See Ferns: *Matteuccia struthiopteris*, p. 137.

D 'Royal Standard' hosta (use 7)
A perennial that bears large white flowers with a pleasant sweet scent from August into September. The large smooth leaves are solid medium green. See *Hosta*, p. 140.

E Spiderwort (use 12)
Unusual three-petaled blue flowers sparkle atop this native perennial, which forms a clump of slender grassy leaves at the front of the bed. See *Tradescantia andersoniana*, p. 152.

F 'Mrs. Moon' lungwort (use 10)
This subtle perennial ground cover features silver-flecked leaves that look good all summer and pink and blue flowers for many weeks in spring. See *Pulmonaria saccharata*, p. 147.

See p. 80 for the following:

G Trellis

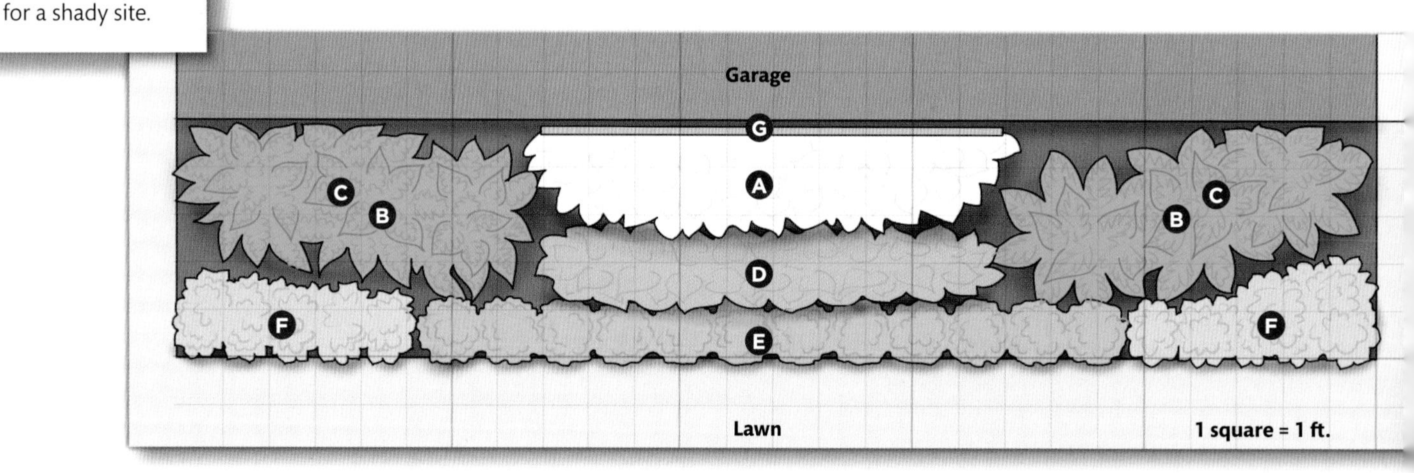

PLANT PORTRAITS

These vines, perennials, and shrubs make a handsome "vertical" garden in sunny or shady conditions.

● = First design, pp. 80–81

▲ = Second design, pp. 82

'Climbing Joseph's Coat' rose (*Rosa*, p. 149) ●

Oriental poppy (*Papaver orientale*, p. 145) ▲

Cushion spurge (*Euphorbia polychroma*, p. 137) ●

'Butterfly Blue' pincushion flower (*Scabiosa columbaria*, p. 150) ●

Spiderwort (*Tradescantia andersoniana*, p. 152) ▲

'Golden Sword' yucca (*Yucca filamentosa*, p. 153) ●

Climbing hydrangea (*Hydrangea petiolaris*, p. 140) ▲

A Shady Hideaway

BUILD A COZY RETREAT IN A CORNER OF YOUR YARD

If your property is long on lawn and short on shade, a bench under a leafy arbor can provide a cool respite from the heat or the cares of the day. Tucked into a corner of the backyard and set among attractive shrubs and vines, the arbor and planting shown here is a desirable destination even when the day isn't sizzling.

The arbor, flagstone paving, and shrubs can be installed in a weekend or two. The kiwi vine will cover the structure in short order, though the shrubs will take longer to provide additional privacy. At maturity, the stepped heights of the shrubs will settle the composition comfortably on its site. The planting could easily be extended along the property lines or merged with an existing planting.

In spring, the shrubs sparkle with small flowers. Summer is lush and cool on the bench. The most colorful season is fall (shown here). It is also the busiest, as birds and other wildlife bustle about the shrubs, harvesting fruits and berries.

Plants & Projects

Once the arbor is built and the young plants are nurtured through their first year, you can relax on your bench and enjoy this carefree planting. From time to time, you'll need to prune dead or weak stems from the shrubs. Every year, you'll need to shear the thymes with hedge shears or a string trimmer.

A Hardy kiwi (use 2 plants)
This hardy vine will quickly cover the arbor. Large heart-shaped deciduous leaves can be green, white, or pink, or a combination of all three. Male plants have flashier leaves, but include a female so you can harvest the edible fruit. See *Actinidia kolomikta*, p. 130.

B 'Sparkleberry' winterberry holly (use 3)
Bunches of bright-red berries shine through the fall and winter days on a mass of twiggy stems after this upright deciduous shrub drops its bright green leaves. With or without leaves, it's a dense screen for the bench. Berries attract a variety of birds. See *Ilex verticillata*, p. 141.

C Purpleleaf sand cherry (use 2)
Reddish purple leaves of this spreading deciduous shrub provide color on each side of the arbor all season. Pale-pink blooms appear in May. Fruits are small, but birds love them. See *Prunus* x *cistena*, p. 147.

D Cranberry bush (use 6)
This native deciduous shrub has it all: beautiful white flowers in June, lovely maplelike leaves through the summer, a fall show of blazing foliage, and red fruits that last all winter. Grows slowly into a broad, upright bush and needs little if any pruning. See *Viburnum trilobum*, p. 152.

E Cranberry cotoneaster (use 2)
Glossy dark-green leaves of this mounding deciduous shrub are the perfect background for small pale-pink flowers in May. Red fruits and red foliage follow in fall; the fruits last into November. Its fine texture contrasts with the cranberry bushes behind. See *Cotoneaster apiculatus*, p. 135.

F Thymes (use several)
Tuck woolly thyme and creeping thyme between the flagstones for a living carpet that releases a pleasing fragrance when you walk on it. Furry gray leaves of woolly thyme contrast nicely with the shiny green leaves of its cousin. Both are evergreen perennials that bear masses of tiny pink, white, or mauve flowers in summer. Shear hard every spring. See *Thymus*, p. 151.

G Arbor
Wide enough to accommodate a 4-ft. bench, the wooden arbor can be painted or left to weather beneath its covering of vines. See p. 185.

H Paving
Neatly fitted irregular flagstones, set in a base of sand, suit the arbor and planting well and make a dry place to stand or walk. See p. 160.

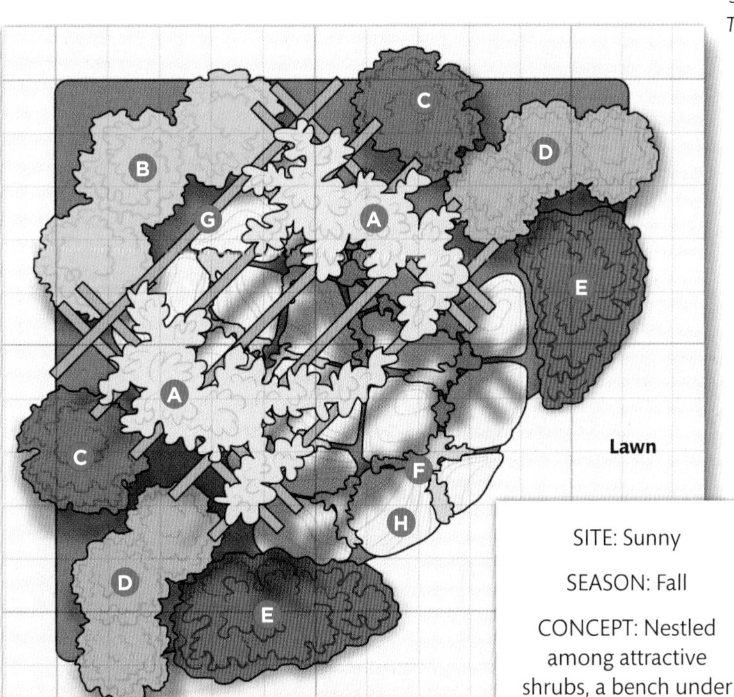

SITE: Sunny

SEASON: Fall

CONCEPT: Nestled among attractive shrubs, a bench under a vine-covered arbor is a restful haven.

A fragrant bower

Few things in life are more pleasant than relaxing in a shaded niche on a summer day while a scented breeze gently stirs the leaves. To provide just such an opportunity, this design envelops the simple wooden arbor and its occupant with fragrant plants.

The planting is most potent in spring and early summer, when clusters of wisteria flowers dangle overhead, their scent mingling with that of the Korean spice viburnum and lilac behind and to the sides of the bench. Lavender, summersweet, and aromatic thyme fill the following months with fragrant flowers and foliage. Like the previous planting, this requires very little maintenance after the plants are established.

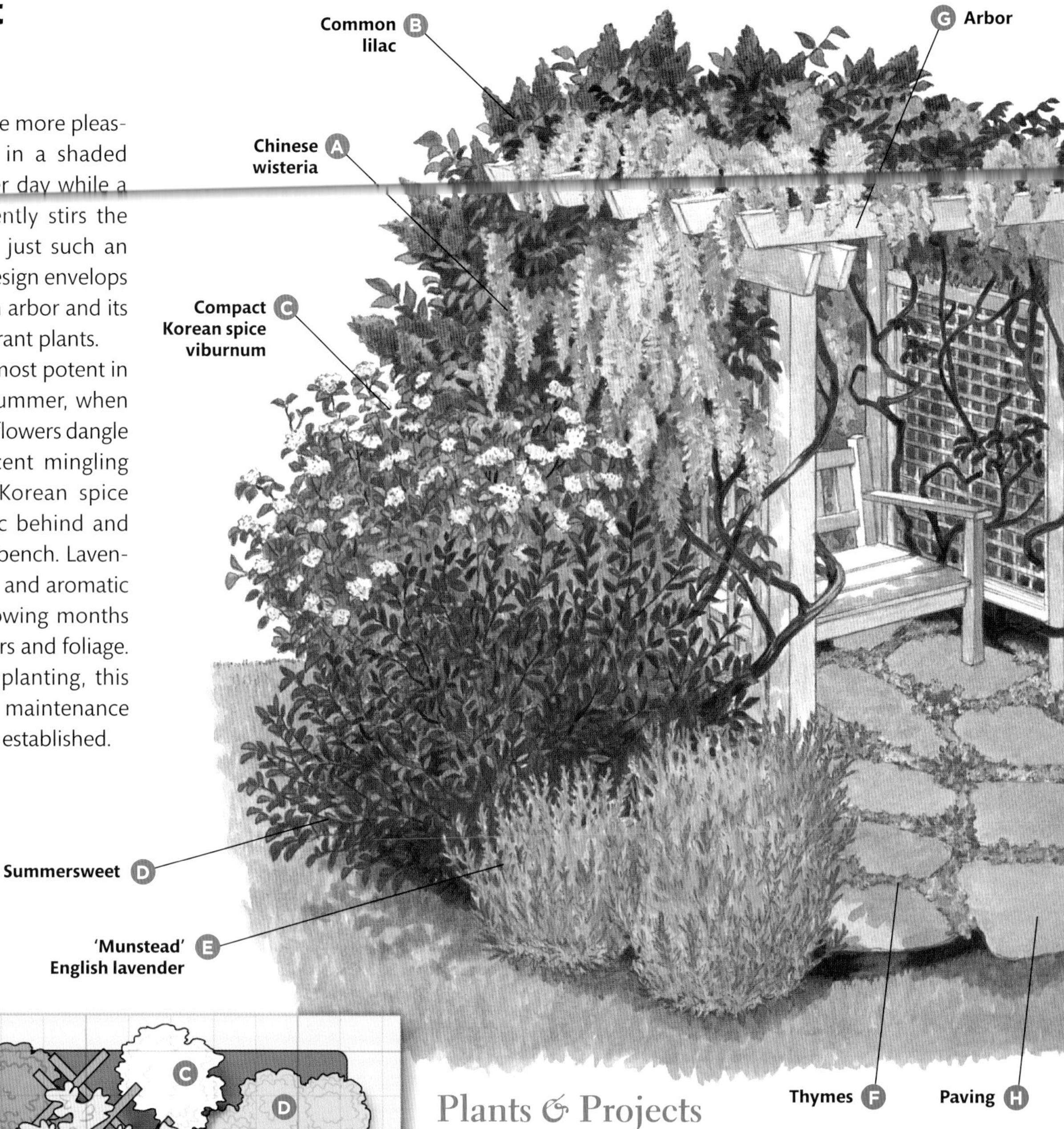

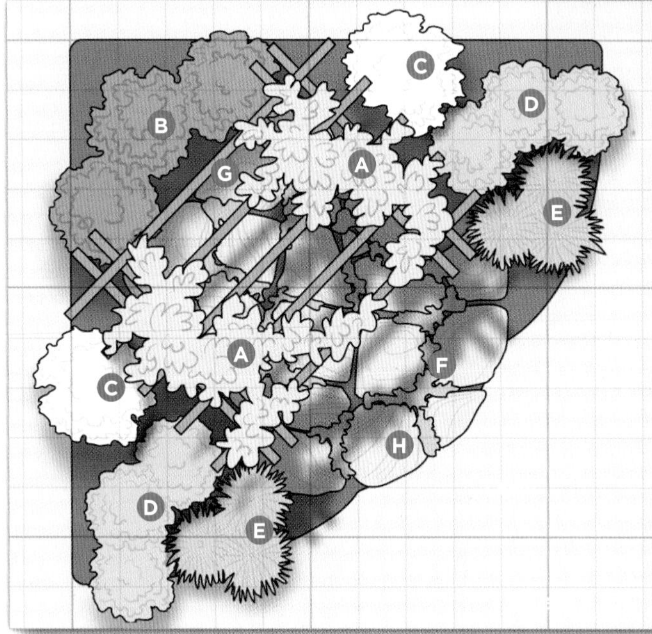

Plants & Projects

A Chinese wisteria (use 2 plants)
A vigorous deciduous vine, it will quickly cover the arbor with lacy foliage. Once established, it blooms in June, with clusters of very fragrant purple, lavender, or white flowers. See *Wisteria sinensis*, p. 153.

B Common lilac (use 3)
The heady scent of the flowers on this old-fashioned deciduous shrub will draw you to the bench in May. It will grow quickly to screen the back of the arbor. Any purple- or white-flowered cultivar will suit the color scheme here. See *Syringa vulgaris*, p. 151.

C Compact Korean spice viburnum (use 2)
The spicy scent of this deciduous shrub's pretty white flower clusters mingles with the fragrance of lilac in May. Its handsome green foliage and tidy compact habit are appealing for the rest of the growing season. See *Viburnum carlesii* 'Compactum', p. 152.

D Summersweet (use 6)
The spicy-scented pink or white flowers on this upright deciduous shrub will cheer you through the August doldrums. Dark glossy leaves turn gold in fall. See *Clethra alnifolia*, p. 134.

SITE: Sunny

SEASON: Spring

CONCEPT: Sheltered in a leafy bower, relax among a potpourri of fragrant plants.

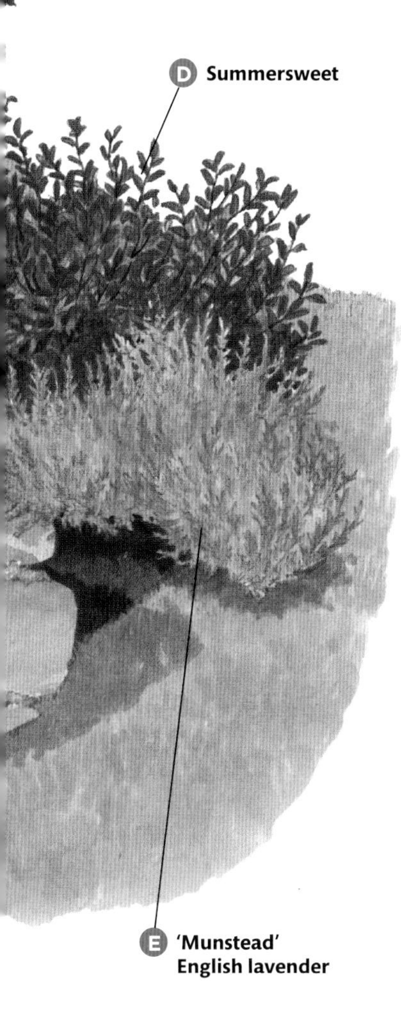

E 'Munstead' English lavender (use 6)
This gray-leaved perennial forms a relaxed mound that drifts gracefully onto the nearby flagstones and lawn. Slender spikes of pale-lavender flowers appear in July and are very fragrant. The foliage smells good, too, when you brush or crush it. See *Lavandula angustifolia*, p. 143.

See p. 85 for the following:

F Thymes

G Arbor

H Paving

PLANT PORTRAITS

These hardy shrubs and vines provide privacy, fruits and berries for you and the birds, and months of fragrant flowers, while demanding little time and attention.

● = First design, pp. 84–85

▲ = Second design, pp. 86–87

Hardy kiwi (*Actinidia kolomikta*, p. 130) ●

Chinese wisteria (*Wisteria sinensis*, p. 153) ▲

Woolly thyme (*Thymus pseudolanuginosus*, p. 151) ● ▲

Compact Korean spice viburnum (*Viburnum carlesii* 'Compactum', p. 152) ▲

Purpleleaf sand cherry (*Prunus x cistena*, p. 147) ●

Cranberry bush (*Viburnum trilobum*, p. 152) ●

Create a "Living" Room

ENCLOSE A PATIO WITH FOLIAGE AND FLOWERS

SITE: Sunny

SEASON: Early summer

CONCEPT: Planting provides privacy and ambiance for entertaining guests or relaxing on your own.

A patio can become a true extension of your living space with the addition of plants for privacy and pleasure. The floral and foliage motifs of the "walls" in the outdoor room shown here are three-dimensional and constantly changing. The handsome flagstone floor accommodates a family barbecue or a large gathering. Stepping-stones extend into the yard and serve to mingle indoors and outdoors.

Scale is particularly important when planting next to the house. The fence and viburnum along the property line won't overwhelm the patio or house while providing privacy. The three planting beds edging the patio combine to create a garden atmosphere as well as a modest sense of enclosure. Something is in bloom from spring to frost, with flowers of white, pink, purple, red, and yellow showcased against handsome foliage. Several of the longest-blooming flowers are also fragrant.

Here, the design shown fading off into the foreground, to indicate that the patio can be made in a range of sizes. If the patio extends farther along the side of the house, you can easily extend the two beds along its edges and, perhaps, around the patio's other end.

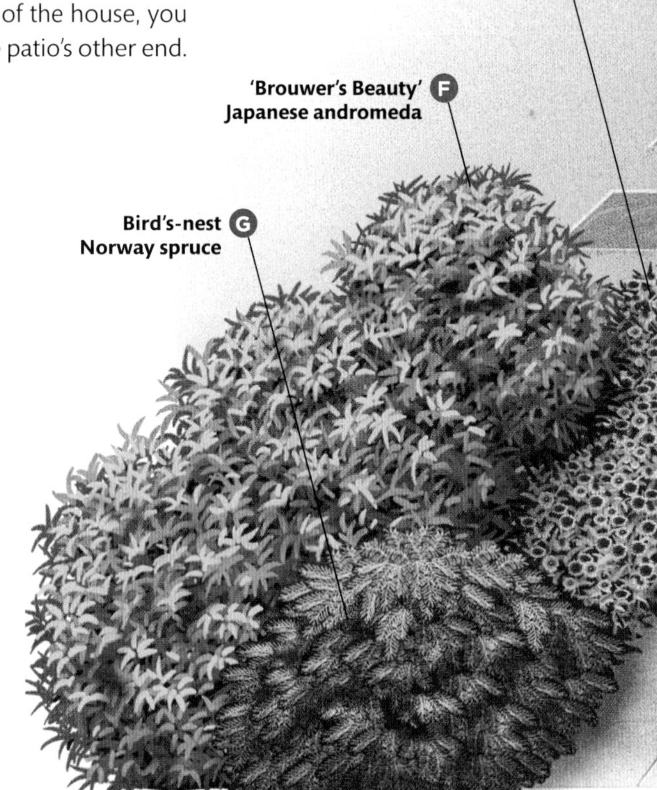

Plants & Projects

The patio and fence are sizable projects, but their rewards are equally great. Check local codes before building the fence. The plants will thrive with little care. The rose needs annual pruning (see p. 206), and as the viburnum matures it may need occasional trimming to keep it in bounds.

A 'Shasta' double-file viburnum (use 1 plant)
Tiered branches smothered with pure-white flowers make this deciduous shrub the patio focal point in late spring. Bright-red fruits in July and purple-red fall color. See *Viburnum plicatum* var. *tomentosum*, p. 152.

B 'New Dawn' rose (use 1)
This deciduous climber covers the fence with glossy green leaves and, for much of the summer, fragrant double pink flowers. In Zones 4 and 5 use the hardier 'William Baffin' rose. See *Rosa*, p. 149.

C Mugo pine (use 5)
A shrublike pine whose dense, light-green foliage makes a low, wide mound, ideal for lining the patio's edge under the overhanging viburnum. See *Pinus mugo*, p. 147.

D Dwarf fountain grass (use 5)
This perennial with arching green leaves and fluffy flower spikes shows well against the fence in summer, turning gold and tan in fall. A handsome presence in winter, too, if snow isn't too heavy. See *Pennisetum alopecuroides* 'Hameln', p. 145.

E 'May Night' salvia (use 10)
Rising above this perennial's dark-green foliage, indigo- purple flower spikes complement the pink roses behind. Blooms in May and repeats all summer if spent flowers are deadheaded. See *Salvia* x *superba*, p. 150.

F 'Brouwer's Beauty' Japanese andromeda (use 5)
This compact hybrid evergreen shrub has shiny leaves. Clusters of reddish flower buds brighten branches through the winter before opening into creamy white flowers in spring. See *Pieris*, p. 146.

G Bird's-nest Norway spruce (use 1)
Slow-growing dwarf evergreen shrub whose "pincushion" look is interesting in every season and makes a pleasing contrast with the andromeda. See *Picea abies* 'Nidiformis', p. 146.

H 'Goblin' blanketflower (use 9)
Large, cheerful red-and-yellow daisylike flowers are crowded atop bushy green mounds of foliage from June until frost on this prairie perennial. See *Gaillardia* x *grandiflora*, p. 138.

I 'Anthony Waterer' spirea (use 4)
The small fine leaves and rosy pink flowers of this compact deciduous shrub belie its tough nature. It thrives in the often hot, dry conditions beneath the eaves. Blooms in midsummer. See *Spiraea* x *bumalda*, p. 150.

J Sweet violet (use 10)
Everyone on the patio will enjoy the sweet fragrance of this perennial's small purple flowers in early spring and again during cool fall days. The dark-green leaves make

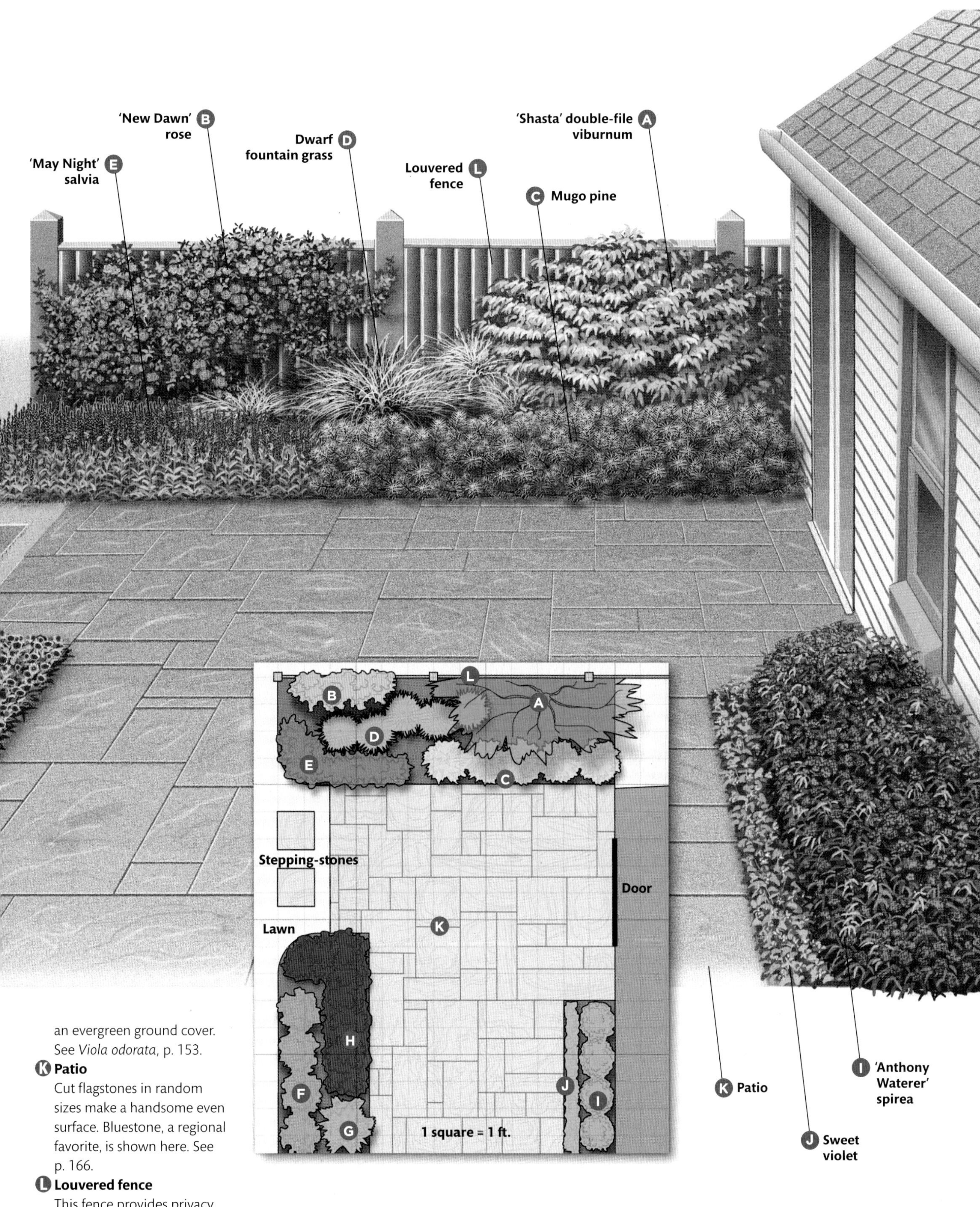

an evergreen ground cover. See *Viola odorata*, p. 153.

K Patio
Cut flagstones in random sizes make a handsome even surface. Bluestone, a regional favorite, is shown here. See p. 166.

L Louvered fence
This fence provides privacy for people and air circulation for nearby plants. See p. 186.

PLANT PORTRAITS

Evergreens and perennials provide year-round presence and plenty of flowers, too.

● = First design, pp. 88–89

▲ = Second design, pp. 90–91

Wild sweet William (*Phlox divaricata*, p. 146) ▲

Mugo pine (*Pinus mugo*, p. 147) ●

'Shasta' double-file viburnum (*Viburnum plicatum* var. *tomentosum*, p. 152) ● ▲

'Hicksii' hybrid yew (*Taxus* x *media*, p. 151) ▲

Weeping hemlock (*Tsuga canadensis* var. *sargentii*, p. 152) ▲

Spreading English yew (*Taxus baccata* 'Repandens', p. 151) ▲

A patio in the shade

If your patio is already blessed with a cool canopy of shade, perhaps from a large tree nearby, consider this design. Here shade-tolerant shrubs and perennials create a more subdued—but equally pleasing—outdoor room.

A tall evergreen hedge replaces the louvered fence, providing privacy along the property line as well as a dark-green backdrop for the shrubs, perennials, and ferns in the planting bed at its feet.

The remaining beds separate the patio from other backyard areas and from the house. These beds also offer a mix of broad- and needle-leaved evergreens and perennials that provide months of colorful flowers and foliage. Aside from maintaining the hedge, this planting requires little care.

Plants & Projects

Ⓐ **'Hicksii' hybrid yew** (use 11 plants) This fast-growing, densely branched evergreen shrub makes a fine dark-green hedge to screen the patio. Its narrow form means you spend less time pruning. See *Taxus* x *media*, p. 151.

Ⓑ **Spreading English yew** (use 3) Dark green needles on a low, spreading evergreen shrub provide year-round color and texture. Grows slowly, so it will not outgrow its place. See *Taxus baccata* 'Repandens', p. 151.

Ⓒ **Cranberry cotoneaster** (use 3) A low, spreading deciduous shrub with glossy dark-green leaves. Cranberry red fruits follow small pink flowers. Fall color is a bright red. See *Cotoneaster apiculatus*, p. 135.

Ⓓ **Marginal wood fern** (use 10) An evergreen fern with leathery, finely divided fronds. An effective backdrop for the cotoneasters. See Ferns: *Dryopteris marginalis*, p. 137.

Ⓔ **Pink astilbe** (use 10) Mounds of this perennial's dark-green, deeply divided leaves dress up

SITE: Shady

SEASON: Late spring

CONCEPT: Foliage sets the tone on a shady site.

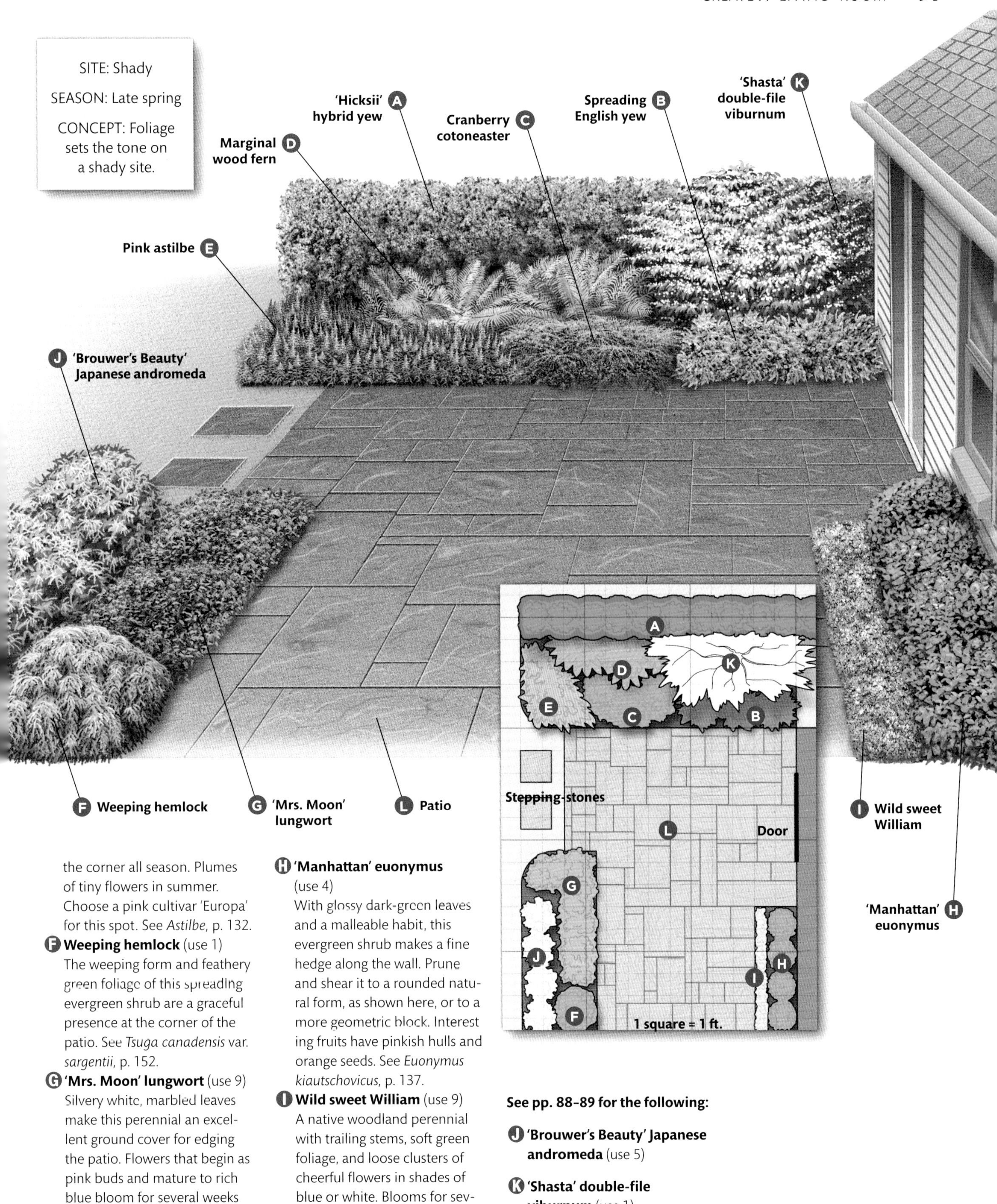

the corner all season. Plumes of tiny flowers in summer. Choose a pink cultivar 'Europa' for this spot. See *Astilbe*, p. 132.

F Weeping hemlock (use 1)
The weeping form and feathery green foliage of this spreading evergreen shrub are a graceful presence at the corner of the patio. See *Tsuga canadensis* var. *sargentii*, p. 152.

G 'Mrs. Moon' lungwort (use 9)
Silvery white, marbled leaves make this perennial an excellent ground cover for edging the patio. Flowers that begin as pink buds and mature to rich blue bloom for several weeks in early spring. See *Pulmonaria saccharata*, p. 147.

H 'Manhattan' euonymus (use 4)
With glossy dark-green leaves and a malleable habit, this evergreen shrub makes a fine hedge along the wall. Prune and shear it to a rounded natural form, as shown here, or to a more geometric block. Interesting fruits have pinkish hulls and orange seeds. See *Euonymus kiautschovicus*, p. 137.

I Wild sweet William (use 9)
A native woodland perennial with trailing stems, soft green foliage, and loose clusters of cheerful flowers in shades of blue or white. Blooms for several weeks in May and June. See *Phlox divaricata*, p. 146.

See pp. 88–89 for the following:

J 'Brouwer's Beauty' Japanese andromeda (use 5)

K 'Shasta' double-file viburnum (use 1)

L Patio

Another "Room" Out Back

CREATE AN IMTIMATE, PLANT COVERED NOOK

In this version of the "living" room, the Japanese tree lilac shades the patio area without overpowering the house. The vine-covered fence and mixed border in front of it function rather like the wall hangings and furniture in a room. Composed of offset rectangles, the patio offers an intimate nook nestled among plants and screened by the fence and a larger area for functions that can spill out onto the lawn.

From early summer through fall the plantings provide a colorful accompaniment to your patio activities. Each season has a special treat—fragrant lilac blossoms in early summer; showy Jackman clematis and purple coneflowers in midsummer; bright asters and aromatic sweet autumn clematis in fall.

Plants & Projects

The patio and fence are sizable projects, but their rewards are large, too. Check local codes before building the fence. Once established, the plants are not demanding. Other than pruning the clematis and roses in late winter or early spring, seasonal cleanup is all that's required.

A Jackman clematis (use 3 plants)
A graceful form, dark-green leaves, and striking, rich-purple summer flowers make this deciduous vine a favorite. See *Clematis x jackmanii*, p. 134.

B Sweet autumn clematis (use 1)
This deciduous but invasive vine will quickly cover the fence. Starry white flowers fill the air in August and September with their pleasing fragrance. See *Clematis terniflora*, p. 134.

C Japanese tree lilac (use 1)
The creamy white, fragrant flowers of this small deciduous tree appear in early summer, weeks after regular lilacs bloom. When the flowers are gone, lush green leaves and shiny reddish-brown bark provide interest for many months. See *Syringa reticulata*, p. 151.

D 'Green Velvet' boxwood (use 4)
A compact evergreen shrub ideal for making a low, natural hedge to create a patio niche. The shiny leaves complement the flowers and foliage of the nearby roses. See *Buxus*, p. 133.

E 'Bonica' rose (use 1)
Clusters of scentless, soft-pink, double flowers cover this carefree shrub rose from June until frost. See *Rosa*, p. 149.

F 'The Fairy' rose (use 2)
This shrub rose's scentless double pink blossoms are borne from early summer to frost on a low, spreading mass of small, shiny leaves. See *Rosa*, p. 149.

G Purple coneflower (use 3)
A native prairie perennial that forms a mound of large green leaves. In late summer, stiff stalks bear large daisylike flowers with deep-pink petals surrounding a large orange-brown central "cone." See *Echinacea purpurea*, p. 136.

H 'Purple Dome' New England aster (use 2)
This compact perennial has dark-green leaves and blooms for weeks in fall, bearing masses of deep-purple daisy flowers, each with a bright-yellow eye. See *Aster novae-angliae*, p. 132.

I 'Blue Clips' Carpathian bellflower (use 5)
Bell-shaped blue flowers on slender stalks rising from this perennial's neat mounds of shiny dark-green foliage show well against the boxwood. You could substitute or combine with 'White Clips', too. *Campanula carpatica*, p. 134.

J 'Moonbeam' coreopsis (use 2)
Nestled by the house, this durable perennial produces masses of small pale-yellow flowers above lacy dark-green foliage. Blooms continually from July into September. See *Coreopsis verticillata*, p. 135.

K Louvered fence
Slanting slats of this 6-ft.-tall fence form an effective visual screen, while allowing air to circulate among the plants and people on the patio. See p. 186.

L Patio
The mellow look and feel of brick combine with almost any architectural style. Dressed flagstones or pavers would work well also. See p. 166.

SITE: Sunny

SEASON: Summer

CONCEPT: Planting provides privacy and a colorful setting for entertaining guests or enjoying the early-morning air on your own.

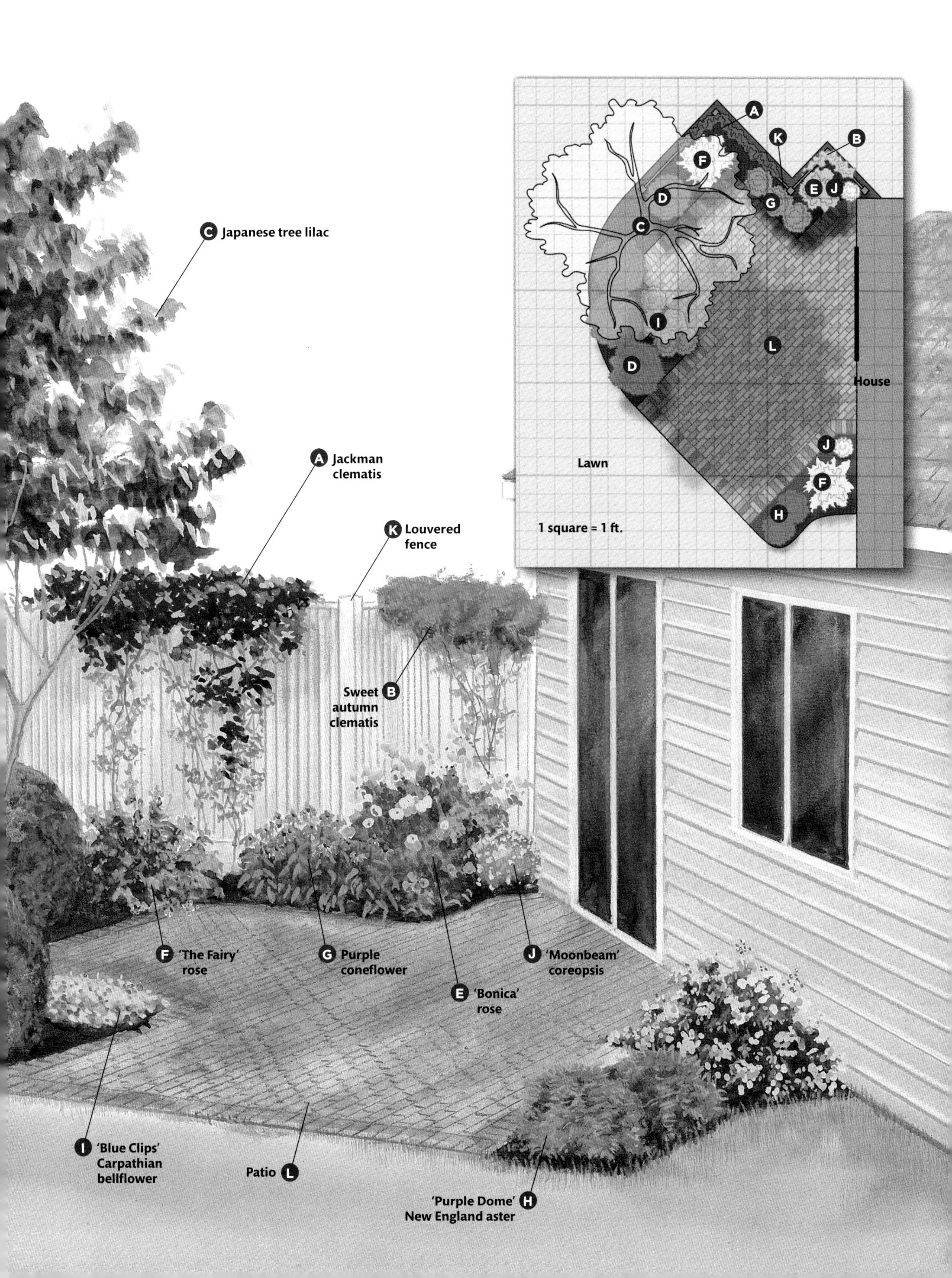
A
K
B
F
E J
D
G
C
I
L
D
House
J
Lawn
F
H
1 square = 1 ft.
C Japanese tree lilac
A Jackman clematis
K Louvered fence
Sweet autumn clematis B
F 'The Fairy' rose
G Purple coneflower
J 'Moonbeam' coreopsis
E 'Bonica' rose
I 'Blue Clips' Carpathian bellflower
Patio L
'Purple Dome' New England aster H

A Big Splash with a Small Pond

ADD AN EXTRA DIMENSION TO YOUR LANDSCAPE

SITE: Sunny

SEASON: Summer

CONCEPT: A backyard focal point, the pond nestles among shrubs and perennials and features striking water plants—even fish.

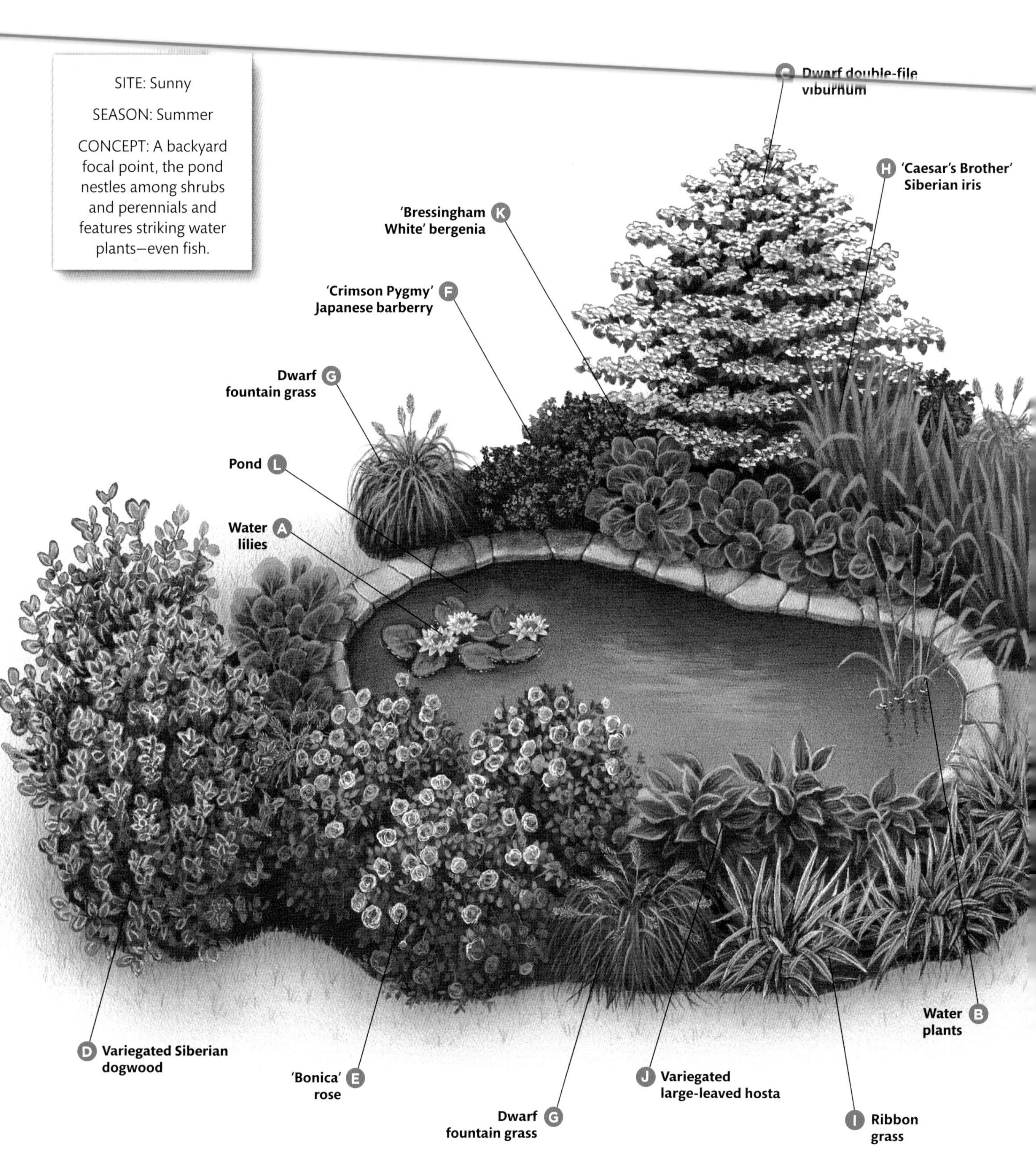

A water garden adds a new dimension to a landscape. It can be the eye-catching focal point of the entire property, a center of outdoor entertainment, or a quiet out-of-the-way retreat. A pond can be a hub of activity—a place to garden, watch birds and wildlife, raise ornamental fish, or stage an impromptu paper-boat race. It just as easily affords an opportunity for some therapeutic inactivity; a few minutes contemplating the ripples on the water's surface make a welcome break in a busy day.

A pond can't be easily moved, so choose your site carefully. Practical considerations are outlined on p. 168 (along with instructions on installation). Think about those first. Then consider how the pond and its plantings relate to the surroundings. Before plopping down a pond in the middle of the backyard, imagine how you might integrate it, visually if not physically, with nearby plantings and structures.

The plantings in this design are intended to settle the pond comfortably into an expanse of lawn. From a distance, the shrubs, ornamental grasses, and perennials that frame the pond resemble an island bed. Sitting at water's edge, however, the plants provide enclosure, a sense of being on an island looking at its flora and fauna.

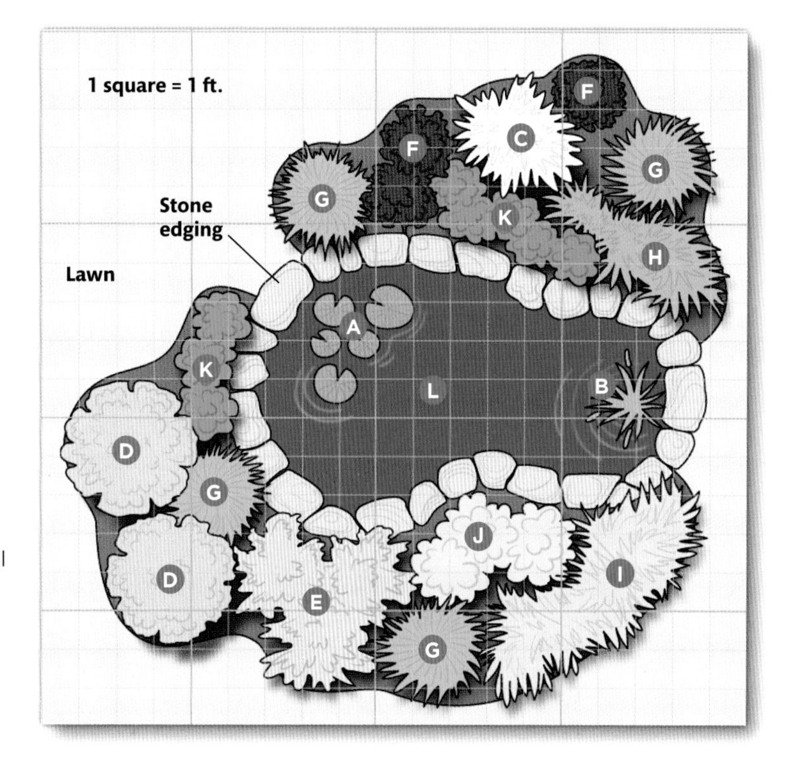

Plants & Projects

Even without the pond, this would be a lovely planting, with something to offer throughout the year. The viburnum and roses guarantee months of flowers, accented for shorter periods by the distinctive blooms of dogwood, iris, and bergenia. Every plant has noteworthy foliage and form, from the tropical lushness of the hostas and bergenias in the summer heat to the rustle of dried grasses and dogwood stems in a winter breeze.

A Water lilies
(use 1 or more plants)
The large cuplike blooms of water lilies glow against their dark-green floating leaves. Visit a specialty nursery or order by mail, and take your pick of white, yellow, or pink cultivars. See *Nymphaea*, p. 145.

B Water plants (as desired)
Along with water lilies, other aquatic plants add visual interest, help keep the pond water clear, and provide oxygen. Here we've shown the upright pokerlike flowers of a miniature cattail, which prefers the shallow water near the shore. If you want to keep fish in your pool, you'll need to add some oxygenating plants, which float underwater. See Water plants, p. 153.

C Dwarf double-file viburnum
(use 1)
The smaller form of a popular deciduous shrub is well suited to the scale here. Tiers of horizontal branches are dotted with clusters of creamy white flowers from June until fall. See *Viburnum plicatum* var. *tomentosum*, p. 152.

D Variegated Siberian dogwood (use 2)
This deciduous shrub is handsome year-round, with green-and-white leaves, clusters of white flowers in spring, then pale-blue berries in late summer and fall. Its best season may be winter, when the bright red stems are truly eye-catching. See *Cornus alba* 'Elegantissima', p. 135.

E 'Bonica' rose (use 3)
Clusters of double, soft-pink flowers cover this carefree shrub rose, providing a colorful accent from June until frost. This compact rose needs little pruning, has healthy foliage, and is quite hardy. See *Rosa*, p. 149.

F 'Crimson Pygmy' Japanese barberry (use 3)
Nestled at the foot of the viburnum, this deciduous shrub makes a low mound of dark maroon leaves all summer, then turns a spectacular crimson in fall, augmented by a crop of bright-red berries. See *Berberis thunbergii*, p. 132.

G Dwarf fountain grass (use 4)
The arching leaves of this clump-forming grass seem right at home at water's edge. Foliage is green in summer, turning gold or tan in fall. Fluffy flower spikes wave in the breeze from midsummer on. See *Pennisetum alopecuroides* 'Hameln', p. 145.

H 'Caesar's Brother' Siberian iris (use 8)
A perennial with elegant dark blue-purple flowers in June. Forms arching clumps of slender leaves that stay green until mid-fall, then turn a rusty brown. See *Iris sibirica*, p. 142.

I Ribbon grass (use 3)
White stripes run the length of the narrow bright-green leaves of this tough, very vigorous perennial, providing a textural contrast to the broad hosta leaves nearby. Spreads invasively, so confine it by planting it in a bottomless pot. See *Phalaris arundinacea* 'Picta', p. 146.

J Variegated large-leaved hosta (use 3)
The outsize leaves of this popular perennial add a lush note to the planting at poolside. Choose any cultivar you like, with green-and-white or green-and-gold leaves. Pale-lilac or -lavender flowers on tall stalks bloom for several weeks in July or August. See *Hosta*, p. 140.

K 'Bressingham White' bergenia (use 8)
Large, rounded, glossy dark green leaves echo the hostas across the water and contrast with the upright iris and fine-textured barberries nearby. The leaves turn garnet or burgundy in fall. Clusters of white flowers appear in spring. See *Bergenia cordifolia*, p. 132.

L Pond
Measuring about 7 ft. by 12 ft., this can be made with a weekend or two of energetic digging, a ready-made plastic pond liner, and flagstones for edging. See p. 168.

A simple pool and planting

This little pool provides the pleasures of water gardening for those without the space or energy required to install and maintain a larger pond. Here, you can enjoy one or more water plants as well as a few fish. Even simpler, have a reflecting pool of clear water, as shown here.

A simple, elegant planting frames the pool. The arching grasses, leaves rippling in the wind, are a natural companion to water. The irises and evening primroses add splashes of rich color to the scene.

The rectangular pool, made from a fiberglass pool shell or agricultural tank, and its plantings can stand alone in an expanse of lawn, but they will look their best integrated into a larger scheme. We've shown it as part of a flagstone patio. If you grow water plants or stock fish, consult local or mail-order suppliers to help you choose a combination that will maintain a healthy balance in the pool.

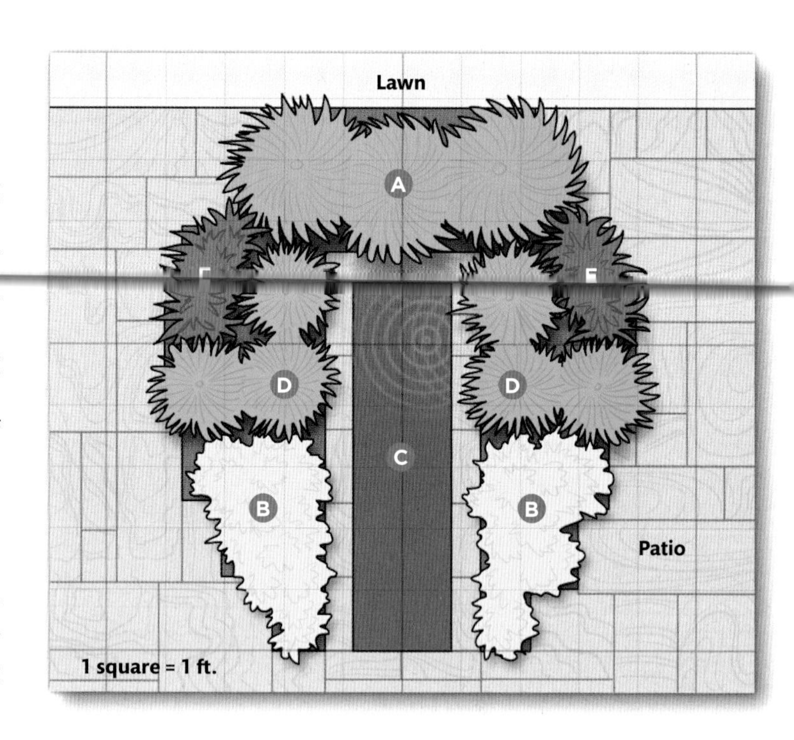

SITE: Sunny

SEASON: Early summer

CONCEPT:
This small-scale design is easy to install and maintain.

Plants & Projects

A 'Karl Foerster' feather reed grass (use 3 plants)
Tall, slim flower spikes appear in June above the slender green leaves. Leaves and spikes change from green to beige as they mature. See *Calamagrostis* x *acutiflora*, p. 134.

B Missouri evening primrose (use 4)
Delicate, cup-shaped, luminous yellow flowers cover the sprawling glossy foliage of this perennial, providing sunny color next to the pool all summer long. See *Oenothera missouriensis*, p. 145.

C Pool
The pool shown is 2 ft. by 6 ft. Adapt the design to suit the shell you buy. See p. 168.

See p. 95 for the following:

D Dwarf fountain grass (use 6)

E 'Caesar's Brother' Siberian iris (use 6)

PLANT PORTRAITS

Whether growing in or near the water, these plants combine fresh foliage and bright flowers for pondside pleasure.

● = First design, pp. 94–95

▲ = Second design, pp. 96

Ribbon grass (*Phalaris arundinacea* 'Picta', p. 146) ●

'Karl Foerster' feather reed grass (*Calamagrostis* x *acutiflora*, p. 134) ▲

Missouri evening primrose (*Oenothera missouriensis*, p. 145) ▲

'Caesar's Brother' Siberian iris (*Iris sibirica*, p. 142) ● ▲

Water lilies (*Nymphaea*, p. 145) ●

Water lilies (*Nymphaea*, p. 145) ●

Garden in the Round

CREATE AN ISLAND BED ATTRACTIVE FROM EVERY SIDE

Plantings in domestic landscapes are usually "attached" to something. Beds and borders hew to property lines, walls, or patios; foundation plantings skirt the house, garage, or deck. Most are meant to be viewed from the front, rather like a wall-mounted sculpture in raised relief.

On the other hand, the planting shown here floats free on the lawn. Called an "island bed," it is an excellent option for those who want to squeeze more gardening space from a small lot, add interest to a rectangular one, or divide a large area into smaller "outdoor rooms." Because you can walk around most of the bed, plants can be displayed in the round, and they can be combined to present different scenes from several vantage points.

Without a strong connection to a structure or other landscape feature, a bed like this requires a particular sensitivity to scale. To be successful, the bed must neither dominate its surroundings nor be lost in them. This planting was designed with a modest or larger suburban property in mind. Evergreen and deciduous shrubs and trees provide form, color, and structure year-round. The combination of large and small, subtle and bold plants makes the island attractive up close or viewed from a distance, and there's always something to admire as you walk around it.

Plants & Projects

You'll visit this island primarily for pleasure. Other than deadheading spent flowers from time to time during the growing season, the only maintenance needed can be accomplished with pruning shears and a rake over a few days in spring and fall.

A Amur maple (use 1 plant)
This small multistemmed deciduous tree offers fragrant flowers in spring and attractive leaves that turn fiery red in fall. See *Acer ginnala*, p. 130.

B Bird's-nest Norway spruce (use 3)
The dark-green pincushion look of this evergreen is interesting in every season. Broader than tall, it makes a good backdrop for nearby plants. See *Picea abies* 'Nidiformis', p. 146.

C 'Carol Mackie' daphne (use 5)
Intensely fragrant bursts of starry pink flowers appear on this compact evergreen shrub and scent the yard for a few weeks in May. Its green leaves edged with gold are equally pleasing the rest of the year. See *Daphne x burkwoodii*, p. 136.

D 'Midnight Wine' Japanese barberry (use 5)
This deciduous shrub bears dark burgundy wine leaves and only reaches about 10 to 12 in. tall. Its light pink blooms appear in late spring. Best foliage color appears in full or partial sun; in shade it may become greenish. See *Weigela florida*, p. 153.

E 'Summer Sun' false sunflower (use 1)
Golden yellow sunflower-like blooms shine light up this bushy perennial in August and September. A great partner for the nearby blazing star. See *Heliopsis helianthoides*, p. 138.

F 'Kobold' blazing star (use 5)
Magenta flower spikes of this native perennial rise above grassy green foliage in midsummer. Flowers will last for weeks in a vase. See *Liatris spicata*, p. 143.

G 'Munstead' English lavender (use 7)
Fragrant pale-lavender flower spikes are only one reason to grow this classic perennial. Its subtle silver-green foliage looks cool on the hottest day and forms loose irregular mounds that make it a great edging plant, and help moor the island bed to the lawn. Foliage is also fragrant. See *Lavandula angustifolia*, p. 143.

H 'Stella d'Oro' daylily (use 5)
One of the longest-blooming of the thousands of cultivars of this popular perennial, daily producing golden yellow flowers from mid-June until fall. Its glowing flowers and grassy foliage look lovely tucked between the daphnes and spruces. See *Hemerocallis*, p. 139.

I Lady's mantle (use 6)
This perennial is worth growing for its mound of lovely ruffled light-green leaves alone. For weeks beginning in June, a profusion of tiny yellow-green flowers floats on the foliage; flowers are good for drying. See *Alchemilla mollis*, p. 130.

J Bloody cranesbill (use 5)
This spreading perennial makes a great ground cover beneath the maple, offering months of soft-pink flowers above mounds of pretty, deeply divided foliage. See *Geranium sanguineum* var. *striatum*, p. 138.

SITE: Sunny

SEASON: Midsummer

CONCEPT: Mix of perennials and woody plants looks good from anywhere on the property.

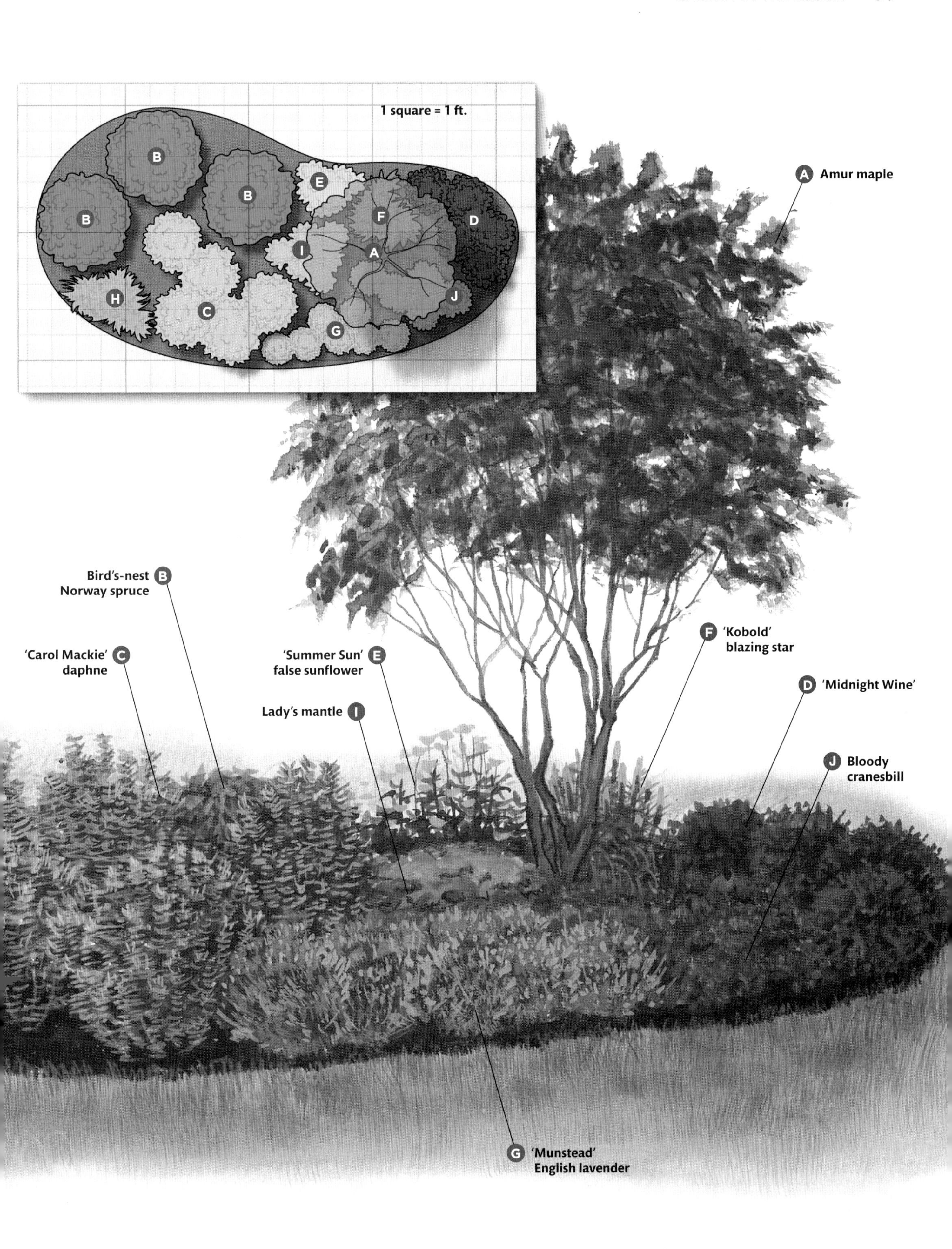
1 square = 1 ft.
B
B
B
E
F
D
I
A
H
C
J
G
Amur maple
Bird's-nest Norway spruce
'Carol Mackie' daphne
'Summer Sun' false sunflower
Lady's mantle
'Kobold' blazing star
'Midnight Wine'
Bloody cranesbill
'Munstead' English lavender

An island in the shade

SITE: Shady

SEASON: Late spring

CONCEPT: Lush foliage and striking flowers reward a visit to this shady island

Island beds are just as versatile and attractive in the shade as they are in full sun. For much of the year, the design shown here exhibits the lush green character expected of a shade planting, but there are times when its color rivals that of an island bathed in sun.

The plants bloom in sequence, starting with the white serviceberry and bergenia blossoms in early spring, followed by the blue Siberian iris and pink-and-white mountain laurel, then continuing into early summer with the chartreuse lady's mantle and rosy pink bleeding heart. In fall, the serviceberry foliage turns red and the frosted fern fronds form a patch of gold. The evergreen mountain laurel, garnet bergenia leaves, and gray-barked serviceberry stand out against the snow in winter.

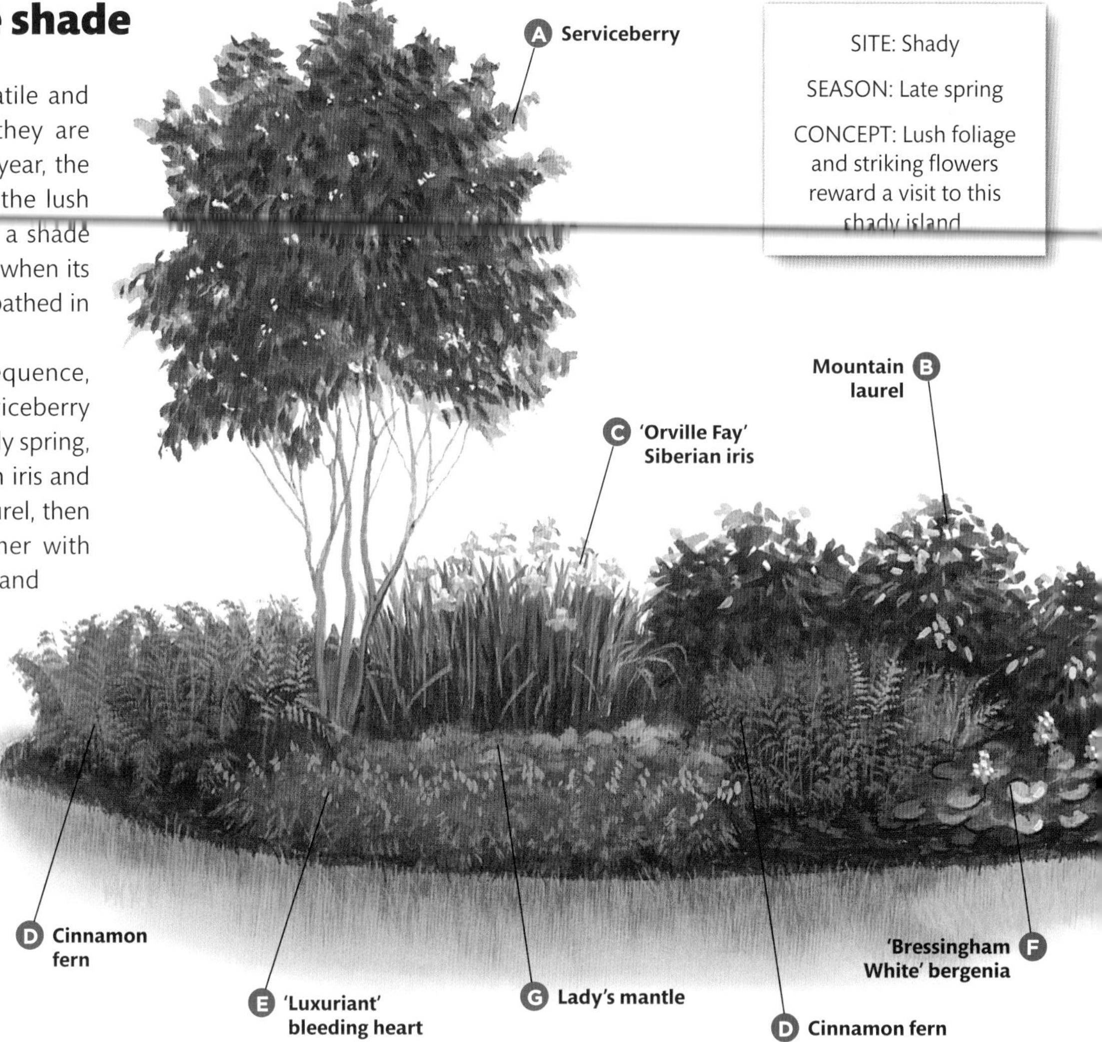

Plants & Projects

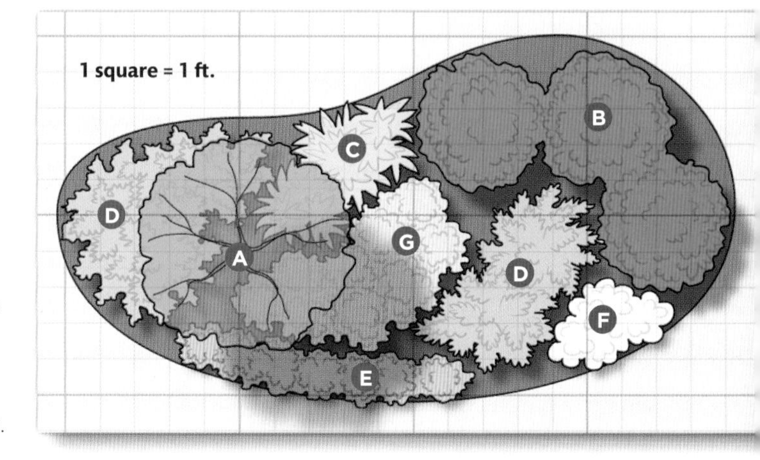

A Serviceberry (use 1 plant)
This small deciduous tree catches the eye with white flowers in early spring, edible berries in summer, and brilliant red fall color. Silhouette looks good in winter, too. See *Amelanchier* x *grandiflora*, p. 131.

B Mountain laurel (use 3)
These evergreen shrubs bloom in June, bearing clusters of small cup-shaped pink-and-white flowers that stand out from a distance in the shade. Leathery dark-green leaves turn green-gold in winter. See *Kalmia latifolia*, p. 142.

C 'Orville Fay' Siberian iris (use 9)
This elegant perennial produces large sky blue flowers atop 3-ft. stalks in early summer. Clumps of slim arching leaves contrast beautifully with the mounded lady's mantle. See *Iris sibirica*, p. 142.

D Cinnamon fern (use 31)
A native fern that forms tall clumps of finely divided fronds that look intriguing as they unfurl in spring, are soft and green all summer, and turn a lovely golden tan after fall frost. Spreads to form a weed-proof patch. See Ferns: *Osmunda cinnamomea*, p. 137.

E 'Luxuriant' bleeding heart (use 7)
This shade-loving perennial has handsome fernlike foliage that makes a great ground cover. From June until October, small but distinctive rose-red flowers dangle in a row from thin arching stalks. See *Dicentra*, p. 136.

F 'Bressingham White' bergenia (use 3)
The large, rounded, glossy dark-green leaves of this perennial turn dark red in late fall and winter. Clusters of white flowers rise above the foliage in late spring. See *Bergenia cordifolia*, p. 132.

See p. 98 for the following:
G Lady's mantle (use 9)

PLANT PORTRAITS

Create islands of beauty in the sun or the shade with these plants, which cruise through the seasons with little care.

● = First design, pp. 98–99

▲ = Second design, p. 100

Bloody cranesbill (*Geranium sanguineum* var. *striatum*, p. 138) ●

'Summer Sun' false sunflower (*Heliopsis helianthoides*, p. 138) ●

Amur maple (*Acer ginnala*, p. 130) ●

Lady's mantle (*Alchemilla mollis*, p. 130) ● ▲

'Kobold' blazing star (*Liatris spicata*, p. 143) ●

'Carol Mackie' daphne (*Daphne x burkwoodii*, p. 136) ●

'Munstead' English lavender (*Lavandula angustifolia*, p. 143) ●

A Beginning Border

CREATE AN INTIMATE, PLANT-COVERED NOOK

A perennial border can be one of the most delightful of all gardens. Indeed, that's usually its sole purpose. Unlike many other types of landscape plantings, a traditional border is seldom yoked to any function beyond that of providing as much pleasure as possible. From the first neat mounds of foliage in the spring to the fullness of summer bloom and autumn color, the mix of flowers and foliage, textures, tones, and hues brings enjoyment.

This border is designed for a beginning perennial gardener, using durable plants that are easy to establish and care for. Behind the planting, screening out distraction, is a simple fence. The border is meant to be viewed from the front, so tall plants go at the back. There, graceful grasses mark the rear corners and center of the bed, framing the grassy foliage and striking flowers of irises, lilies, and daylilies. Your choice of lily and daylily cultivars—bright and bold or muted pastels—plays a big role in determining the planting's character.

Arrayed in front of these plants, at the center of the bed, coreopsis and blazing star offer additional bloom from midsummer on. Plants edging the front of the bed are chosen primarily for their attractive foliage, a mixture of greens punctuated by silvery mounds; they also provide a bonus of pink and chartreuse flowers.

Plants & Projects

No garden is carefree, but this one comes close. Removing spent flowers and foliage is the main chore. Don't cut back the grasses or sedum until spring, or you'll miss their buff and brown winter hues. And be sure to place markers where the lilies are planted, so you won't damage emerging shoots during spring cleanup.

A Variegated Japanese silver grass (use 3 plants)
This perennial grass makes a graceful sheaf of long arching cream-colored leaves with vertical green stripes. Tall stalks rise in late summer or fall carrying fluffy seed heads that last through winter and look good in dried arrangements. See *Miscanthus* 'Variegatus', p. 144.

B 'Caesar's Brother' Siberian iris (use 3)
Prized for its striking dark blue-purple June flowers, this perennial forms an arching mound of tall slender leaves that is attractive all season long. See *Iris sibirica*, p. 142.

C Daylily (use 9)
For an extended show of cheerful trumpet-shaped flowers, combine early- and late-blooming cultivars of this dependable perennial. Stick to one or two colors that will combine well with the white and yellow blooms nearby. See *Hemerocallis*, p. 139.

D Lily (use 13 or more)
Indulge yourself with as many of these flamboyant perennials as possible, selecting from the wide range of cultivars available. The large flowers are borne on erect narrow stalks, so you can fit quite a few along the fence. With careful choices, you can ensure bloom most of the summer. See *Lilium*, p. 143.

E White blazing star (use 5)
Choose a white-flowered form of this perennial for a vertical accent in the middle of the border from late July. Its flower spikes are great for cutting and drying, and butterflies love them. See *Liatris spicata*, p. 143.

F 'Autumn Joy' sedum (use 6)
One of the best perennials for fall bloom, with flat-topped pink flower clusters that become rust-colored seed heads. Thick stalks and light-green fleshy leaves are also disinctive. See *Sedum*, p. 150.

G 'Moonbeam' coreopsis (use 3)
The fine, dark-green foliage of this tough perennial contrasts with the lady's mantle, and its tiny pale-yellow flowers go with anything. Blooms from July into September. See *Coreopsis verticillata*, p. 135.

H Lady's mantle (use 3)
The front of the border is the ideal spot for enjoying this perennial's mounds of ruffled light-green leaves. In June, a froth of tiny yellow-green flowers covers the foliage. See *Alchemilla mollis*, p. 130.

I Coralbells (use 5)
The tiny flowers of this low-growing perennial hover like a swarm of bees above clumps of dark-green, leathery, almost evergreen leaves. Bloom begins in June and lasts through the summer. Use any cultivar with pink flowers here. See *Heuchera* x *brizoides*, p. 139.

J Lamb's ears (use 4 large or 12 small plants)
Children love the large, soft, silver-gray leaves of this spreading perennial. Gardeners value it as an edging and say the gray color enhances the hues of neighboring plants. See *Stachys byzantina*, p. 150.

K Fence
Topped with a strip of lattice, this 6-ft.-tall fence functions both as a privacy screen and as a backdrop for the border. See p. 187.

L Stepping-stones
Flagstones provide access for filling the birdbath and maintaining plants at the back of the border. See p. 165.

M Birdbath
If you provide a little water, birds will love your border, too. Choose a sturdy design to prevent thirsty raccoons from toppling it over.

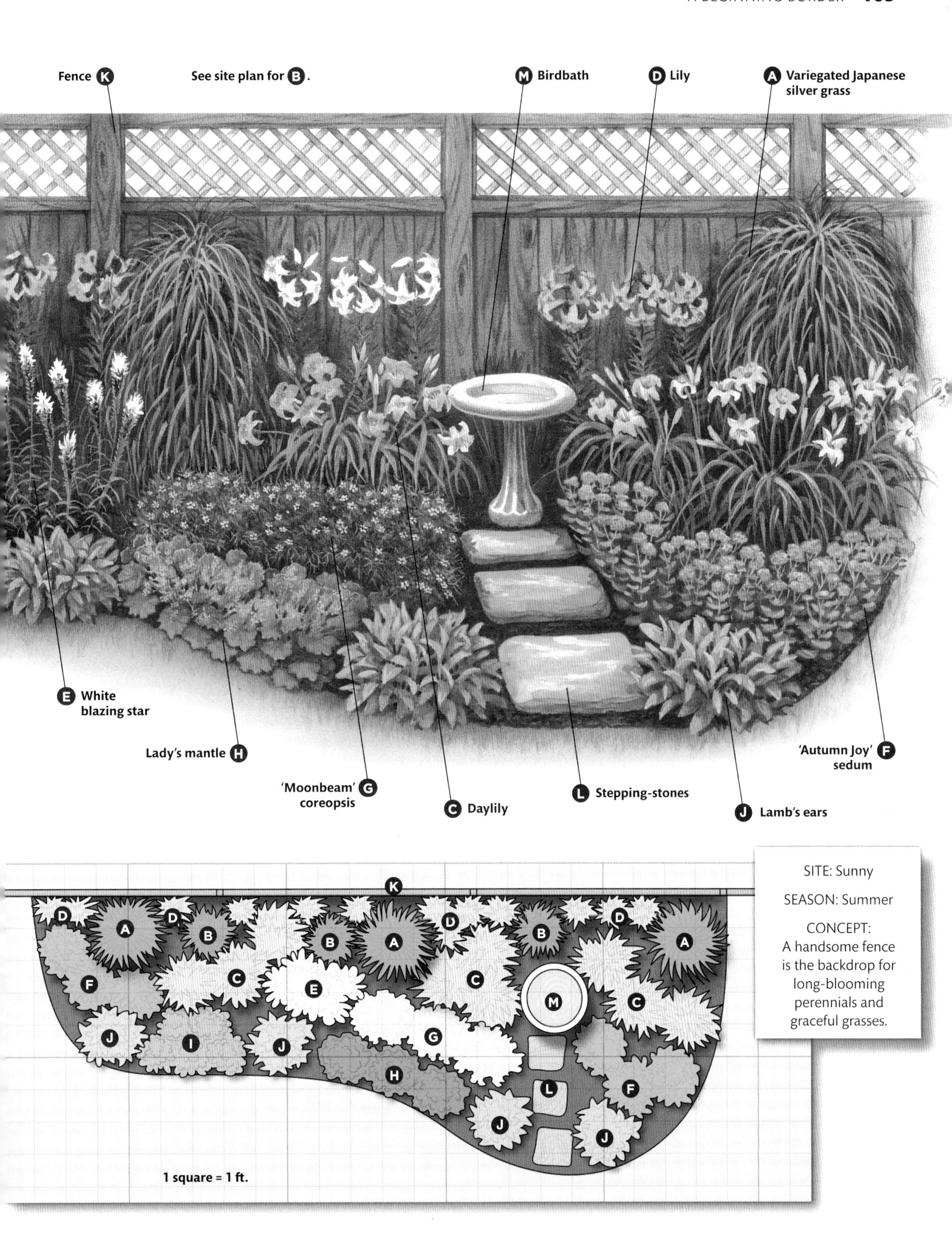

SITE: Sunny

SEASON: Summer

CONCEPT:
A handsome fence is the backdrop for long-blooming perennials and graceful grasses.

Mixing it up

In a mixed border, shrubs and small trees join perennials, seasonal bulbs, and even annuals. Because of the all-season physical presence of woody plants, mixed borders are sometimes called upon to perform functional tasks, such as for screens or barriers.

This design, however, like the previous one, is intended primarily to be beautiful. Now conical spruces and broad rose-of-Sharon alternate along the fence at the back of the planting. Daylilies, here with brightly colored flowers, run like a ribbon across the planting and are still the summertime showstopper. Earlier, daffodils, tulips, and others of your favorite bulbs, planted behind and between the daylilies, brighten the spring border. The grassy daylily leaves appear just in time to hide the dying bulb foliage.

Ornamental grasses add an eye-catching range of foliage shapes, textures, and colors, particularly fall tans and golds. Like shrubs, they give the garden a winter presence, too.

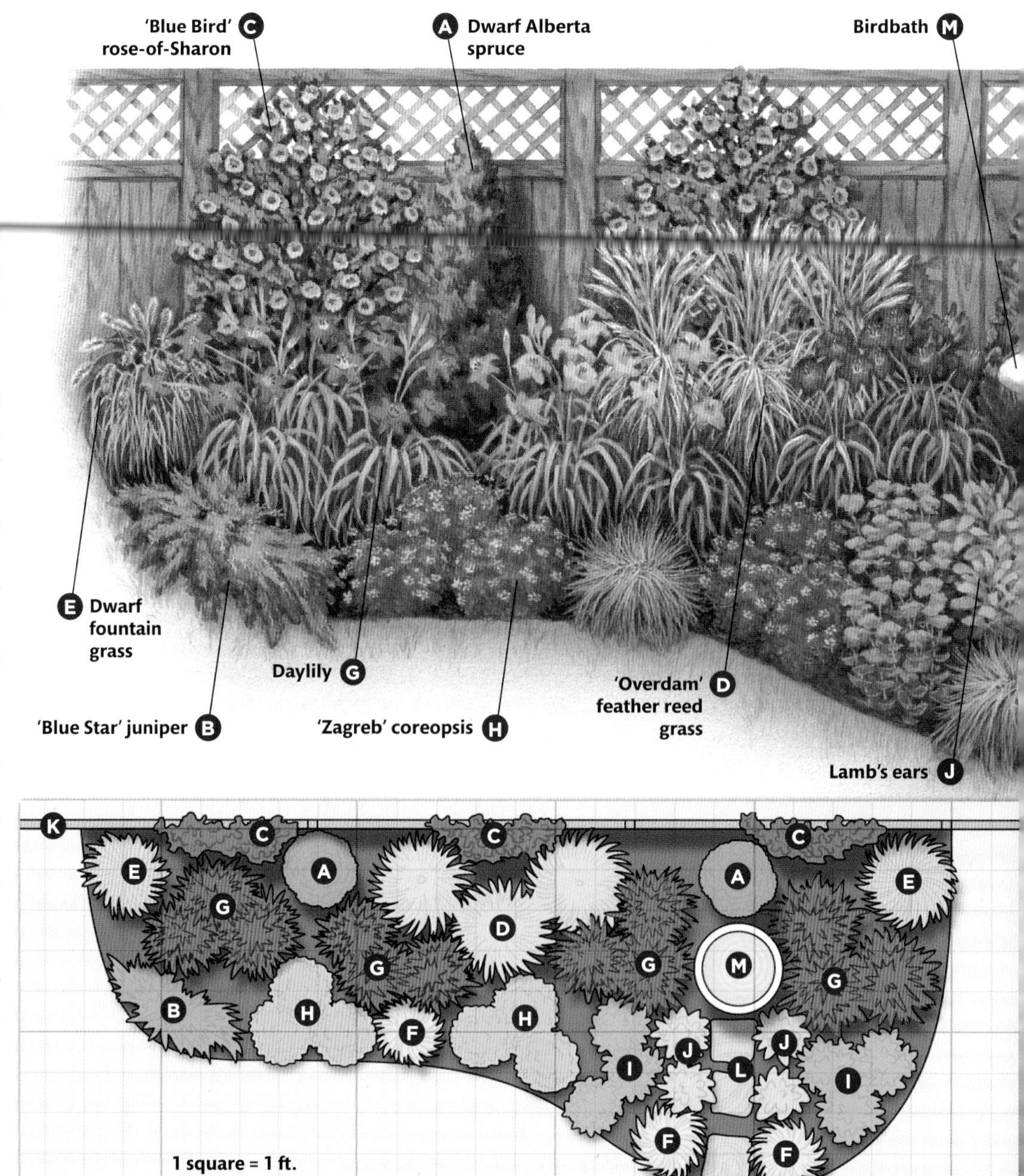

Plants & Projects

A Dwarf Alberta spruce (use 2)
Standing like sentinels at the back of the border, these attractive dwarf evergreen trees form tight dense cones of light green needles. See *Picea glauca* 'Conica', p. 146.

B 'Blue Star' juniper (use 1)
The rich blue needles of this low mounded evergreen shrub almost sparkle, adding a dash of year-round color to the end of the border. See *Juniperus squamata*, p. 142.

C 'Blue Bird' rose-of-Sharon (use 3)
Train this deciduous shrub flat against the fence by clipping off any branches that stick out too far. It will reward you with lovely violet-blue flowers from midsummer to fall. See *Hibiscus syriacus*, p. 139.

D 'Overdam' feather reed grass (use 3)
The white-edged leaves of this perennial grass form compact clumps. Leave or trim off the flower plumes according to your taste. See *Calamagrostis* x *acutiflora*, p. 134.

E Dwarf fountain grass (use 2)
Fluffy flower spikes arch above this perennial's flowing fountain of narrow leaves from midsummer on. See *Pennisetum alopecuroides* 'Hameln', p. 145.

F Blue oat grass (use 3)
This perennial grass makes a striking mound of wiry powder blue leaves that hold their color well in mild winters. Flowers are sparse. See *Helictotrichon sempervirens*, p. 138.

G Daylily (use 12)
Cultivars of this versatile perennial in bright, bold colors will look good in this design; mix early and late cultivars for long bloom. For a spring show, underplant daylilies with daffodils and other spring bulbs. See *Hemerocallis*, p. 139.

H 'Zagreb' coreopsis (use 6)
A superb perennial for the front of the border, with bright

SITE: Sunny

SEASON: Summer

CONCEPT: Adding woody plants and more grasses gives the border a different character.

golden yellow flowers that keep coming from July through September. Its lacy dark-green foliage is attractive, too. See *Coreopsis verticillata*, p. 135.

See p. 102 for the following:

I 'Autumn Joy' sedum (use 6)

J Lamb's ears (use 4)

K Fence

L Stepping-stones

M Birdbath

PLANT PORTRAITS

Whether you are a beginning gardener or an old hand, you'll appreciate the long season of bloom these plants provide, with so little care.

● = First design, pp. 102–103

▲ = Second design, pp. 104–105

'Autumn Joy' sedum (*Sedum*, p. 150) ● ▲

'Blue Bird' rose-of-Sharon (*Hibiscus syriacus*, p. 139) ▲

Variegated Japanese silver grass (*Miscanthus* 'Variegatus', p. 144) ●

'Zagreb' coreopsis (*Coreopsis verticillata*, p. 135) ▲

Daylily (*Hemerocallis*, p. 139) ● ▲

Back to Nature

CREATE A WOODED RETREAT IN YOUR BACKYARD

The open spaces and squared-up property lines in many new developments (and some old neighborhoods as well) can make a homeowner long for the seclusion and intimacy of a wooded landscape. It may come as a surprise that you can create just such a retreat on even a modest property. With a relatively small number of trees and shrubs and a selection of understory perennials, you can have your own backyard nature park.

The woodland surrounds a grassy peninsula, creating a private, shady niche, complete with bench to enjoy the sights. During the year, these woody plants provide fragrant and colorful flowers, blazing fall foliage, and attractive bark. At their feet, shade-loving wildflowers and ferns carpet the ground with dainty spring flowers and, as summer progresses, lush foliage.

Many of the plants provide birds and other animals with nesting sites and a diet of fruits and berries. In winter, the conifers and broad-leaved evergreens furnish the wildlife with shelter, while offering you a colorful backyard view.

Because a mature woodland is what you dream of when you plant small trees and shrubs, we've shown the planting here as it will appear after it has grown for 12 to 15 years. But the young planting offers its own distinctive attractions. For a look at them, turn to the following pages.

Plants & Projects

Although this is a large planting, it can be installed in several weekends. Annual maintenance includes pruning away dead and damaged branches and cleaning up the understory plantings in spring and fall.

A River birch (use 1 plant)
The lustrous green leaves of this fast-growing deciduous tree turn a pretty gold or tan color in fall. In winter, the peeling bark reveals layers of beige, tan, and copper. See *Betula nigra*, p. 132.

B Eastern white pine (use 1)
A native evergreen tree with soft, bright-green needles and a handsome branching pattern. It will grow quickly to provide year-round screening and seclusion for the sitting area. See *Pinus strobus*, p. 147.

C 'Golden Glory' cornelian cherry dogwood (use 1)
This small deciduous tree, often with multiple trunks, provides yellow flowers in very early spring followed by handsome foliage and red berries in summer and bright-red leaves in fall. The flaky bark and multitrunked profile lend winter interest. See *Cornus mas*, p. 135.

D Washington hawthorn (use 1)
In early June this small deciduous tree is a cloud of small white flowers that give rise in late summer to glossy red fruits popular with birds. The red-tinged young leaves become dark green in summer and turn red in autumn. See *Crataegus phaenopyrum*, p. 136.

E Arrowwood viburnum (use 1)
The arrow-straight stems of this deciduous shrub are clothed in dark-green leaves that turn maroon in fall. Creamy white June flowers produce blue-black berries in September. See *Viburnum dentatum*, p. 152.

F Summersweet (use 1)
Just when you begin to tire of summer's heat, the pink or white, spicy-sweet flower spikes of this upright deciduous shrub will draw you to the garden. Glossy foliage is dark green in summer, gold in fall. See *Clethra alnifolia*, p. 134.

G Inkberry holly (use 4)
The glossy evergreen leaves of this adaptable native shrub add green to the winter garden. It forms a thicket full of blue-black berries that is a haven for birds. See *Ilex glabra*, p. 141.

H Mountain laurel (use 16)
Repeating groups of this lovely broad-leaved evergreen shrub give structure to the planting. In late spring, clusters of cup-shaped white (or pink or rosy) flowers stand out against the leathery dark-green leaves. Winter color is green-gold. See *Kalmia latifolia*, p. 142.

I 'Brilliantissima' chokeberry (use 3)
This broad deciduous shrub offers white flowers in spring and narrow leaves that turn red in fall. Red berries decorate the bare branches all winter. See *Aronia arbutifolia*, p. 131.

J Wildflowers and ferns
As the trees and shrubs mature, you'll want to replace sun-loving wildflowers with shade lovers. You can expand the fern plantings described on p. 109 and add wild ginger (*Asarum canadense*, p. 131), sweet woodruff (*Galium odoratum*, p. 138), and foamflower (*Tiarella cordifolia*, p. 152), all excellent perennial ground covers.

K Stepping-stones
Flagstone path provides entry for woodland strolls and maintenance. See p. 165.

L Soil mounds
Varying the height of the two planting areas adjacent to the narrow entry creates additional interest on a flat site. Mound the soil in the center of each area to a height of 18 to 24 in., tapering it out over a radius of 6 to 8 ft. Large stones embedded here and elsewhere add a natural touch.

See site plan for E G I.

Eastern white pine B
Mountain laurel H
Mountain laurel H
Ferns J

SITE: Sunny

SEASON: Late spring

CONCEPT: Mixed planting across the back of a lot attracts birds and wildlife. Shown after 12 to 15 years.

A colorful sunny start

The trees and shrubs in this planting will need a number of years to create a shady woodland. While they're small, you can take advantage of the sunny site to make this meadow garden, filled with wildflowers, grasses, and ferns.

A real meadow is difficult to duplicate. To achieve the look and feel of a meadow, it's best to choose dependable garden relatives of wild plants. Use the plants and plan here, or ones of your choice. (Note that we've indicated areas for types of plants on the plan.) As the shade increases, expand the fern plantings and replace sun-loving wildflowers with the shade-tolerant ones mentioned in the previous pages.

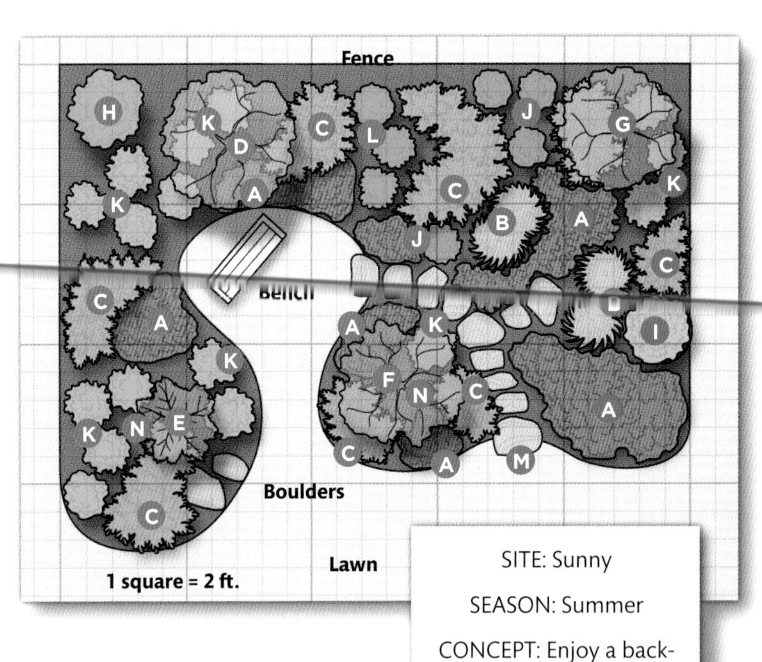

SITE: Sunny

SEASON: Summer

CONCEPT: Enjoy a backyard full of wildflowers while your trees and shrubs are growing.

Plants & Projects

A Wildflowers (as needed; space plants sold in gallon containers 2 to 3 ft. apart) Masses of perennial wildflowers arranged in large clumps or patches make a striking sight. Choose several kinds from the following list and plant them in groups of 3, 5, 7, or more.

- Both purple coneflower (*Echinacea purpurea*, p. 136) and coneflower (*Rudbeckia fulgida*, p. 149) have large daisylike flowerheads.
- Butterfly weed (*Asclepias tuberosa*, p. 131) displays flat clusters of striking bright orange flowers that are irresistible to butterflies.
- Bee balm (*Monarda didyma*, p. 144) entices hummingbirds with brightly colored moplike flowerheads.
- Blazing star (*Liatris spicata*, p. 143) and false indigo (*Baptisia australis*, p. 132) display showy

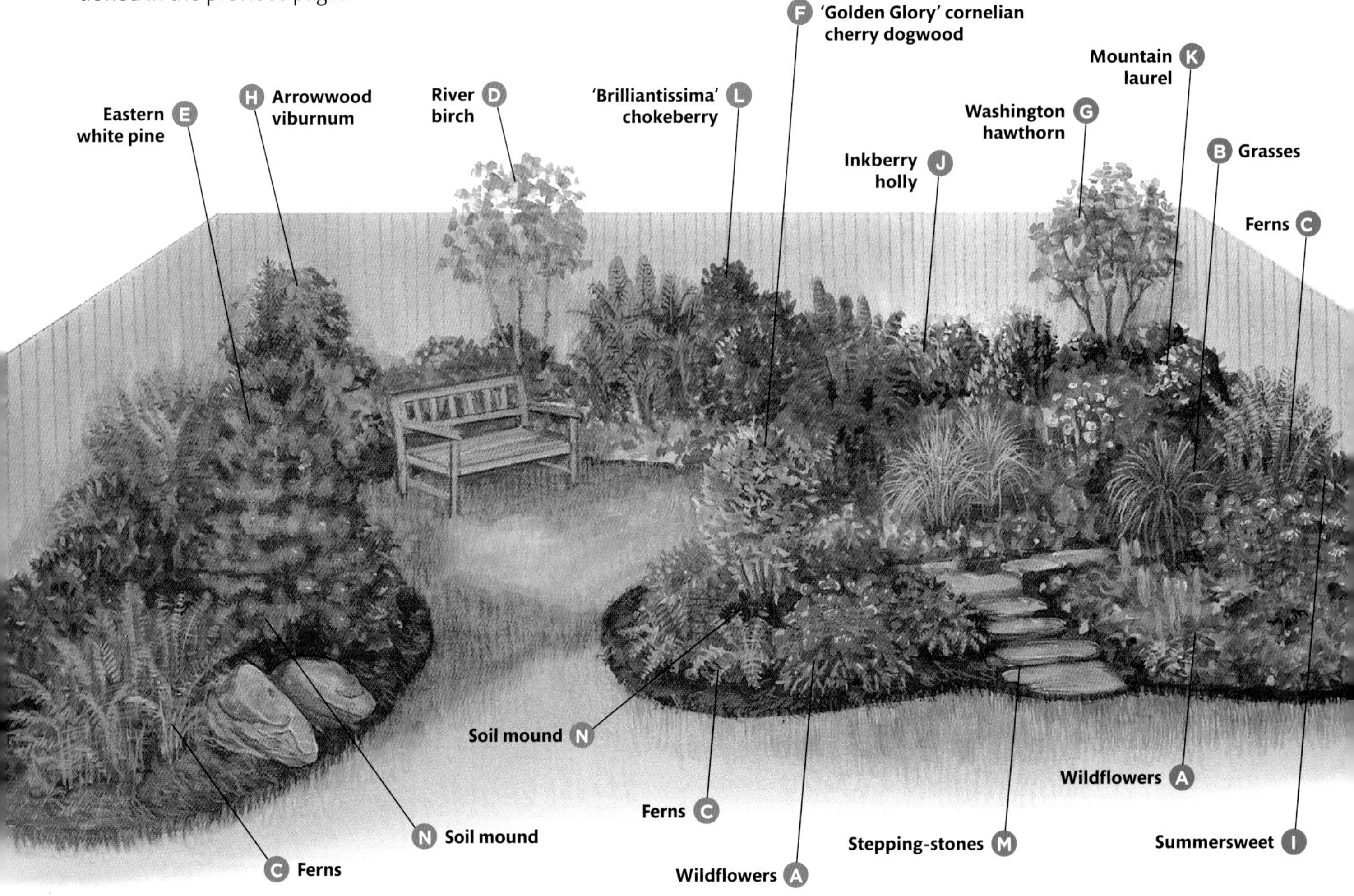

spikes of flowers, the former carried on narrow leafy stems, the latter hovering over an attractive mound of blue-green leaves.

- Columbine (*Aquilegia canadensis*, p. 131) and fringed bleeding heart (*Dicentra eximia*, p. 136) both produce exquisite flowers that demand closer inspection.

Ⓑ **Grasses** (as needed; space plants from gallon containers 3 to 4 ft. apart)
No meadow is complete without grasses. Here the long arching leaves and tall fluffy seed heads of Japanese silver grass (*Miscanthus*, p. 144) rustle in the wind. This aristocratic grass is attended by drifts of the shorter but no less attractive fountain grass (*Pennisetum alopecuroides*, p. 145). Tawny dried foliage and seed heads of both grasses look good in the winter.

Ⓒ **Ferns** (as needed; space plants from gallon containers about 2 ft. apart)
These trouble-free plants of woodland edges and understory are the meadow's link to its shady future.

- Maidenhair fern (*Adiantum pedatum*, p. 137) is the shortest and needs more shade than the others, which will do well in partial shade.
- Marginal wood fern (*Dryopteris marginalis*) and cinnamon fern (*Osmunda cinnamomea*) grow 2 to 3 ft. tall, while the broad plumes of ostrich fern (*Matteuccia struthiopteris*) stretch up to 5 ft. See Ferns, p. 137.

See p. 106 for the following:

Ⓓ **River birch**
Ⓔ **Eastern white pine**
Ⓕ **'Golden Glory' cornelian cherry dogwood**
Ⓖ **Washington hawthorn**
Ⓗ **Arrowwood viburnum**
Ⓘ **Summersweet**
Ⓙ **Inkberry holly**
Ⓚ **Mountain laurel**
Ⓛ **'Brilliantissima' chokeberry**
Ⓜ **Stepping-stones**
Ⓝ **Soil mounds**

PLANT PORTRAITS

A nature park calls for the relaxed, informal look of these trees, shrubs, and perennials. Most are native plants, and many offer fruits to entice birds and other wildlife.

● = Older view, pp. 106–107
▲ = Younger view, pp. 108–109

Butterfly weed (*Asclepias tuberosa*, p. 131) ▲

Eastern white pine (*Pinus strobus*, p. 147) ● ▲

Coneflower (*Rudbeckia fulgida*, p. 149) ▲

Maidenhair fern (Ferns: *Adiantum pedatum*, p. 137) ▲

'Brilliantissima' chokeberry (*Aronia arbutifolia*, p. 131) ● ▲

River birch (*Betula nigra*, p. 132) ●

Under the Old Shade Tree

CREATE A COZY GARDEN IN A COOL SPOT

SITE: Shady

SEASON: Early summer

CONCEPT: Woodland understory plants make a lovely shade garden and private haven.

This planting is designed to help homeowners blessed with a large shade tree make the most of their good fortune. A bench is included, of course. There's no better spot to rest on a hot summer day. But why stop there? The tree's high, wide canopy provides an ideal setting for a planting of understory shrubs, perennials, and ferns. The result is a woodland garden that warrants a visit any day of the year.

The planting roughly coincides with the pool of shade cast by the tree. A selection of medium-to-large evergreen shrubs extends about halfway around the perimeter. You can position these to provide privacy, screen a view from the bench, or block early-morning or late-afternoon sun.

The planting blooms for weeks in spring and early summer, highlighted by the distinctive flowers of the rhododendrons and mountain laurels. During summer, the little woodland is an oasis of cool foliage, brightened by colorful clumps of hosta. As fall shifts to winter, the tracery of bare branches in the canopy overhead is nicely balanced by evergreen foliage below.

Plants & Projects

For best results, thin the tree canopy, if necessary, to produce dappled rather than deep shade. Also remove limbs to a height of 8 ft. or more to provide headroom. Although the oak we've shown here has deeper roots than some shade trees, it still competes for moisture with nearby plants. Judicious supplemental watering and moisture-conserving mulch will help get plants started and improve their performance. (For more on planting under a shade tree, see p. 201)

A Eastern red cedar (use 5 plants)
A tough, pyramid-shaped native evergreen with fragrant foliage. Use the cultivars 'Canaertii' or 'Keteleeri', both of which hold their green color through the winter. See *Juniperus virginiana*, p. 142.

B 'Scintillation' rhododendron (use 3)
The handsome foliage of this vigorous evergreen shrub is covered with lovely pink flowers in June. See *Rhododendron*, p. 148.

C Mountain laurel (use 6)
Less well known than the rhododendrons it resembles, but just as lovely, this native evergreen shrub displays clusters of small cup-shaped pink-and-white flowers in June. See *Kalmia latifolia*, p. 142.

D 'PJM' rhododendron (use 5)
One of the hardiest of these evergreen shrubs, this compact plant features vivid magenta flowers in April or May and maroon winter foliage. 'Olga Mezitt' is a good substitute. See *Rhododendron*, p. 148.

E Large-leaved hosta (use 13)
One of the best perennials for shade. Choose a cultivar such as 'Elegans', the huge blue-gray textured leaves of which look great against the rhododendrons and add color to the shade from spring until frost. See *Hosta sieboldiana*, p. 140.

F Variegated small-leaved hosta (use 8)
Contrasts with its nearby relative in color, size, and texture. Choose a cultivar such as 'Ginko Craig', which has narrow green-and-white leaves. See *Hosta*, p. 140.

G Lenten rose (use 11)
Among the first flowers to appear in spring are the nodding cuplike blooms of this perennial. Flower colors range from white through pink and rose to green. The large, leathery evergreen leaves combine well with the nearby ferns, hostas, and rhododendrons. See *Helleborus orientalis*, p. 139.

H Cinnamon fern (use 10)
A native fern that spreads to form a patch. Clumps of tall, fine-cut fronds are bright green in summer, gold in fall. If the site is very dry, plant interrupted fern (*Osmunda claytonia*) instead. See Ferns: *Osmunda cinnamomea*, p. 137.

I Christmas fern (use 10)
The glossy evergreen fronds of this easy native fern are attractive tucked in between the small-leaved hostas and Lenten rose. See Ferns: *Polystichum acrostichoides*, p. 137.

J Maidenhair fern (use 5)
One of the most elegant ferns. Slowly it forms a patch of lacy, bright-green fronds on shiny black stems. See Ferns: *Adiantum pedatum*, p. 137.

K Bench
A comfortable wooden bench provides a place to rest and enjoy the scenery in this shady garden oasis.

A
C
K
C
B
D
H
Tree
I
Path
H
E
D
E
G
I
F
J
G
1 square = 1 ft.
Bench K
B 'Scintillation' rhododendron
'PJM' D rhododendron
Lenten G rose
H Cinnamon fern
E Large-leaved hosta
J Maidenhair fern
I Christmas fern
G Lenten rose
F Variegated small-leaved hosta

Simple and cool

This simple symmetrical design, with its cool color scheme, is a more formal alternative to the woodsy feeling of the previous planting. Here, by using raised beds and selecting tough plants, we also offer a solution to the problem of planting in the dry, root-clogged soil found beneath trees such as beeches and maples. Encircling the tree, an octagonal bench allows you to sit always on the shady side while enjoying the scenery.

Wood-chip paths radiate out from the tree trunk, creating four identical beds. In each, a whiskey-barrel planter serves as focal point, set among low mounds of large green-and-white hosta leaves, colors that echo those of the ivy and impatiens filling the planter. A ring of evergreen euonymus with green-and-white foliage defines the perimeter of the planting.

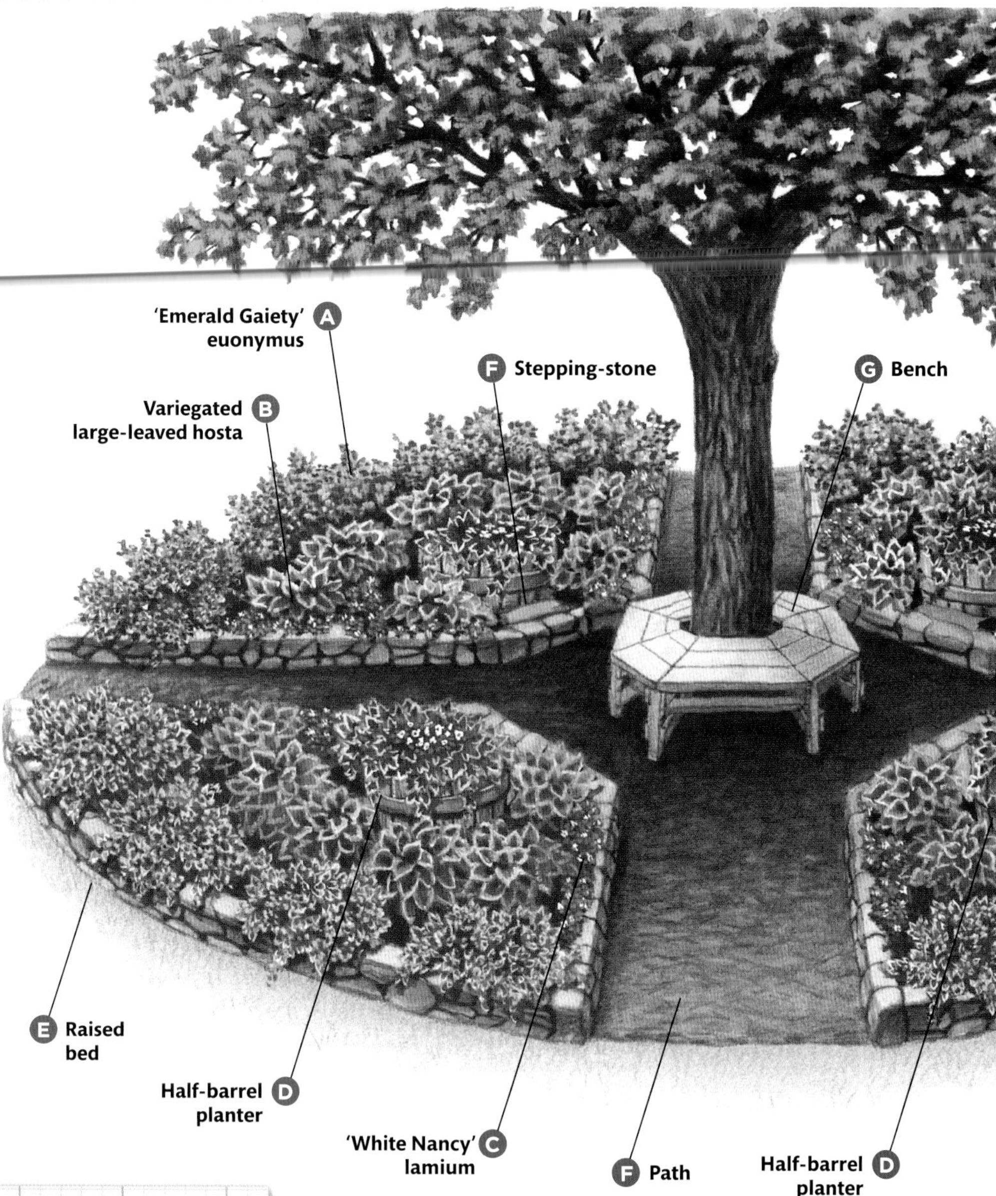

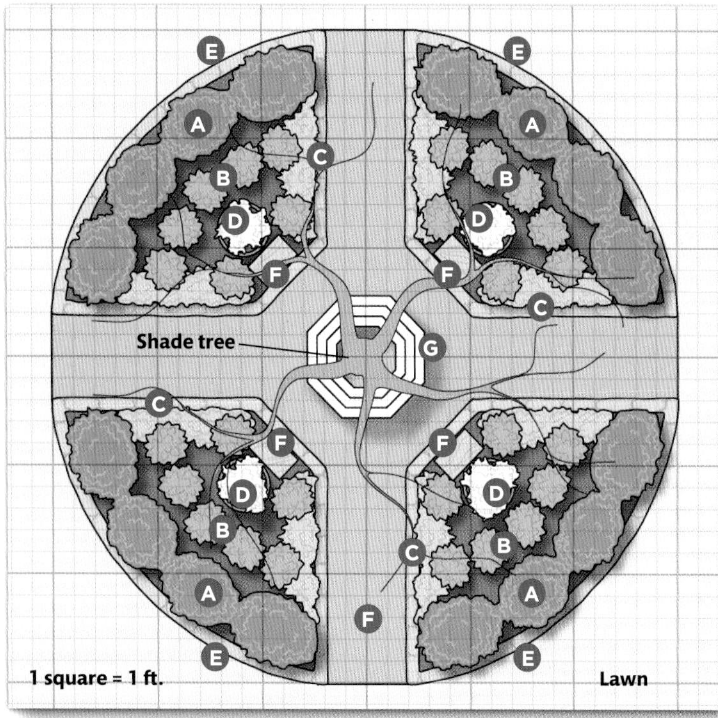

Plants & Projects

A 'Emerald Gaiety' euonymus (use 16 plants)
A ring of these mounded evergreen shrubs encircles the planting. The small dark-green leaves have white margins that turn pinkish in winter. You can let the plants spread naturally or prune them into distinct rounded shapes. See *Euonymus fortunei*, p. 136.

B Variegated large-leaved hosta (use 28)
In the heat of summer, this perennial's mounds of large white-and-green leaves bring a cool, lush quality to the shady spot. Plant the same cultivar in each bay, or mix several together. See *Hosta*, p. 140.

C 'White Nancy' lamium (use 72)
Small silvery leaves with green margins edge each bed. This perennial ground cover also provides pure-white flowers in early summer. Plant on 1-ft. centers. See *Lamium maculatum*, p. 143.

D Half-barrel planter (use 4)
These large containers, available at many local garden centers, make great planters. Here we've planted four English ivies and three impatiens in each. Choose a white impatiens; these bushy annuals will fill the planter with flowers all summer long. Plant the ivy around the perimeter so it trails over the edge. See *Hedera helix*, p. 138.

SITE: Shady

SEASON: Summer

CONCEPT: A simple design and a limited palette of plants make a restful shade garden.

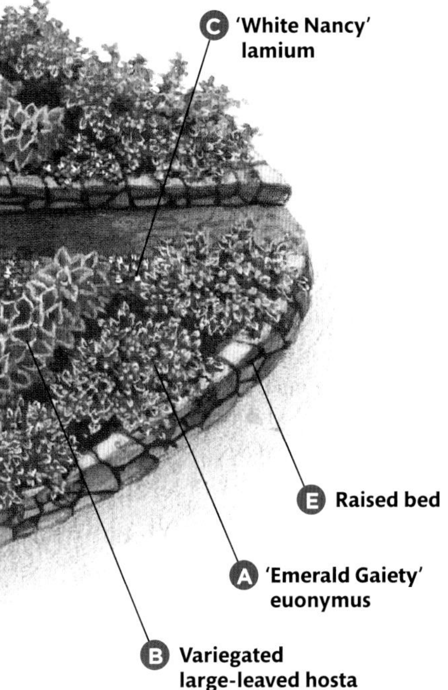

E Raised beds
Plantings under beeches, maples, and some other trees must contend with dry soil and competition from surface roots. Adding 4 to 6 in. of topsoil in raised, fieldstone-edged beds and mulching generously helps overcome these problems.

F Paths and stepping-stones
The fieldstone edging separates the raised beds and wood-chip paths. A stepping-stone in each bed provides easy access to the planters. See p. 165.

G Bench
Encircling the tree, this octagonal wooden bench suits the symmetrical planting and isn't difficult to build. See p. 188.

PLANT PORTRAITS

Whether in a casual woodland setting or a more formal display, these plants offer a wide range of foliage shapes, textures, and colors to liven up any shady spot.

● = First design, pp. 110–111

▲ = Second design, pp. 112–113

Variegated large-leaved hosta (*Hosta 'Antioch'*, p. 140) ● ▲

Christmas fern
(Ferns: *Polystichum acrostichoides*, p. 137) ●

Eastern red cedar
(*Juniperus virginiana*, p. 142) ●

Variegated English ivy (*Hedera helix*, p. 138) ▲

'Scintillation' rhododendron
(*Rhododendron*, p. 148) ●

Down to Earth

HARMONIZE YOUR DECK WITH ITS SURROUNDINGS

A second-story deck is a perfect spot for viewing your garden and yard. Too often, however, the view of the deck from the yard is less pleasing. Perched atop skinny posts, towering over a patch of lawn, an elevated deck looks out of place, an ungainly visitor that is uncomfortable in its surroundings.

In the design shown here, attractive landscaping brings the deck, house, and yard into balance. Plants, including vine-covered trellises, form a broad pedestal of visual support for the deck. Decreasing in height from the deck to the yard, they make it easier for your eyes to move between the levels.

The planting is pretty as well as functional. At one corner, a magnolia tree provides delightful spring flowers that can be enjoyed from the deck above or lawn below. The vines make a handsome backdrop for evergreen shrubs, lacy ferns, and a clump of ornamental grass.

Tucked beneath the deck, snug in a wood-paneled niche, a bench looks out on the backyard, providing a comfortable spot for watching kids play or just enjoying the landscape.

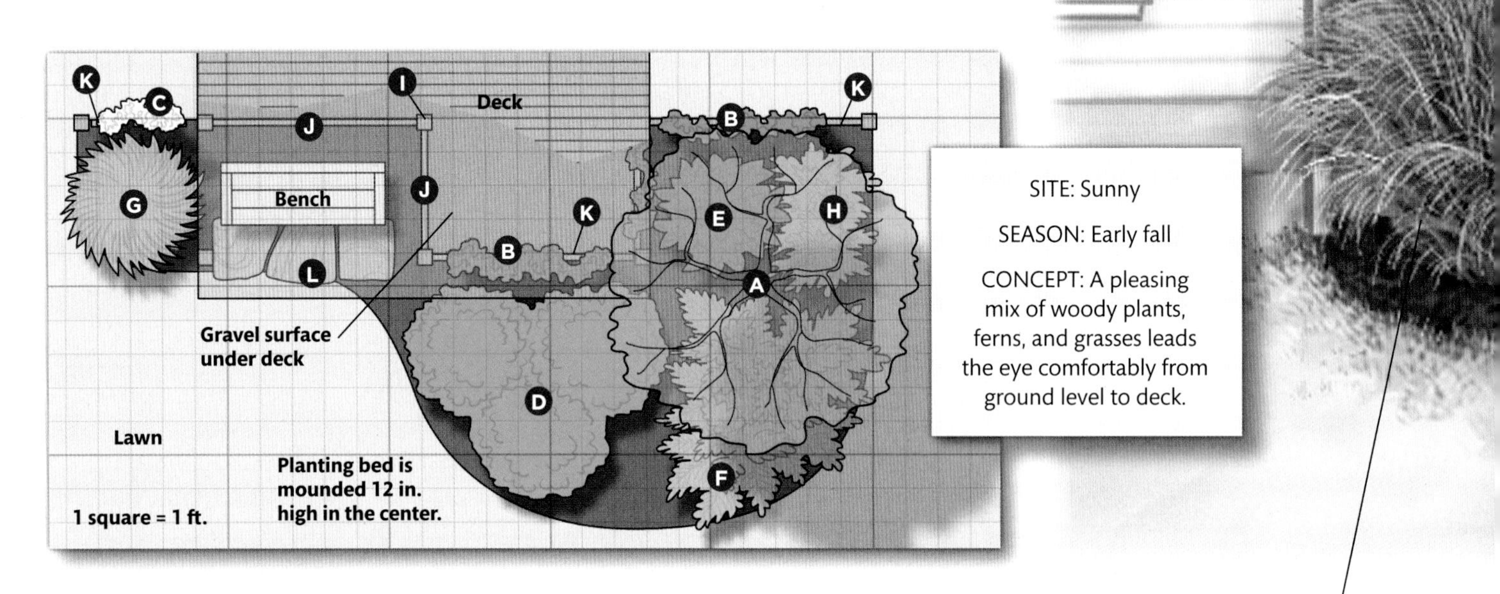

SITE: Sunny

SEASON: Early fall

CONCEPT: A pleasing mix of woody plants, ferns, and grasses leads the eye comfortably from ground level to deck.

Sweet autumn clematis (C)

Ladder trellis (K)

'Gracillimus' Japanese silver grass (G)

Plants & Projects

The trellises and partitions for the bench niche aren't difficult to install, and you can use the area they enclose under the deck near the house for storage. Mound up the soil in the large planting bed about a foot in the center to give the bed added interest. The vines and grass will need annual pruning.

A 'Dr. Merrill' magnolia (use 1)
This small deciduous tree is just right for close viewing from the deck, offering bright-white spring flowers, nice summer foliage, and, in winter, handsome smooth bark and big fuzzy buds. Grows quickly into a narrow upright shape and needs little pruning. See *Magnolia* x *loebneri*, p. 144.

B Trumpet creeper (use 3)
This fast-growing deciduous vine, up to 40 ft., suckers widely especially in good soil. It's 12 in. leaves are glossy and dark green, toothed along the margins. Bunches of conspicuously bright orange or scarlet, trumpet-shaped flowers, bloom in summer. Successful in most types of soil. Best bloom in full sun. Deer-resistant. See *Campsis radicans*, p. 134.

C Sweet autumn clematis (use 1)
A vigorous deciduous vine, it covers the trellis with fragrant starry white flowers in September and fluffy seed heads later. Its small green leaves make a backdrop for the fountain of silver grass. See *Clematis terniflora*, p. 134.

D Compact inkberry holly (use 3)
The neat habit and glossy evergreen leaves of this adaptable shrub fill the space beneath the magnolia with green all year. You can let the plants merge into a single irregular mound, as shown here, or prune them as you choose. See *Ilex glabra* 'Compacta', p. 141.

E Mountain laurel (use 1)
Clusters of very pretty cup-shaped white, pink, or rosy

flowers stand out in the shade of the magnolia in June. The leathery dark-evergreen leaves of this native shrub look good year-round. See *Kalmia latifolia*, p. 142.

F Ostrich fern (use 3)
A tall fern at home in the shade of the magnolia. Its bright-green fronds look like large feathers and can turn a pretty yellow in fall. Spreads to form a patch. See Ferns: *Matteuccia struthiopteris*, p. 137.

G 'Gracillimus' Japanese silver grass (use 1)
Narrow, arching silvery green leaves of this perennial grass form a large clump that provides privacy for the bench. Fluffy seed heads rise above the foliage in late summer. The whole plant turns beige in fall and stands up partway through the winter. See *Miscanthus*, p. 144.

H Cinnamon fern (use 2)
Like a shorter version of ostrich fern. Forms clumps of finely divided fronds. See Ferns: *Osmunda cinnamomea*, p. 137.

I Posts
To make the 4x4 deck posts look more substantial, we've added a 1x3 centered on each face. See p. 187.

J Partitions
Two fencelike wooden partitions create a niche for the bench beneath the deck. Made of vertical boards, they extend between posts and to within a foot of the underside of the deck. See p. 189.

K Ladder trellises
These simple-to-construct open frameworks of 2x2s support the vines. The trellises span the space between some of the existing deck posts as well as the new posts added on both sides of the deck. See p. 189.

L Paving
Large flagstones support the bench and delineate the sitting area. See p. 161.

A shady understory

This planting also integrates the deck with its surroundings, but it does so in a shady environment, produced perhaps by large trees nearby. The deck supports virtually disappear in this design, masked by a creative mix of trellises and shade-tolerant plants.

Here the ladder trellises expand the visual base of the deck in front as well as to the sides. The bench again has a private niche formed by wooden partitions and a large shrub, but now it sits in front of, rather than under, the deck.

Vines, ferns, and the evergreen foliage of mountain laurel make a serene shade garden, sparkling with flowers in spring and lush foliage through the summer. Soil in the larger bed is built up to form a mound about 2 ft. high in the center. This planting is bisected by the vine-covered trellis, creating a little private area near the house where you might put another bench or a table and chairs. The area beneath the deck provides well-screened storage space.

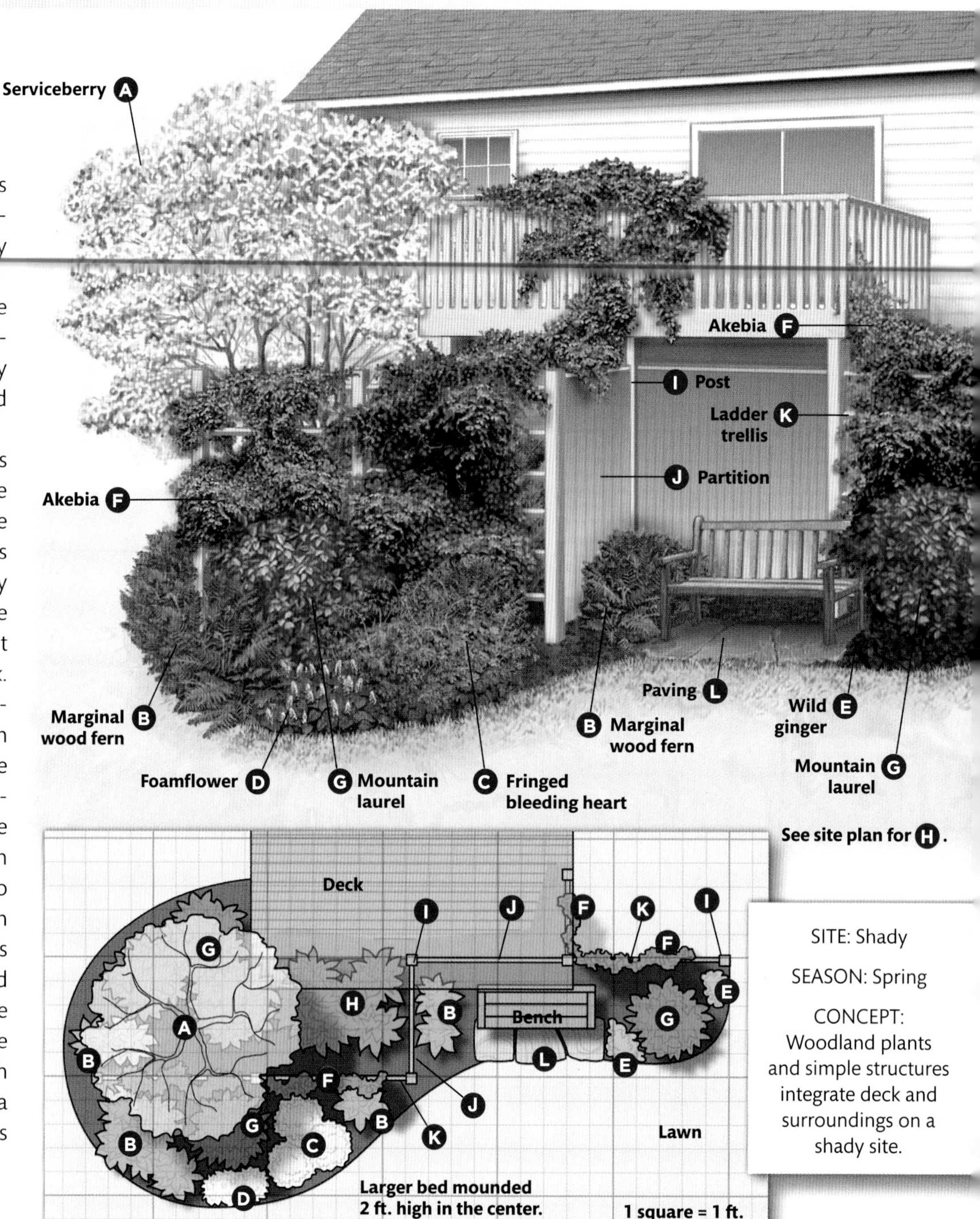

SITE: Shady

SEASON: Spring

CONCEPT: Woodland plants and simple structures integrate deck and surroundings on a shady site.

Plants & Projects

A Serviceberry (use 1 plant)
This small deciduous tree is a focal point for months, with white flowers in spring, good foliage and edible berrylike fruit in summer, brilliant red fall color, and attractive gray bark in winter. Choose one with multiple trunks. See *Amelanchier* x *grandiflora*, p. 131.

B Marginal wood fern (use 10)
The lustrous, dark blue-green fronds of this hardy fern are a graceful presence next to the bench and an attractive ground cover beneath the serviceberry. See Ferns: *Dryopteris marginalis*, p. 137.

C Fringed bleeding heart (use 3)
This native perennial offers delicate lacy foliage and adds color to the shade garden all summer with its lovely heart-shaped pale pink flowers. See *Dicentra eximia*, p. 136.

D Foamflower (use 6)
Erect fluffy spikes of starry white flowers hover above this perennial's evergreen leaves in late spring. A native woodland wildflower, it spreads to form a ground cover in the shade of the serviceberry. See *Tiarella cordifolia*, p. 152.

E Wild ginger (use 10)
This woodland perennial is another excellent native ground cover for the shaded area near the bench, where you can have a close-up view of its large, elegant heart-shaped leaves. Spreads slowly, forming a dense mat. See *Asarum canadense*, p. 131.

See pp. 114–115 for the following:

F Trumpet creeper (use 7)

G Mountain laurel (use 5)

H Ostrich fern (use 6)

I Posts

J Partitions

K Ladder trellises

L Paving

PLANT PORTRAITS

These trees, shrubs, ferns, and perennials accommodate the mix of sun and shade found in the two designs.

● = First design, pp. 114–115

▲ = Second design, pp. 116

Sweet autumn clematis (*Clematis terniflora*, p. 134) ●

'Dr. Merrill' magnolia (*Magnolia x loebneri*, p. 144) ●

Trumpet creeper (*Campsis radicans*, p. 134) ● ▲

Fringed bleeding heart (*Dicentra eximia*, p. 136) ▲

Cinnamon fern (Ferns: *Osmunda cinnamomea*, p. 137) ●

Ostrich fern (Ferns: *Matteuccia struthiopteris*, p. 137) ● ▲

Foamflower (*Tiarella cordifolia*, p. 152) ▲

Integrated Deck

ENHANCE THE LOOK OF YOUR DECK WITH LANDSCAPING

Combined with a simple homemade lattice skirting attached to the porch, plants in this upper-deck design form a broad pedestal of visual support for the deck. Decreasing in height from the deck to the yard, the planting makes it easier for our eyes to move between the levels.

The planting is as pretty as it is functional. Anchoring one side, at the corners of house and deck, are a lilac and a viburnum. Their scented flowers sweeten the springtime air. On the other side, tall ornamental grasses sway and rustle in the breeze, their clouds of pinkish flowers greeting viewers looking down from the deck. On the lattice (and the deck railing if you wish), fragrant roses bloom from early summer, joined in late August by scented clematis flowers.

Completing the planting, perennials provide bursts of summer color and low-growing junipers form a rough-textured "throw rug" at the base of deck and house, tying the taller elements of the design together. Grass paths lead to the enclosed area beneath the deck. Cover the ground there with crushed stone and use the space to store garden tools or bicycles.

SITE: Sunny

SEASON: Summer

CONCEPT: A pleasing mix of shrubs, perennials, and grasses leads the eye comfortably from ground to deck.

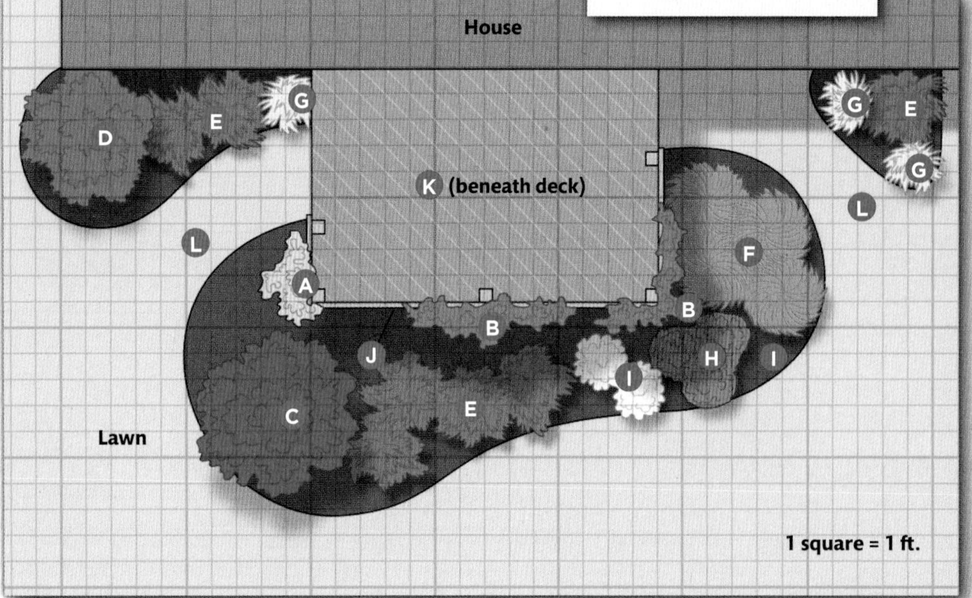

Plants & Projects

The shrubs, rose, and clematis will take a few years to fill out, during which time you can fill in the open spaces with low-growing annuals. (See p. 197 for more on this maturing process.) Once established, the planting requires only seasonal pruning and cleanup.

A 'Zéphirine Drouhin' rose (use 1 plant)
This deciduous climber covers its portion of the lattice with long, nearly thornless canes; shiny green leaves; and fragrant rose-pink flowers that bloom from early summer to frost. See *Rosa*, p. 149.

B Sweet autumn clematis (use 2)
This twining deciduous vine will clothe the lattice and deck railing with its small light-green leaves. Starry white flowers fill the air with their sweet scent in August and September. See *Clematis terniflora*, p. 134.

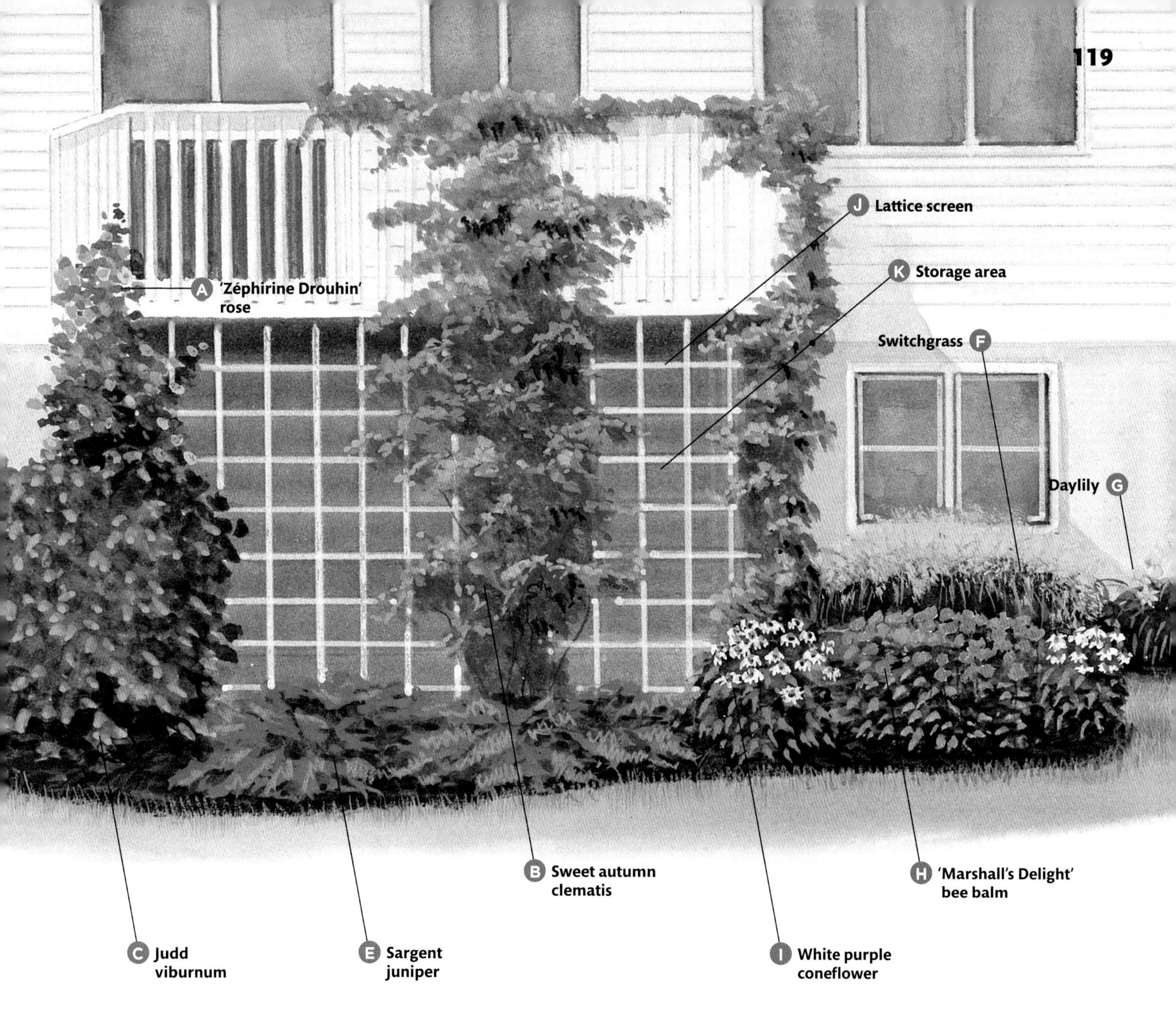

C Judd viburnum (use 1)
This large deciduous shrub helps broaden the visual base of the deck. Its dark-green leaves are an ideal backdrop to the spicy-scented white flowers that appear in May. See *Viburnum* x *juddii*, p. 152

D Dwarf lilac (use 1)
Forming a bushy clump at the corner of the house, this deciduous shrub bears fragrant lilac flowers in May and offers purple fall foliage. See *Syringa meyeri* 'Palibin', p. 150.

E Sargent juniper (use 7)
This low-growing, spreading evergreen shrub provides year-round color and texture to the planting. See *Juniperus chinensis* var. *sargentii*, p. 142.

F Switchgrass (use 4)
This native perennial grass forms graceful upright clumps of narrow leaves topped in late summer by a cloud of pinkish flowers. Foliage turns from bright green in summer to gold in autumn and tan in winter. See *Panicum virgatum*, p. 145.

G Daylily (use 3)
Choose from this dependable perennial's nearly limitless variety of flower colors. All have long, grasslike leaves that are attractive after the flowers have finished. Shown here is 'Hyperion', which bears scented pale-yellow flowers in July. See *Hemerocallis*, p. 139.

H 'Marshall's Delight' bee balm (use 3)
This perennial forms clumps of mintlike foliage topped in July and August with big, globe-shaped, pink flowers that may attract hummingbirds and butterflies to the deck area. See *Monarda*, p. 144.

I White purple coneflower (use 3)
Use a white-flowered cultivar of this native prairie perennial. Flowers are carried on sturdy stalks above large clumps of coarse green leaves. Blooms in July and August; dry seed heads provide winter interest and food for birds. See *Echinacea purpurea*, p. 136.

J Lattice screen
Easy to make and attach to the deck posts, this lattice dresses up the deck and provides support for the clematis vines and rose canes. Stain to match your house, or let the natural wood weather. See p. 184.

K Storage area
For a durable tidy surface, cover the ground beneath the deck with 2 in. of crushed stone. Use a wooden edging to keep the stone out of the surrounding beds.

L Path
Access to the storage area can be a strip of lawn, as shown here. Install a crushed-stone surface (see p. 161) if traffic is too heavy for a grass path.

Elegant Symmetry

FIT A FORMAL GARDEN INTO YOUR BACKYARD

Formal landscaping often lends dignity to the public areas around a home (see pp. 20–23 and 34–35). Formality can also be rewarding in a more private setting. There, the groomed plants, geometric lines, and symmetrical layout of a formal garden can help to organize the surrounding landscape, provide an elegant area for entertaining, or simply be enjoyed for their own sake.

Wide pathways divide this 25-ft.-square garden into identical quadrants, creating a central island where a sculpted rosebush serves as a focal point. The plantings in each quadrant are nearly identical, with flowers and foliage in several colors and textures to provide interest. A neatly sheared evergreen hedge defines the outer perimeter; a double row of perennials makes a looser border next to the path. At the center of this frame, like a jewel on display, sits a small conical evergreen tree on a grassy silver-and-green carpet.

Formal gardens like this one look self-contained on paper, neatly packaged within rigid boundaries. But even more than other types of landscaping, actual formal gardens work well only when carefully correlated with other elements in the landscape, such as the house, patio, and major plantings. Transitions, both physical and visual, between formal and more casual areas are particularly important. An expanse of lawn, changes of level that separate one area from another, or plantings that screen sight lines can all help formal and informal elements coexist comfortably.

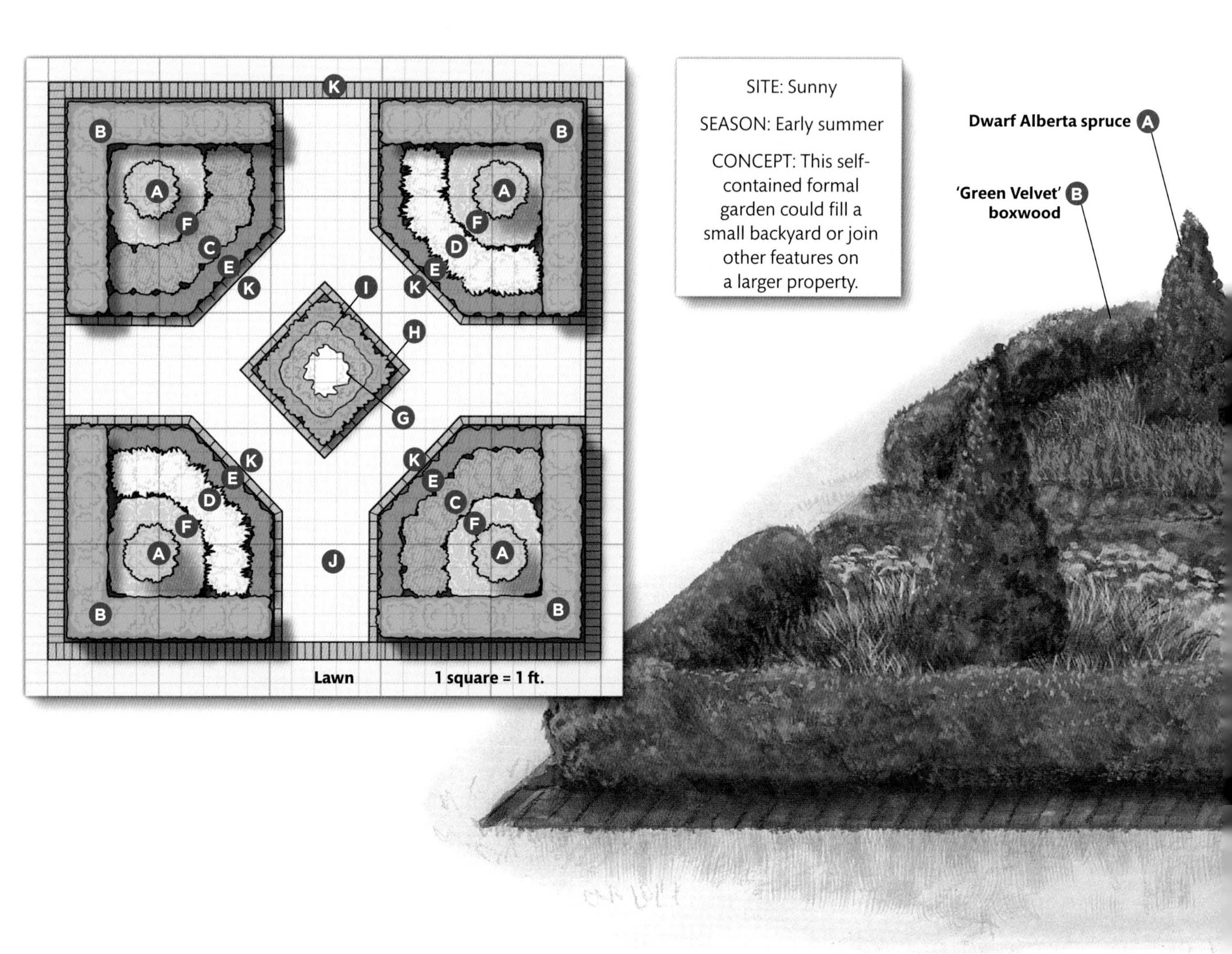

Plants & Projects

Of all gardens, a formal garden most obviously reflects the efforts of its makers. After the hedge has filled in, this garden requires attention mostly to keep it looking neat: shearing the hedge, removing spent flowers, pruning stray foliage, and maintaining the paths.

A Dwarf Alberta spruce (use 4 plants)
The dense, light-green foliage of this small evergreen tree naturally forms a conical shape, so it requires no pruning. See *Picea glauca* 'Conica', p. 146.

B 'Green Velvet' boxwood (use 36)
Dense branching and small leaves make this shrub an excellent hedge plant. Leaves hold their good green color through the winter. Trim the hedge about 18 in. high and 12 in. wide. See *Buxus*, p. 133.

C 'Dropmore' catmint (use 18)
Loose spikes of violet-blue flowers bloom above this perennial's silver-green aromatic foliage for most of the summer; heaviest in June. See *Nepeta* x *faassenii*, p. 144.

D 'Moonbeam' coreopsis (use 18)
This easy perennial produces masses of tiny pale-yellow flowers above threadlike dark-green foliage. Blooms from July into September. See *Coreopsis verticillata*, p. 135.

E Dwarf Chinese astilbe (use 48)
The pink fluffy spires of this low-growing perennial color the edges of the paths in late summer. Lacy dark-green foliage looks good the rest of the season. Spreads quickly, so you'll need to pull up stray shoots regularly. See *Astilbe chinensis* var. *pumila*, p. 132.

F 'Silvery Sunproof' lilyturf (use 60)
This useful perennial forms grasslike clumps of green-and-white-striped semievergreen leaves that set off the spruce beautifully. Purplish hyacinth-like flowers in August. See *Liriope muscari*, p. 143. In Zones 4 and 5, substitute *Dianthus* 'Bath's Pink'.

G Standard rose (use 1)
A standard is a bushy mass of foliage and flowers perched atop a single tall stem. Available at local nurseries; buy a pink- or white-flowered one. Grown in a container, a standard rose can survive mild winters outdoors, but in Zones 4 and 5, substitute statuary, a birdbath, or a large urn planted with annuals. See *Rosa*, p. 149.

H Evergreen candytuft (use 16)
This spreading evergreen perennial forms a low, glossy green edging around the central square. It bears masses of bright-white flowers in the spring. See *Iberis sempervirens*, p. 140.

I Annuals (use 12)
Plant petunias or dwarf snapdragons to form a colorful patch of flowers beneath the rose all summer long.

J Paths
The fine-textured, uniform surface of crushed-rock paths goes well with the simplicity of the formal design. See p. 160.

K Edging
Brick edging defines the paths, keeps the crushed rock out of the adjacent beds, and forms a mowing strip around the outside of the planting. Place the bricks on edge, with the long side perpendicular to the path or hedge. See p. 162.

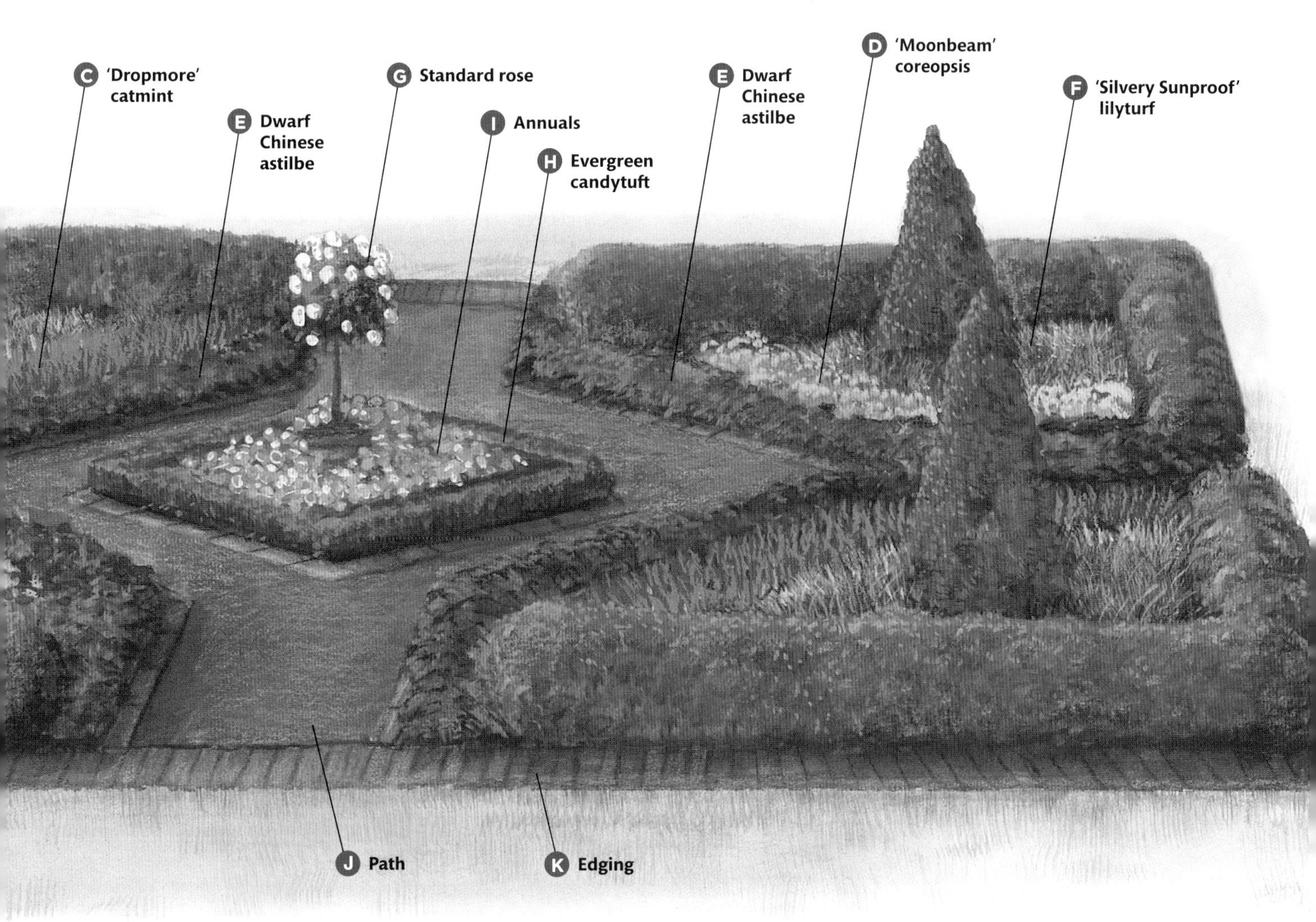

PLANT PORTRAITS

These plants are right at home in a formal setting, but they aren't fussy about the care they need.

● = First design, pp. 120–121

▲ = Second design, pp. 122–123

'Silvery Sunproof' lilyturf (*Liriope muscari*, p. 143) ●

Evergreen candytuft (*Iberis sempervirens*, p. 140) ● ▲

Chinese juniper (*Juniperus chinensis*, p. 142) ▲

'Dropmore' catmint (*Nepeta* x *faassenii*, p. 144) ●

'Bath's Pink' dianthus (*Dianthus*, p. 136) ▲

Dwarf Chinese astilbe (*Astilbe chinensis* var. *pumila*, p. 132) ●

A formal patio

In this design, a brick patio large enough for a small table and chairs is the centerpiece of the formal garden, providing a lovely spot for an intimate lunch or a restful hour with a favorite book.

A single entrance interrupts the clipped boxwood hedge. Even though the hedge is low, it creates a sense of enclosure. White-flowered evergreen candytuft and violet-blue catmint edge the flagstones. In each corner is a juniper, trained and sheared to a geometric shape, surrounded by a carpet of fragrant pink flowers.

Plants & Projects

A Chinese juniper (use 4 plants)
You can usually find trained and sheared specimens of these hardy evergreen shrubs at nurseries, but four matching ones may require a special order. See *Juniperus chinensis*, p. 142.

B 'Bath's Pink' dianthus (use 60)
The pink flowers of this perennial resemble small carnations and have a wonderful fragrance. The grassy gray-green foliage goes well with the junipers. See *Dianthus*, p. 136.

C Patio
The 12-ft.-square brick patio has a border of large flagstones and, on the perimeter, an edging of additional bricks in a single row. See p. 166.

See p. 121 for the following:

D 'Green Velvet' boxwood (use 45)

E 'Dropmore' catmint (use 36)

F Evergreen candytuft (use 52)

G Edging

SITE: Sunny

SEASON: Early summer

CONCEPT: A low hedge and plantings in four quadrants frame a small patio.

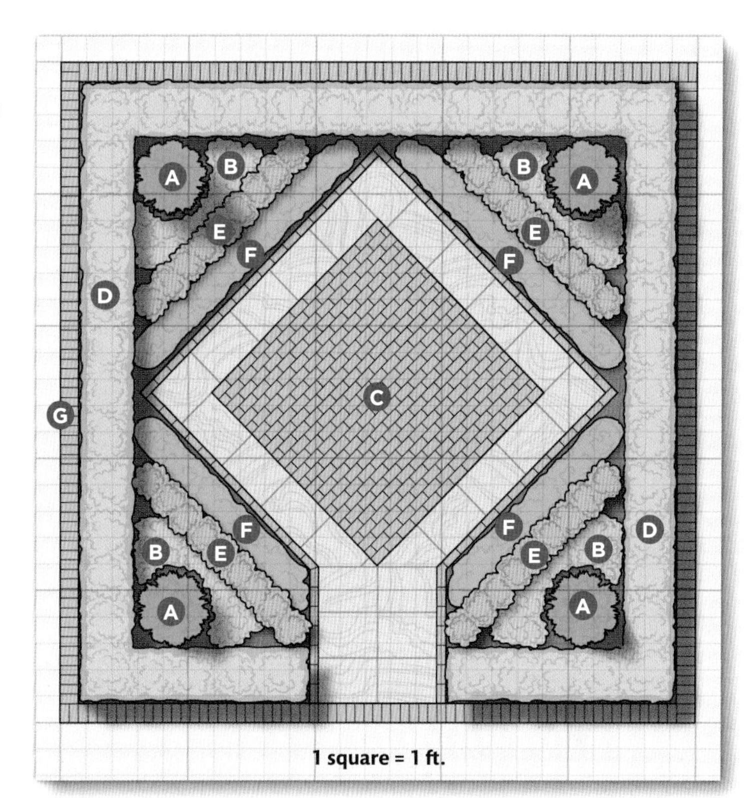

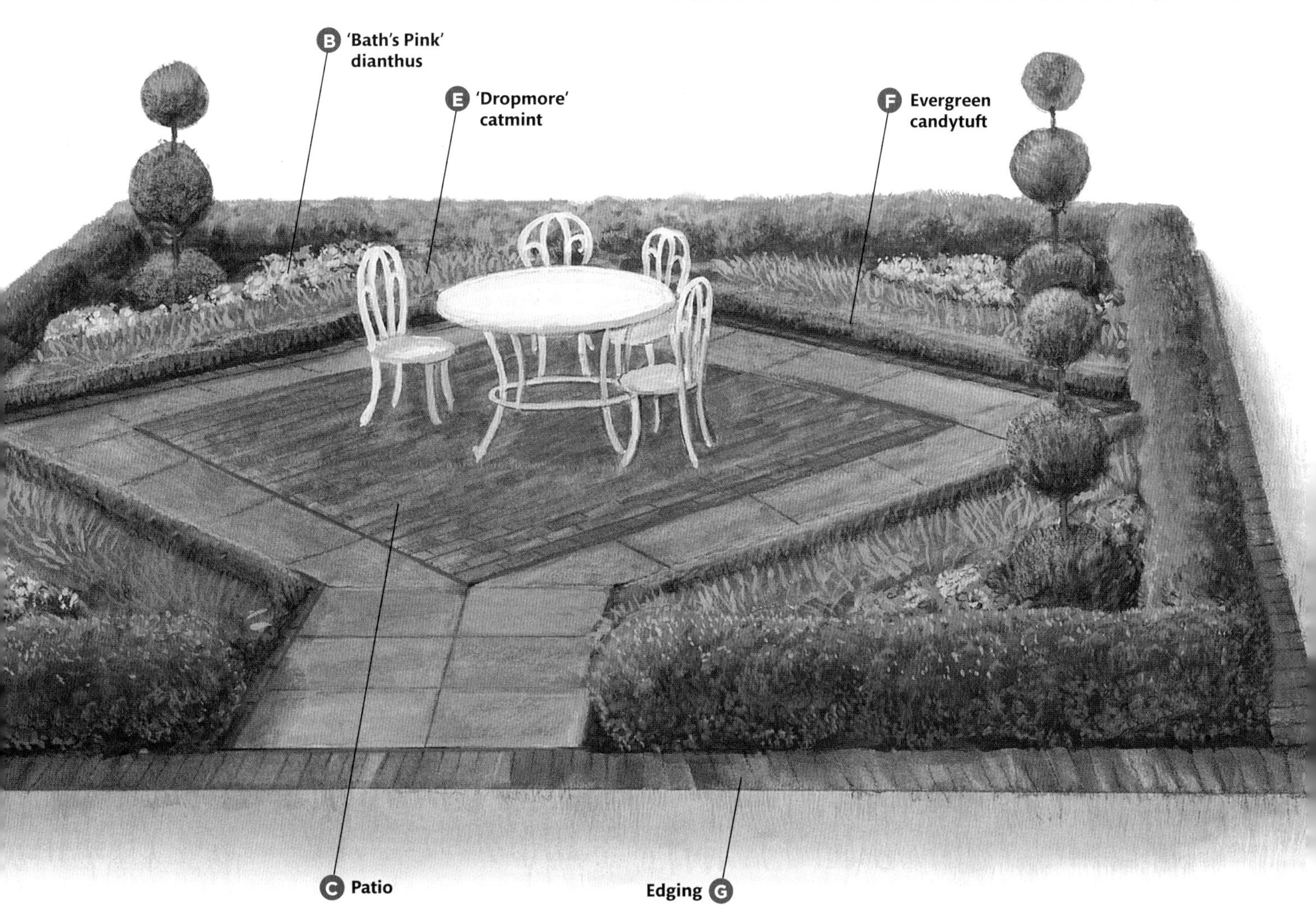

A Woodland Link

CREATE A SHRUB BORDER OF NEARBY WOODS

The woodlands and forests of the Northeast are treasured by all who live in the region. Many subdivisions, both new and old, incorporate woodland areas, with homes bordering landscapes of stately trees and large shrubs. In older neighborhoods, mature trees on adjacent lots create almost the same woodland feeling.

The planting shown here integrates a domestic landscape with a woodland at its edge. It makes a pleasant transition between the open area of lawn, with its sunny entertainments, and the cool, secluded woods beyond. The design takes inspiration from the border of small trees and shrubs nature provides at the sunny edge of a wood, and it should have the same attraction to birds and wildlife as its natural counterpart does.

Shrubs of various sizes mingle in the planting, larger ones toward the back, imitating natural layered growth. Whether viewed up close from the meandering path or from across the yard, the planting is appealing all year. A succession of bloom begins with a spectacular show in early spring and continues into early summer. The foliage is attractive from spring's tender greens to fall's yellows and deep reds. Winter snow makes a pristine backdrop for patterns of bare branches, including the dogwood's bright-red stems.

Plants & Projects

Even though this design calls for relatively few plants in a large area, preparing the entire planting bed by tilling and amending the soil will pay off in the long run with healthy vigorous growth (see p. 192). If you plant in the spring, fill in between small trees and shrubs with ground covers. Then, in the fall, plant as many bulbs as you can afford and enjoy the lovely show the following spring. Once the woody plants are established, in a year or so, just devote a weekend each spring and fall to mulching and basic pruning.

A 'Regent' shadblow (use 2 plants)
This deciduous shrub forms a bushy clump of numerous erect stems. Long clusters of white spring flowers give way to sweet edible black fruits. Fall foliage is yellow or gold. See *Amelanchier canadensis*, p. 131.

B Arrowwood viburnum (use 3)
Another thicket-forming deciduous shrub with stems so straight they once were used for arrow shafts. Native to the region, it produces small white flowers in June, blue berries for the birds, and deep-green leaves that turn maroon in fall. See *Viburnum dentatum*, p. 152.

C Siberian dogwood (use 1)
Placed at the center of the curving path, this lovely deciduous shrub is an ideal focal point, especially in winter, when its bright-red stems gleam in the sun. See *Cornus alba* 'Sibirica', p. 135.

D Compact inkberry holly (use 3)
The planting's only evergreen, this shrub offers small, shiny dark-green leaves on a bushy round shrub. See *Ilex glabra* 'Compacta', p. 141.

E Variegated weigela (use 6)
An old-fashioned favorite, this fast-growing deciduous shrub has eye-catching green-and-gold leaves and pink flowers in summer. Prune hard every few years to keep it neat and vigorous. See *Weigela florida* 'Variegata', p. 153.

F 'Northern Sun' forsythia (use 3)
The bright-yellow flowers on this adaptable deciduous shrub are an early-spring eye-opener next to the path. An especially hardy cultivar. See *Forsythia* x *intermedia*, p. 137.

G 'Rosy Lights' azalea (use 3)
A hardy deciduous shrub whose clusters of fragrant dark-pink flowers appear on leafless stems in May, making quite a show at the front of the planting. See *Rhododendron:* Northern Lights, p. 148.

H 'Spicy Lights' azalea (use 3)
Same as above, with soft orange blooms. See *Rhododendron:* Northern Lights, p. 148.

I Bulbs and ground covers
Between the trees and shrubs, plant drifts of spring bulbs among ground covers, such as myrtle (see p. 153), which will cover the faded bulb foliage in summer. See Bulbs, p. 133.

J Path
A path of wood chips maintains the woodland flavor of the planting. See p. 160.

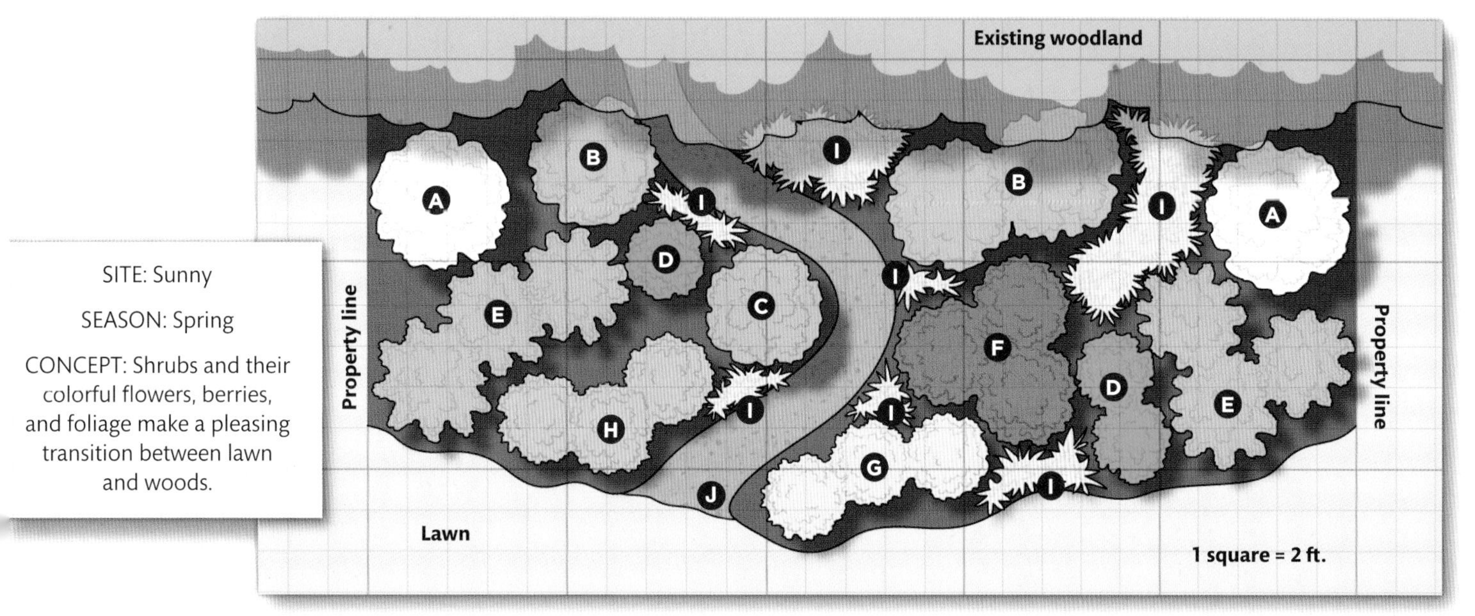

SITE: Sunny

SEASON: Spring

CONCEPT: Shrubs and their colorful flowers, berries, and foliage make a pleasing transition between lawn and woods.

Evergreens for shade

If your lot is on the shady side of a woodland or you prefer a look with more evergreen foliage, try this design. Here evergreen plants of the woodland understory replace many of the deciduous shrubs in the previous planting.

Large conifers anchor each end of the planting, with broad-leaved evergreens in between and along the front. A few deciduous shrubs add pleasing contrast, especially in winter, when the dogwood's showy red stems and the sparkleberry's red fruits stand out amidst all the greens.

The mountain laurels, rhododendrons, and andromeda combine beautifully at the front of the border, and their pink and white flowers offer a dazzling spring display.

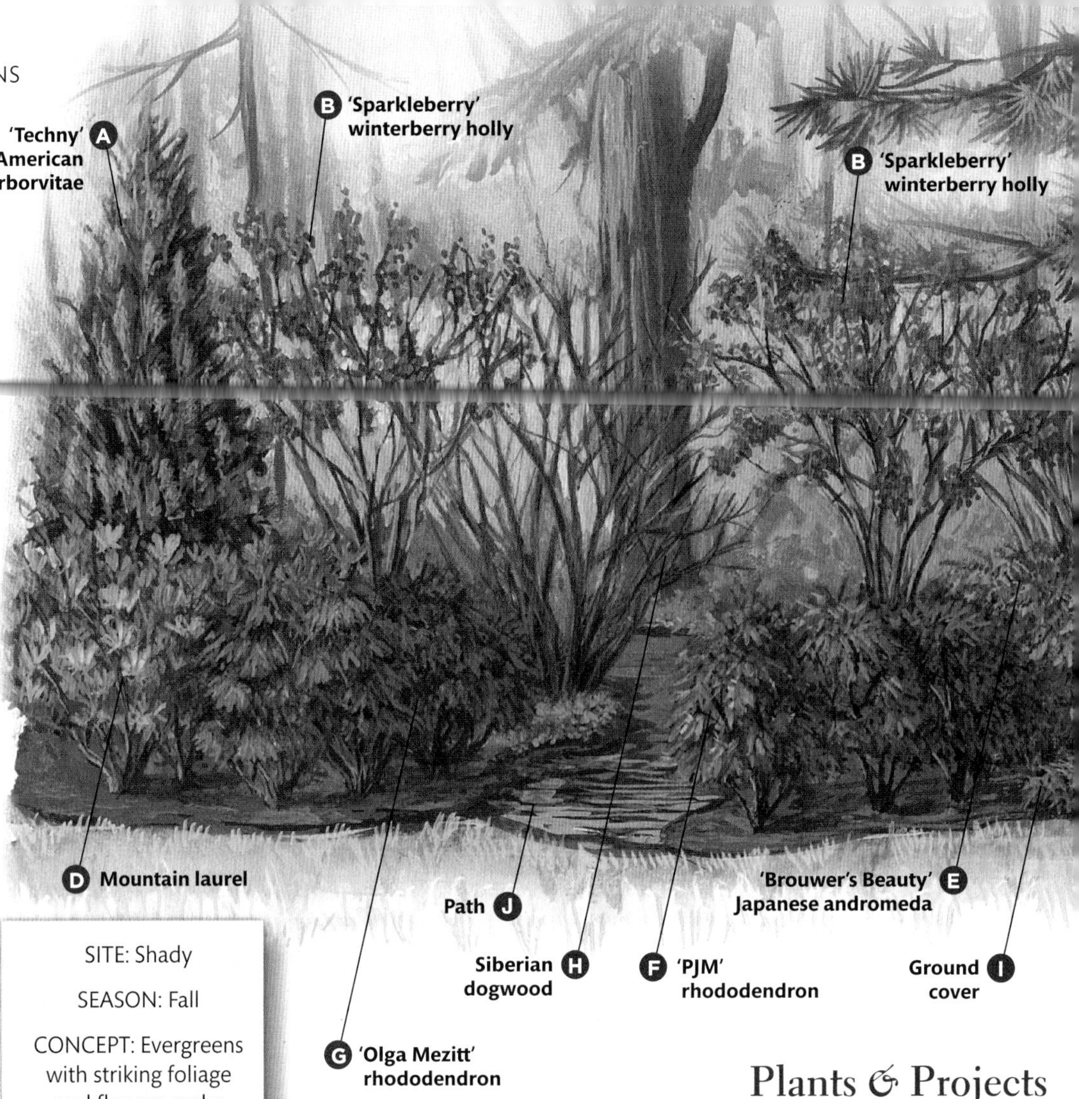

SITE: Shady

SEASON: Fall

CONCEPT: Evergreens with striking foliage and flowers make this woodland edge pretty year-round.

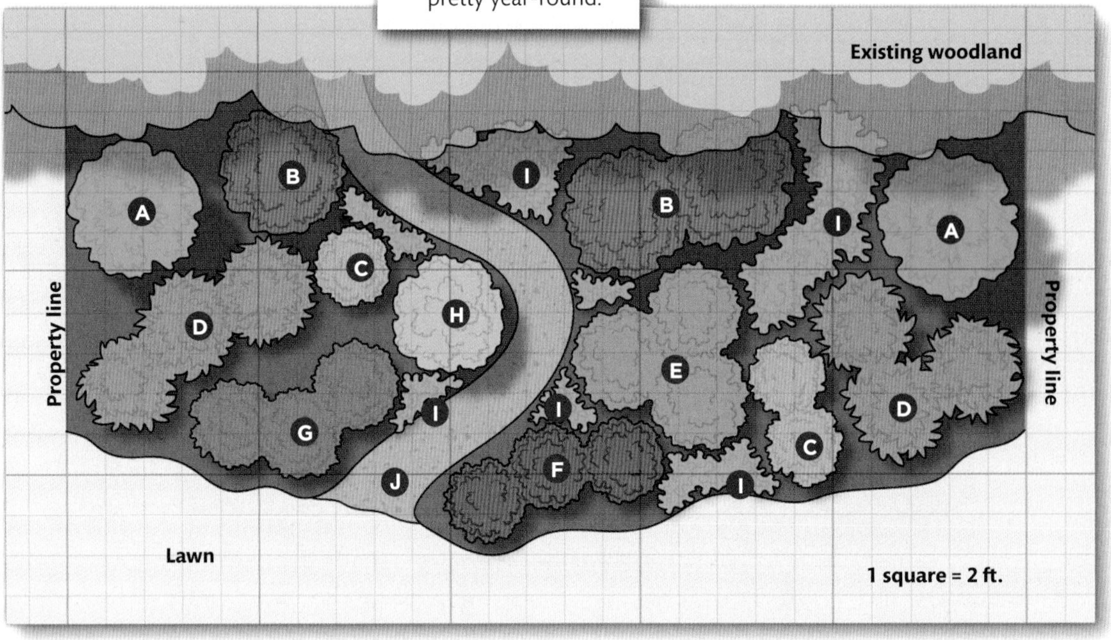

Plants & Projects

A 'Techny' American arborvitae (use 2 plants)
A handsome, pyramid-shaped evergreen shrub that holds its good green color through the winter and acts as a transition to the adjacent woodland. See *Thuja occidentalis*, p. 151.

B 'Sparkleberry' winterberry holly (use 3)
A large deciduous shrub with shiny red berries in fall and winter. Plant one male cultivar to ensure berry production. See *Ilex verticillata*, p. 141.

C Japanese holly (use 3)
This evergreen shrub forms an eye-catching dense mass of shiny dark-green leaves. Choose a low, spreading cultivar. In Zone 4, substitute a compact inkberry holly. See *Ilex crenata*, p. 140.

D Mountain laurel (use 6)
In June, this native evergreen shrub displays lovely clusters of small cup-shaped flowers (in white, pale pink, or bright

pink) against dark-green foliage. See *Kalmia latifolia*, p. 142.

E 'Brouwer's Beauty' Japanese andromeda (use 3)
A handsome, compact evergreen shrub with narrow shiny green leaves. Winter's attractive reddish flower buds become fragrant white flowers in June. See *Pieris*, p. 146.

F 'PJM' rhododendron (use 3)
A compact, rounded evergreen shrub with small dark-green leaves that turn maroon in winter. Its vivid lavender-pink flowers light up the front of the border in early spring. See *Rhododendron*, p. 148.

G 'Olga Mezitt' rhododendron (use 3)
Showcased against small dark-green leaves, the pink flowers of this compact evergreen shrub complement those of its relative across the path. See *Rhododendron*, p. 148.

See p. 124 for the following:

H Siberian dogwood (use 1)

I Bulbs and ground cover

J Path

PLANT PORTRAITS

Deciduous or evergreen, these shrubs offer good-looking flowers and foliage for sun or shade.
● = First design, pp. 124–125
▲ = Second design, pp. 126–127

'Northern Sun' forsythia (*Forsythia* x *intermedia*, p. 137) ●

Siberian dogwood (*Cornus alba* 'Sibirica', p. 135) ● ▲

'Rosy Lights' azalea (*Rhododendron:* Northern Lights, p. 148) ●

'PJM' rhododendron (*Rhododendron*, p. 148) ▲

'Sparkleberry' winterberry holly (*Ilex verticillata*, p. 141) ▲

Variegated weigela (*Weigela florida* 'Variegata,' p. 153) ●

Plant Profiles

Plants are the heart of the designs in this book. In this section you'll find descriptions of all the plants used in the designs, along with information on planting and maintaining them. These trees, shrubs, perennials, grasses, bulbs, and vines have all proved themselves as dependable performers in the region. They offer a wide spectrum of lovely flowers and fruits, handsome foliage, and striking forms. Most contribute something of note in at least two seasons. You can use this section as an aid when installing the designs in this book and as a reference guide to desirable plants for other home landscaping projects.

Using the plant profiles

All of these plants are proven performers in many of the soils, climates, and other conditions commonly found in the Northeast region. But they will perform best if planted and cared for as described in the Guide to Installation. In these descriptions and recommendations, the term "garden soil" means soil that has been prepared for planting by digging or tilling and adding some organic matter so that it's loose enough for roots and water to penetrate easily. Here also, "full sun" means a site that gets at least eight hours a day of direct sun throughout the growing season. "Partial sun" and "partial shade" both refer to sites that get direct sun for part of the day but are shaded the rest of the time by a building, fence, or tree. "Full shade" means sites that don't receive direct sunlight.

The plants are organized here alphabetically by their scientific name. If you're browsing, page references direct you to the designs in which the plants appear. Those in ***bold italic*** type indicate the page where a photo of the plant can be found

Abies balsamea 'Nana'

DWARF BALSAM FIR. A compact form of the popular Christmas tree. Glossy dark-green needles have a wonderful aroma. Needs full sun and moist, well-drained soil. Forms a broad low mound, gradually reaching 2 to 3 ft. tall and 3 to 5 ft. wide. Grows only a few inches a year, so buy the biggest you can afford to start with. Pages: 59, 67, ***69***.

Acer ginnala

AMUR MAPLE. A deciduous tree that's smaller, tougher, and more adaptable than our native sugar maples but just as colorful in fall. Usually grown with multiple trunks as a bushy specimen 15 to 25 ft. tall and wide; 'Compactum' grows 10 to 15 ft. tall and wide. Has conspicuous, sweet-scented, pale-colored flowers in spring; showy clusters of red fruits in summer; and crimson fall foliage. Needs full sun and a well-drained site; tolerates poor, dry soil. Prune in summer, removing weak or crossing limbs. Pages: 98, ***101***.

Acer palmatum

JAPANESE MAPLE. A small deciduous tree with fine-textured foliage. There are many fine cultivars, with green or dark red leaves. Mature sizes range from 10 to 25 ft. tall and wide. Adapts to full sun or partial shade; needs fertile, moist, well-drained soil. Prune with respect for its natural shape, removing only crossing or damaged limbs. Pages: 37, ***39***.

Achillea

YARROW. Long-blooming perennials with flat clusters of small flowers on stiff stalks and finely divided gray-green leaves that have a pungent aroma. 'Moonshine' (pp. 25, 49, ***51***) has lemon yellow flowers. *A. millefolium* 'Summer Pastels' (p. 53) has creamy, pale yellow, or pale pink flowers. All need full sun. Cut off old flower stalks when the blossoms fade. Divide every few years in spring or fall. Most yarrows grow 2 to 3 ft. tall.

Actinidia kolomikta

HARDY KIWI. A robust vine with woody stems and large deciduous leaves that are medium green splashed with pink-and-white patches. If you plant both male and female vines, you can pick tasty little fruits in the fall. Needs full sun. Climbs by twining, reaching 15 to 20 ft. or more. Prune in early spring, removing weak or dead stems. Pages: 84, ***87***.

Ajuga reptans 'Burgundy Glow'

'BURGUNDY GLOW' BUGLEWEED. A low, mat-forming perennial used as a ground cover. Erect 6-in. spikes densely packed with blue flowers are very showy for a few weeks in May or June. The glossy leaves are marked with purple, green, and white. Other cultivars have plain green or dark purplish bronze foliage. Tolerates full sun in rich, moist soil; needs partial or full shade in garden or dry soil. After flowers fade, cut them off with a string trimmer, lawn mower, or hedge shears. Spreads quickly and will invade a lawn unless you keep cutting along the edge or install a mowing strip. Pages: 38, ***39***.

Alchemilla mollis

LADY'S MANTLE. A perennial that forms clumps of gray-green leaves with a pleated texture and bears foamy sprays of lemon yellow flowers in June. Takes full or partial sun. Remove flower stalks after bloom to prevent the plant spreading by self- seeding. Cut leaves to the ground in late fall or early spring. Divide clumps every few years, in spring or right after the flowers fade. Grows about 1 ft. tall and 2 ft. wide. Pages: 29, 47, 65, 98, ***101***, 102.

Amelanchier canadensis 'Regent'

'Regent' shadblow. A deciduous shrub that forms a small thicket 4 to 5 ft. tall and 5 ft. or wider. Resembles serviceberry and needs the same care. (See below.) Page: 124.

Amelanchier x *grandiflora*

Serviceberry. A small deciduous tree, typically grown with multiple trunks. Bears white flowers in early spring and edible blue or purplish berries in summer; bright-red fall foliage. Needs full sun or partial shade. Grows fairly slowly, so buy a good-size specimen. Needs little pruning: just remove any crossing branches. May grow up to 25 ft. tall, 15 ft. wide. Pages: 23, 100, 116.

Aquilegia canadensis

Columbine. A native perennial wildflower with red and yellow flowers on erect branching stalks 2 to 3 ft. tall. Blooms in early summer. Forms a low clump of lacy foliage that looks good in fall and spring but often dies down in summer. Takes full sun or partial shade, well-drained soil. Needs no care. Individual plants live only a few years, but they self-sow readily if you let the seedpods ripen. Page: 109.

Aristolochia durior

Dutchman's pipe. A vigorous vine with large heart-shaped leaves that provide cool shade all summer and drop in winter. Bears pipe-shaped flowers in early summer. Climbs by twining and grows at least 10 ft. tall. Tolerates sun or shade, any garden soil. Prune young plants so they branch out at the base. Prune older plants to limit their size. Page: 29, ***29***.

Armeria maritima

Thrift. A perennial that forms a neat tuft of evergreen grassy leaves and bears spherical flower heads on stiff stalks about 1 ft. tall. Blooms generously in June, with scattered blossoms throughout the summer and fall, in shades of rose, pink, and white. Needs full sun and very well-drained soil. Remove flowers as they fade, and shear off old foliage in early spring. Pages: 63, ***64***.

Aronia arbutifolia 'Brilliantissima'

'Brilliantissima' chokeberry. A deciduous native shrub that grows erect, up to about 10 ft. tall and 8 ft. wide, with white flowers in late spring, crimson fall foliage, and small red berries that last all winter. Grows in sun or shade, in almost any soil. Carefree. Pages: 35, 106, ***109***.

Artemisia schmidtiana 'Silver Mound'

'Silver Mound' artemisia. An eye-catching perennial that makes a low mound, about 1 ft. tall and 2 ft. wide, of very fine-textured, silvery white foliage. Needs full sun, good air circulation, and very well drained soil; otherwise the foliage is liable to rot, especially in humid weather. Shear off the tops of the stems once or twice in spring and summer. Pages: 45, ***46***.

Artemisia stelleriana

Beach wormwood. A low, shrubby perennial with silver-gray, soft-textured leaves like the annual dusty miller. If you can find it, buy 'Silver Brocade' (pp. 53, ***55***), a cultivar with especially attractive foliage. Grows about 1 ft. tall, 2 to 3 ft. wide. Treat it like 'Silver Mound' artemisia. (See above.)

Asarum canadense

Wild ginger. A low-growing deciduous perennial with large heart-shaped leaves and inconspicuous flowers. Grows wild in the woods. Spreads slowly but gradually forms an excellent three-season ground cover. Needs partial or full shade and rich, moist, well-drained soil. Carefree. Can be divided in spring to make new plants. Grows about 6 in. tall and spreads up to 1 ft. wide. Pages: 56, ***58***, 106, 116.

Asclepias tuberosa

Butterfly weed. A perennial wildflower with flat heads of bright-orange flowers in early summer and attractive pods in fall. Forms a clump up to 2 ft. tall and wide, with more stems each year. Needs full sun. Carefree. Pages: 108, ***109***.

Amelanchier x *grandiflora*
Serviceberry

Bergenia cordifolia 'Bressingham White' BERGENIA

Aster novae-angliae 'Purple Dome'

'PURPLE DOME' NEW ENGLAND ASTER. A compact form of the popular perennial wildflower, this aster forms a dense mound of dark-green foliage all summer, then bears thousands of dark-purple flowers for a month or so in early fall. Grows about 2 ft. tall and wide. Needs full sun and good air circulation because it is subject to mildew in shady or too-sheltered sites. Grows best in rich, moist soil but adapts to garden soil. Divide every year or two in early spring. Pages: 49, ***51***, 68, 92.

Astilbe

ASTILBE. Among the best perennials for shady or partly shady sites, astilbes have fluffy plumes of tiny flowers in June or July and healthy, glossy, compound leaves all season. There are many kinds of hybrid astilbes, sold by cultivar name, that grow from 18 to 42 in. tall and have white, pale-pink, rose, or red flowers. Choose whatever size and color you prefer (p. 26, 90). A related plant, the dwarf Chinese astilbe, *A. chinensis* var. *pumila* (pp. 56, 121, ***122***), grows only 1 ft. tall and has mauve flowers in August. Spreads fast. All astilbes prefer rich, moist, well-drained soil and need shade from midday sun. Cut foliage to the ground in late fall or early spring. Divide every three to five years in spring or late summer, using a sharp spade, ax, or old pruning saw to cut the tough woody rootstock into a few large chunks.

Astilbe chinensis var. *pumila* ASTILBE

Aurinia saxatilis

BASKET-OF-GOLD. One of the first perennials to bloom in spring, it needs full sun and well-drained soil. Cut stems back halfway after it blooms and again in summer if the leaves get diseased during a spell of hot, humid weather. This is a fast-growing but short-lived plant, so buy replacements every few years. Grows about 6 to 8 in. tall, spreads 2 to 3 ft. wide. Pages: 25, 79.

Baptisia australis

FALSE INDIGO. A perennial prairie wildflower that's unusually carefree and long-lived. Forms a mushroom-shaped mound of blue-green foliage, topped in early summer with showy spikes of indigo-blue flowers, followed by clusters of decorative seedpods that last through the fall. Adapts to full sun or partial shade. Grows about 3 ft. tall and 3 to 6 ft. wide. Page: 53, ***55***, 108.

Bergenia cordifolia 'Bressingham White'

'BRESSINGHAM WHITE' BERGENIA. A perennial with unusually large, thick, glossy leaves that are fresh green in summer and turn garnet in winter. Clusters of white flowers are held above the foliage for a few weeks in late spring. Forms a clump about 1 ft. tall and 2 ft. wide. Prefers partial shade and moist soil but tolerates sun and garden soil. Divide every few years in spring or fall. Pages: 47, 56, 95, 100.

Betula nigra

RIVER BIRCH. A deciduous tree with very attractive beige, tan, or coppery bark that peels off in curly strips. The leaves are an attractive glossy green all summer and turn tan or gold in fall. Grows 1 to 2 ft. a year, reaching 60 ft. tall and almost that wide when mature. Needs full sun, prefers moist soil but adapts to garden soil. Subject to various diseases and insects, but usually the damage is minor. Train young trees as described on p. 207 to eliminate narrow crotches, which break apart in ice storms. Pages: 106, ***109***.

Betula platyphylla 'White Spire'

'WHITE SPIRE' BIRCH. A deciduous tree with bright-white bark and fresh green leaves that turn yellow in fall. Grows about 40 ft. tall, 25 ft. wide, with a narrow profile. Needs full sun and well-drained garden soil. Train young trees to eliminate narrow crotches (p. 207), which often break apart in ice storms. Pages: 32, 40, **42**.

Recommended bulbs and corms

***Colchicum autumnale*, Meadow saffron**
A fall-blooming corm with rosy pink or lilac flowers like giant crocuses on 6-in. stalks in O ctober. Plant corms 4 in. deep, 6 in. apart. Forms large clumps after a few years. Thick straplike leaves develop in early spring and die down in July. Page: 53.

***Crocus*, Crocus**
Cup-shaped flowers on 4-in. stalks in March. Available in white, yellow, lilac, and purple. Plant corms 4 in. deep, 4 in. apart. Forms large clumps after a few years. Slender grassy leaves die down in June. Pages: 53, 71.

***Endymion hispanica*, Spanish bluebell**
Bell-shaped blue flowers dangle from 18-in. stalks in April. Plant bulbs 5 in. deep, 5 in. apart. Forms large clumps after a few years and also spreads by seed. Flat grassy leaves die down in June, or you can pull them out earlier. Pages: 67, ***69***.

***Galanthus nivalis*, Snowdrop**
Bright-white flowers droop from 6-in. stems in March or April. Plant 3 in. deep, 3 in. apart. Page: 71.

***Muscari armeniacum*, Grape hyacinth**
Grapelike clusters of sweet-scented purple flowers on 6-in. stalks last for several weeks in April and May. Plant bulbs 3 in. deep, 3 in. apart. Grassy foliage appears in fall, survives until spring, and dies down in June. Pages: 67, 71.

***Narcissus*, Daffodils, jonquils, and narcissus**
Bright-yellow, white, or bicolor flowers, often fragrant, on stalks 6 to 18 in. tall. Different kinds bloom in sequence from early February through early May. Leaves die down in June to July. Plant bulbs 4 to 6 in. deep, 4 to 6 in. apart, depending on their size. Very reliable, carefree, and long-lived. Use dwarf daffodils such as 'Baby Moon', 'February Gold', and 'Tête `a Tête' close to the house, because after they bloom, their short leaves are less conspicuous. Use larger daffodils such as 'King Alfred' or 'Mt. Hood' for plantings viewed from a distance. Pages: 67, ***69***, 71.

***Tulipa*, Tulip**
Cup- or bell-shaped flowers on short or tall stalks in April or May. Plant the bulbs 3 to 4 in. deep, 3 to 4 in. apart. They seldom bloom the second year. Page: 71.

Boltonia asteroides 'Snowbank'

'SNOWBANK' BOLTONIA. A perennial wildflower that blooms for many weeks in fall, bearing thousands of small white asterlike blossoms. Forms an erect clump of many stems. Foliage is pale green and stays healthy all summer. Takes full or partial sun, garden or moist soil. Grows 3 to 4 ft. tall, 2 to 4 ft. wide. Cut stems back partway in late spring to reduce height of clump, if desired. Pages: 53, ***55***.

Bulbs

The bulbs recommended in this book are all perennials that come up year after year and bloom in late winter, spring, or early summer. After they flower, their leaves keep growing and stay growing until sometime in summer, when they gradually turn yellow and die down to the ground. To get started, you must buy bulbs from a garden center or catalog sometime in the fall. Plant them promptly in a sunny or partly sunny bed with well-prepared soil, burying them two to three times as deep as the bulb is high. Water well. In subsequent years, all you have to do is pick off the faded flowers in spring and remove (or ignore, if you choose) the old leaves after they turn brown in summer. For more information on bulbs, see the box above.

Buxus

BOXWOOD. Very popular and highly prized shrubs that form a dense mass of neat, small, glossy evergreen leaves. The leaves, and also the small white flowers in spring, have a distinct fragrance. Boxwood forms soft mounded shapes if left alone or can be sheared into formal globes, cones, hedges, or topiary. There are many kinds of boxwood, differing in rate of growth, size of leaf, natural habit (upright or spreading), and winter foliage color (green or bronzy). 'Green Velvet' boxwood has small leaves that stay bright green in winter and forms a globe about 3 ft. tall (pp. 75, 92, 121). 'Wintergreen' littleleaf boxwood (*B. microphylla;* pp. **32**, 33, 63) is similar but smaller, about 2 ft. tall. Boxwoods grow slowly, so buy the largest plants you can afford. They need well-drained soil and grow best in full or partial sun. Use mulch to protect their shallow roots. Shear in early summer, if desired.

Buxus 'Green Velvet'
BOXWOOD

Calamagrostis x *acutiflora*

FEATHER REED GRASS. A perennial grass that forms narrow, erect clumps. Leaves develop early in the season. Slender stalks topped with flower spikes that resemble pipe cleaners form in midsummer. The whole plant gradually turns beige or tan by late summer, but it stands up well into the winter. Cut it all down to the ground before new growth starts in spring. Can be divided every few years if you want more plants. Otherwise, leave it alone. Adapts to most soils but needs full or partial sun. Flower stalks reach 5 to 6 ft. tall, foliage spreads about 2 ft. wide. 'Karl Foerster' (pp. 96, **97**) has plain green leaves. 'Overdam' (p. 104) has green-and-white striped leaves.

Chamaecyparis pisifera 'Boulevard'
DWARF FALSE CYPRESS

Campanula carpatica

CARPATHIAN BELLFLOWER. A short, compact perennial that blooms for most of the summer. 'Blue Clips' (pp. 45, **46**, 72, 75, 92) has sky blue flowers; 'White Clips' (pp. 49, **51**) has white flowers. Both have medium-green foliage. Prefers full sun and well-drained soil. Divide clumps every few years in spring. Grows about 1 ft. tall and wide.

Campsis radicans

TRUMPET CREEPER. This fast-growing deciduous vine, up to 40 ft., suckers widely especially in good soil. It's opposite, pinnately compound, 12 in. leaves are glossy and dark green, toothed along the margins. Bunches of conspicuously bright orange or scarlet, trumpet-shaped flowers, bloom in summer and are pollinated by hummingbirds. Successful in most types of soil, but tolerates infertile, droughty or wet conditions. Best bloom in full sun. Deer-resistant.Pages: 114, **117**.

Clethra alnifoli
SUMMERSWEET

Cercis canadensis

REDBUD. A small deciduous tree native to the Northeast and surrounding region. Clusters of bright pink-purple flowers line the twigs in midspring, before the leaves unfold. Heart-shaped leaves are medium green all summer and turn gold in fall. Tolerates partial shade and grows in any well-drained soil. Available with single or multiple trunks. Grows quickly, so it's reasonable to start with a small plant. Prune every summer, removing limbs that hang too low and dead twigs that accumulate inside the crown. May reach 20 to 25 ft. tall and wide. Pages: 20, **23**.

Chamaecyparis pisifera 'Boulevard'

'BOULEVARD' DWARF FALSE CYPRESS. A slow-growing conifer with soft-textured blue foliage. Grows naturally into a narrow cone but can be sheared for extra neatness if you choose. Prefers partial sun and moist, well-drained soil. Buy the largest plant you can afford to start with because it grows only a few inches a year. Takes decades to grow larger than 10 ft. tall, 5 ft. wide. Pages: 37, 59.

Chrysanthemum x *superbum* 'Alaska'

'ALASKA' SHASTA DAISY. A popular perennial with large daisy blossoms on stalks 2 ft. tall, good for bouquets as well as in the garden. Blooms in July. Forms a low mat of glossy foliage that looks good all season. Needs full sun. Cut down the flower stalks after it blooms. Divide every year or two in early spring. Sometimes listed as *Leucanthemum* x *superbum*. Pages: 63, **64**.

Clematis x *jackmanii*

JACKMAN CLEMATIS. A deciduous vine with large velvety blue-purple flowers in summer. Climbs a trellis or support up to 8 ft. tall. Needs full or partial sun and good garden soil amended with a cupful of ground limestone. When planting clematis, dig the hole deep enough to cover the root-ball and base of the stem with about 2 in. of soil. Cut the stem back to the lowest set of healthy leaves to encourage the plant to branch out near the base. Guide the new stems into position, and use twist-ties to secure them to the support. In subsequent years, prune all stems down to 1 ft. tall in spring, just as the buds begin to swell. Pages: 30, **32**, 92.

Clematis terniflora

SWEET AUTUMN CLEMATIS. A deciduous vine that is covered with countless clusters of small fragrant white flowers in September. Self-seeds very freely. Climbs quickly and can reach 25 ft. or higher. Often sold under the name *C. paniculata*. Grow like Jackman clematis. (See above.) Pages: 60, 63, 92, 114, **117**, 118.

Clethra alnifolia

SUMMERSWEET. A deciduous shrub with very sweet-scented white or pink flowers in the heat of August. Glossy dark foliage develops late in spring but looks fresh all summer and turns gold in fall. Very adaptable—tolerates sun or shade, garden or damp soil. Prune each year in early spring, cutting

Campsis radicans TRUMPET CREEPER

Coreopsis verticillata 'Moonbeam'
THREAD-LEAVED COREOPSIS

some of the older stems to ground level and cutting new stems back by one-third. Sends up suckers around the base and gradually forms a patch. Regular summersweet grows 6 to 10 ft. tall and wide (pp. 86, 106). 'Hummingbird' (pp. 38, ***39***) is a dwarf cultivar that grows about 3 to 4 ft. tall and spreads 5 to 8 ft. wide.

Convallaria majalis

LILY-OF-THE-VALLEY. A perennial that forms a patch, with large smooth leaves held in a vertical position and very fragrant nodding white flowers in spring. Prefers a shady site with garden or moist soil. Makes a good ground cover, although in hot, dry years the leaves may wither early, leaving the ground bare until the next spring. Needs no routine care. Can be (but doesn't have to be) divided every few years in spring or summer. May become invasive. Grows about 8 in. tall, spreads indefinitely. Pages: 60, 75, ***77***.

Coreopsis verticillata

THREAD-LEAVED COREOPSIS. A long-blooming perennial that bears hundreds of small daisylike blossoms in July and August and into September. 'Moonbeam' (pp. 23, 25, 45, 72, 92, 102, 121) has lemon yellow flowers. 'Zagreb' (pp. 104, ***105***) has gold flowers. The dark-green leaves are short and threadlike. Spreads to form a patch but isn't invasive. Needs full sun. Grows about 18 in. tall and wide.

Cornus alba

SIBERIAN DOGWOOD. A deciduous shrub with stems that turn bright red in winter, white flowers in spring, pale-blue berries in late summer, and crimson foliage in autumn. Forms a vase-shaped clump with many erect or arching stems. 'Sibirica' (pp. 124, ***127***) is a popular cultivar that has especially vivid bark in winter. 'Elegantissima' (pp. 33, 41, ***42***, 95) has pretty bark in winter and variegated green-and-white leaves in summer. If these are unavailable, other cultivars are good substitutes. Needs full or partial sun, garden or moist soil. Cut all the stems down close to the ground every few years (or every year, if you want to) in early spring. After a few weeks, the plant will send up vigorous new shoots. These young shoots develop the brightest-colored bark. Grows 6 to 8 ft. tall and 8 to 12 ft. wide.

Cornus mas 'Golden Glory'
CORNELIAN CHERRY DOGWOOD

Cornus mas 'Golden Glory'

'GOLDEN GLORY' CORNELIAN CHERRY DOGWOOD. A small deciduous tree with fluffy yellow flowers in early spring (even earlier than forsythia), edible red berries in late summer, and crimson foliage in late fall. Grows narrowly upright, reaching about 20 ft. tall and 12 to 15 ft. wide. Takes sun or shade, any garden soil. Needs only minimal routine pruning. Pages: 32, 106.

Cotoneaster apiculatus

CRANBERRY COTONEASTER. A deciduous shrub with low, spreading limbs. Grows only 1 to 3 ft. tall, spreads 4 to 6 ft. wide. Small glossy leaves appear in early spring and turn bright red before dropping in fall. Dainty pale-pink flowers mature into red berries that last until November. Needs full or partial sun and fertile, well-drained soil. Prune as desired to control size and shape. Pages: 23, 72, **73**, 85, 90.

Cotoneaster apiculatus
CRANBERRY COTONEASTER

Cotoneaster dammeri 'Lowfast'

'LOWFAST' COTONEASTER. A low shrub that grows sideways and makes a good ground cover, dotted with red berries in late summer and fall. Stays under 1 ft. tall but spreads several feet wide. Small glossy leaves are evergreen through mild winters. Not hardy in northern or western New England; substitute cranberry cotoneaster there. Grow like cranberry cotoneaster. (See previous page.) Page: 37.

Crataegus phaenopyrum

WASHINGTON HAWTHORN. A small deciduous tree with white flowers in late spring, red foliage in fall, and small red berries that attract birds in winter. Birds also nest in this tree because its thorny twigs provide safety from predators. Prefers full sun and well-drained soil. Pages: 54, ***55***, 106.

Daphne x *burkwoodii* 'Carol Mackie'

'CAROL MACKIE' DAPHNE. A small, slow-growing, rounded shrub with lovely variegated green-and-white foliage that looks good all year, plus clusters of deliciously fragrant pale flowers in May. Needs well-drained soil and prefers partial shade. Try not to disturb the thick fleshy roots when planting it, and be sure not to plant it too deep. Once established, needs no pruning or routine care. Gradually reaches 3 ft. tall, 3 to 5 ft. wide. Pages: 98, ***101***.

Dendranthema x *grandiflorum* 'Sheffield'

'SHEFFIELD' CHRYSANTHEMUM, 'SHEFFIELD' DAISY. A hardy chrysanthemum that bears single pink daisylike flowers for almost two months in the fall. Soft, gray-green, aromatic foliage is quietly attractive throughout the summer. Forms a rounded clump 2 to 3 ft. tall, 3 to 4 ft. wide. Needs full sun and garden soil. Leave bloom stalks in place over the winter, then cut them down in early spring. A few weeks later, divide the clump and replant the most vigorous-looking shoots. (Nurseries often sell these chrysanthemums under their former name, *Chrysanthemum* x *morifolium*.) Pages: 26, ***29***.

Dianthus 'Bath's Pink'

'BATH'S PINK' DIANTHUS. A low-growing perennial with very fragrant flowers resembling small pink carnations in June. The grassy blue-green evergreen foliage forms a dense mat a few inches tall and 1 to 3 ft. wide. Needs full sun and well-drained soil. After it blooms, shear off the flower stalks and cut the leaves back halfway. Shear foliage again in early spring. Divide every few years. Pages: ***122,*** 123.

Dicentra

BLEEDING HEART. Perennials that form rounded clumps of soft-textured lacy foliage, topped with heart-shaped flowers that dangle from delicate stalks. They grow 2 to 3 ft. tall and wide, and bloom from late spring until fall. Keep removing the old faded flowers to the base. Fringed bleeding heart, *D. eximia* (pp. 109, 116, ***117***), has pale-pink flowers. 'Luxuriant' (pp. ***46,*** 47, 56, 100) has rose-red flowers. Both need partial shade and fertile, moist, well-drained soil. Divide every few years in spring or fall.

Echinacea purpurea

PURPLE CONEFLOWER. A prairie wildflower that thrives in gardens and blooms for several weeks in July and August. Large pink daisylike blossoms are held on stiff branching stalks above a basal mound of dark green foliage. Needs full sun. Cut back flower stalk, or let the seed heads ripen for winter interest and birds. Numerous, new named hybrids in assorted flower colors. May self-sow but isn't weedy. Grows about 3 ft. tall, 2 ft. wide. Pages: 49, ***51***, 72, ***73***, 92, 108, 119.

Euonymus alatus 'Compactus'

COMPACT BURNING BUSH. A deciduous shrub with unusually colorful fall foliage, turning from green in midsummer to coppery in September and vivid crimson in October. Grows naturally into a neat sphere of layered branches. Needs full sun or partial shade to produce its color, adapts to almost any soil. Carefree. Eventually reaches 6 ft. tall and wide but can be sheared to keep it smaller if you choose. Considered invasive in some places. Pages: 21, 23, 67, ***69***, 72.

Euonymus fortunei 'Emerald Gaiety'

'EMERALD GAIETY' WINTER CREEPER, EUONYMUS. An evergreen that can be trained as a low shrub, ground cover, or climbing vine. Its rounded leaves have white markings that turn pinkish in winter. It grows slowly, forming a mounded shrub at least 3 ft. tall and wide and sometimes climbing up a tree or fence. Tolerates sun or shade, any well-drained soil. Shear or prune at any time to control size or shape. Where deer are a problem, plant pachysandra or myrtle instead of euonymus. Pages: 45, ***46***, 112.

Recommended ferns

Adiantum pedatum, Maidenhair fern
Spreads slowly, forming a continuous patch of lacy-textured deciduous fronds. Grows 1 to 2 ft. tall, spreads 2 to 3 ft. wide. Pages: 109, ***109***, 110.

Athyrium goeringianum 'Pictum', Japanese painted fern
A colorful fern that forms rosettes of finely cut fronds marked in shades of green, silver, and maroon. They look almost iridescent. Deciduous. Grows about 1 ft. tall, 2 ft. wide. Pages: 56, ***58***.

Dryopteris marginalis, Marginal wood fern
A native fern with glossy, evergreen, finely divided fronds. Forms clumps about 2 to 3 ft. tall, 1 ft. wide. Pages: 90, 109, 116.

Matteuccia struthiopteris, Ostrich fern
An especially luxurious fern that forms large clumps of bright-green deciduous fronds. Needs moist soil or it will turn yellow and go dormant before the end of summer. Grows 3 to 5 ft. tall; over time, spreads to form a patch 3 to 5 ft. wide. Pages: 82, 115, ***117***.

Osmunda cinnamomea, Cinnamon fern
A native fern that forms erect clumps of finely divided deciduous fronds. Needs moist soil. Pages: 100, 109, 110, 115, ***117***. *O. claytoniana*, interrupted fern, looks similar but tolerates drier sites. Both species grow 3 to 4 ft. tall, 2 ft. wide.

Polystichum acrostichoides, Christmas fern
A native fern with glossy evergreen fronds. New fronds are held upright in summer but flop down onto the ground in winter. Grows about 2 ft. tall and wide. Pages: 110, ***113***.

Dryopteris marginalis
MARGINAL WOOD FERN

Euonymus kiautschovicus 'Manhattan'

'MANHATTAN' EUONYMUS. An evergreen shrub with thick, glossy, rounded, medium-green leaves and small but showy pink-and-orange fruits that ripen in the fall. Tolerates sun or shade, any well-drained soil. Grows natually as an upright shrub, reaching about 6 ft. tall and 4 ft. wide, but can be sheared, pruned, or trained as you choose. Substitute mountain laurel in northern and western New England, where 'Manhattan' is not hardy, and wherever deer are a problem. Pages: 28, 91.

Euphorbia polychroma

CUSHION SPURGE. A perennial that's attractive all season. Forms a dome-shaped clump 1 to 2 ft. tall and wide, topped with bright-yellow flowers in spring. Leaves turn red in fall. Needs full or partial sun. Cut the stems back partway after it blooms to keep the clump compact and tidy. Pages: 49, 80, ***83***.

Ferns

Ferns are carefree, long-lived perennials for shady sites. Despite their delicate appearance, they're among the most durable and trouble-free plants you can grow. Almost all ferns need shade from the midday and afternoon sun. They grow best in soil that's been amended with extra organic matter. You can divide them every few years in early spring if you want more plants, or can leave them alone. See the box above for more information on specific ferns.

Festuca ovina var. *glauca*

BLUE FESCUE GRASS. A neat, compact grass that forms a dense tuft of hair-thin, blue-green leaves. Slender flower spikes appear in early summer and soon turn tan. 'Sea Urchin' is a popular cultivar with especially blue-colored foliage. Needs full sun and well-drained soil. Cut old foliage to the ground in late winter. Divide every few years in early spring. Grows about 1 ft. tall and wide. Pages: 26, ***29***.

Forsythia x *intermedia* 'Northern Sun'

'NORTHERN SUN' FORSYTHIA. A deciduous shrub beloved for its bright-yellow flowers in April. Most forsythias are damaged in severely cold winters, but 'Northern Sun' is hardy throughout New England. Also, it doesn't grow too fast and stays under 8 ft. tall and wide. Other forsythias get much larger and need frequent pruning to keep them under control. Full sun. Carefree. Pages: 124, ***127***.

Euonymus kiautschovicus 'Manhattan'
EUONYMUS

Gaillardia x *grandiflora* 'Goblin'

'GOBLIN' BLANKETFLOWER. A perennial prairie wildflower with cheerful red-and-yellow flowers all summer long. Needs full sun and well-drained soil. Remove old flowers to the topmost leaf as they fade. Forms a clump about 1 ft. high and wide. Divide every year or two in early spring. Pages: 45, **46**, 88.

Galium odoratum

SWEET WOODRUFF. A deciduous perennial ground cover that spreads quickly, needs no care, and lasts for decades. Fine-textured foliage is bright green throughout the growing season, then turns beige or tan in late fall. Thousands of tiny white flowers sparkle above the fresh new foliage in May. Adapts to most soils, prefers partial or full shade. Shear or mow close to the ground in early spring and rake away the old foliage. Easily divided in spring or fall to make more plants for other spots. Buy just a few plants to start with and you'll have all you want in a year or two. Grows about 6 in. tall, spreads indefinitely. Pages: **58**, 59, 106.

Geranium macrorrhizum

BIGROOT GERANIUM. A short, compact perennial that forms bushy clumps of fragrant semievergreen foliage, with magenta or pink flowers in June. Grows about 12 in. tall, 18 to 24 in. wide, and makes a good ground cover. Prefers partial shade and well-drained soil. Divide clumps every few years in spring or late summer. Page: 23, **23**.

Gypsophila paniculata
BABY'S BREATH

Geranium sanguineum var. *striatum*

BLOODY CRANESBILL. A perennial that forms a low mound or mat of small, very finely cut leaves, topped with pale-pink flowers in May and June. Stays under 1 ft. tall but can spread 2 ft. wide. Prefers full sun and well-drained soil. Divide every few years in spring or late summer. This plant is often sold under the cultivar name 'Lancastriense'. Pages: 98, **101**.

Gypsophila paniculata

BABY'S BREATH. A showy perennial that forms a vase-shaped or domelike clump 3 ft. tall and wide. Its fine-textured twiggy stems are covered with thousands of bright white flowers in summer. Needs full sun and deep, fertile, well-drained soil. Amend the planting hole by mixing in a cupful of ground limestone. Cut stalks to the ground in fall or spring. Pages: 49, 65.

Hedera helix

ENGLISH IVY. An aggressive evergreen vine that trails attractively over the rim of a container. 'Baltica' has large green leaves and may survive the winter outdoors in its container. 'Glacier' has smaller leaves mottled with green, gray, and white. It is less likely to survive the winter, so treat it as an annual. Both need full or partial shade in summer and protection from the winter sun. Pages: 112, **113**.

Helictotrichon sempervirens

BLUE OAT GRASS. A clump-forming grass with thin, wiry, pale-blue evergreen leaves. Blooms sparsely, with thin flower spikes that turn beige or tan. Needs full sun and well-drained or dry soil. Do not cut down in spring; simply comb your fingers through the clump to pull out any loose, dead leaves. Old clumps may die out in the middle; if they do so, divide them in early spring. Grows 18 to 24 in. tall and wide. Pages: 41, **42**, 49, 104.

Heliopsis helianthoides 'Summer Sun'

'SUMMER SUN' FALSE SUNFLOWER. A carefree perennial wildflower with large gold flowers for several weeks in August and September. Forms an erect clump about 3 to 5 ft. tall. Prefers full sun. Remove spent flowers to promote continued bloom. Divide every few years in spring. Pages: 98, **101**.

Helleborus orientalis

Lenten rose. A clump-forming perennial with dark leathery evergreen leaves and clusters of pink, rose, white, or greenish flowers that last for weeks in April and May. Needs partial shade and rich, well-drained soil. Grows slowly but self-sows and gradually spreads to form a patch. Individual plants grow 1 to 2 ft. tall and 2 to 3 ft. wide. Pages: 56, ***58***, 110.

Hemerocallis

Daylily. Some of the most reliable and popular perennials, with large lilylike flowers in summer, held above dense clumps or patches of grassy arching leaves. The common roadside daylily has orange flowers for about two weeks in July, but cultivated kinds come in many other colors and bloom for a longer season. Each bloom lasts only one day. There are many daylily nurseries scattered around the Northeast; watch for ads in local or regional papers. Go to the nursery in summer when the plants are in bloom, and choose the colors and types you want (pp. 37, 43, 49, 102, 104, ***105***). 'Stella d'Oro' (pp. 25, 68, 80, 98) is special because it bears gold flowers from early June until October on stalks 18 to 24 in. tall. Most daylilies are odorless, but 'Hyperion' (pp. 54, ***55***, 119) has sweet-scented pale- yellow flowers in late July on stalks 40 in. tall. All prefer full sun and garden soil. Cut off flower stalks after blooming is finished. Divide every few years in late summer. When planting, space shorter daylilies about 1 ft. apart, taller kinds 2 ft. apart. Protect from deer.

Heuchera x *brizoides*

Coralbells. A perennial that forms low clumps of almost evergreen foliage and blooms for most of the summer, bearing sprays of tiny pink, rose, coral, or white flowers on slender stalks 18 in. tall. Prefers full sun and moist, well-drained soil. Remove flower stalks as the blossoms fade. Cut last year's leaves to the ground in early spring. Divide every few years, and contrary to normal rules, replant the divisions an inch or two deeper than they were growing before. Pages: 56, ***58***, 79, 102.

Heuchera micrantha 'Palace Purple'

'Palace Purple' heuchera. A clumping perennial with dark bronzy purple leaves, shaped like maple leaves, and sprays of tiny white flowers in summer. Grows about 1 ft. tall and wide. Looks best in partial shade, because the leaves tend to scorch or fade if exposed to too much sun. Grow like coralbells. (See above.) Pages: 47, 75, ***77***.

Hibiscus syriacus

Rose-of-Sharon. A deciduous shrub with large hollyhock-like flowers from late July through mid-September. 'Blue Bird' (pp. 104, ***105***) has violet-blue flowers. 'Diana' (pp. ***64***, 65) has pure-white flowers. Grows 8 to 10 ft. tall, 6 to 8 ft. wide. Needs full sun. Prune in early spring by cutting some of the oldest stems down to the ground. Japanese beetles chew on the flowers in midsummer but less so as the weather cools off. Their damage looks ugly but doesn't really hurt the plant.

Native vs. Invasive Plants

A native plant is one that occurs naturally and has existed for many years in an area. These plants can be trees, flowers, grasses, or any other plant. It is adapted to the climate and soil of the region over millennia and is in sync with the needs of specific flora and fauna, especially pollinators. Native plants provide food and shelter for countless native birds, butterflies, pollinators, and other animals. That is not to say that a particular native plant cannot grow in other areas or under different conditions. Often, they are grown in different regions, ideally with similar climates and soil conditions. As gardeners, it is important to grow plants native to our region to mitigate storm runoff and flooding, as well as natural erosion.

Invasive plant species usually refer to non-native plants that have become out of control. By contrast, native plants that spread widely, including the seed-spreading brown-eyed Susan (Rudbeckia trifolia), are mostly called "nuisance" plants, although the result is more-or-less the same. Both spread rapidly by underground runners, running stems above ground, or by releasing copious amounts of wind-borne seed. Non-native invasives often may have escaped from gardens or parks where they were planted as interesting ornamentals. In time they overrun huge areas and crowd out native plants that have evolved as food for native birds and pollinators. Major examples include Japanese barberry, sweet autumn clematis, English ivy, multiflora roses, some honeysuckles, Japanese knotweed, garlic mustard, Japanese wisteria, and Oriental bittersweet.

To clear out invasives, be sure to remove the plants, root and all; this is not always easy, especially on deep-rooted species. Cut your lawn grass before the plants go to seed. Likewise, any plants that have become a nuisance and are blooming should be cut before the seeds scatter. Routine deadheading is critical. Potentially invasive plants, such as beebalm, mint, and some ornamental grasses, are often planted inside a bottomless container to corral the roots.

Hosta

HOSTA. Hostas are long-lived, carefree, shade-tolerant perennials with beautiful leaves in a wide variety of colors and sizes. The plants can be small or large. They form dome-shaped clumps or spreading patches of foliage that looks good from spring to fall and dies down in winter. Stalks of lavender, purple, or white flowers appear in mid- to late summer. Some hostas tolerate full sun, but most grow better in partial or full shade. All need fertile, moist, well-drained soil. Cut off flower stalks before seedpods ripen. Clumps can be divided every few years in early spring if you want to make more plants; otherwise, leave them alone. Where deer are a problem, plant astilbe, heuchera, Lenten rose, or ferns instead of hostas. See box at left for more information on specific hostas.

Recommended hostas

Hosta sieboldiana 'Elegans'

Large, round, puckered leaves are blue-gray. Forms a large specimen 2 to 3 ft. tall, 4 to 6 ft. wide. Pages: 56, 110.

'Royal Standard' hosta

Leaves are medium green. Large white flowers have a sweet aroma. Forms a leafy mound under 2 ft. tall, about 3 ft. wide. Pages: 77, **77**, 82. If space is restricted, try 'Halcyon', which forms a low mound 1 ft. tall and 2 ft. wide, with powder blue leaves in spring changing to darker blue-green in summer.

Variegated hostas

Many hostas have leaves with white or gold stripes down the middle or around the leaf edges. Good larger cultivars (pp. 95, 112), growing about 2 ft. tall and 2 to 3 ft. wide, are *H. fortunei* 'Aureo-marginata' and 'Wide Brim' hosta, both with dark-green leaves edged with gold or yellow bands. 'Antioch' (pp. ***113***) and 'Francee' are similar in size but have white leaf edges. Two popular smaller hostas are 'Ginko Craig' (pp. 75, 110), which has slender green leaves with a thin white border, and *H. undulata* 'Variegata', which has broad wavy-edged leaves with green and white stripes. Both grow about 1 ft. tall and wide.

Hosta sieboldiana 'Elegans' HOSTA

Hydrangea petiolaris

CLIMBING HYDRANGEA. A long-lived vine that has a thick trunk with peeling bark, large glossy leaves that open in early spring and don't drop until late fall, and lacy clusters of white flowers in June. Clings to a tree or wall and climbs by itself. Tolerates sun or shade; prefers moist, well-drained soil. Grows slowly for the first few years, then climbs several feet a year, eventually reaching 40 ft. or more. Needs no pruning, but you can cut it back if it goes too far. Pages: 82, ***83***.

Iberis sempervirens

EVERGREEN CANDYTUFT. A bushy perennial that forms a low or sprawling mound of slender glossy evergreen foliage, topped for several weeks in May or June with clusters of bright-white flowers. 'Snowflake' is a popular cultivar with larger-than-average flowers. Needs full or partial sun, well-drained soil. Shear off the top half of the plants after they bloom. Needs no other care. Don't try to divide candytuft; buy new plants if you want more. Stays under 1 ft. tall, spreads 2 to 3 ft. wide. Pages: 21, 121, ***122***.

Ilex crenata

JAPANESE HOLLY. A compact shrub with dense twiggy growth and small evergreen leaves, good for formal specimens, hedges, and foundation plantings. Some cultivars, like 'Hoogendorn' or 'Soft Touch,' spread wider than tall, others grow upright and conical; ask your nursery for help in choosing plants that are suitable for your design. Adapts to full sun or partial shade, needs well-drained soil. Can be pruned or sheared to shape as you choose, or not at all. Can't survive severe winters, so substitute compact inkberry holly in northern New England. Pages: 21, 37, 60, 126.

Ilex glabra

INKBERRY HOLLY. A native holly that's hardy throughout New England, with small glossy evergreen leaves and inconspicuous black berries. The wild-type plants (p. 106) grow 6 ft. or taller and sometimes get leggy at the base. 'Compacta' (pp. 28, 76, 114, 124) stays under 6 ft. and grows round and bushy. Adapts to sun or shade, garden or moist soil. Prune or shear in late winter to control size and shape, if desired.

Ilex x *meserveae* 'China Girl' and 'China Boy'

'CHINA GIRL' AND 'CHINA BOY' HOLLIES. Dense bushy shrubs with glossy evergreen leaves that have a few spines around the edge. If pollinated, 'China Girl' bears big crops of red berries that last all winter. Both plants grow fairly slowly but can reach 8 to 10 ft. tall and wide. They need full or partial sun and well-drained soil. Prune in late winter to control size and shape, if desired. Pages: ***32***, 33.

Ilex verticillata 'Sparkleberry'

'SPARKLEBERRY' WINTERBERRY HOLLY. A deciduous shrub with many twiggy stems and soft spineless leaves. This hybrid female cultivar bears clusters of small bright-red berries that ripen in September and last until the birds eat them. 'Sunset' and 'Winter Red' are other good female cultivars. To get berries, there has to be a male plant, such as 'Apollo', 'Early Male', or 'Southern Gentleman', within 200 yd. Adapts to sun or shade, garden or damp soil. Rather slow-growing, so start with the largest, fullest plants you can find. Prune only to remove dead or damaged shoots. Eventually reaches 8 to 12 ft. high, depending on site, and usually spreads wider than tall. Pages: 85, 126, ***127***.

Ilex crenata 'Hetzii' JAPANESE HOLLY

Ilex glabra
INKBERRY HOLLY

Ilex crenata 'Compacta'
JAPANESE HOLLY

Recommended junipers

Juniperus chinensis, Chinese juniper
This is typically an upright shrub or small tree with fine-textured green or gray-green foliage. It can be sheared into formal shapes. For that purpose, choose a plant that's already been shaped by the nursery and ask their advice on how to maintain it. Pages: **122**, 123.

J. chinensis, 'Maney' juniper
A vase-shaped shrub about 6 ft. tall and wide, with prickly foliage. Page: 79.

J. chinensis, 'Sea Green' juniper
A compact, vase-shaped shrub with arching limbs, usually about 4 ft. tall, 6 ft. wide. Page: 24.

_J. c._ var. _sargentii_, Sargent juniper
A low evergreen shrub, usually grown as a ground cover, that forms a patch of short upright stems. Regular Sargent juniper has dark-green foliage (p. 119). 'Glauca' (pp. 37, **39**) has a blue-green color. Grows 1 to 2 ft. tall, 3 ft. or more wide.

J. horizontalis, 'Blue Chip' juniper
A low, spreading juniper with blue-gray or blue-green foliage. Forms a mound about 1 ft. tall, 4 ft. wide. If it is unavailable, 'Bar Harbor' is a good substitute. Page: 51.

J. procumbens 'Nana', Dwarf creeping juniper
A creeping juniper that forms an irregular mound of prickly bright-green foliage. Stays under 1 ft. tall but can spread several feet wide. Pages: 21, **23**, 30.

J. sabina, 'Arcadia' juniper
A low, spreading shrub, 12 to 18 in. tall and 3 to 4 ft. wide, with scaly, bright-green foliage. Page: 35.

J. sabina, 'Broadmoor' juniper
A low spreading shrub that forms a flat mound of feathery gray-green foliage. Grows 1 to 2 ft. tall, can reach 8 to 10 ft. wide. Page: 79.

J. scopulorum, 'Skyrocket' juniper
A narrow, upright shrub, 10 to 15 ft. tall but only 2 ft. wide at the base, wth blue-green foliage. Page: 60.

J. scopulorum, 'Wichita Blue' juniper
A slow-growing upright juniper that forms a cone of silvery blue foliage dotted with blue berries in fall and winter. Eventually can reach 20 ft. tall, 6 ft. wide. Page: 26.

J. squamata, 'Blue Star' juniper
A small, slow-growing juniper that makes an irregular mound of sparkling blue, prickly textured foliage. Reaches 1 to 2 ft. tall, 2 to 4 ft. wide after several years. Pages: 26, 30, 41, **42**, 104.

J. virginiana, Eastern red cedar
An upright juniper that grows wild in abandoned fields and pastures. 'Canaertii' and 'Keteleeri' are desirable cultivars with attractive foliage that keeps its green color in winter (unlike wild trees, which turn a dirty brown in winter). Both reach 12 to 15 ft. or taller. Protect from deer. Pages: 110, **113**.

Iris sibirica
SIBERIAN IRIS. A perennial that forms a large arching clump of tall slender leaves. Blooms for a few weeks in June. 'Caesar's Brother' (p. 65, 95, **97**, 102) has dark blue-purple flowers. 'Orville Fay' (p. 100) has especially large sky blue flowers. Other kinds have pale-blue or white flowers. Needs full or partial sun and moist, fertile, well-drained soil. Remove flower stalks after the blooms fade, or let the seedpods develop if you like their looks. Divide large clumps every few years in late summer. Grows 2 to 3 ft. tall, 2 to 4 ft. wide.

Juniperus
JUNIPER. A large group of shrubs and trees with scaly or needlelike evergreen foliage, often quite fragrant, and small berrylike fruits. All need full sun and well-drained soil. They rarely require pruning, but they can be pruned or sheared if you want to control their size or shape. Subject to various insects and diseases but generally carefree. See box at left for more information on specific junipers.

Kalmia latifolia
MOUNTAIN LAUREL. A native shrub with smooth evergreen leaves and very showy clusters of white, pale-pink, or rosy flowers in June. (The cultivar pictured on this page has bright-red flower buds, too.) Adapts to shade but blooms much more profusely in partial or full sun; needs moist, well-drained soil. Snap off flower stalks as soon as the petals drop (if you let the seedpods form, the plant will bloom only every other year). Prune at the

Kalmia latifolia 'Ostbo Red' MOUNTAIN LAUREL

same time. Normally reaches 10 ft. tall and wide after many years. Some of the new cultivars, which have brighter-colored flowers, are more compact plants and get only about 6 ft. tall. Pages: 56, 100, 106, 110, 114, 126.

Lamium maculatum 'White Nancy'

'WHITE NANCY' LAMIUM. A creeping perennial that forms low mats of foliage that looks good from early spring until late fall. Heart-shaped leaves are silver with a thin green band around the edge. Clusters of white flowers bloom in early summer. 'Beacon Silver' is a good substitute that has pink flowers. Prefers partial shade and garden or moist soil. Cut off flower stalks after it blooms. Divide every few years in spring or fall. Under 6 in. tall but spreads to 2 ft. or wider. Pages: ***46***, 47, 112.

Lavandula angustifolia 'Munstead'

'MUNSTEAD' ENGLISH LAVENDER. A small shrub that freezes back partway and is treated more like an annual where winters are cold. Forms a bushy mound about 1 ft. tall and 2 ft. wide. Fragrant silver-gray foliage is topped in July with countless long-stalked spikes of very fragrant pale lavender flowers. Needs full sun and well-drained soil. Shear off the tops of the plants in early May, removing any frozen stems. Shear flower stalks even with the foliage when the flower petals fade. Not hardy in northern and western New England, but you can buy little plants each spring and treat it as an annual there. Pages: 49, 80, 87, 98, ***101***.

Liatris spicata

BLAZING STAR. A perennial prairie wildflower that blooms in late July and August, with dense spikes of small flowers on stiff stalks about 3 ft. tall, arising from a clump or tuft of grassy dark-green foliage. Needs full sun. Typically has purple flowers (p. 108), but a few cultivars, such as 'Floristan White', have white flowers (p. 102). 'Kobold' (pp. 49, 72, ***73***, 98, ***101***) has magenta flowers and is about 2 ft. tall. Cut off the flower stalks after it blooms. Plant corms in fall. Needs no other care.

Lilium

HYBRID LILY. There are hundreds of wonderful lily cultivars, all with large flowers on leafy stalks ranging from 2 to 6 ft. tall (p. 102). Flower colors include white, yellow, gold, orange, pink, red, and magenta. Different kinds bloom in sequence from June through late August. 'Casablanca' (p. 63) is a favorite with large, flat, sweet-scented, clear-white flowers on stalks 3 to 4 ft. tall in August. 'Stargazer' (p. 72) flowers are dark crimson-pink edged with white on stalks 2 to 3 ft. tall. All lilies prefer full sun and deep, fertile, well-drained soil. Plant bulbs when they are available in late fall or early spring, burying them about 6 in. deep. Lilies multiply slowly and can remain in the same place for years (unless they get eaten by deer, voles, woodchucks, or other varmints). Sprinkle some bulb fertilizer on the soil each fall. May need to be staked.

Liriope muscari 'Silvery Sunproof'

'SILVERY SUNPROOF' LILYTURF. A perennial that forms clumps of grasslike evergreen leaves marked with lengthwise white stripes. Bears spikes of small violet flowers in late summer. Clumps grow about 1 ft. tall and wide. Prefers partial sun or shade. Mow or shear off old foliage in early spring. If unavailable, 'Variegata' is a good substitute. Not hardy in northern and western New England; substitute a small variegated hosta there. Pages: 121, ***122***.

Lonicera x *heckrottii*

GOLDFLAME HONEYSUCKLE. A woody vine that grows fast enough to make an impressive display in just a few years but is not aggressive and will not take over your garden. It climbs about 10 ft. high. Leafs out in early spring, grows all summer, and doesn't freeze back until early winter. Blooms heavily in late spring and fall, off and on all summer, with clusters of pink-and-yellow flowers that smell sweet on warm nights. Needs full or partial sun. Prune young plants hard, repeating two or three times the first year if needed to encourage lots of branching near the base. Prune older plants once a year in late winter. Pages: ***64,*** 65.

Lilium 'Casablanca'
HYBRID LILY

Magnolia

MAGNOLIA. Star magnolia, *M. stellata* (pp. 30, 67, **69**), is a deciduous small tree or shrub that's covered with fresh white flowers in early spring, before the leaves appear. It grows slowly, eventually reaching up to 15 ft. tall and wide. 'Dr. Merrill' magnolia, *M.* x *loebneri* (pp. 114, **117**), has similar flowers but grows much faster and reaches 25 to 30 ft. tall and wide. Both need full or partial sun and well-drained soil. Plant in spring. Prune in early summer, removing only weak or crossing limbs.

Malus

CRAB APPLE. 'Centurion' (p. 67, **69**) is neat, upright deciduous tree with rosy pink flowers in May, foliage that stays healthy all summer, and small red fruits that ripen in early fall and last all winter unless consumed by birds. Grows about 20 ft. tall, 15 ft. wide. Needs full sun. Prune off any suckers that sprout from the base of the tree and any shoots that grow straight up. 'Pink Spires' (p. 78) grows about 25 ft. tall and has lavendar-pink flowers, purple-red fruits, and foliage tinged with red.

Malva alcea 'Fastigiata'

HOLLYHOCK MALLOW. A perennial that blooms abundantly in midsummer, with dozens of erect flower stalks bearing hundreds of clear-pink hollyhock-like flowers. In spring and fall, it forms a low mound of medium green foliage. Needs full or partial sun. Cut flower stalks to the ground after it blooms. Often self-sows but isn't weedy. Grows about 3 to 4 ft. tall, 2 to 3 ft. wide. Pages: 63, **64**, 79.

Miscanthus sinensis
'Gracillimus'
JAPANESE SILVER GRASS

Miscanthus

JAPANESE SILVER GRASS, MAIDENGRASS. A showy grass that forms vase-shaped or rounded clumps of long arching leaves. Blooms in late summer or fall and has fluffy seed heads that last through the winter (p. 109). 'Gracillimus' (pp. 30, 41, 73, 115) has very narrow leaves with a white stripe up the middle. 'Variegatus' (pp. 102, **105**) has wider leaves with white along the edge. Miscanthus need full sun. Cut old leaves and stalks close to the ground in late winter or early spring. Divide clumps in early spring every few years. May seed about.

Monarda didyma

BEE BALM, MONARDA. A spreading perennial that forms a patch of erect stems topped with moplike clusters of bright-colored flowers that attract hummingbirds. Blooms in midsummer. Common bee balm (p. 108) has scarlet flowers. 'Marshall's Delight' (pp. **64,** 65, 79, 119), a hybrid, has pink flowers. Adapts to sun or shade but needs fertile, moist, well-drained soil. Cut old stalks to the ground in fall. Divide the plants every few years in early spring. Good mildew resistance.

Myrica pensylvanica

BAYBERRY. A deciduous native shrub with an irregular mounded profile, wider than tall. Fragrant leaves develop late in spring but are glossy green all summer, turn maroon or purple in fall, and last partway into the winter. Small, waxy, silver-gray berries form along the stems of female plants. Adapts to almost any soil, in sun or shade. Doesn't need pruning or regular care. Unpruned, plants may grow 8 to 10 ft. tall and wide. Pages: 38, **39**.

Nepeta x *faassenii*

CATMINT. A perennial that forms a bushy mound of soft gray foliage topped with spikes of small violet-blue flowers. Blooms most in early summer but continues or repeats throughout the season. Needs full sun and well-drained soil. Shear plants back halfway after the first blooming to keep them tidy and to promote new growth. Cut to the ground in late fall or winter. May self-sow. 'Dropmore' (pp. 121, **122**) grows about 2 ft. tall and wide; if it is unavailable, 'Blue Wonder' (p. 35) is a good substitute. 'Six Hills Giant' grows 3 ft. tall and wide (pp. 30, 43). 'Walker's Low' grows 2 to 2.5 ft. tall and 1.5 ft. wide.

Nepeta x *faassenii* 'Six Hills Giant' CATMINT

Nymphaea

WATER LILY. There are two main groups of water lilies: tropical and hardy. Tropical water lilies need hot summers and don't thrive in the Northeast. Hardy water lilies survive outdoors from year to year. They bloom in midsummer, in shades of white, yellow, and pink. Water lilies need full sun. (See p. 169 for a discussion of planting water lilies.) Pages: 95, ***97***.

Oenothera missouriensis

MISSOURI EVENING PRIMROSE. A perennial with sprawling stems, good for the front of a border or edge of a raised bed. Forms a patch about 8 in. tall, 2 ft. wide. It bears big yellow flowers day after day from late June through August and has glossy foliage all growing season. Needs full sun. Carefree. Pages: 45, 49, 96, ***97***.

Pachysandra terminalis

PACHYSANDRA. A tough, adaptable ground cover with glossy evergreen leaves. Creeps slowly to form dense patches. Prefers partial shade or shade, well-drained soil. Does well under and around trees and shrubs. Plant rooted cuttings in spring or fall, spaced four cuttings per square foot. Grows about 8 in. tall. Pages: 21, ***32***, 33.

Paeonia

PEONY. A long-lived perennial that forms a bushy clump of many stems, with spectacular large, fragrant, white, pink, or rosy flowers in June and dark glossy foliage that turns purple or gold before it dies down in fall. 'Sarah Bernhardt' (pp. 26, ***29***) is an old favorite with big pink double flowers. Needs full sun and deep, well-drained, fertile soil. Plant in late summer, and position the thick rootstock so the pink buds are no more than 1 in. deep. (If planted too deep, peonies may not bloom.) Established clumps are typically 2 to 3 ft. tall, 3 to 4 ft. wide. Deer resistant.

Panicum virgatum

SWITCHGRASS. Forms a dense upright clump of foliage that is bright green in summer, gold in fall, and tan in winter. Topped with a cloudlike mass of fine-textured flower stalks that are pink when they appear in late summer and fade to tan in winter. Mature clumps stand 4 to 6 ft. tall, 2 to 3 ft. wide. They last well into the winter and aren't knocked over by wind, rain, or snow. Needs full or partial sun and well-drained soil. Cut to the ground in early spring. Divide every few years in spring. Page: 119.

Papaver orientale

ORIENTAL POPPY. A hardy perennial with very large and showy flowers in June on stalks about 3 ft. tall. Old-fashioned poppies were bright orange, but new cultivars come in shades of red or pink also. The large hairy leaves die down in summer. Needs full or partial sun. Plant in late summer or fall. Carefree. Pages: 82, ***83***.

Pennisetum alopecuroides

FOUNTAIN GRASS. A grass that forms a hassocklike clump of arching leaves, green in summer and gold or tan in fall. Blooms over a long season from midsummer to fall, with fluffy spikes on arching stalks. Needs full sun. Cut old leaves to the ground in late winter, or sooner if storms knock them down. Can go many years without being divided but may become invasive. 'Hameln' (pp. 88, 95, 104), a dwarf cultivar, grows about 2 ft. tall, 3 ft. wide. Regular fountain grass (p. 109) gets about 3 ft. tall, 5 ft. wide.

Penstemon digitalis 'Husker Red'

'HUSKER RED' PENSTEMON. A perennial with dark red-purple foliage all season and spikes of small white flowers on 3-ft. stalks in midsummer. Forms erect clumps about 3 ft. tall. Needs full or partial sun. Cut down flower stalks after bloom. Divide every few years in early spring. Pages: 63, ***64***.

Pennisetum alopecuroides 'Hameln' FOUNTAIN GRASS

Phlox subulata
MOSS PHLOX

Phalaris arundinacea 'Picta'

'PICTA' RIBBON GRASS. A fast-growing grass that spreads to form a patch of bright green-and-white striped foliage. Can grow 3 to 4 ft. tall but looks better if you shear it back once or twice during the growing season. Needs full or partial sun; adapts to almost any soil. Ribbon grass is very invasive, so plant it in a bottomless 5-gal. pot. Lift, divide, and replant it every year in early spring. Pages: 95, **97**.

Phlox divaricata

WILD SWEET WILLIAM. A woodland wildflower with pale-blue, white, or blue-purple flowers for several weeks in May and June. Forms a patch a few inches tall and about 2 ft. wide. Small, oval, dark-green leaves are almost evergreen. Needs partial shade and rich, moist, well-drained soil. Divide every few years to expand the patch. Pages: **90**, 91.

Phlox paniculata

GARDEN PHLOX. A perennial with dense clusters of small fragrant flowers atop slender erect stalks in August and September. Forms a clump or patch. 'Bright Eyes' (p. 63) has two-tone pink flowers and grows about 2 ft. tall. 'David' (p. 77, **77**) has pure white flowers and grows 3 to 4 ft. tall. Needs full or partial sun; rich, moist soil is best, but adapts to ordinary garden soil. Cut off flowers after they fade. Divide clumps every few years in spring. Prone to powdery mildew.

Phlox subulata

MOSS PHLOX. A low perennial that forms dense mats of prickly looking evergreen foliage. Pink, magenta, lilac-blue, or white flowers completely cover the leaves for a few weeks in spring. Needs full or partial sun and garden or dry soil. Shear the plants back halfway after they bloom to promote neat, compact growth. Divide every few years in fall or early spring. Grows about 6 in. tall, spreads to form a patch 2 to 3 ft. wide in a few years. Page: 77.

Picea abies 'Nidiformis'

BIRD'S-NEST NORWAY SPRUCE. A dwarf conifer with sharp, dark-green needles. Grows wider than tall, typically reaching about 2 to 3 ft. tall and 3 to 5 ft. wide, and is flat or slightly concave on top. Needs full sun and well-drained soil. Grows slowly, so buy the biggest you can afford to start with. Doesn't need pruning and is otherwise carefree—just keep other plants pulled away so they don't flop onto it. Pages: 50, 88, 98.

Picea glauca 'Conica'

DWARF ALBERTA SPRUCE. A dwarf conifer with close-set pale green needles. Forms a dense cone that gets a few inches taller each year, eventually reaching 8 to 10 ft. or taller. Grow like bird's-nest Norway spruce. (See above.) Pages: 104, 121.

Pieris 'Brouwer's Beauty'

'BROUWER'S BEAUTY' JAPANESE ANDROMEDA. An evergreen shrub, 3 to 5 ft. tall and wide, with neat, glossy foliage, beadlike flower buds that are conspicuous all winter, and spreading clusters of white flowers in June. New leaves are pale yellow-green in summer, darkening to olive green by winter. Needs partial or full shade and rich, moist, well-drained soil. Slow-growing, so buy the biggest plants you can find. Be sure to split and tease apart the roots of container-grown specimens when you plant them. Prune in early summer, removing spent flowers and trimming any wayward shoots. Not reliably hardy in northern and western New England; substitute mountain laurel there. Pages: 28, 38, 88, 127.

Picea abies 'Nidiformis'
BIRD'S-NEST NORWAY SPRUCE

Picea abies 'Conica'
DWARF ALBERTA SPRUCE

Pinus mugo

MUGO PINE. A slow-growing pine that forms an irregular shrubby mound, not a conical tree. Needles are dark green. Needs full sun and well-drained soil. Doesn't need pruning, but you can shear it in early summer, cutting new growth back by less than one-half. Typically grows just a few inches a year, but some plants are faster than others. Usually stays under 3 to 6 ft. tall and 5 to 10 ft. wide for several years. Pages: 88, ***90***.

Pinus strobus

EASTERN WHITE PINE. A native pine, common throughout the Northeast, appreciated for its fast growth and soft blue-green needles. Young trees grow 1 to 2 ft. a year and have a neat "Christmas tree" shape. Mature trees reach up to 80 ft. tall, with a thick trunk and limbs, and distinctive irregular profiles. Needs full sun. Plant in September or as soon as the ground thaws in spring. Damaged by road salt and air pollution but otherwise trouble-free. Pages: 106, ***109***.

Prunus x *cistena*

PURPLELEAF SAND CHERRY. A deciduous shrub with rich red-purple foliage that keeps its color all season. Pale-pink flowers line the stems in spring, just as the leaves expand. Needs full sun for good foliage color, and well-drained soil. Grows 8 to 10 ft. tall and wide or can be kept smaller by pruning. Otherwise carefree. Pages: 85, ***87***.

Pulmonaria saccharata 'Mrs. Moon'

'MRS. MOON' LUNGWORT. A perennial that blooms for many weeks in spring, with masses of tiny pink-and-blue flowers. The large, white-spotted leaves make a good ground cover throughout the summer and fall. Needs partial shade and rich, moist, well-drained soil. Cut off flower stalks when the petals fade. Divide every few years in late summer. Wear gloves when handling this plant because it is covered with prickly hairs. Pages: ***46***, 47, 82, 91.

Rhododendron

RHODODENDRON AND AZALEA. An especially diverse and popular group of shrubs with very showy flowers between early spring and early summer. The leaves can be small or large, deciduous or evergreen. The plants can be short, medium-size, or tall, with spreading, mounded, or erect habits. See box on page 148 for information on specific varieties.

All rhododendrons and azaleas do best with partial shade and need fertile, moist, well-drained soil. Mix a 3-in. layer of peat moss or compost into the soil to prepare a bed for these plants. Plant rhododendrons and azaleas in spring or early fall. Be sure not to plant them too deep—the top of the root-ball should be level with, or a little higher than the surrounding soil. Azaleas are usually sold in containers. When planting them it's very important that you make a few deep cuts down the root-ball and tease apart some of the roots; otherwise typically azaleas do not root well into the surrounding soil. Treat container-grown rhododendrons the same way. Large rhododendron plants are often sold balled-and-burlapped; the roots were cut when the plants were dug and need no further attention. They will grow out through the burlap in time, but if wrapped in plastic or other impervious material, this must be removed.

Use a 2 in. layer of mulch to keep the soil cool and damp around your azaleas and rhododendrons, and water the plants during any dry spell for the first few years. If the site is exposed to winter sun and wind, protect evergreen azaleas and rhododendrons for the first few winters by spraying the leaves with an antitranspirant in late fall or by erecting a burlap cage or plywood A-frame around the plants. Plants on sheltered sites and plants that have had a few years to get established do not need protection. Prune or shear off the flower stalks as soon as the petals fade to prevent seed formation and to neaten the plants. Prune or shear to control the size and shape of the plant at the same time (in early summer).

Deer sometimes eat rhododendrons, especially in severe winters. Spraying the plants with a deer repellent offers some protection. If you live in northern or western New England, ask a local nursery to recommend hardy substitutes for the rhododendrons listed on page 148.

Rhus aromatica 'Gro-low'

'GRO-LOW' SUMAC. A deciduous shrub that spreads to form a low mounded patch under 2 ft. tall but 6 to 8 ft. wide. Scalloped leaves are glossy dark green all summer and turn scarlet in fall. Small clusters of fuzzy red fruits add interest in summer. Takes full or partial sun, any well-drained soil. Doesn't need pruning, but you can shear or shape it if you want to. Pages: 37, ***39***, 50.

Recommended rhododendrons and azaleas

'Boule de Neige' rhododendron
Pure-white flowers in late spring on a compact rounded shrub about 5 ft. tall and wide. Large evergreen leaves. Not hardy in northern New England. Pages: 32, 59.

'Dora Amateis' rhododendron
Creamy white flowers in late spring on an upright shrub about 3 ft. tall and wide. Small evergreen leaves. Not hardy in northern New England. Page: 56.

'Janet Blair' rhododendron
Frilly, pale-pink flowers in late spring on a compact rounded shrub that reaches about 4 ft. tall and wide. Large evergreen leaves. Not hardy in northern New England. Page: 21.

Northern Lights azaleas
Masses of fragrant bright-colored flowers in midspring on upright shrubs 4 to 6 ft. tall. Small deciduous leaves. There are several cultivars with different-colored flowers—'Rosy Lights', 'Golden Lights', 'White Lights', 'Spicy Lights', etc. All are highly recommended and very hardy. Pages: 59, 124, **127**.

'Olga Mezitt' rhododendron
Clear-pink flowers in midspring; otherwise just like 'PJM' rhododendron. Very hardy. Pages: 23, 38, 71, **73**, 75, 127.

'PJM' rhododendron
Magenta flowers in very early spring on an upright shrub about 4 ft. tall and 3 ft. wide. Small evergreen leaves turn maroon in winter. Very hardy. Pages: 26, 110, 127, **127**.

***Rhododendron laetivirens*, Wilson rhododendron**
Small rose-pink flowers in late spring on a compact mounded shrub that reaches about 3 ft. tall, 4 to 5 ft. wide. Small evergreen leaves. Not hardy in northern and western New England. Page: 38.

'Scintillation' rhododendron
Clear-pink flowers in late spring on a vigorous shrub that grows at least 6 ft. tall and wide. Large evergreen leaves. Not hardy in northern and western New England. Pages: 28, 110, **113**.

Rhododendron 'Boule de Neige'
RHODODENDRON

Rhododendron 'Olga Mezitt'
RHODODENDRON

Rosa

ROSE. Fast-growing deciduous shrubs with glossy compound leaves, thorny stems or canes, and very showy, often fragrant flowers. (See box on facing page for information on specific roses.) In the spring, many garden centers stock bare-root roses, with their roots wrapped in a plastic bag and packed in a cardboard box. These are a good investment if you buy them right after they arrive in the stores and plant them promptly, but their quality deteriorates with every day in the box. Nurseries may sell bare-root roses in the spring but usually grow the plants in containers. If you buy a potted rose, you can plant it anytime from spring to late summer, but keep well watered.

Many roses are propagated by grafting and have a swollen place on the stem called the bud union where the graft was inserted. When planting, place the bud union at ground level, then heap an inch or more of soil up over it. All roses grow best in full sun and well-amended, well-drained soil topped with a few inches of mulch. Once established, the roses recommended in this book require no more care than many other shrubs. Prune them once a year in spring, before new growth starts. (See p. 206 for information on pruning roses.)

These roses have good resistance to various fungal diseases but may have problems some years when the weather is especially humid. To control fungus, mix ¼ cup baking soda plus a few drops of salad oil in 1 gal. of water and spray the rose foliage until it's dripping wet. Repeat every 10 days.

Aphids—soft-bodied insects the size of a pinhead—may attack the new growth on roses but do little serious damage. You can wash them away with plain or soapy water. Japanese beetles are a major problem in some areas, and unfortunately there isn't much you can do but go out every morning and knock them into a pail of hot soapy water, where they drown. Other beetle-control methods such as traps and sprays all have significant drawbacks. Swarms of beetles eat rosebuds, blossoms, and foliage in July and August but are fairly uncommon in June or from September onward, so early and late blossoms may be untouched. Deer eat rosebushes, despite the thorns. Where deer are a problem, consider planting lilacs, spireas, clematis, or other plants instead of roses.

Recommended roses

'Blaze' rose
A "climbing" rose with flexible canes about 8 ft. long. Can be attached and trained up a trellis or sideways on a fence. Flowers are red, semidouble, only slightly fragrant. Blooms most in June, with scattered flowers the rest of the summer. Pages: 41, ***42***.

'Bonica' rose
A broad bush, about 5 ft. tall and wide, with clusters of small double pink flowers all summer. Flowers are scentless. Pages: 30, 50, 92, 95.

'Climbing Joseph's Coat' rose
A multicolored rose with scentless flowers that shade from gold to orange to red. Blooms all summer. Easily trained as a climber. Pages: 80, **83**.

'Frau Dagmar Hartop' rose
A rugosa-type rose with large, fragrant, single pink flowers June through September and disease-resistant foliage. Forms an upright or rounded bush up to 5 ft. tall and wide. Pages: 25, 43, 65, 79.

'New Dawn' rose
A climbing rose with glossy, dark, healthy foliage and fragrant double pink flowers that bloom off and on all summer. Page: 88.

'The Fairy' rose
A low, spreading shrub, about 2 ft. tall and 3 to 4 ft. wide, with small shiny leaves and masses of small, scentless, light-pink flowers from early summer until hard frost. Pages: 30, **32**, 92.

'White Meidiland' rose
A low, spreading shrub, about 2 ft. tall and 5 ft. wide, with healthy foliage and clusters of scentless white flowers all summer. Page: 30.

'William Baffin' rose
A very hardy, vigorous, climbing rose with large, fragrant, double pink flowers. 'John Cabot' has fuchsia flowers. Highly recommended for northern gardens. Page: 79.

'Zéphirine Drouhin' rose
With sweet-scented semidouble rose-pink flowers on long, arching, almost thornless canes, it "climbs" about 12 ft. tall. Blooms well even in partial shade. Not reliably hardy in Zone 4; substitute 'William Baffin' there. Pages: 60, 118.

Standard roses
Nurseries produce several kinds of roses in this style. Sometimes called tree roses, they have a stiff naked trunk about 3 ft. tall topped with a ball-shaped or drooping crown of foliage and flowers. These plants need special care, depending on what cultivar you choose and how severe your climate is. Ask the nursery how to prune the flowering shoots and how to protect the plants in the winter. Page: 121.

Rosa 'Bonica' ROSE

Rosa rugosa 'Frau Dagmar Hartop' ROSE

Rosa 'William Baffin' ROSE

Rudbeckia fulgida
CONEFLOWER, BLACK-EYED SUSAN. A popular perennial wildflower that blooms for several weeks in late summer. 'Goldsturm' (p. 25) is a cultivar that forms an especially robust clump, with large dark-green leaves at the base and stiff, erect, branching flower stalks. Adapts to most soils but needs full or partial sun. Cut down the flower stalks in fall, or spring to provide winter food for seed-eating birds. Divide every few years in spring. Pages: 108, ***109***.

Salvia officinalis

COMMON SAGE. A shrubby perennial with fragrant, gray-green, oval leaves and spikes of lovely blue flowers in June. Grows 1 to 2 ft. tall, 2 to 3 ft. wide. Needs full sun and well-drained soil. Cut frozen stems back to live buds in early spring, and cut off flower stalks after they bloom. Use pine boughs or a temporary shelter to protect it from severe winters in northern and western New England. Pages: 75, ***77***.

Salvia x *superba* 'May Night'

'MAY NIGHT' SALVIA. A long-blooming perennial that forms a patch of dark-green foliage topped with countless spikes of dark indigo-purple flowers. Starts blooming in May and continues off and on through summer and fall. Grows 18 to 24 in. tall, spreads 2 ft. wide. Prefers full sun and well-drained soil. Shear or trim off the old flower stalks to the next leaf to keep it blooming. Divide every few years in spring or fall. Pages: 45, 51, 68, 88.

Scabiosa columbaria 'Butterfly Blue'

'BUTTERFLY BLUE' PINCUSHION FLOWER. A compact perennial that forms a neat clump of bright-green foliage and blooms all season from May to hard frost. The round, sky blue flowers really do attract butterflies and make good cut flowers, too. 'Pink Mist' has pink flowers. Grows about 1 ft. tall and spreads 1 ft. wide. Needs full sun and well-drained soil. Keep picking off the old flowers as they fade. Divide every few years in early spring. Pages: 65, 77, 80, ***83***.

Sedum

SEDUM. A perennial that forms a vase-shaped clump of thick stems lined with large, fleshy, gray-green leaves. Broad flat clusters of buds form at the top of each stem in late summer and gradually change from creamy white to pink to rust as the flowers open and mature. 'Autumn Joy' flowers are pale pink at their peak (pp. 43, 102, ***105***). 'Brilliant' (pp. 23, 68) has darker rosy-pink flowers. Both are excellent plants that need full sun. Cut stems back partway in early summer to keep them from flopping over and to make the clump bushier. In late fall or spring, cut old stems to the ground. Divide clumps every few years in early spring. Grows about 2 ft. tall and 2 to 3 ft. wide.

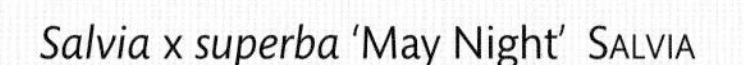

Salvia x *superba* 'May Night' SALVIA

Spiraea x *bumalda* 'Anthony Waterer'

'ANTHONY WATERER' SPIREA. A small deciduous shrub with a neat rounded habit, fine-textured foliage, and round clusters of dark-pink flowers for several weeks in July and early August. Grows about 2 ft. tall and 3 ft. wide. Thrives in garden soil with full or partial sun. Shear off the tops of the stems after the flowers fade. May get uneven or straggly- looking after several years. When that happens, cut the bush to the ground in early spring and it will grow back good as new. Pages: 37, ***39***, 79, 88.

Spiraea japonica

LITTLE PRINCESS SPIREA. Grows about 18 in. tall and 2 ft. wide, with dark-green foliage and pink flowers during June and July. Page: 25.

Stachys byzantina

LAMB'S EARS. A mat-forming perennial whose large oval leaves are densely covered with soft white fuzz. Typically the leaves are 3 to 4 in. long, and the plant spreads about 18 in. wide. 'Helene von Stein' (also called 'Big Ears') is a cultivar with leaves 6 to 8 in. long. It spreads about 3 ft. wide. Blooms in early summer, with small purple flowers on thick stalks about 1 ft. tall. Needs full or partial sun. Cut off the bloom stalks when the flowers fade, or sooner if you prefer. Use a soft rake to clean away the old leaves in early spring. Divide clumps every few years. Pages: 49, ***51***, 68, 102.

Syringa patula 'Miss Kim'

'MISS KIM' LILAC. An excellent lilac with graceful clusters of wonderfully fragrant lilac-blue flowers in May, plus a compact habit and disease-resistant leaves that turn purple before dropping in fall. Grows about 5 ft. tall and wide. Needs full sun for maximum bloom. After the flowers drop, prune off the clusters of developing seedpods and cut back any limbs that are too long. Needs little other pruning. If it gets straggly after several years, cut the whole bush to the ground in early summer to renew it. Pages: 63, 67, ***69***.

Syringa meyeri 'Palibin'

DWARF LILAC, DWARF KOREAN LILAC. A deciduous shrub with fragrant lilac flowers in May and small, glossy dark green leaves that turn purple in fall. Forms a busy clump with many erect stems 4 to 6 ft. tall. Needs full sun for maximum flowering. Pages: 35, 119.

Syringa reticulata

Japanese tree lilac. A small deciduous tree with clusters of fragrant creamy white flowers in June, later than other lilacs. Often trained with multiple trunks because the dark peeling bark is attractive. Grows about 25 ft. tall, with an upright oval crown. (p. 92). 'Ivory Silk' (pp. 75, **77**) is a popular cultivar with especially nice flowers and bark. Grow like 'Miss Kim' lilac. (See previous page.)

Syringa vulgaris

Common lilac. A large deciduous shrub valued for its sweet-scented flowers in May. There are dozens of cultivars with single or double flowers in shades of lilac, purple, pink, and white. Most grow 10 to 20 ft. tall, with many erect stems. Grow like 'Miss Kim' lilac (see previous page). Page: 86.

Taxus

Yew. Evergreen shrubs and trees with flat sprays of dark-green needlelike foliage. Yews tolerate repeated pruning and are often sheared into formal or geometric shapes and used for specimens, hedges, and foundation plantings. Some kinds are naturally compact and don't need to be sheared. Female yews produce red berries that are attractive but poisonous. (See box above for information on particular yews.) Yews adapt to full sun, partial sun, or shade but must have well-drained soil. They are sold in containers or balled-and-burlapped. Large plants are readily available and transplant well, if you want fast results. To maintain a formal look, shear back the new growth in early summer, before it has hardened. For a natural look, prune individual branches as needed to maintain the desired shape. Where deer are a problem, plant boxwood, andromeda, or other evergreens instead of yews.

Recommended yews

***Taxus baccata* 'Repandens', Spreading English yew**
A low-growing, wide-spreading yew with unusually large needles that stay dark green all year. Grows about 2 ft. tall, 6 to 8 ft. wide after many years. Not hardy in northern and western New England; substitute 'Nana' yew there. Page: 90, ***90***.

***T. cuspidata* 'Nana', Dwarf Japanese yew**
A compact yew, wider than tall, with green needles all year. Slow-growing. Reaches 3 to 4 ft. tall, 4 to 5 ft. wide after several years. Pages: 38, ***39***.

***T.* x *media*, 'Hicksii' hybrid yew, 'Densiformis' hybrid yew**
Fast-growing and good for hedges 4 to 8 ft. tall. ('Hicksii' grows up to 20 ft. if unpruned.) Stays green all year. Pages: 71, ***73***, 90, ***90***.

Teucrium chamaedrys

Germander. A low, mounded shrub with small, glossy, dark evergreen leaves and pink-purple flowers in August and September. Grows about 1 ft. tall and 2 ft. wide if unpruned. Needs full or partial sun and well-drained soil. Shear stems back partway every spring to keep the plant compact and bushy. Provide winter protection in northern New England. Pages: 26, ***29***, 77.

Thuja occidentalis

Arborvitae. A plump, cone-shaped evergreen shrub with glossy green scalelike foliage that releases a pleasant aroma when touched. Keeps its color all winter. Needs full or partial sun, garden or moist but well-drained soil. Plant in spring or fall. 'Techny' eventually reaches 10 to 15 ft. tall, 6 ft. or more wide, but is fairly slow-growing, so buy the biggest plant you can afford. Needs no routine care. Where deer are a problem, plant a spruce or juniper instead. Pages: 26, 35, 126. 'Nigra' can reach 25 ft. or taller. Page: 35.

Thymus

Thyme. A shrubby perennial that forms a tangle of wiry twigs covered with tiny evergreen leaves that have a pleasant fragrance. Blooms profusely in July or August, with pink, mauve, rose, or white flowers. There are many kinds from which to choose at any herb nursery or the herb section of a garden center, usually sold by common names. Woolly thyme (pp. 85, **87**) has fuzzy gray leaves. Mother-of-thyme or creeping thyme (p. 85) has shiny green leaves that turn maroon in cold weather. Both form low mats a few inches tall and 1 ft. or more wide. All thymes need full sun and well-drained soil. Shear old growth back halfway in early spring. Shear again in summer as soon as the flowers fade. Divide every few years in spring.

Thuja occidentalis 'Techny'
American arborvitae

Viburnum dentatum
ARROWWOOD VIBURNUM

Tiarella cordifolia

FOAMFLOWER. A perennial woodland native that spreads quickly to form a dense low patch of evergreen foliage, covered with spikes of dainty white flowers in late spring. Prefers partial shade and moist, well-drained soil. Divide every few years in spring or fall if you want to make more plants or if the patch has gotten crowded and stopped flowering. Grows about 8 in. tall, at least 2 ft. wide. Pages: 56, 106, 116, ***117***.

Tradescantia andersoniana

SPIDERWORT. A lush-looking perennial that forms a soft clump of bright-green leaves, dotted with three-petaled flowers in shades of blue, pink, or white. Grows about 1 ft. tall, spreads 2 to 3 ft. wide. Prefers full sun or partial shade and moist, well-drained garden soil. Divide every few years in spring. Trouble-free. Pages: 82, ***83***.

Tsuga canadensis* var. *sargentii

WEEPING HEMLOCK. A selected form of the native hemlock that grows wild throughout the Northeast, with limbs that arch gracefully out and down, forming a mounded specimen. Grows slowly and spreads wider than tall, eventually reaching up to 10 ft. tall and 20 ft. wide. Buy the largest specimen you can afford. Takes sun or shade but needs moist, well-drained soil. Requires no pruning and is generally trouble-free, but it is subject to the woolly adelgid, an aphidlike pest that's hard to control. A local nursery can advise you if adelgids occur in your area; if so, plant a bird's-nest Norway spruce instead. Pages: ***90,*** 91.

***Veronica* 'Sunny Border Blue'**

'SUNNY BORDER BLUE' VERONICA. A perennial that blooms all summer. Needs full or partial sun; 2 ft. tall. Keep cutting off the old flower spikes. Divide every few years in early spring. Page: 72.

***Viburnum carlesii* 'Compactum'**

COMPACT KOREAN SPICE VIBURNUM. A deciduous shrub with stiff twigs and a dense habit. Clusters of pretty pink buds open into spice-scented white flowers in May. Leaves are plain green all summer and fall. Blooms best in full sun, with moist, well-drained soil. Fairly slow-growing, so start with the biggest one you can buy. Prune in early summer, right after it blooms, to shape a neat sphere, or let it grow naturally, if you prefer. Grows about 4 ft. tall and wide. Pages: 56, 71, 76, 86, ***87***.

Viburnum dentatum

ARROWWOOD VIBURNUM. A deciduous shrub native to the Northeast, very hardy and adaptable, with white flowers in June and blue berries in September. Glossy dark-green leaves turn maroon in fall. Grows about 8 ft. tall, with straight, erect stems. Thrives in full sun or partial shade. Carefree. Needs only routine pruning. Pages: 106, 124.

***Viburnum opulus* 'Compactum'**

COMPACT EUROPEAN CRANBERRY BUSH. A neat, rounded deciduous shrub with lacy clusters of white flowers in June, maplelike leaves that turn red in fall, and bright-red berries in fall and winter. Grows about 6 ft. tall and wide. Needs full or partial sun. Carefree. Pages: ***58***, 59.

***Viburnum opulus* 'Nanum'**

DWARF CRANBERRY BUSH. A small, twiggy shrub, 2 ft. tall and wide. Rarely flowers or fruits. Page: 25.

Viburnum plicatum* var. *tomentosum

DOUBLE-FILE VIBURNUM. A deciduous shrub valued especially for its lovely flowers. 'Shasta' (pp. 88, ***90***) is a popular cultivar that grows about 6 ft. tall and 10 to 12 ft. wide, with long horizontal limbs, and bears clusters of large pure-white flowers in May or June. It needs plenty of space to spread sideways. Dwarf cultivars (pp. 21, ***23***, 95) are harder to find at nurseries but better suited to small gardens. Look for 'Summer Snowflake' or 'Watanabei', which have creamy white flowers all summer. They grow about 6 ft. tall but spread only 6 ft. wide. All double-file viburnums prefer partial sun and moist, well-drained garden soil. Prune only to remove damaged or crossing limbs.

Viburnum trilobum

CRANBERRY BUSH, HIGHBUSH CRANBERRY. A native deciduous shrub with lacy clusters of white flowers in June, attractive maplelike leaves that turn crimson in fall, and bright-red fruits that ripen in early fall and last all winter. The fruits are edible but very tart. Grows 10 to 12 ft. tall and wide. Needs full or partial sun. Little pruning required. Pages: 85, ***87***. *V. trilobum* 'Compactum' grows 4 to 6 ft. tall and wide. Page: 60.

Viburnum* x *juddii

JUDD VIBURNUM. A hybrid with Korean spice viburnum, this has similar fragrant flowers, but its dark-green foliage is glossier and more attractive. It grows 6 to 8 ft. tall and 4 to 6 ft. wide. Page: 119.

Vinca minor

MYRTLE. An evergreen ground cover with small, glossy, leathery, dark-green leaves. Gradually forms a thick mass of foliage about 6 in. tall. Blooms in late spring, with round lilac flowers. Adapts to most soils, in partial sun or shade. Once established, needs absolutely no care. Pages: 23, 38, 47, 54, ***55***.

Viola odorata

SWEET VIOLET. A low-growing perennial that spreads by seeds and runners to make a patch or ground cover. Dark-green, heart-shaped leaves are evergreen in mild winters. Blooms in late fall and again in early spring, with fragrant purple flowers that perfume the whole garden. Adapts to most soils, in sun or shade. Invasive, but too short (under 4 in.) to be much of a threat. Pull up runners and seedlings that stray into a path or lawn. Pages: 56, 88.

Water plants

Most water plants are fast-growing, even weedy, so you need only one of each kind to start with. Some kinds are tender to frost, but you can overwinter them indoors in a pot or an aquarium. Marginal or emergent plants grow well in containers covered with 2 in. or more of water; their leaves and flower stalks stick up into the air. For example, dwarf cattail (*Typha minima*) looks like regular cattails but grows only 2 ft. tall and has finger-size seed heads. Oxygenating or submerged plants grow underwater; they help keep the water clear and provide oxygen, food, and shelter for fish. Anacharis (*Elodea canadensis*) is a popular oxygenator with tiny dark-green leaves. (For water lilies, see *Nymphaea*.) Page: 95.

Weigela florida

WEIGELA. A small, rounded deciduous shrub that blooms in June. 'Minuet' (p. 37) has dark purple-green foliage and dark-red flowers. 'Rhumba' (p. 67) has green leaves with a purple stripe around the edge and dark-red flowers. Both are compact cultivars that grow only 3 ft. tall and wide. 'Variegata' (pp. 60, 124, ***127***) gets larger, reaching 6 to 8 ft. tall and wide, and has green-and-gold leaves and pink flowers. All need full or partial sun (foliage turns green if it isn't getting enough sun). Prune by cutting out some of the older stems (They have rougher-textured bark.) to the ground in early spring. These are fast-growing, trouble-free shrubs.

Weigela florida 'Midnight Wine'

'MIDNIGHT WINE.' This easy-to-grow, dwarf rounded deciduous shrub bears dark burgundy wine leaves and only reaches about 10 to 12 in. tall. Its light pink blooms appear in late spring. Prune lightly after bloom time. Best foliage color appears in full or partial sun; in shade it may become greenish. Well-drained average soil is ideal but tolerates most. Resistant to deer; attracts hummingbirds and butterflies. Pages: 21, ***23***, 98.

Wisteria sinensis

CHINESE WISTERIA. A vigorous woody vine with dangling clusters of fragrant purple, lavender, or white flowers in June and deciduous compound leaves. Climbs by twining around a trellis, tree, or other support and can reach 30 ft. or taller. Needs full sun to flower well, and well-drained soil. May not flower for several years after you plant it, but the lacy foliage is attractive meanwhile. Prune the new growth back hard in late August to stimulate flowering. Otherwise needs no care. Not hardy in northern New England; substitute Japanese wisteria, *W. floribunda*, a similar but even more vigorous vine, there. Pages: 86, ***87***.

Yucca filamentosa 'Golden Sword'

'GOLDEN SWORD' YUCCA. An unusual shrub with daggerlike leaves, 2 ft. long, that stick out in all directions from a short thick trunk. Green-and-gold striped leaves are evergreen but get droopy in cold weather. Blooms in June, with bunches of large white flowers on stiff stalks 4 to 6 ft. tall. The woody seedpods are decorative, too. Needs full or partial sun. Cut down the old flower stalks whenever you choose, and peel dead leaves from around the base of the plant in spring. Not hardy in northern New England; substitute a clump of Siberian iris there. Pages: 80, ***83***.

Viola odorata
SWEET VIOLET

Guide *to* Installation

In this section, we introduce the hard but rewarding work of landscaping. Here, you'll find information on all the tasks you need to install any of the designs in this book, organized in the order in which you'd most likely tackle them. Clearly written text and numerous illustrations help you learn how to plan the job; clear the site; construct paths, patios, ponds, fences, arbors, and trellises; prepare the planting beds; and install and maintain the plantings. Roll up your sleeves and dig in. In just a few weekends, you can create a landscape feature that will provide years of enjoyment.

Organizing Your Project

If your gardening experience is limited to mowing the lawn, pruning the bushes, and growing some flowers and vegetables, the thought of starting from scratch and installing a whole new landscape feature might be intimidating. But in fact, adding one of the designs in this book to your property is completely within reach, if you approach it the right way. The key is to divide the project into a series of steps and take them one at a time. This is how professional landscapers work. It's efficient and orderly, and it makes even big jobs seem manageable.

On this and the facing page, we'll explain how to think your way through a landscaping project and anticipate the various steps. Subsequent topics in this section describe how to do each part of the job. Detailed instructions and illustrations cover all the techniques you'll need to install any design from start to finish.

The step-by-step approach

Choose a design, and adapt it to your site. The designs in this book address parts of the home landscape. In the most attractive and effective home landscapes, all the various parts work together. Don't be afraid to change the shape of beds; alter the number, kinds, and positions of plants; or revise paths and structures to bring them into harmony with their surroundings.

To see the relationships with your existing landscape, you can draw the design on a scaled plan of your property. Or you can work on the site itself, placing wooden stakes, pots, tricycles, or whatever is handy to represent plants and structures. With a little imagination, either method will allow you to visualize basic relationships.

Lay out the design on-site. Once you've decided what you want to do, you'll need to lay out the paths and structures and outline the beds. Some people are comfortable laying out a design "freehand," pacing off distances and relying on their eye to judge sizes and relative positions. Others prefer to transfer the grid from the plan full size onto the site in order to place elements precisely. (Garden lime, a grainy white powder available at nurseries, can be used like chalk on a blackboard to "draw" a grid or outlines of planting beds.)

Clear the site. (See pp. 158–159.) Sometimes you have to work around existing features—a nice big tree, a building or

DIGGING POSTHOLES

AMENDING SOIL

fence, a sidewalk—but it's usually easiest to start a new landscaping project if you clear as much as possible, down to ground level. That means removing unwanted structures or pavement and killing, cutting down, or uprooting all the plants. Needless to say, this can generate a lot of debris, and you'll need to figure out how to dispose of it all. Still, it's often worth the trouble to make a fresh start.

Build the "hardscape." (See pp. 160–191.) "Hardscape" means anything you build as part of a landscape—a fence, trellis, arbor, retaining wall, walkway, edging, outdoor lighting, or whatever. If you're going to do any building, do it first, and finish the construction before you start any planting. That way you won't have to worry about stepping on any of the plants, and they won't be in the way as you work.

Prepare the soil. (See pp. 192–195.) On most properties, it's uncommon to find soil that's as good as it should be for growing plants. Typically, the soil around a house is shallow, compacted, and infertile. It may be rocky or contain buried debris. Some plants tolerate such poor conditions, but they don't thrive. To grow healthy, attractive plants, you need to improve the quality of the soil throughout the entire area that you're planning to plant.

Do the planting, and add mulch. (See pp. 197–200.) Putting plants in the ground usually goes quite quickly and gives instant gratification. Spreading mulch over the soil makes the area look "finished" even when plants are still small.

Maintain the planting. (See pp. 201–214.) Most plantings need regular watering and occasional weeding for the first year or two. After that, depending on the design you've chosen, you'll have to do some routine maintenance—pruning, shaping, cutting back, and cleaning up—to keep the plants looking their best. This may take as little as a few hours a year or as much as an hour or two every week throughout the growing season.

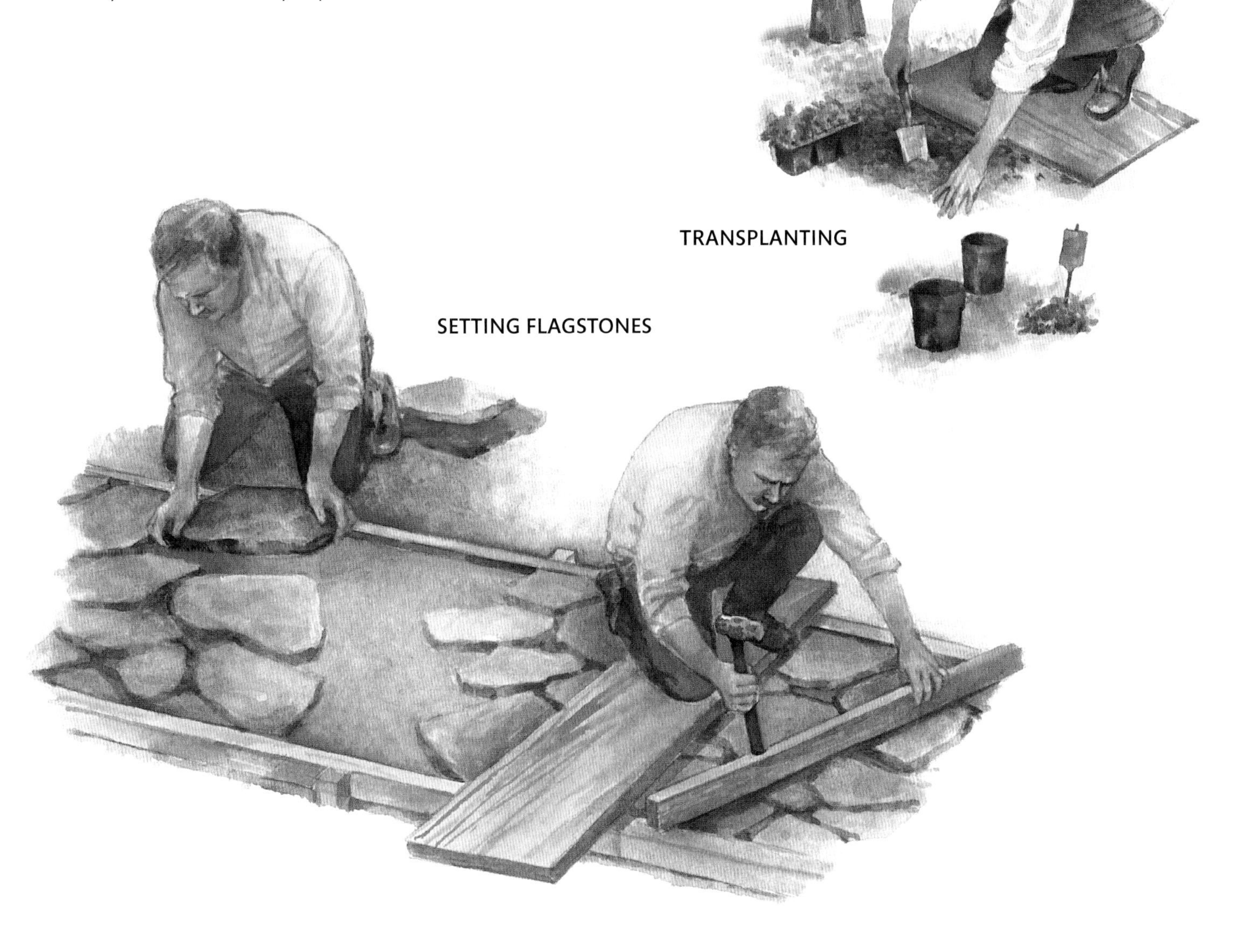

TRANSPLANTING

SETTING FLAGSTONES

Clearing the Site

The site you've chosen for a landscaping project may or may not have any man-made objects (fences, old pavement, trash, etc.) to be removed, but it will almost certainly be covered with plants.

Before you start cutting down plants, try to find someone—a friend or neighbor who enjoys gardening—to identify these plants for you. As you walk around together, make a sketch that shows which plants are where, and attach labels to the plants, too. Determine if there are any desirable plants worth saving—mature shade trees that you should work around, shapely shrubs that aren't too big to dig up and relocate or give away, worthwhile perennials and ground covers that you could divide and replant, healthy sod that you could lay elsewhere. Likewise, decide which plants have to go—diseased or crooked trees, straggly or overgrown shrubs, weedy brush, invasive ground covers, tattered lawn.

You can clear small areas yourself, bundling the brush for pickup and tossing soft-stemmed plants on the compost pile, but if you have lots of woody brush or any trees to remove, you might want to hire someone else to do the job. A crew armed with power tools can turn a thicket into a pile of wood chips in just a few hours. Have them pull out the roots and grind the stumps, too. Save the chips; they're good for surfacing paths, or you can use them as mulch.

Working around a tree

If there are any large, healthy trees on your site, be careful as you work around them. It's okay to prune off some of a tree's limbs, as shown on the facing page, but respect its trunk and roots. Never cut or wound the bark on the trunk (don't nail things to a tree), as that exposes the tree to disease organisms. Don't pile soil or mulch against the trunk, because that keeps the bark wet and can make it rot.

Killing perennial weeds

Some common weeds that sprout back from perennial roots or runners are bedstraw, bindweed, blackberry and other briers, ground ivy, poison ivy, quack grass, and sorrel. Garden plants that can become weedy include ajuga, akebia, bamboo, bishop's weed, English ivy, Japanese honeysuckle, Japanese knotweed, lily-of-the-valley, loosestrife, sundrops, and tansy. Once they get established, perennial weeds are hard to eliminate. You can't just cut off the tops, because they keep sprouting back. You have to dig the weeds out, smother them with mulch, or kill them with an herbicide, and it's better to do this before rather than after you plant a bed.

Smothering weeds

This technique is easier than digging, particularly for eradicating large infestations, but much slower. First mow or cut the tops of the weeds as close to the ground as possible ❶. Then cover the area with sections from the newspaper, overlapped like shingles ❷, or flattened-out cardboard boxes and top with a layer of mulch, such as straw, grass clippings, tree leaves, wood chips, or other organic material spread several inches deep ❸.

Smothering works by excluding light, which stops photosynthesis. If any shoots reach up through the covering and produce green leaves, pull them out immediately. Wait a few months, until you're sure the weeds are dead, before you dig into the smothered area and plant there.

Digging. In many cases, you can do a pretty good job of removing a perennial weed if you dig carefully where the stems enter the ground, find the roots, and follow them as far as possible through the soil, pulling out every bit of root that you find. Some plant roots go deeper than you can dig, and most plants will sprout back from the small bits that you miss, but these leftover sprouts are easy to pull.

Spraying. Herbicides are easy, fast, and effective weed killers when chosen and applied with care. Look for those that break down quickly into more benign substances, and make sure the weed you're trying to kill is listed on the product label. Apply all herbicides exactly as directed by the manufacturer. After spraying, you usually have to wait from one to four weeks for the weed to die completely, and some weeds need to be sprayed a second or third time before they give up. Some weeds just "melt away" when they die, but if there are tough or woody stems and roots, you'll need to dig them up and discard them.

Replacing turf

If the area where you're planning to add a landscape feature is currently part of the lawn, you have a fairly easy task ahead. How to proceed depends on the condition of the turf and on what you want to put in its place. If the turf is healthy, you can "recycle" it to replace, repair, or extend the lawn elsewhere.

The drawing below shows a technique for removing relatively small areas of strong, healthy turf for replanting. First, with a sharp shovel, cut it into squares or strips about 1 to 3 ft. square (these small pieces are easy to lift) ❶. Then slice a few inches deep under each square, and lift the squares, roots and all, like brownies from a pan ❷. Quickly transplant the squares to a previously prepared site; water them well until the roots are established.

If you don't need the turf, or if it's straggly or weedy, leave it in place and kill the grass. Spraying with a herbicide kills most grasses within one to two weeks. Or cover it with a tarp or a sheet of black plastic for two to four weeks during the heat of summer (it takes longer in cool weather). Then dig or till the bed, shredding the turf, roots and all, and mixing it into the soil.

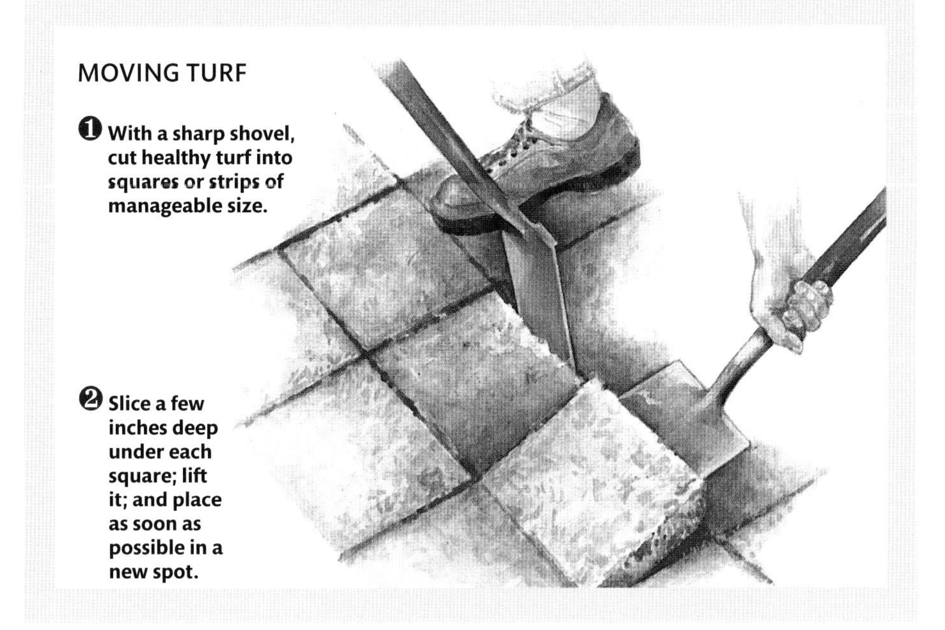

Removing large limbs

If there are large trees on your property now, you may want to remove some of the lower limbs so light can reach your plantings. Major pruning of large trees is a job for a professional arborist, but you can remove limbs smaller than 4 in. in diameter and less than 10 ft. above the ground yourself with a simple bow saw or pole saw.

Use the three-step procedure shown below to remove large limbs safely. First, saw partway through the bottom of the limb, approximately 1 ft. out from the trunk ❶. This keeps the bark from tearing down the trunk when the limb falls. Then make a corresponding cut down through the top of the limb ❷—be prepared to get out of the way when the limb drops. Finally, remove the stub ❸. Undercut it slightly or hold it as you finish the cut so that it doesn't fall away and peel bark off the trunk. Note that the cut is not flush with the trunk but is just outside the thick area at the limb's base, called the "branch collar." Leaving the branch collar helps the wound heal quickly and naturally. Wound dressing is considered unnecessary today.

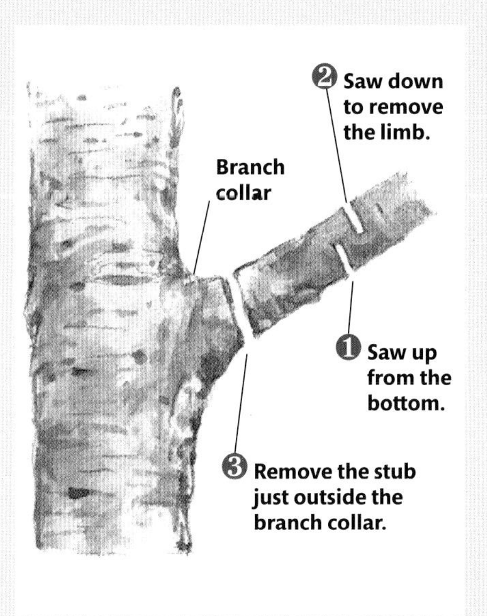

Making Paths and Walkways

Every landscape needs paths and walkways if for no other reason than to keep your feet dry as you move from one place to another. A path can also divide and define the spaces in the landscape, orchestrate the way the landscape is viewed, and even be a key element enhancing its beauty.

Whether it is a graceful curving garden path or a utilitarian slab leading to the garage, a walk has two main functional requirements: durability and safety. It should hold up through seasonal changes. It should provide a well-drained surface that is easy to walk on and to maintain.

A path's function helps determine its surface and its character. In general, heavily trafficked walkways leading to a door, garage, or shed need hard, smooth (but not slick) surfaces and should take you where you want to go fairly directly. A path to a backyard play area could be a strip of soft wood bark, easy on the knees of impatient children. A relaxed stroll in the garden might require only a hop-scotch collection of flat stones meandering from one prized plant to another.

Before laying out a walk or path, spend some time observing existing traffic patterns. If your path makes use of a route people already take (particularly children), they'll be more likely to stay on the path and off the lawn or flowers. Avoid areas that are slow to drain. When determining width, consider whether the path must accommodate rototillers or several strollers walking abreast, or just provide access for plant maintenance.

Dry-laid paths

You can make a path simply by laying bricks or spreading wood chips on top of bare earth. While quick and easy, this method has serious drawbacks. Laid on the surface, with no edging to contain them, loose materials are soon scattered, and solid materials are easily jostled out of place. If the earth base doesn't drain very well, the path will be a swamp or sheet of ice after rain or snowmelt. And in cold-winter areas, repeated expansion and contraction of the soil will heave bricks or flagstones out of alignment, making the path unsightly and dangerous.

The method we recommend—laying surface material on an excavated sand-and-gravel base—minimizes these problems. The sand and gravel improve drainage and provide a cushion against the freeze-thaw movement of the soil. Excavation can place the path surface at ground level, where the surrounding soil or an installed edging can contain loose materials and prevent hard materials from shifting.

All styles, from a "natural" wood-bark path to a formal cut-stone entry walk, and all the materials discussed here can be laid on an excavated base of gravel and sand.

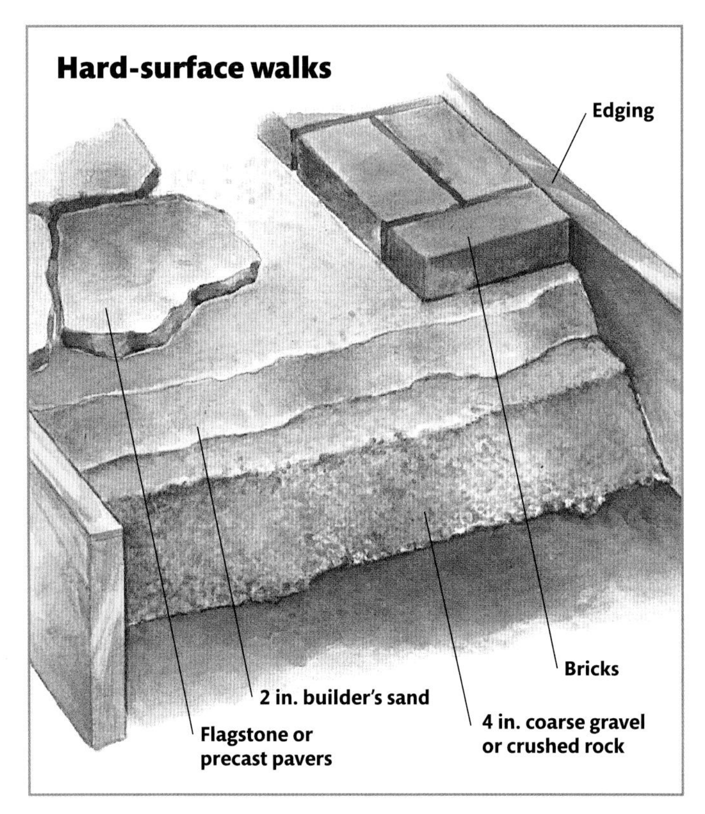

Choosing a surface

Walkways and paths can be made of either hard or soft material. Your choice of material will depend on the walkway's function, your budget, and your personal preferences.

Soft materials, including bark, wood chips, pine needles, and loose gravel, are best for informal and low-traffic areas. Inexpensive and simple to install, they settle, scatter, or decompose and must be replenished or replaced every few years.

Hard materials, such as brick, flagstone, and concrete pavers, are more expensive and time-consuming to install, but they are permanent, requiring only occasional maintenance. (Compacted crushed stone can also make a hard-surface walk.) Durable and handsome, they're ideal for high-traffic, high-profile areas.

Bark, wood chips, and pine needles

Perfect for a natural look or a quick temporary path, these loose materials can be laid directly on the soil or, if drainage is poor, on a gravel bed. Bagged materials from a nursery or garden center will be cleaner, more uniform, and considerably more expensive than bulk supplies bought by the cubic yard. Check with local tree services to find the best prices on bulk material.

Gravel and crushed rock

Loose rounded gravel gives a bit underfoot, creating a soft but messy path. The angular facets of crushed stone eventually compact into a hard and tidier path that can, if the surrounding soil is firm enough, be laid without an edging. Gravel and stone type and color vary from area to area. Buy materials by the ton or cubic yard.

Concrete pavers

Precast concrete pavers are versatile, readily available, and often the least expensive hard-surface material. They come in a range of colors and shapes, including interlocking patterns. Precast edgings are also available. Most home and garden centers carry a variety of precast pavers, which are sold by the piece.

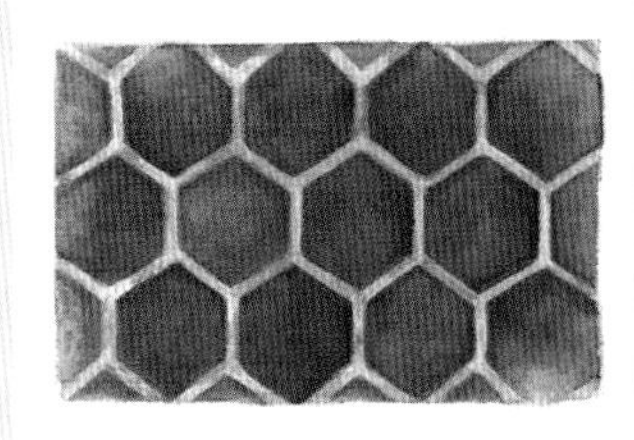

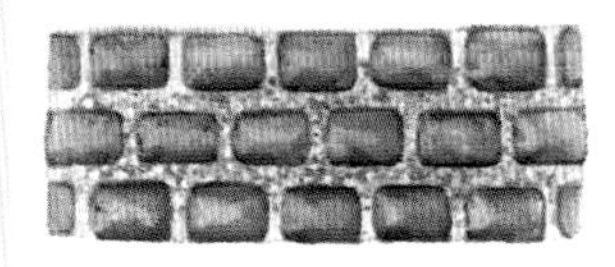

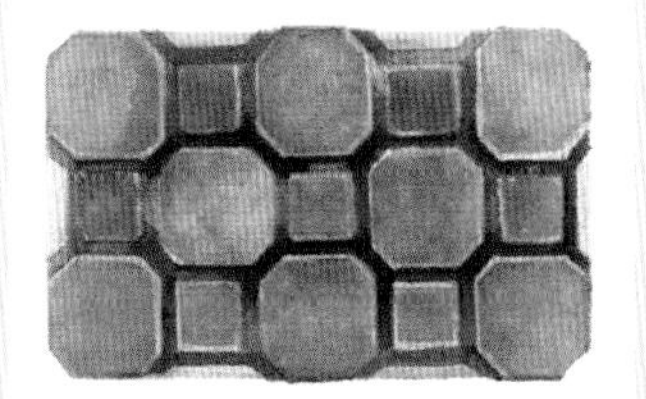

PRECAST PAVERS

Brick

Widely available in a range of sizes, colors, and textures, brick complements many design styles. When carefully laid on a well-prepared sand-and-gravel base, brick provides an even, safe, and long-lasting surface. Buy paving brick instead of the softer "facing" brick, which may break up after a few freeze-thaw cycles. (If you buy used brick, pick the hardest.) Avoid glazed brick; the glaze traps moisture and salts, which will damage the brick.

RUNNING BOND

TWO-BRICK BASKET WEAVE

HERRINGBONE

DIAGONAL HERRINGBONE

Flagstone

"Flagstone" is a generic term for stratified stone that can be split to form pavers. Limestone, sandstone, and bluestone are common paving materials. The surfaces of marble and slate are usually too smooth to make safe paving. Cut into squares or rectangles, flagstone can be laid as individual stepping-stones or in interesting patterns. Flagstones come in a range of colors, textures, and sizes. Flags for walks should be at least 2 in. thick. Purchased by weight, surface area, or pallet load, flagstones are usually the most expensive paving choice.

CUT FLAGSTONE

CUT AND IRREGULAR FLAGSTONE

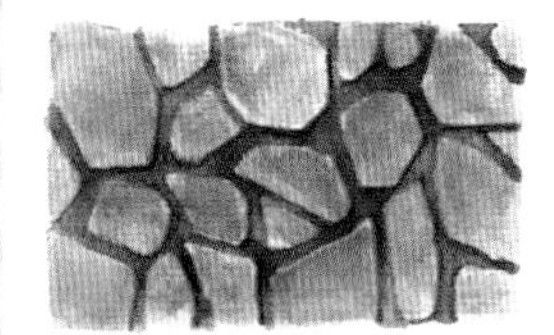

IRREGULAR FLAGSTONE

Drainage

Few things are worse than a path dotted with puddles or icy patches. To prevent these from forming, the soil around and beneath the path should drain well. The path's location and construction should ensure that rainwater and snowmelt do not collect on the surface. Drainage also affects frost heaving. In cold-winter areas, the soil expands and contracts as the water in it freezes and thaws. As the soil moves, so do path and walkway materials laid on it. The effect is minimal on loose materials, such as wood chips or gravel, but frost heaving can shift brick and stone significantly.

Before you locate a path, observe runoff and drainage on your property during and after heavy rains or snowmelt. Avoid routing a path where water courses collects, or is slow to drain.

While both loose and hard paving can sometimes be successfully laid directly on well-drained soil, laying surface materials on a base of gravel and sand will help improve drainage and minimize frost heaving. In most situations, a 4-in. gravel bed topped with 2 in. of sand will be sufficient. Water moves through these materials quickly, and they cushion the surface materials from the expansion and contraction of the underlying soil. Very poorly drained soils may require more gravel, an additional layer of coarse rock beneath the gravel, or even drain tiles—if you suspect your site has serious drainage problems, consult a specialist for advice.

Finally, keep water from pooling on a walk by making its surface higher in the center than at the edges. The center of a 4-ft.-wide walk should be at least ½ in. higher than its edges. If you're using a drag board to level the sand base, curve its lower edge to create this crown. Otherwise crown the surface by eye.

Edgings

All walk surfaces need to be contained in some fashion along their edges. Where soil is firm or tightly knit by turf, neatly cut walls of the excavation can serve as edging. An installed edging often provides more effective containment, particularly if the walk surface is above grade. It also prevents damage to bricks or stones on the edges of paths. Walkway edgings are commonly made of 1- or 2-in.-thick lumber, thicker landscaping timbers, brick, or stone.

Wood edging

Wood should be rot-resistant redwood, cedar, cypress, or pressure-treated lumber for ground-contact use. If you're working in loose soils, fix a deep wooden edging with double-headed nails to support stakes. When the path is laid, pull the nails, and fill behind the edging. Then drive the stakes below grade. In firmer soils, or if the edging material is not wide enough, install it on top of the gravel base. Position the top of the edging at the height of the path. One-by lumber is pliable enough to bend around gradual curves.

Treated dimensional lumber with support stakes

Landscape timbers with cross ties laid on gravel base

Brick and stone edging

In firm soil, a row of bricks laid on edge and perpendicular to the length of the path adds stability. For a more substantial edging, stand bricks on end on the excavated soil surface; add the gravel base and tamp earth around the base of the bricks on the outside of the excavation. Stone edgings laid on end can be set in the same way. "End-up" brick or stone edgings are easy to install on curved walks.

Bricks on edge, laid on gravel base

Bricks on end, laid on soil

Preparing the base

Having decided on the location and the materials, you can get down to business. The initial steps of layout and base preparation are much the same for all surface materials.

Layout

Lay out straight sections with stakes and string, turning 90-degree corners with batter boards. (See below.) You can plot curves with stakes and lay out the curve with a garden hose, or outline the curve with hose alone, marking it with lime or sand ❶.

Excavation

The excavation depth depends on how much sand-and-gravel base your soil's drainage calls for, the thickness of the surface material, and its position above or below grade ❷. Mark the depth on a stake or stick, and use this to check depth as you dig. Walking surfaces are most comfortable if they are reasonably level across their width. Check the bottom of the excavation with a level as you dig. If the walk cuts across a slope, you'll need to remove soil from the high side and use it to fill the low side to produce a level surface. If you've added soil or if the subsoil is loose, compact it by tamping.

Edging installation

Some edgings can be installed immediately after excavation; others are placed on top of the gravel portion of the base ❸. (See the sidebar "Edgings" on the facing page.) If the soil's drainage permits, you can lay soft materials now on the excavated, tamped, and edged soil base. To control weeds, and to keep bark, chips, or pine needles from mixing with the subsoil, spread water-permeable landscape fabric over the gravel or the excavated base.

Laying the base

Now add gravel (if required); rake it level; and compact it ❹. Use gravel up to 1 in. in diameter or ¼- to ¾-in. crushed stone, which drains and compacts well. You can rent a hand tamper (a heavy metal plate on the end of a pole) or a machine compactor if you have a large area to compact.

If you're making a loose-gravel or crushed-stone walk, add the surface material on top of the base gravel. (See "Loose Materials" page 164.) For walks of brick, stone, or pavers, add a 2-in. layer of builder's sand, not the finer sand masons use for mixing mortar.

Rake the sand smooth with the back of a level-head rake. You can level the sand with a wooden drag board, also called a screed ❺. Nail together two 1x4s or notch a 1x6 to place the lower edge at the desired height of the sand, and run the board along the path edging. To settle the sand, dampen it thoroughly with a hose set on fine spray. Fill any low spots, rake or drag the surface level, and then dampen it again.

PREPARING THE BASE

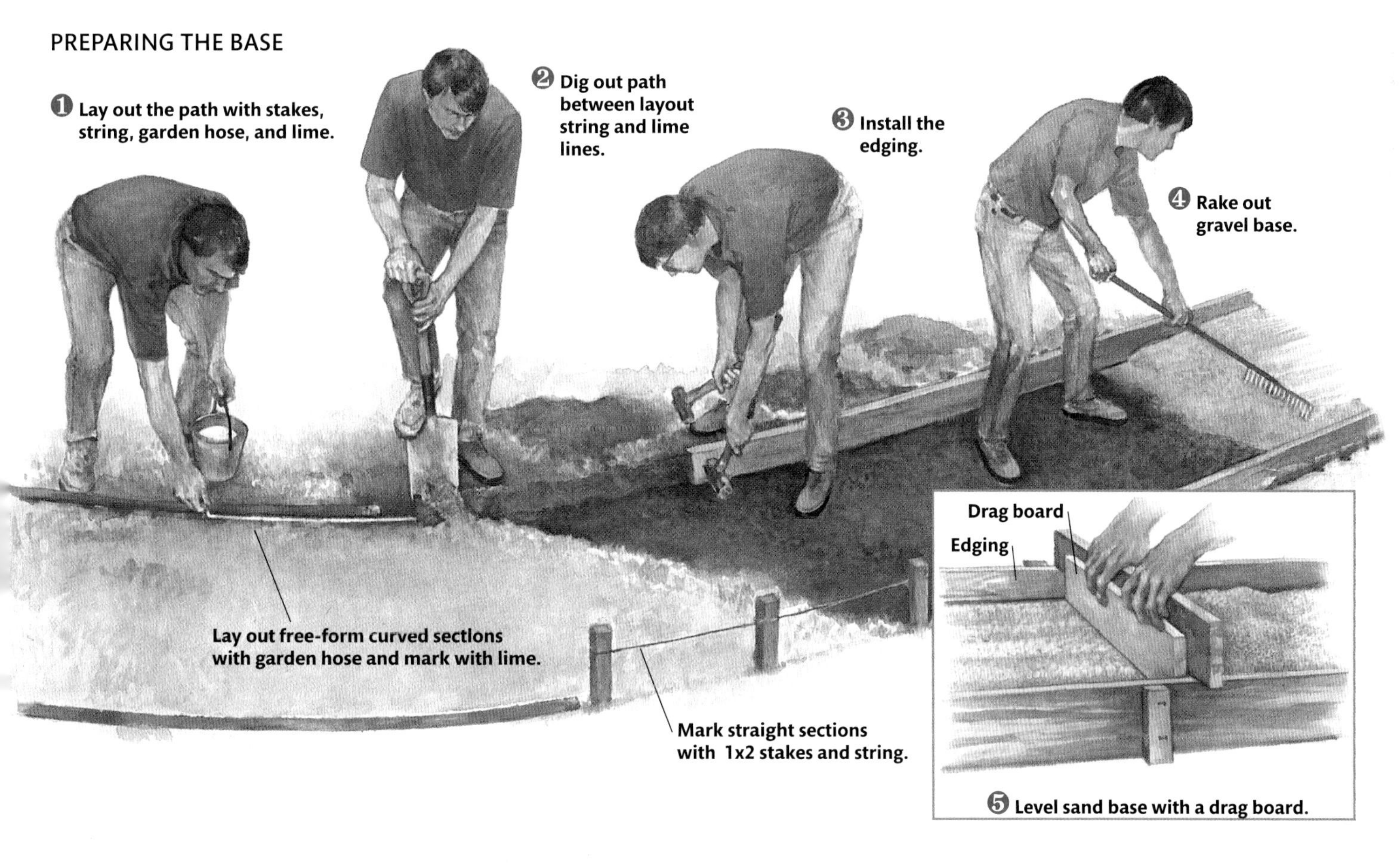

Laying the surface

Whether you're laying loose or hard material, take time to plan your work. Provide access for delivery trucks, and have materials deposited as close to the worksite as possible.

Loose materials

Install water-permeable landscape fabric over the gravel base to prevent gravel from mixing with the surface material. Spread bark or wood chips 2 to 4 in. deep. For a pine-needle surface, spread 2 in. of needles on top of several inches of bark or chips. Spread loose pea gravel about 2 in. deep. For a harder, more uniform surface, add ½ in. of fine crushed stone on top of the gravel. You can let traffic compact crushed-rock surfaces, or compact them by hand or with a machine.

Bricks and precast pavers

Take time to figure out the pattern and spacing of the bricks or pavers by laying them out on the lawn or driveway, rather than disturbing your carefully prepared sand base. When you're satisfied, begin in a corner, laying the bricks or pavers gently on the sand so the base remains even ❶. Lay full bricks first; then cut bricks to fit as needed along the edges of the patio. To produce uniform joints, space bricks with a piece of wood cut to the joint width. You can also maintain alignment with either a straightedge or a string stretched across the path between nails or stakes. Move the string along the path as you proceed with the work.

As you complete a row or section, bed the bricks or pavers into the sand base with several firm raps of a rubber mallet or a hammer on a scrap 2x4. Check with a level or straightedge to make sure the surface is even ❷. (You'll have to do this by feel or eye across the width of a crowned path.) Lift low bricks or pavers carefully and fill beneath them with sand; then reset them. Don't stand on the walk until you've filled the joints.

When you've finished a section, sweep fine, dry mason's sand into the joints, working across the surface of the path in all directions ❸. Wet thoroughly with a fine spray and let dry; then sweep in more sand if necessary. If you want a "living" walk, sweep a loam-sand mixture into the joints and plant small, tough, ground-hugging plants, such as thyme, in them.

Rare is the brick walk that can be laid without cutting something to fit. To cut brick, mark the line of the cut with a dark pencil all around the brick. With the brick resting firmly on sand or soil, score the entire line by rapping a wide mason's chisel called a *brickset* with a heavy wooden mallet or a soft-headed steel hammer as shown on the facing page. Place the brickset in the scored line across one face, and give it a sharp blow with the hammer to cut the brick.

If you have a lot of bricks to cut, or if you want greater accuracy, consider renting a masonry saw. Whether you work by hand or machine, always wear safety glasses.

Stepping-stones

A stepping-stone walk set in turf creates a charming effect and is very simple to lay. You can use cut or irregular flagstones or fieldstone, which is irregular in thickness as well as in outline. Arrange the stones on the turf; then set them one by one. Cut into the turf around the stone with a sharp flat shovel or trowel; remove the stone; then dig out the sod with the shovel. Placing stones at or below grade will keep them away from mower blades. Fill low spots beneath the stone with earth or sand so the stone doesn't move when you step on it.

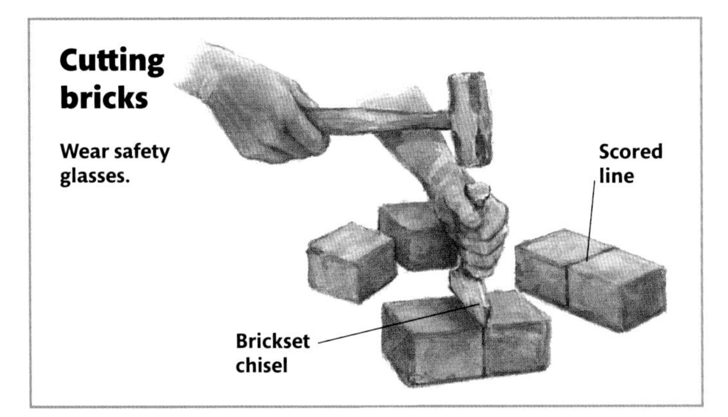

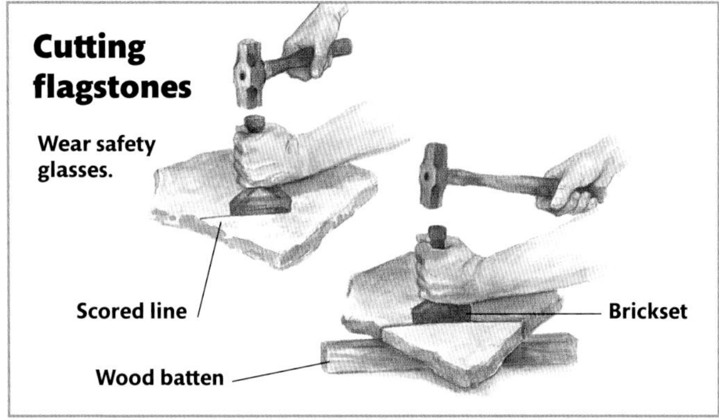

Flagstones

Install cut stones of uniform thickness as described for bricks and pavers. Working out patterns beforehand is particularly important—stones are too heavy to move around more than necessary. To produce a level surface with cut or irregular stones of varying thickness, you'll need to add or remove sand for each stone. Set the stone carefully on sand; then move it back and forth to work it into place ➊. Lay a level or straightedge over three or four stones to check the surface's evenness ➋. When a section is complete, fill the joints with sand or with sand and loam as described for bricks and pavers.

You can cut flagstone with a technique similar to that used for bricks. Score the line of the cut on the top surface with a brickset and hammer. Prop the stone on a piece of scrap wood, positioning the line of cut slightly beyond the edge of the wood. Securing the bottom edge of the stone with your foot, place the brickset on the scored line and strike sharply to make the cut.

FLAGSTONES

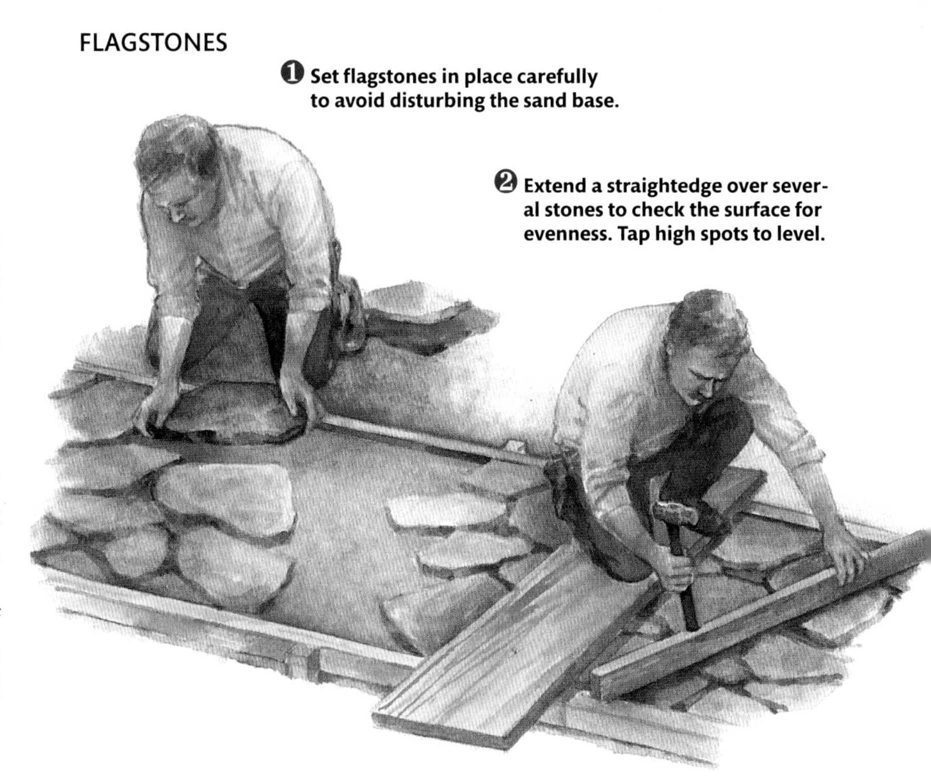

Laying a Patio

You can make a simple patio using the same techniques and materials we have discussed for paths. To ensure good drainage, an even surface, and durability, lay hard surfaces such as brick, flagstone, and pavers on a well-prepared base of gravel, sand, and compacted soil. (Crushed-rock and gravel surfaces likewise benefit from a sound base.) Make sure the surface drains away from any adjacent structure (house or garage); a drop-off of ¼ in. per foot is usually adequate. If the patio isn't near a structure, make it higher in the center to avoid puddles.

Establish the outline of the patio as described for paths; then excavate the area roughly to accommodate 4 in. of gravel, 2 in. of sand, and the thickness of the paving surface. (Check with a local nursery or landscape contractor to find out if local conditions require alterations in the type or amounts of base material.) Now grade the rough excavation to provide drainage, using a simple 4-ft. grid of wooden stakes as shown in the drawings.

Drive the first row of stakes next to the house (or in the center of a freestanding patio), leveling them with a 4-ft. builder's level or a smaller level resting on a straight 2x4. The tops of these stakes should be at the height of the top of the sand base (finish grade of the patio less the thickness of the surface material) ❶. Working from this row of stakes, establish another row about 4 to 5 ft. from the first. Make the tops of these stakes 1 in. lower than those of the first row, using a level and spacer block, as shown in the box below. Continue adding rows of stakes, each

LAYING A SIMPLE PATIO

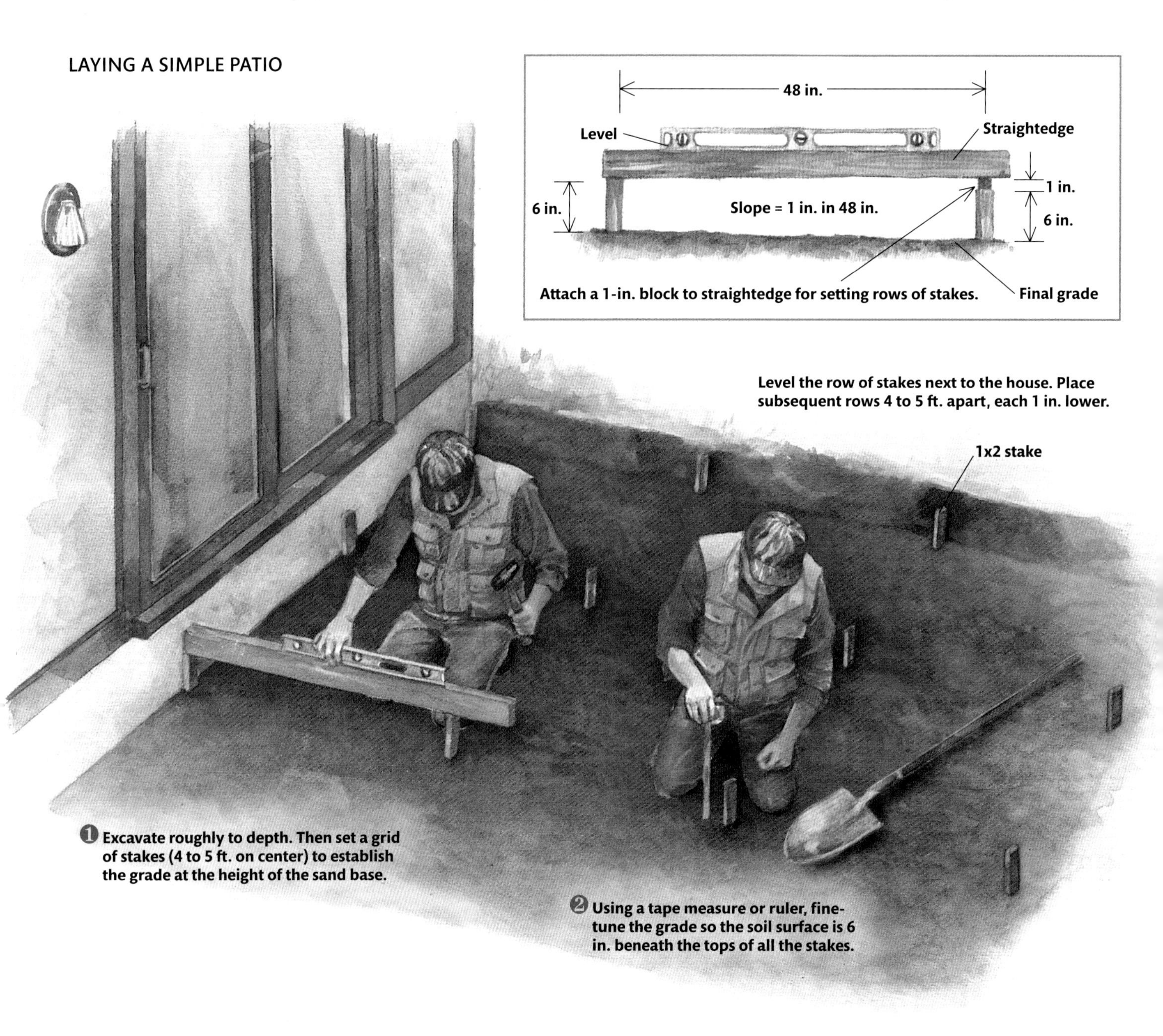

❶ Excavate roughly to depth. Then set a grid of stakes (4 to 5 ft. on center) to establish the grade at the height of the sand base.

❷ Using a tape measure or ruler, fine-tune the grade so the soil surface is 6 in. beneath the tops of all the stakes.

1 in. lower than the previous row, until the entire area is staked. Then, with a tape measure or ruler and a shovel, fine-tune the grading by removing or adding soil until the excavated surface is 6 in. (the thickness of the gravel-sand base) below the tops of all the stakes ❷.

When installing the sand-and-gravel base, you'll want to maintain the drainage grade you've just established and produce an even surface for the paving material. If you have a good eye or a very small patio, you can do this by sight. Otherwise, you can use the stakes to install a series of 1x3 or 1x4 "leveling boards," as shown in the drawing below. (Before adding gravel, you may want to cover the soil with water-permeable landscape fabric to keep perennial weeds from growing; just cut slits to accommodate the stakes.)

Add a few inches of gravel ❸. Then set leveling boards along each row of stakes, with the boards' top edges even with the top of the stakes ❹. Drive additional stakes to sandwich the boards in place (don't use nails). Distribute the remaining inch or so of gravel and compact it by hand or machine, then the 2 in. of sand. Dragging a straight 2x4 across two adjacent rows of leveling boards will produce a precise grade and an even surface ❺. Wet the sand and fill low spots that settle.

You can install the patio surface as previously described for paths, removing the leveling boards as the bricks or pavers reach them ❻. Disturbing the sand surface as little as possible, slide the boards out from between the stakes and drive the stakes an inch or so beneath the level of the sand. Cover the stakes and fill the gaps left by the boards with sand, tamped down carefully. Then continue laying the surface. Finally, sweep fine sand into the joints.

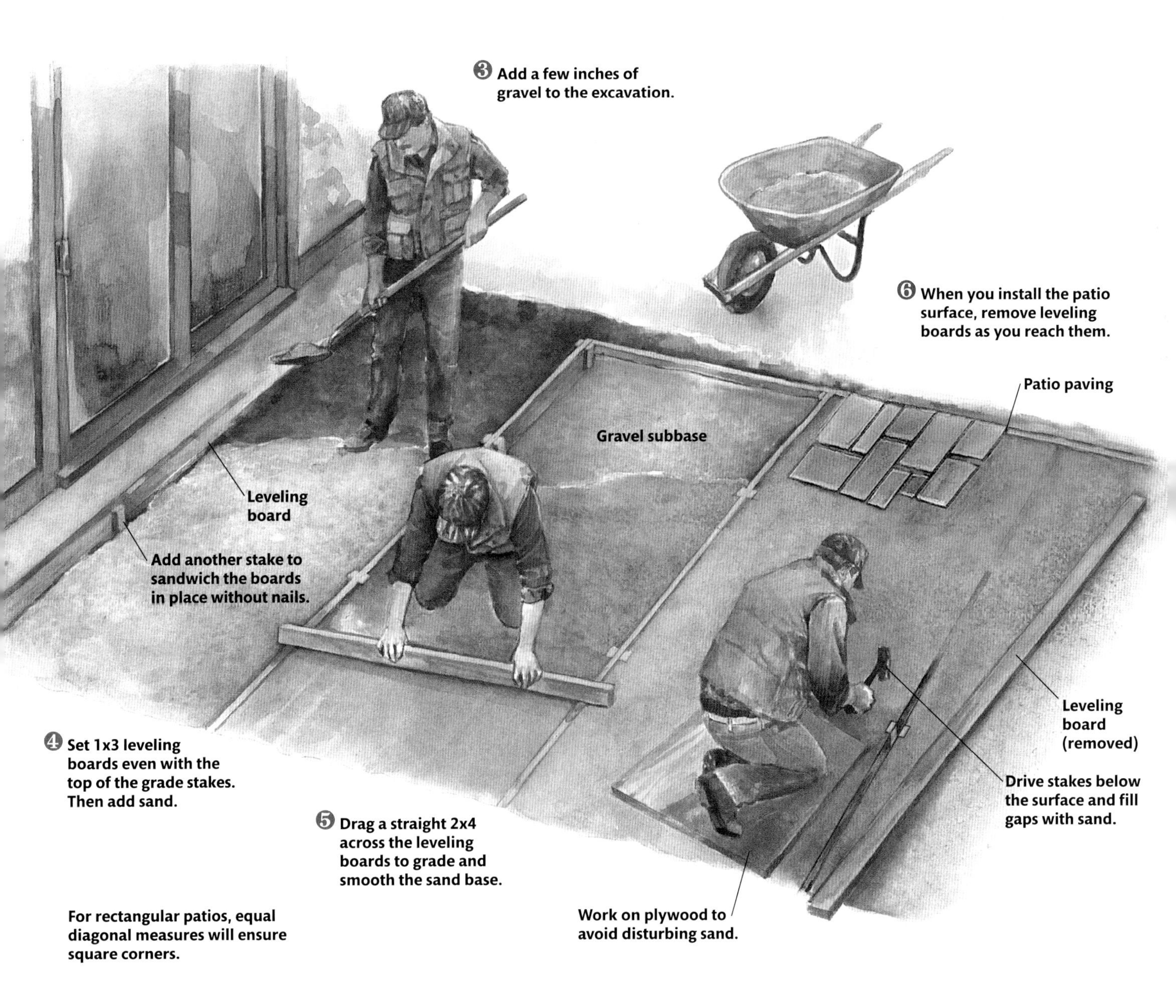

Installing a Pond

It wasn't so long ago that a garden pond like the one in this book required yards of concrete, an expert mason, and deep pockets. Today's strong, lightweight, and long-lasting synthetic liners and rigid fiberglass shells have put garden pools in reach of every homeowner. Installation does require some hard labor, but little expertise: just dig a hole; spread the liner or seat the shell; install edging; and plant. We'll discuss installation of a linered pond in the main text; see below for installing a smaller, fiberglass pool.

Liner notes

More and more nurseries and garden centers are carrying flexible pond liners; you can also buy them from mail-order suppliers specializing in water gardens. Synthetic rubber liners are longer lasting but more expensive than PVC liners. (Both are much cheaper than rigid fiberglass shells.) Buy only liners specifically made for garden ponds—don't use ordinary plastic sheeting. Many people feel that black liners look best; blue liners tend to make the pond look like a swimming pool.

Before you dig

First, make sure you comply with any rules your town may have about water features. Then keep the following ideas in mind when locating your pond. Avoid trees whose shade keeps sun-loving water plants from thriving; whose roots make digging a chore; and whose flowers, leaves, and seeds clog the water, making it unsightly and inhospitable to plants or fish. Avoid the low spot on your property; otherwise your pond will be a catch basin for runoff. Select a level spot; the immediate vicinity of the pond must be level, and starting out

Small reflecting pool

A fiberglass shell or agricultural tank about 6 ft. long, 18 to 24 in. wide, and 15 to 30 in. deep is ideal for the small pool on p. 96. To install it, dig a hole about 6 in. wider on all sides than the shell or tank. Its depth should equal that of the shell plus 1 in. for a sand base, plus the thickness of the fieldstone edging. Compact the bottom of the hole and spread the sand; then lower the shell into place. Add temporary wedges or props if necessary to orient and level the shell. Slowly fill it with water, backfilling around it with sand or sifted soil, tamped carefully in place, keeping pace with the rising water level. Excavate a wide relief for the edging stones, laying them on as firm a base as possible, slightly overhanging the rim of the shell.

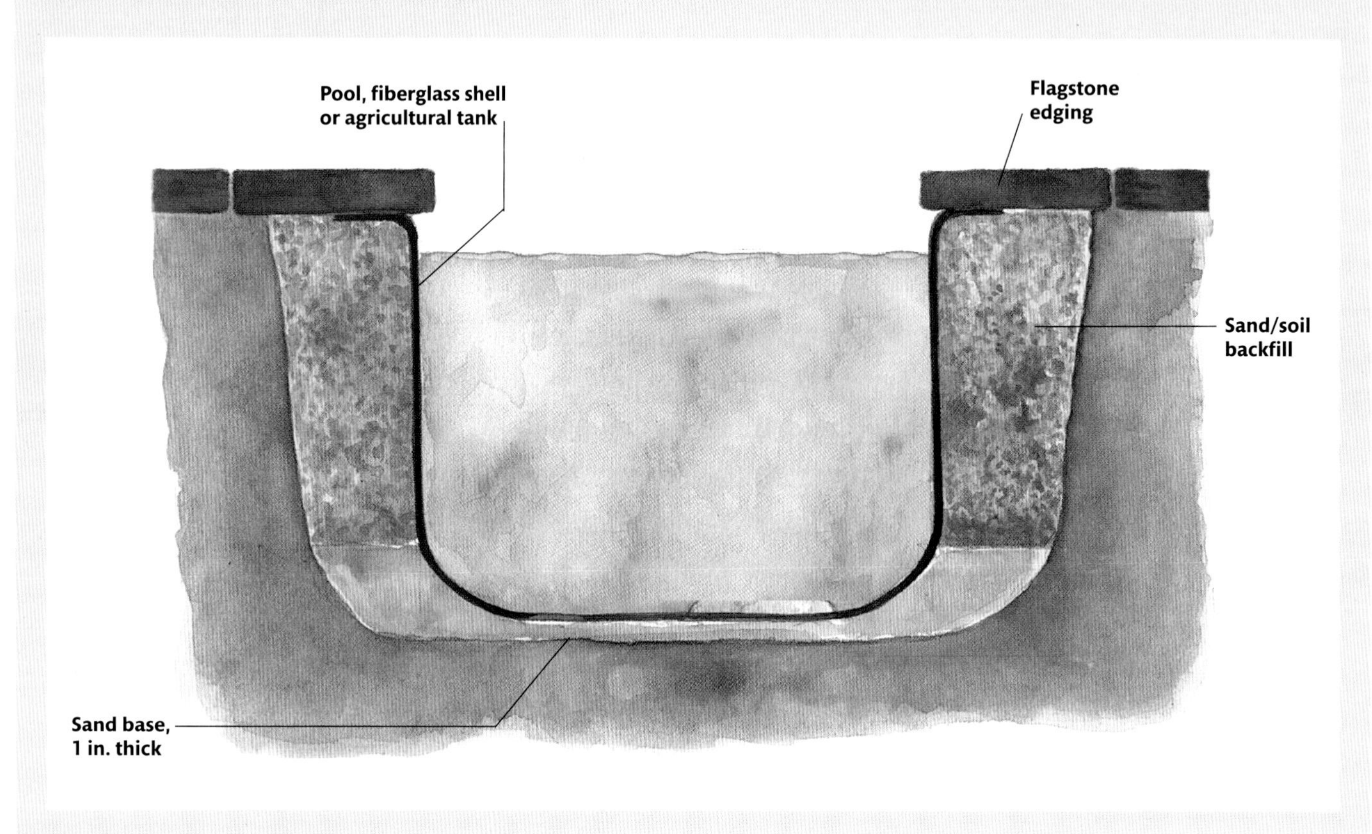

that way saves a lot of work. (Remember that you can use excavated soil to help level the site.)

Using graph paper, enlarge the outline of the pond provided on the site plan on p. 95, altering it as you wish. If you change the size or depth of the pond or are interested in growing a wider variety of water plants or in adding fish, remember that a healthy pond must achieve a balance between the plants and fish and the volume, depth, and temperature of the water. Even if you're not altering size or pond plants and fish, it's a good idea to consult with a knowledgeable person at a nursery or pet store specializing in water-garden plants and animals.

Calculate the liner width by adding twice the maximum depth of the pool plus an additional 2 ft. to the width. Use the same formula to calculate the length. So, for a pond 2 ft. deep, 6 ft. wide, and 12 ft. long, the liner width would be 4 ft. plus 6 ft. plus 2 ft. (or 12 ft.). The length would be 4 ft. plus 12 ft. plus 2 ft. (or 18 ft.).

Water work

Unless you are a very tidy builder, the water you used to fit the liner will be too dirty to leave in the pond. (Spilled mortar can also make the water too alkaline for plants or fish.) Siphon or pump out the water; clean the liner; and refill the pond. If you're adding fish to the pond, you'll need to let the water stand for a week or so to allow any chlorine (which is deadly to fish) to dissipate. Check with local pet stores to find out if your water contains chemicals that require commercial conditioners to make the water safe for fish.

Installing the pond and plants is only the first step in water gardening. It takes patience, experimentation, and usually some consultation with experienced water gardeners to achieve a balance between plants, fish, and waterborne oxygen, nutrients, and waste that will sustain all happily while keeping algae, diseases, insects, and predators at acceptable levels.

Growing pond plants

One water lily, a few upright-growing plants, and a bundle of submerged plants (which help keep the water clean) are enough for a medium-size pond. An increasing number of nurseries and garden centers stock water lilies and other water plants. For a larger selection, your nursery or garden center may be able to recommend a specialist supplier.

These plants are grown in containers filled with heavy garden soil (not potting soil, which contains ingredients that float). You can buy special containers designed for aquatic plants, or simply use plastic pails or dishpans. Line basketlike containers with burlap to keep the soil from leaking out the holes. A water lily needs at least 2 to 3 gal. of soil; the more, the better. Most other water plants, such as dwarf papyrus, need 1 to 2 gal. of soil.

After planting, add a layer of gravel on the surface to keep soil from clouding the water and to protect roots from marauding fish. Soak the plant and soil thoroughly. Then set the container in the pond, positioning it so the water over the soil is 6 to 18 in. deep for water lilies, 0 to 6 in. for most other plants.

For maximum bloom, push a tablet of special water-lily fertilizer into the pots once or twice a month throughout the summer. Most water plants are easy to grow and carefree, although many are tropicals that die after hard frost, so you'll have to replace them each spring.

PLANTING WATER PLANTS

Set water plants in a container of heavy garden soil. Then cover soil surface with gravel to keep soil from floating away.

Excavation

If your soil isn't too compacted or rocky, a good-size pond can be excavated with a shovel or two in a weekend ❶. (Energetic teenagers are a marvelous pool-building resource.) If the site isn't level, you can grade it using a stake-and-level system such as the one described on pp. 166–167 for grading the patio.

Outline the pond's shape with garden lime, establishing the curves freehand with a garden hose or by staking out a large grid and plotting from the graph-paper plan. The pond has two levels. The broad end, at 2 ft. deep, accommodates water lilies and other plants requiring deeper water as well as fish. Make the narrow end 12 to 16 in. deep for plants requiring shallower submersion. (You can put plant pots on stacks of bricks or other platforms to vary heights as necessary.) The walls will be less likely to crumble as you dig and the liner will install more easily if you slope them in about 3 to 4 in. for each foot of depth. Make the walls smooth, removing roots, rocks, and other sharp protrusions.

Excavate a shallow relief about 1 ft. wide around the perimeter to contain the liner overlap and stone edging. (The depth of the relief should accommodate the thickness of the edging stones.) Somewhere along the perimeter, create an overflow channel to take runoff after a heavy rain. This can simply be a 1- to 2-in. depression a foot or so wide spanned by one of the edging stones. Lengths of PVC pipe placed side by side beneath the stone (as shown in the drawing opposite) will keep the liner in place. The overflow channel can open onto a lower area of lawn or garden adjacent to the pond or to a rock-filled dry well.

Fitting the liner

When the hole is complete, cushion the surfaces to protect the liner ❷. Here we show an inch-thick layer of sand on the bot-

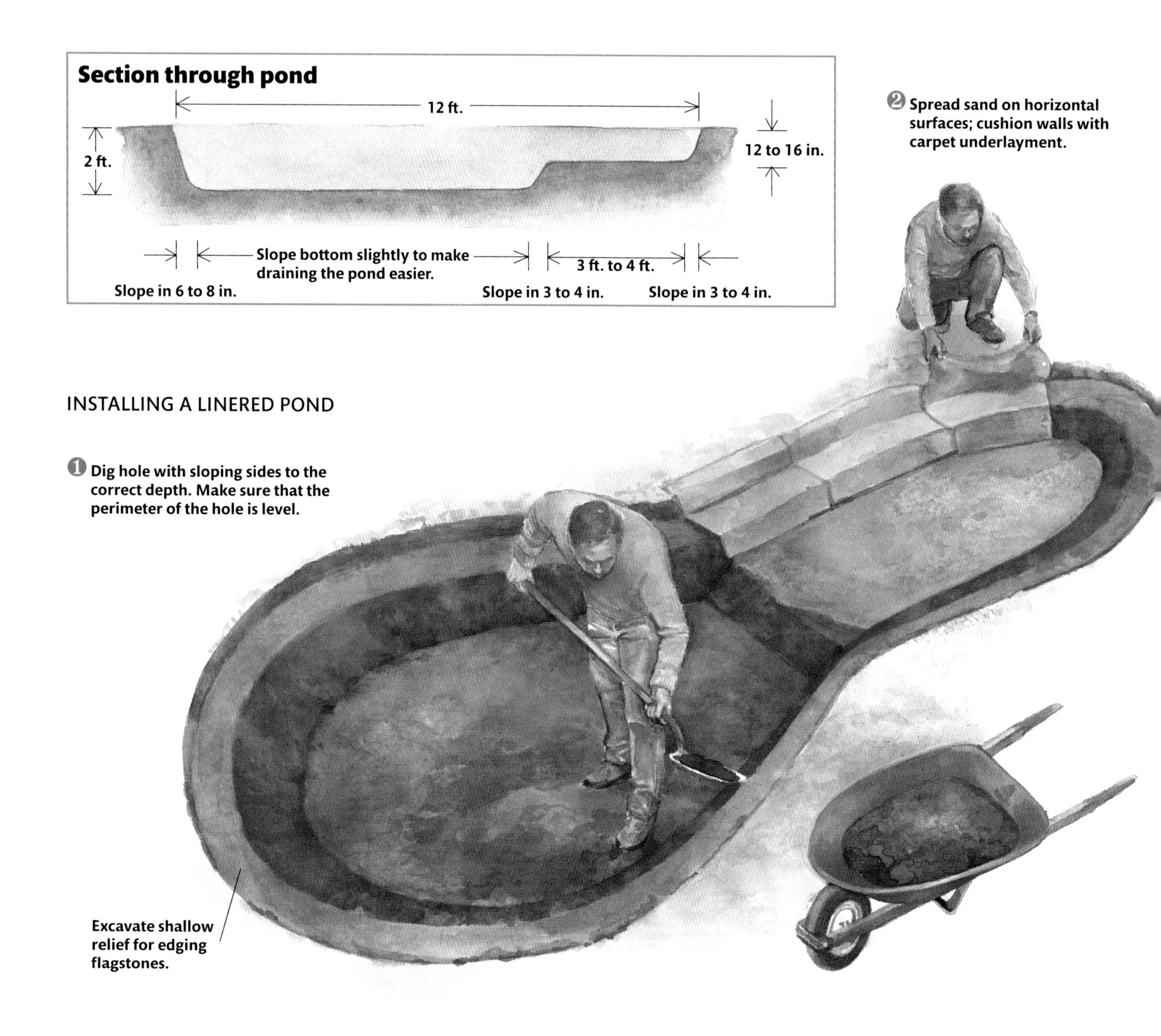

INSTALLING A LINERED POND

tom surfaces and carpet underlayment on the sloping walls. Fiberglass batting insulation also works well, as do old blankets or even heavy landscaping fabric.

Stretch the liner across the hole, letting it sag naturally to touch the walls and bottom but keeping it taut enough so it does not bunch up. Weight its edges with bricks or stones; then fill it with water ❸. The water's weight will push the liner against the walls; the stones will prevent it from blowing around. As it fills, tuck and smooth out as many creases as you can; the weight of the water makes this difficult to do after the pond is full. If you stand in the pond to do so, take care not to damage the liner. Don't be alarmed if you can't smooth all the creases. Stop filling when the water is 2 in. below the rim of the pond, and cut the liner to fit into the overlap relief ❹. Hold it in place with a few long nails or large "staples" made from coat hangers while you install the edging.

Elevation detail of pond overflow

Edging the pond

Finding and fitting flagstones so there aren't wide gaps between them is the most time-consuming part of this task. Cantilevering the stones an inch or two over the water will camouflage the liner somewhat.

The stones can be laid directly on the liner, as shown ❺. Add sand under the liner to level the surface where necessary so that the stones don't rock. Such treatment will withstand the occasional light traffic of pond and plant maintenance but not the wear and tear of young children or large dogs regularly running across the edging. (The liner won't go long without damage if used as a wading pool.) If you anticipate heavier traffic, you can bed the stones in 2 to 3 in. of mortar. It's prudent to consult with a landscape contractor about whether your intended use and soil require some sort of footing for mortared stones.

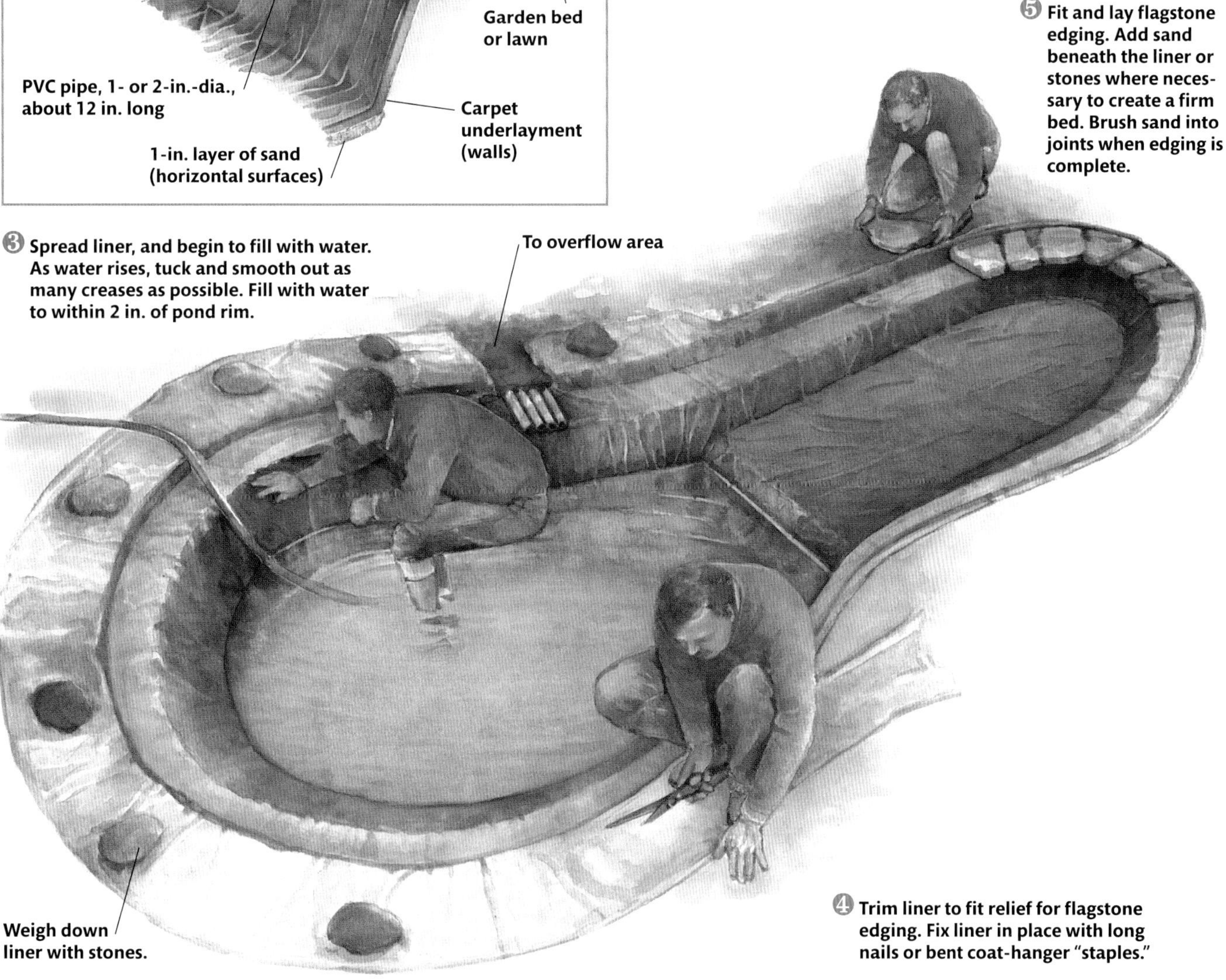

Building a Retaining Wall

Contours and sloping terrain can add considerable interest to a home landscape. But you can have too much of a good thing. Two designs in this book employ retaining walls to alter problem slopes. The wall shown on p. 48 eliminates a small but abrupt grade change, producing two almost level surfaces and the opportunity to install an attractive planting. On p. 36, a gently curved retaining wall helps turn a steep slope into a showpiece planting.

Retaining walls can be handsome landscape features in their own right. Made of cut stone, fieldstone, brick, landscape timbers, or concrete, they can complement the materials and style of your house or nearby structures. However, making a stable, long-lasting retaining wall of these materials can require tools and skills many homeowners do not possess.

For these reasons we've instead chosen retaining-wall systems made of precast concrete for designs in this book. Readily available in a range of sizes, surface finishes, and colors, these systems require few tools and no special skills to install. They have been engineered to resist the forces that soil, water, freezing, and thawing bring to bear on a retaining wall. Install these walls according to the manufacturer's specifications, and you can be confident that they will do their job for many years.

A number of systems are available in the region through nurseries, garden centers, and local contracting suppliers. (Check online.) But they all share basic design principles. Like traditional drystone walls, these systems rely largely on weight and friction to contain the weight of the soil. In many systems, interlocking blocks or pegs help align the courses and increase the wall's strength. In all systems, blocks must rest on a solid, level base. A freely draining backfill of crushed stone is essential to avoid buildup of water pressure (both liquid and frozen) in the retained soil, which can buckle even a heavy wall.

The construction steps shown here are typical of those recommended by most system manufacturers for retaining walls up to 3 to 4 ft. tall; be sure to follow the manufacturer's instructions for the system you choose. (Some installation guides are excellent; others are less helpful. Weigh the quality of instructions in your decision of which system to buy.) For higher walls, walls on loose soil or heavy clay soils, and walls retaining very steep slopes, it is prudent to consult with a landscape architect or contractor.

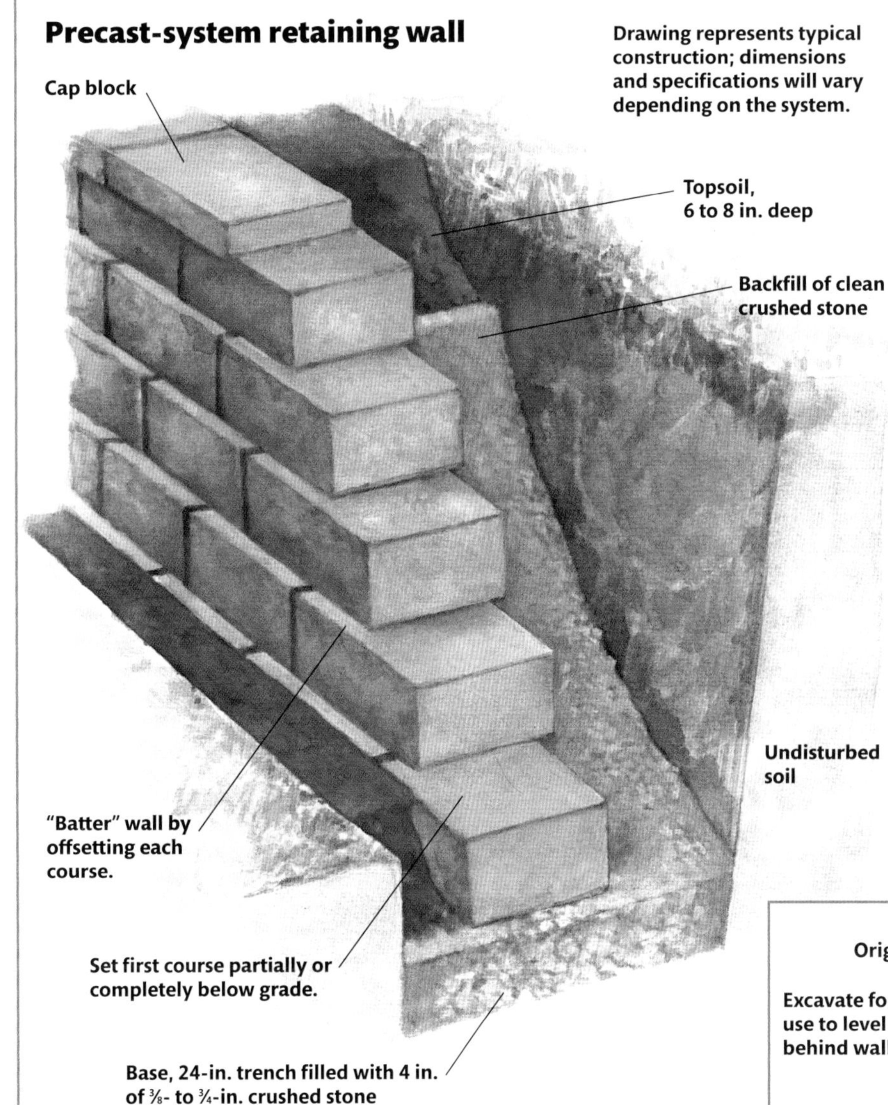

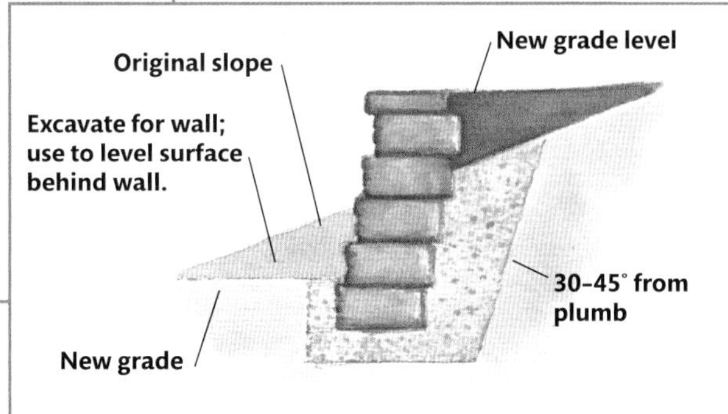

Building a wall

Installing a wall system is just about as simple as stacking up children's building blocks. The most important part of the job is establishing a firm, level base. Start by laying out the wall with string and hose (for curves) and excavating a base trench.

As the boxed drawing shows, the position of the wall in relation to the base of the slope determines the height of the wall, how much soil you move, and the leveling effect on the slope. Unless the wall is very long, it is a good idea to excavate along the entire length and fine-tune the line of the wall before beginning the base trench. Remember to excavate back far enough to accommodate the stone backfill. Systems vary, but a foot of crushed-stone backfill behind the blocks is typical. (For the two-wall design, build the bottom wall first, and then the top.)

Systems vary in the width and depth of trench and type of base material, but in all of them, the trench must be level across its width and along its length. We've shown a 4-in. layer of ⅜- to ¾-in. crushed stone (blocks can slip sideways on rounded aggregate or pea gravel, which also don't compact as well). Depending on the system and the circumstances, a portion or all of the first course lies below grade, so the soil helps hold the blocks in place.

Add crushed stone to the trench; level it with a rake; and compact it with a hand tamper or mechanical compactor. Lay the first course of blocks carefully ❶. Check frequently to make sure the blocks are level across their width and along their length. Stagger vertical joints as you stack subsequent courses. Offset the faces of the blocks so the wall leans back into the retained soil. Some systems design this "batter" into their blocks; others allow you to choose from several possible setbacks.

As the wall rises, shovel backfill behind the blocks ❷. Clean crushed rock drains well; some systems suggest placing a barrier of landscaping fabric between the rock and the retained soil to keep soil from migrating into the fill and impeding drainage.

Thinner cap blocks finish the top of the wall ❸. Some wall systems recommend cementing these blocks in place with a weatherproof adhesive. The last 6 to 8 in. of the backfill should be topsoil, firmed into place and ready for planting.

BUILDING A WALL

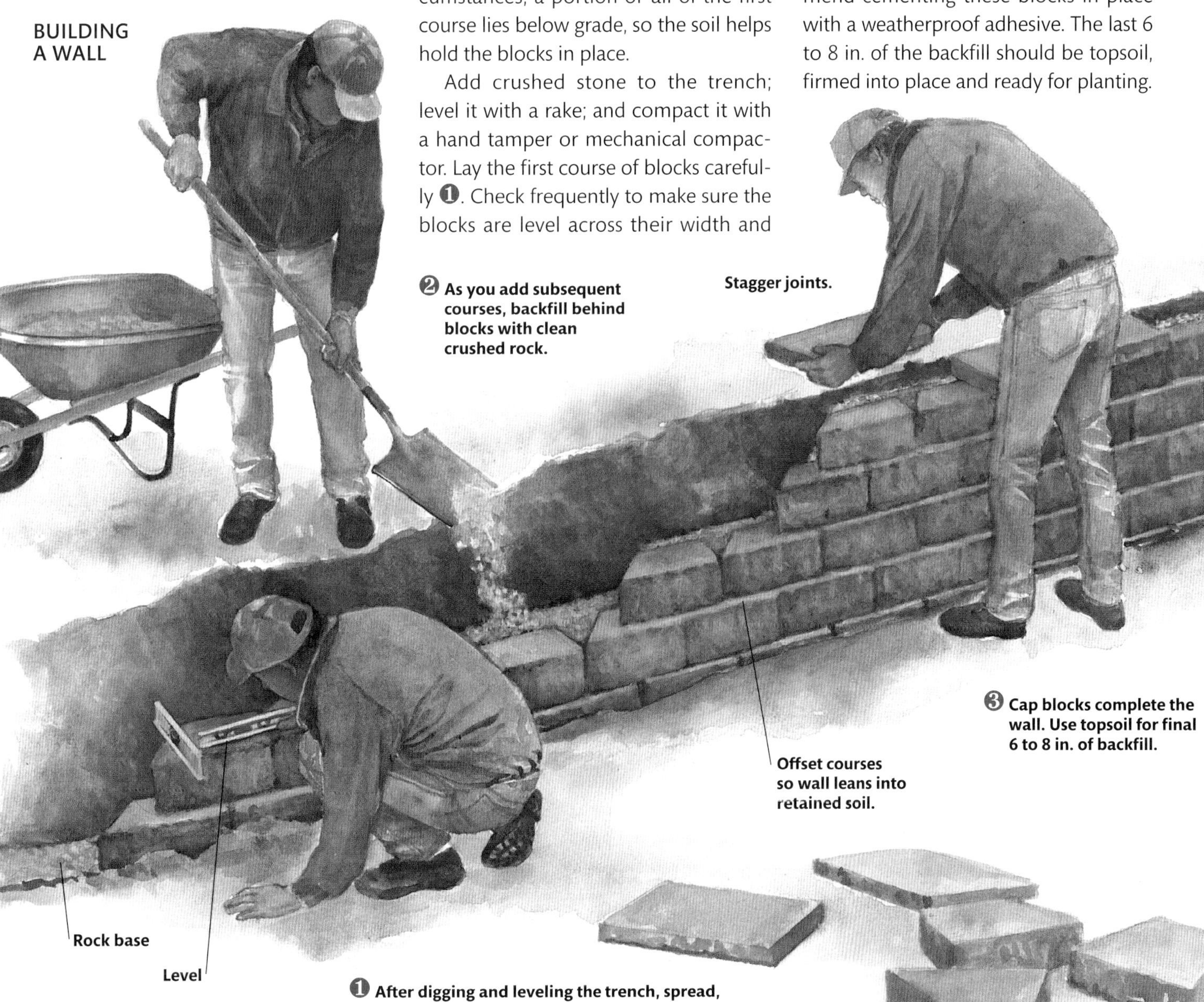

Wall parallel with a slope: Stepped base

Construct walls running parallel to a slope in steps, each with a level base.

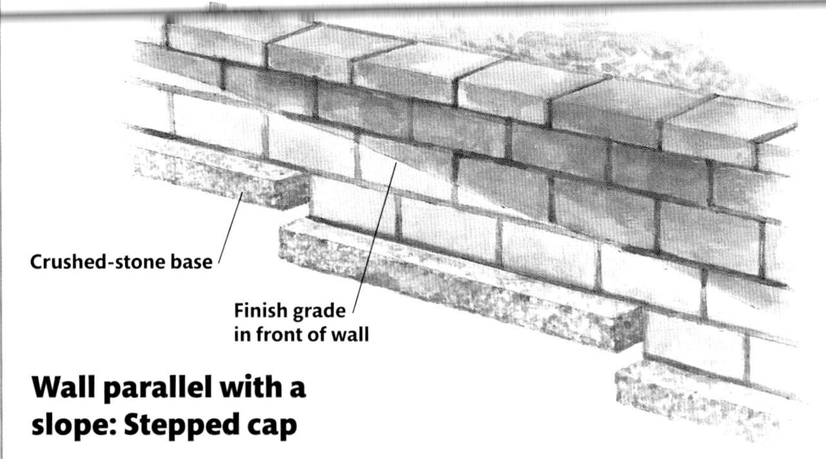

Wall parallel with a slope: Stepped cap

Sometimes the top of a wall needs to step up or down to accommodate grade changes in the slope behind.

A "return" corner

Where you want the slope to extend beyond the end of the wall, make a corner that cuts into the slope.

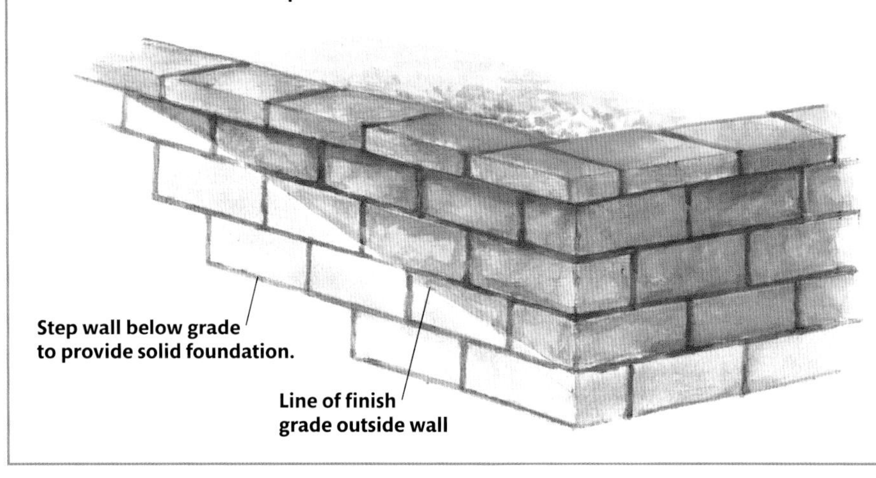

Sloped sites

If your site slopes along the wall's length, you'll need to "step" the bottom of the wall, as shown at top left. Create a length of level trench along the lowest portion of the site; then work up the slope, creating steps as necessary.

The top of the wall can also step if the slope dissipates at one end. This is common on sites such as the one on p. 36, which slopes away from the house. and toward the driveway. Here the base of the wall will rest on level ground, but the slope behind the wall decreases along the wall's length. The design on p. 36 shows one solution to this dilemma—a wall of uniform height with a "return" corner at the street end (see bottom left), backfilled to raise the grade behind to the top of the wall. Another solution, shown at center left, is to step the wall down as the slope decreases, which saves material and produces a different look but still works with the planting design.

Curves and corners

Wall-system blocks are designed so that curves are no more difficult to lay than straight sections. Corners may require that you cut a few blocks or use specially designed blocks, but they are otherwise uncomplicated. If your wall must fit a prescribed length between corners, consider working from the corners toward the middle (after laying a base course). Masons use this technique, which also avoids exposing cut blocks at the corners.

You can cut blocks with a mason's chisel and mallet or rent a mason's saw. Chiseling works well where the faces of the blocks are rough textured, so the cut faces blend with them. A saw is best for smooth-faced blocks and projects requiring lots of cutting.

Where the wall doesn't run the full length of the slope, the best-looking and most structurally sound termination is a corner constructed to cut back into the slope, as shown at bottom left.

Steps

Steps in a low retaining wall are not difficult to build, but they require forethought and careful layout. Systems differ on construction details. The drawing below shows a typical design where the blocks and stone base rest on steps cut into firm subsoil. If your soil is less stable or is recent fill, you should excavate the entire area beneath the steps to the same depth as the wall base and build a foundation of blocks, as shown in the boxed drawing.

These steps are independent of the adjacent return walls, which are vertical, not battered (stepped back). In some systems, steps and return walls are interlocked. To match a path, you can face the treads with the same stone, brick, or pavers, or you can use the system's cap blocks or special treads.

SOLID FOUNDATION: CROSS SECTION

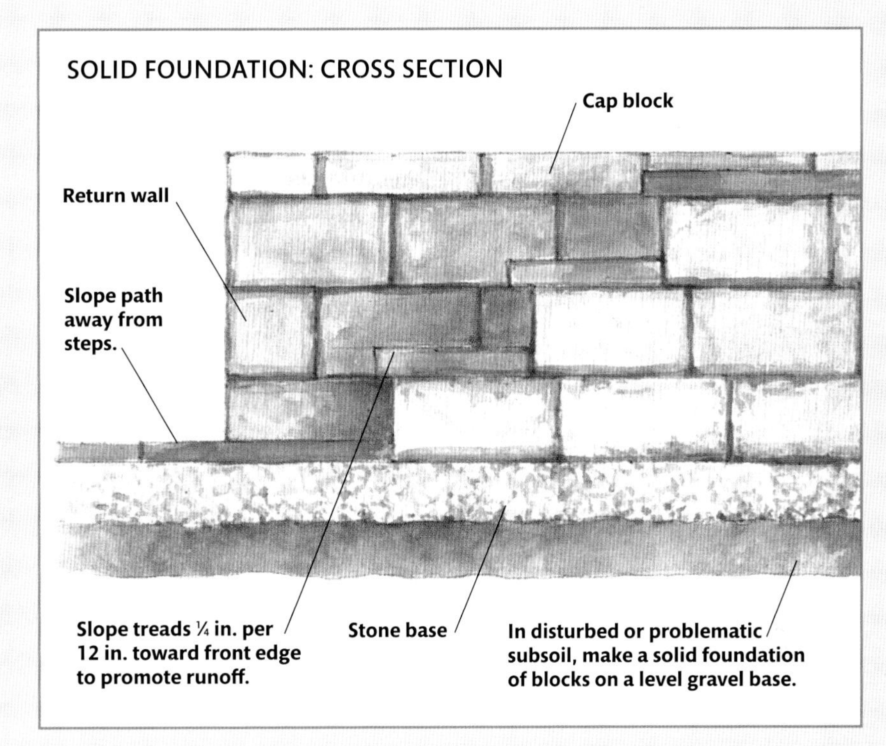

"Stepped" foundation

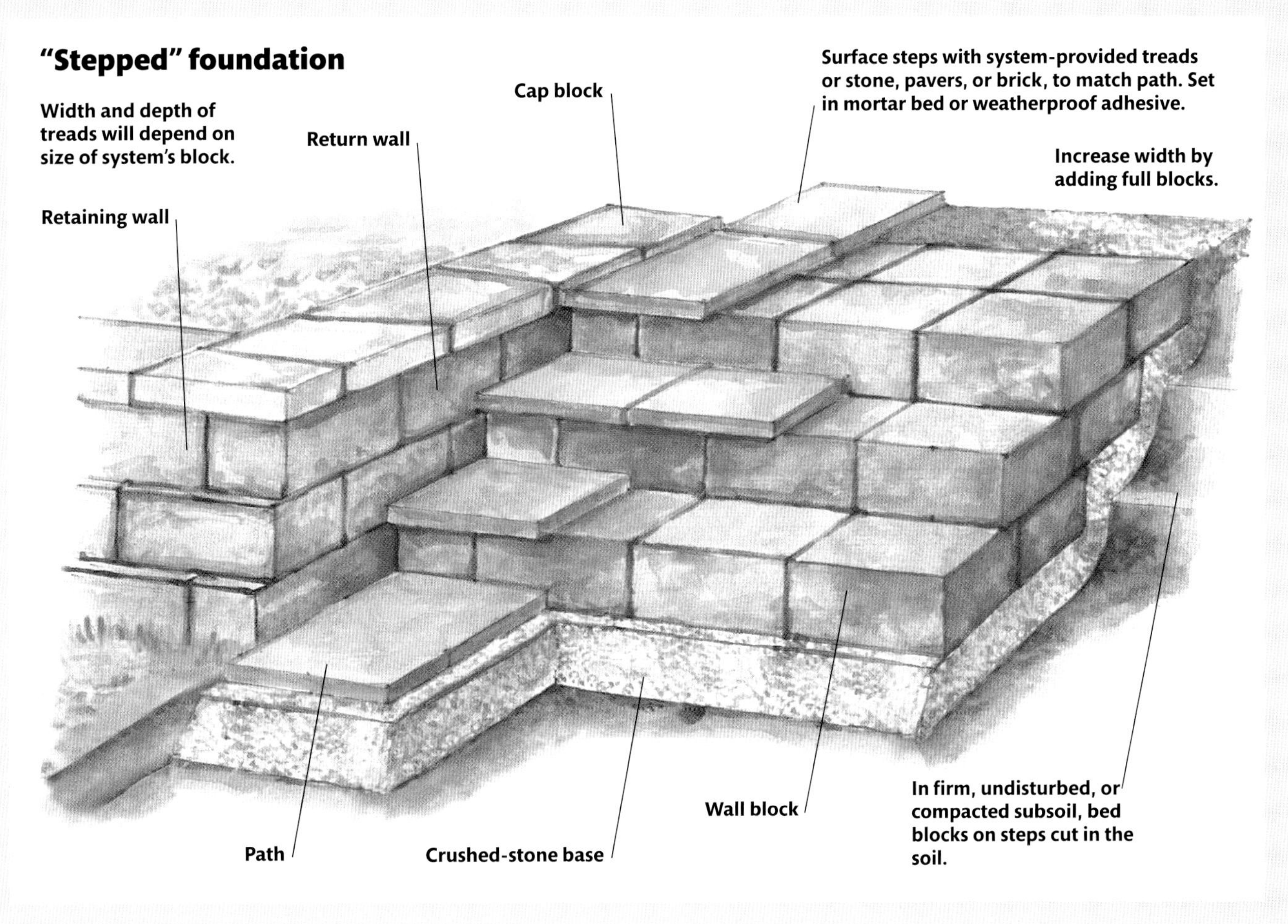

Fences, Arbors, and Trellises

Novices who have no trouble tackling a simple flagstone path often get nervous when it comes time to erect a fence, an arbor, or even a trellis. While such projects can require more skill and resources than others in the landscape, the ones in this book have been designed with less-than-confident do-it-yourself builders in mind. The designs are simple, the materials are readily available, and the tools and skills will be familiar to anyone accustomed to ordinary home maintenance.

First we'll introduce you to the materials and tools needed for the projects. Then we'll present the small number of basic operations you'll employ when building them. Finally, we'll provide drawings and comments on each of the projects.

Tools and materials

Even the least-handy homeowner is likely to have most of the tools needed for these projects: claw hammer, crosscut handsaw, brace-and-bit or electric drill, adjustable wrench, combination square, measuring tape, carpenter's level, and sawhorses. You may even have Grandpa's old posthole digger. Many will have a handheld power circular saw, which makes faster (though noisier) work of cutting parts to length. A cordless drill/screwdriver is invaluable if you're substituting screws for nails. If you have more than a few holes to dig, consider renting a gas-powered posthole digger. A 12-in.-diameter hole will serve for 4x4 posts; if possible, get a larger-diameter digger for 6x6 posts.

Materials

Of the materials offering strength, durability, and attractiveness in outdoor settings, wood is the easiest to work and affords the quickest results. While almost all commercially available lumber is strong enough for landscape structures, most decay quickly when in prolonged contact with soil and water. Cedar, cypress, and redwood, however, contain natural preservatives and are excellent for landscape use. Alternatively, a range of softwoods (such as pine, fir, and hemlock) are pressure treated with preservatives and will last for many years. Parts of structures that do not come in contact with soil or are not continually wet can be made of ordinary construction-grade lumber, but unless they're regularly painted, they will not last as long as treated or naturally decay-resistant material.

In addition to dimension lumber, several of the designs incorporate lattice, which is thin wooden strips crisscrossed to form patterns of diamonds or squares. Premade lattice is widely available in sheets 4 ft. by 8 ft. and smaller. Lattice comes in decay-resistant woods as well as in treated and untreated softwoods. Local supplies vary, and you may find lattice made of thicker or narrower material.

Fasteners

For millennia, even basic structures such as these would have been assembled with complicated joints. Today, using simple nailed, bolted, or screwed joints, a few hours' practice swinging a hammer or wielding a cordless electric screwdriver is all the training necessary.

All these structures can be assembled using nails. But screws are stronger and, if you have a cordless screwdriver, make assembly easier. Buy common or box nails that are galvanized to prevent rust. Self-tapping screws ("deck" screws) require no pilot holes. For rust resistance, buy galvanized screws or screws treated with zinc dichromate.

Galvanized metal connectors are available to reinforce the joints used in these projects. For novice builders, connectors are a great help in aligning parts and making assembly easier. (Correctly fastened with nails or screws, the joints are strong enough without connectors.)

Finishes

Cedar, cypress, and redwood are handsome when left unfinished to weather, when treated with clear or colored stains, or when painted. Pressure-treated lumber is best painted or stained.

Outdoor stains are becoming increasingly popular. Clear or lightly tinted stains can preserve or enhance the rich reddish browns of cedar, cypress, and redwood. Stains also come in a range of colors that can be used like paint. Because they penetrate the wood rather than forming a film, stains don't form an opaque surface, but stains won't peel or chip like paint and are therefore easier to touch up and refinish.

When choosing a finish, take account of what plants are growing on or near the structure. It's a lot of work to remove yards of vines from a trellis or squeeze between a large shrub and a fence to repaint; consider an unfinished, decay-resistant wood or an initial stain that you allow to weather.

Setting posts

All the projects are anchored by firmly set, vertical posts. In general, the taller the structure, the deeper the post should be set. For the arbors and the tallest fences, posts should be at least 3 ft. deep. Posts for fences up to 4 ft. tall can be set 2 ft. deep. To avoid post movement caused by expansion and contraction of the soil during freeze-thaw cycles, it's a good idea to set all arbor posts below the frost line. This depth is greater in colder climates; check with local building authorities.

The length of the posts you buy depends, of course, on the depth at which they are set and their finished heights. When calculating lengths of arbor posts, remember that the tops of the posts must be level. The easiest method of achieving this is to cut the posts to length after installation. For example, buy 12-ft. posts for an arbor finishing at 8 ft. above grade and set 3 ft. in the ground. The convenience is worth the expense of the foot or so you remove. The site and personal preference can determine whether you cut fence posts to length after installation or buy them cut to length and add or remove fill from the bottom of the hole to position them at the correct heights.

Arbor posts

Take extra care when positioning arbor posts. The corners of the structure must be right angles, and the sides must be parallel. Locating the corners with batter boards and string is fussy but accurate. Make the batter boards by nailing 1x2 stakes to scraps of 1x3 or 1x4, and position them about 1 ft. from the approximate location of each post as shown in the boxed drawing at right. Locate the exact post positions with string; adjust the string so the diagonal measurements are equal, which ensures that the corners of the structure will be at right angles.

At the intersections of the strings, locate the postholes by eye or with a plumb bob ❶. Remove the strings and dig the holes; then reattach the strings to position the posts exactly ❷. Plumb and brace the posts carefully. Check positions with the level and by measuring between adjacent posts and across diagonals. Diagonal braces between adjacent posts will stiffen them and help align their faces ❸. Then add concrete ❹ and let it cure for a day.

To establish the height of the posts, measure up from grade on one post; then use a level and straightedge to mark the heights of the other posts from the first one. Where joists will be bolted to the faces of the posts, you can install the joists and use their top edges as a handsaw guide for cutting the posts to length.

SETTING ARBOR POSTS

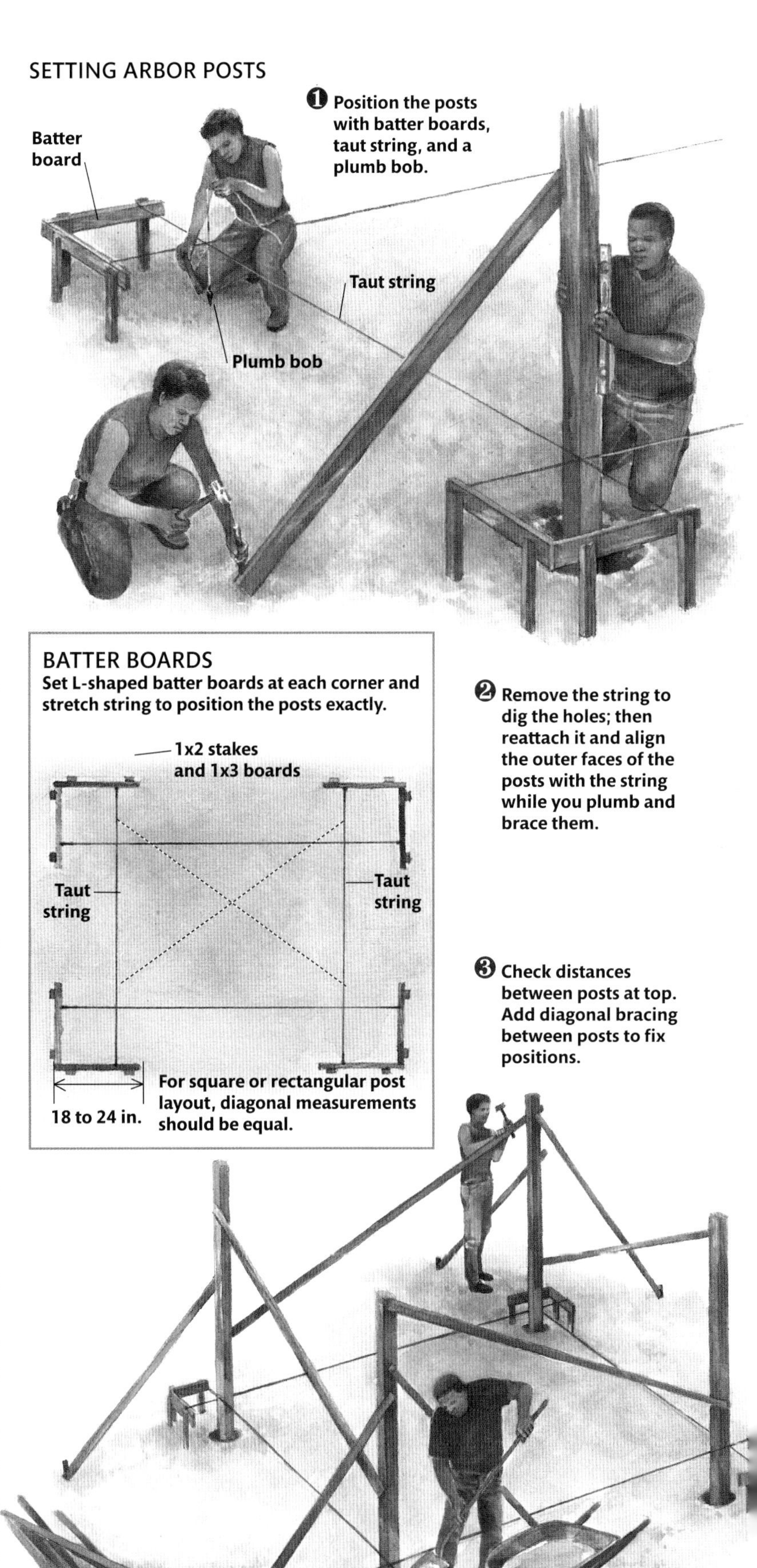

Fence posts

Lay out and set the end or corner posts of a fence first; then add the intermediate posts. Dig the holes by hand or with a power digger ❶. To promote drainage, place several inches of gravel at the bottom of the hole to rest the post. Checking with a carpenter's level, plumb the post vertically and brace it with scrap lumber nailed to stakes ❷. Then add a few more inches of gravel around the post's base.

If your native soil compacts well, you can fix posts in place with tamped earth. Add the soil gradually, tamping it continuously with a heavy iron bar or 2x4. Check regularly with a level to see that the post doesn't get knocked out of plumb. This technique suits rustic or informal fences, where misalignments caused by shifting posts aren't noticeable or damaging.

For more formal fences, or where soils are loose or fence panels are buffeted by winds or snow, it's prudent to fix posts in concrete ❸. Mix enough concrete to set the two end posts; as a rule of thumb, figure one 80-lb. bag of premixed concrete per post. As you shovel it in, prod the concrete with a stick to settle it, particularly if you've added rubble to extend the mix. Build

SETTING A FENCE POST

❶ Position the end or corner posts; then dig holes for them.

❷ Plumb the post, checking on adjacent faces with a level. Hold it in position with stakes and braces.

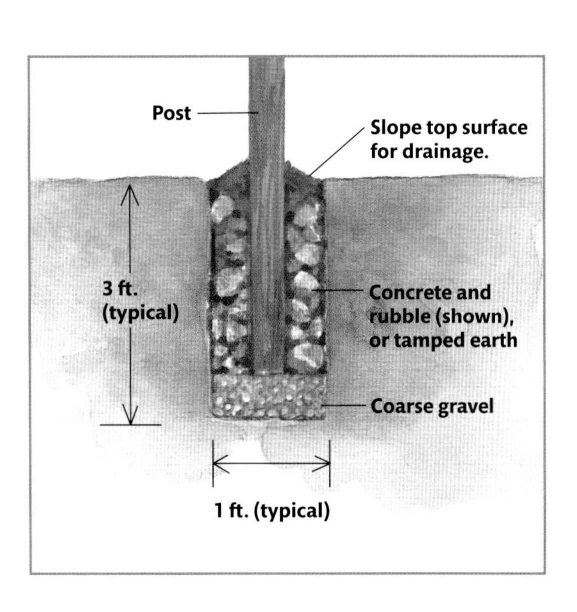

❸ Fill the hole with concrete and rubble.

the concrete slightly above grade and slope it away from the post to aid drainage.

Once the end posts are set, stretch a string between the posts. (The concrete should cure for 24 hours before you nail or screw rails and panels in place, but you can safely stretch string while the concrete is still wet.) Measure along the string to position the intermediate posts; drop a plumb bob from the string at each intermediate post position to gauge the center of the hole below ❹. Once all the holes have been dug, again stretch a string between the end posts, near the top. Set the intermediate posts as described previously; align one face with the string and plumb adjacent faces with the carpenter's level ❺. Check positions of intermediate posts a final time with a tape measure.

If the fence is placed along a slope, the top of the slats or panels can step down the slope or mirror it (as shown in the bottom drawing). Either way, make sure that the posts are plumb, rather than leaning with the slope.

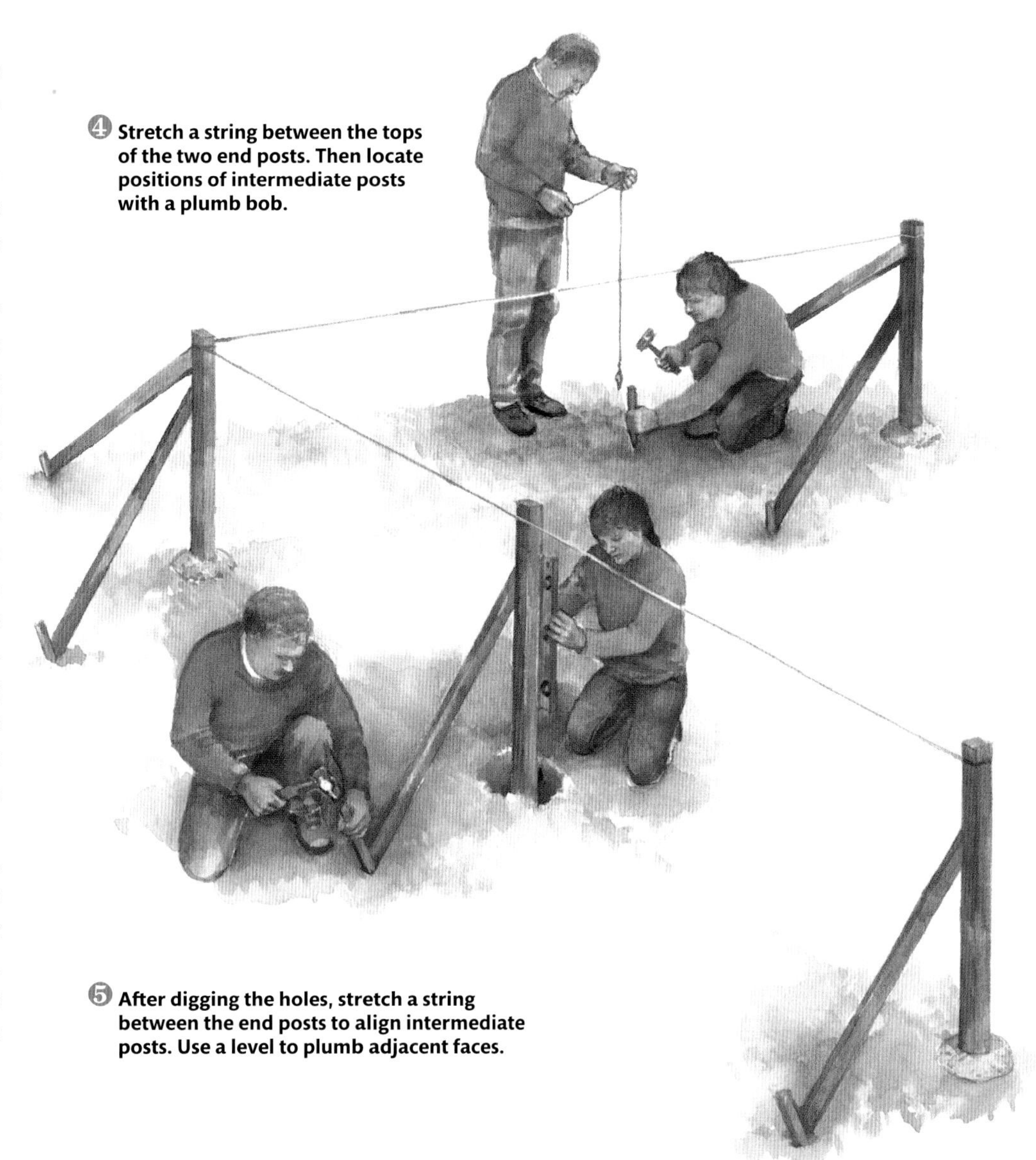

❹ **Stretch a string between the tops of the two end posts. Then locate positions of intermediate posts with a plumb bob.**

❺ **After digging the holes, stretch a string between the end posts to align intermediate posts. Use a level to plumb adjacent faces.**

Fencing a slope

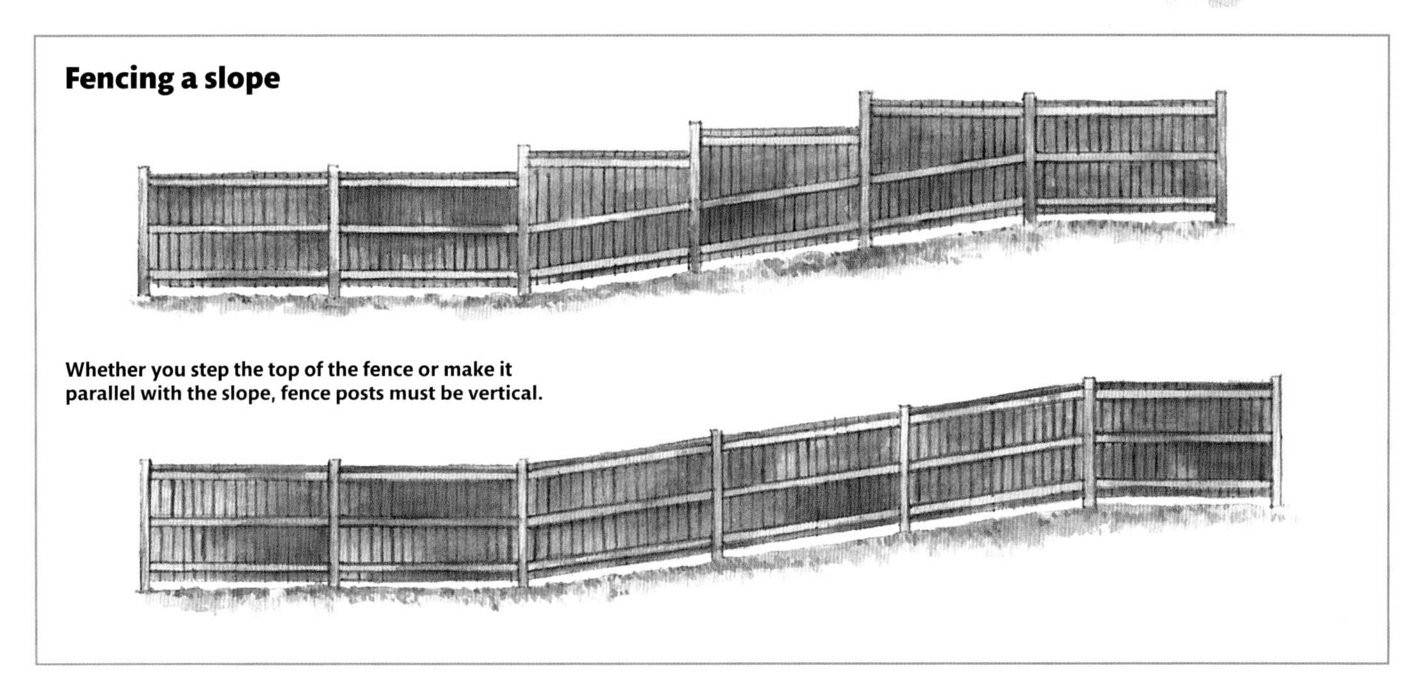

Whether you step the top of the fence or make it parallel with the slope, fence posts must be vertical.

Joints

The components of the fences, arbors, and trellises used in this book are attached to the posts and to each other with the simple joints shown below. Because all the parts are made of dimensioned lumber, the only cuts you'll need to make are to length. For strong joints, cut ends as square as you can, so the mating pieces make contact across their entire surfaces. If you have no confidence in your sawing, many lumberyards will cut pieces to length for a modest fee.

Novices often find it difficult to keep two pieces correctly positioned while trying to drive a nail into them, particularly when the nail must be driven at an angle, called "toenailing". If you have this problem, consider assembling the project with screws, which draw the pieces together, or with metal connectors, which can be nailed or screwed in place on one piece and then attached to the mating piece.

For several designs, you need to attach lattice panels to posts. The panels are made by sandwiching store-bought lattice

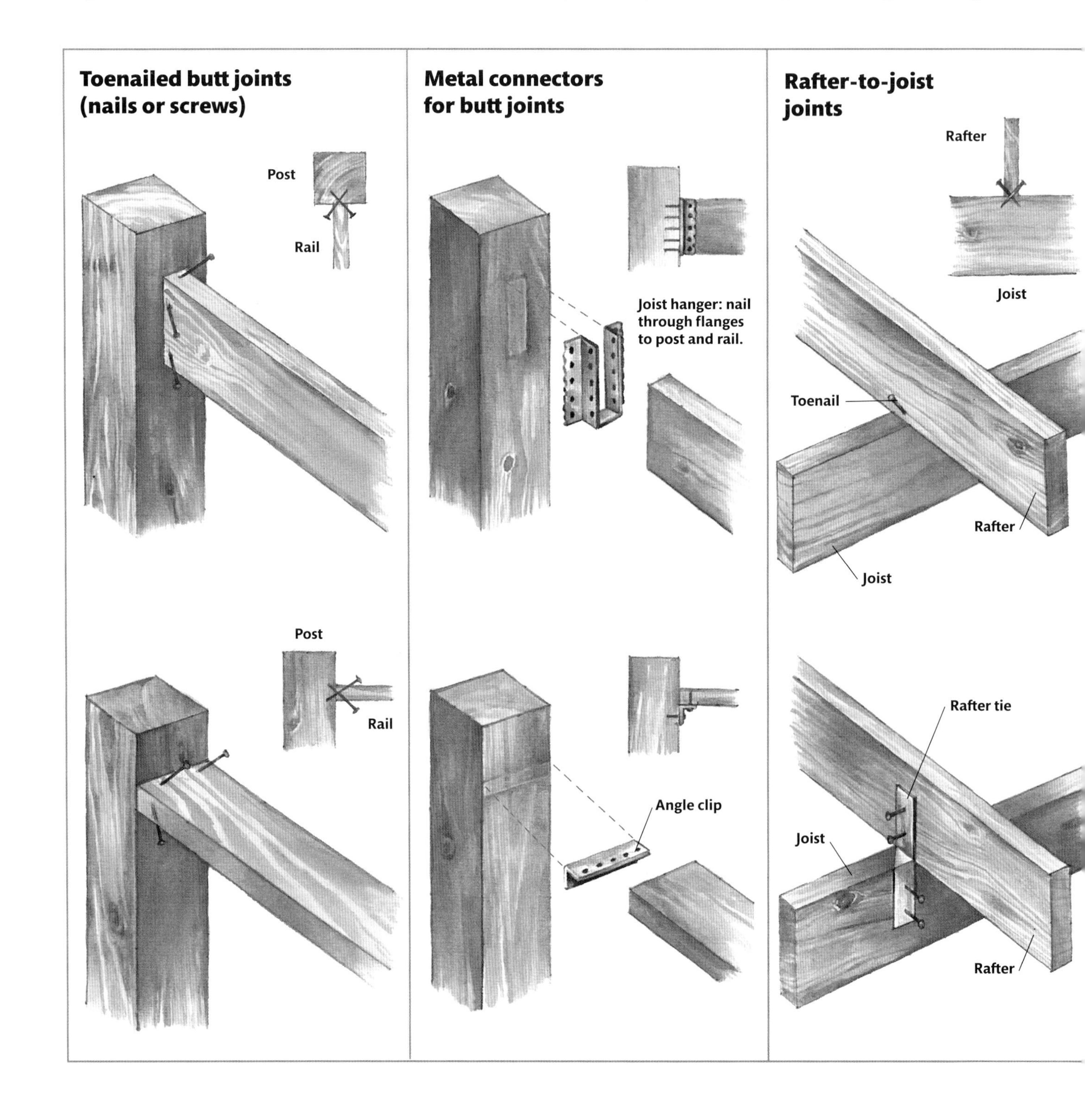

between frames of dimension lumber (construction details are given on the following pages). While the assembled panels can be toenailed to the posts, novices may find that the job goes easier using one or more types of metal connector, as shown in the drawing below right. Attach the angle clips or angle brackets to the post; then position the lattice panel and fix it to the connectors. For greatest strength and ease of assembly, attach connectors with self-tapping screws driven by an electric screwdriver.

In the following pages, we'll show construction details of the fences, arbors, and trellises presented in the Portfolio of designs. (The page number indicates the design.) Where the basic joints discussed here can be used, we have shown the parts but left the selection of fasteners to you. Typical fastenings are indicated for other joints. We have kept the constructions shown here simple and straightforward. They are not the only possibilities, of course, and we encourage builders and homeowners with experience to adapt and alter constructions as well as designs to suit different situations and personal preferences.

Frame corner with metal connector

Nailing plate

Angled plate

Attaching framed lattice panels to posts

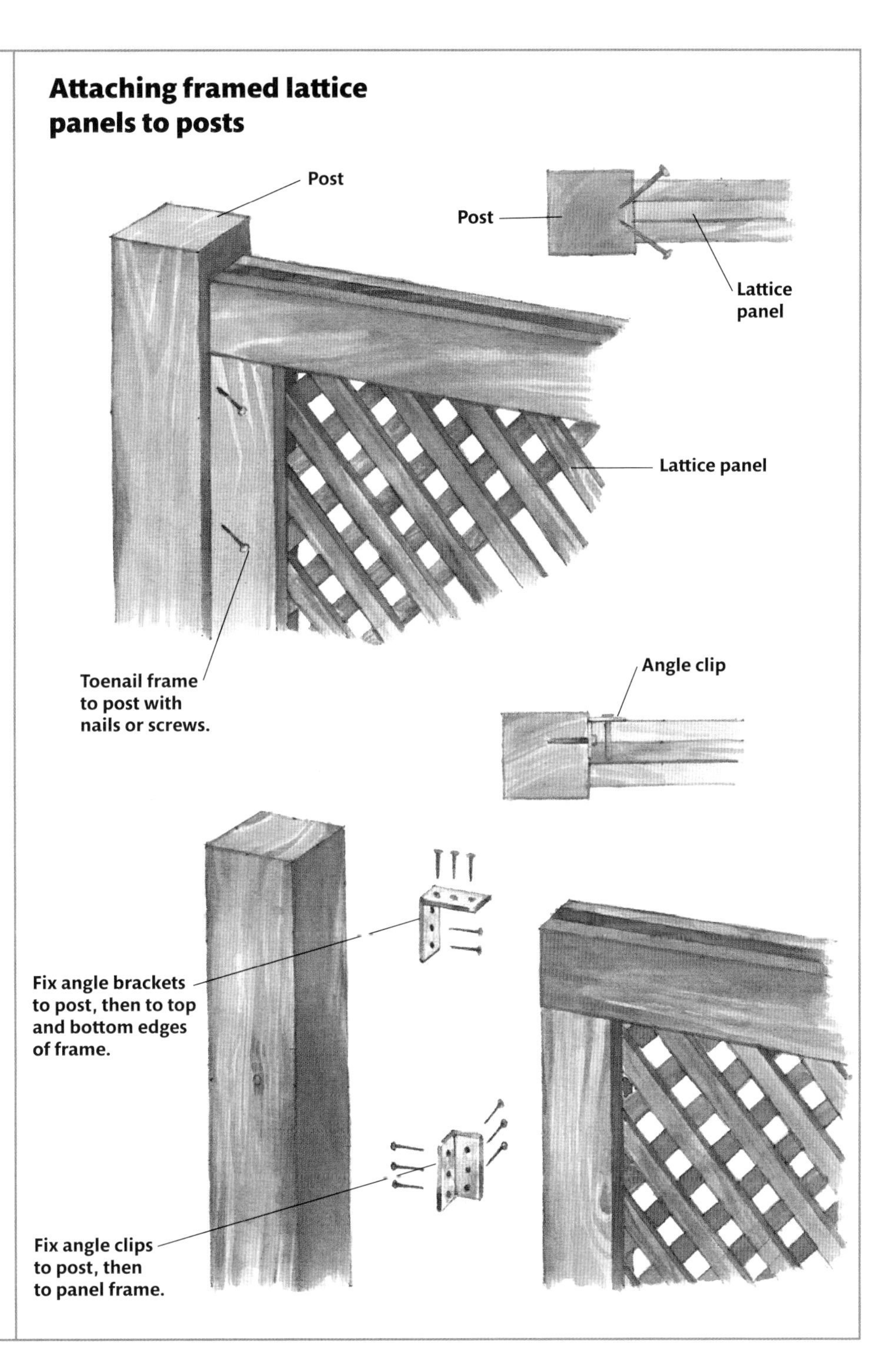

Planters

(pp. 30–33 and 66–67)

The planting boxes in this book bring colorful vines and annuals right up next to a front door and onto a small patio. Commercially made planters are available in a wide range of sizes, shapes, and materials. But a do-it-yourselfer can make one of the simple sturdy boxes shown here in just an hour or so.

The boxes are made in the same way, and the design can be enlarged or reduced to make planters of any size you need. For longevity, use cedar, cypress, redwood, or pressure-treated lumber for all the wooden parts. You can nail the boxes together, but the job will be easier and the boxes stronger if they are assembled with screws and an electric screwdriver. Whether you opt for nails or screws, be sure to use fasteners treated against rust.

Begin by assembling battens and boards to make a pair of opposing sides and the box bottom ❶. On a rectangular box, make the long sides first. Note that on the box sides, the ends of the 1x2 battens stop short of the two edges. Position the box bottom against the bottom ends of these battens ❷ and screw the sides to the bottom. (The top ends stop short so you can cover them with soil, which results in a neater appearance inside the box.) Complete the box by fastening the end boards to the edges of the battens on the ends of the sides and bottom ❸.

To ensure good drainage, bore ¾-in. holes in the box bottom on a 6-in. grid. Cover the holes with pieces of window screen; fill the boxes with damp potting soil; and plant. A box full of soil is heavy, so position the empty boxes where you want them first.

BASIC BOX CONSTRUCTION

❶ Assemble sides and bottom by nailing or screwing battens to boards.

Add intermediate battens for long boxes with sides of two or more boards.

SIDE

1½ in.

1x2 batten

1½ in.

END

❷ Fasten bottom to sides; position it against bottom ends of side battens.

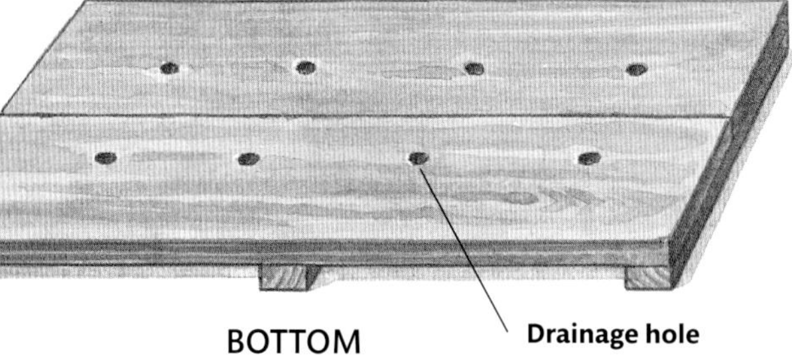

❸ Fix end boards to edges of battens.

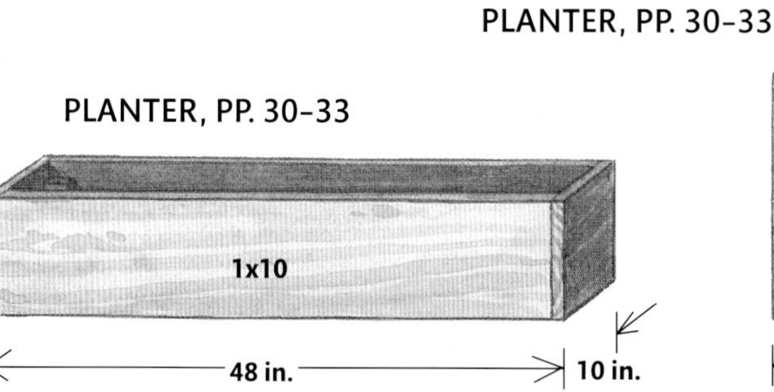

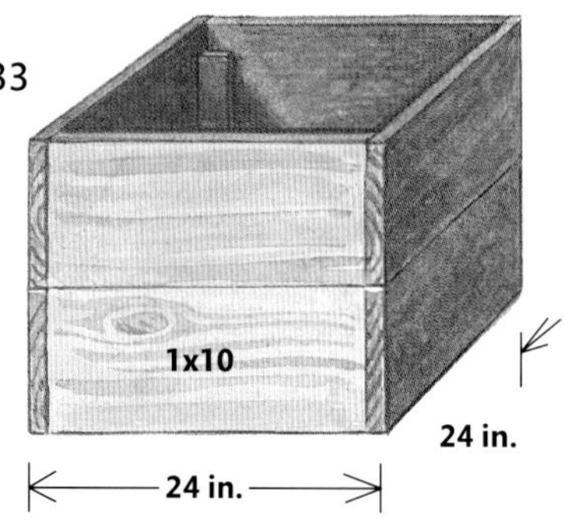

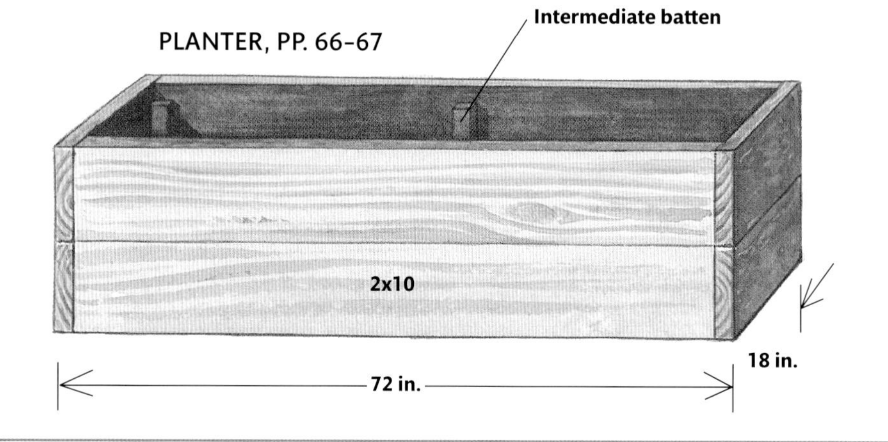

Lattice-panel fence
(pp. 74–75)

Separating the driveway from the backyard, this handsome fence is a barrier to balls and animals. The lattice is held in a frame made of 1x2s sandwiched between 1x3s and 1x4s. (The 1x4s add visual weight to the bottom of the fence.) Note how the parts overlap at the corners of the frame to form an interlocking joint.

Panels wider than 6 ft. are awkward to construct and to install. It is easiest to construct the panels on a large flat surface (a garage or basement floor). Lay out the 1x3s and 1x4 that form one face of the panel frame ❶; then position and nail the 1x2s to them ❷. Add the lattice, then the other layer of 1x3s and 1x4 ❸. As you work, regularly check that the panel is square, its corners at right angles. (Use a framing square or measure across the diagonals to check that they are equal.) Lattice varies in thickness; if yours rattles in its groove, you can add ¾-in. quarter round as shown in the fence construction detail.

Depending on whether you have more confidence as a post setter or as a panel builder, you can build the panels first and then use them to space the posts, or you can set the posts first (see pp. 177–179) and build the panels to fit. Either way, attach the panels to the posts by toenailing (with nails or screws) or with metal connectors along the lengths of the upright members. Add the 1x4 cap after attaching the panels to the posts. Finials in a variety of styles are available at home and garden stores.

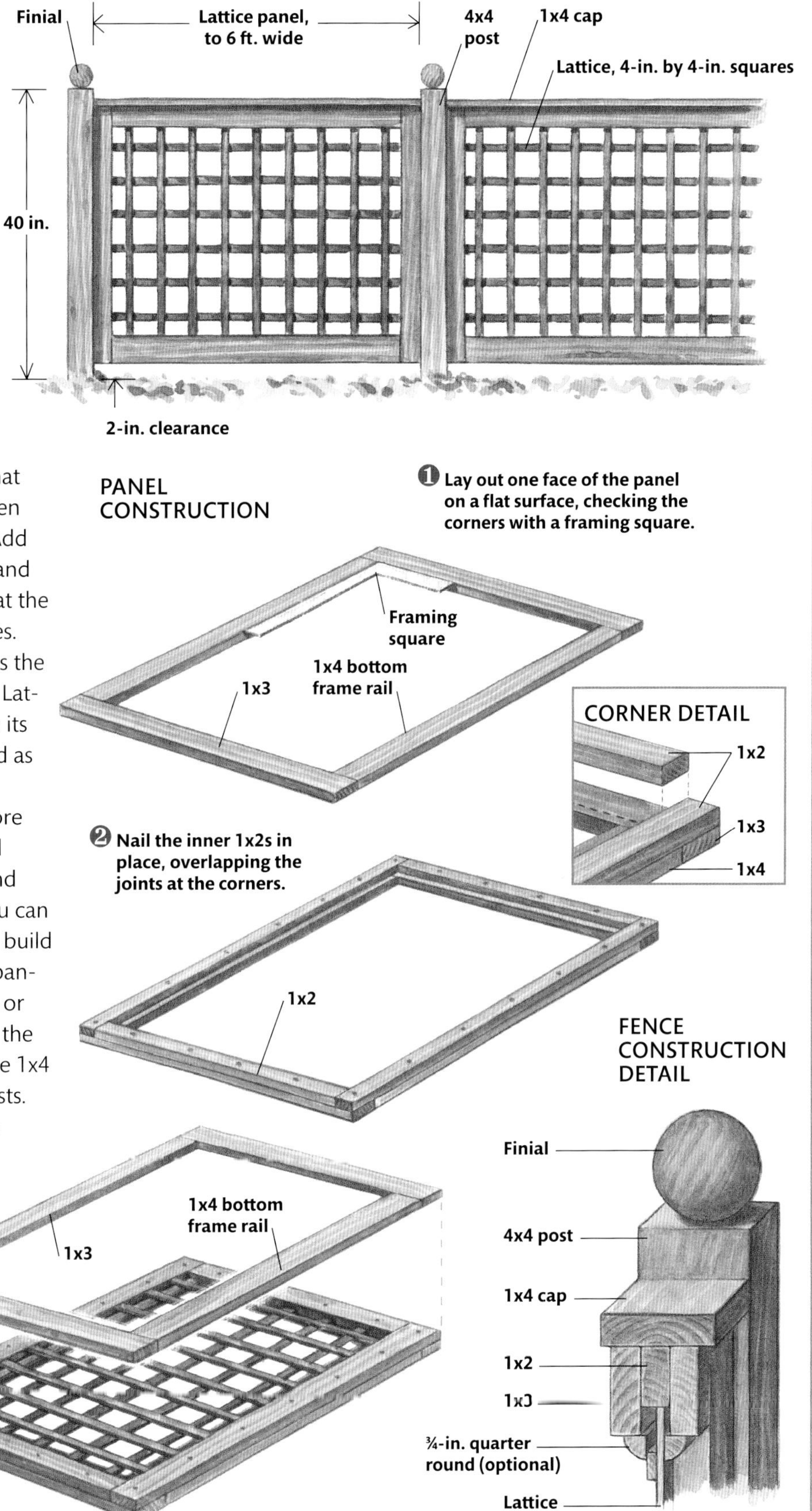

Homemade lattice trellis (pp. 78–82)

The trellis shown here supports climbing plants to make a vertical garden of a blank wall. The design can be altered to fit different-size walls while keeping its pleasing proportions. (You could use a smaller version for the trellis on pp. 118–119.) The four narrow modules are simpler to make than a single large trellis. Hung on L-hangers, they're easy to remove when you need to paint the wall behind them.

Start by cutting all the pieces to length. (Here we'll call the horizontal members "rails" and the vertical members "stiles.") Working on a large flat surface, nail or screw the two outer stiles to the top and bottom rails. These rails are 2x2s to provide ample material to house the L-hangers.

Next, attach the 1x2 rails, then the three intermediate stiles. Cut a piece of scrap 6 in. long to use as a spacer. Then cut and fix the diagonal across the top. (Note how a pair of diagonals forms a rooflike "gable.") Position the panels on the wall so the L-shaped hangers are fixed to 2x4 studs inside the wall. Buy hangers long enough to hold the trellis several inches away from the wall.

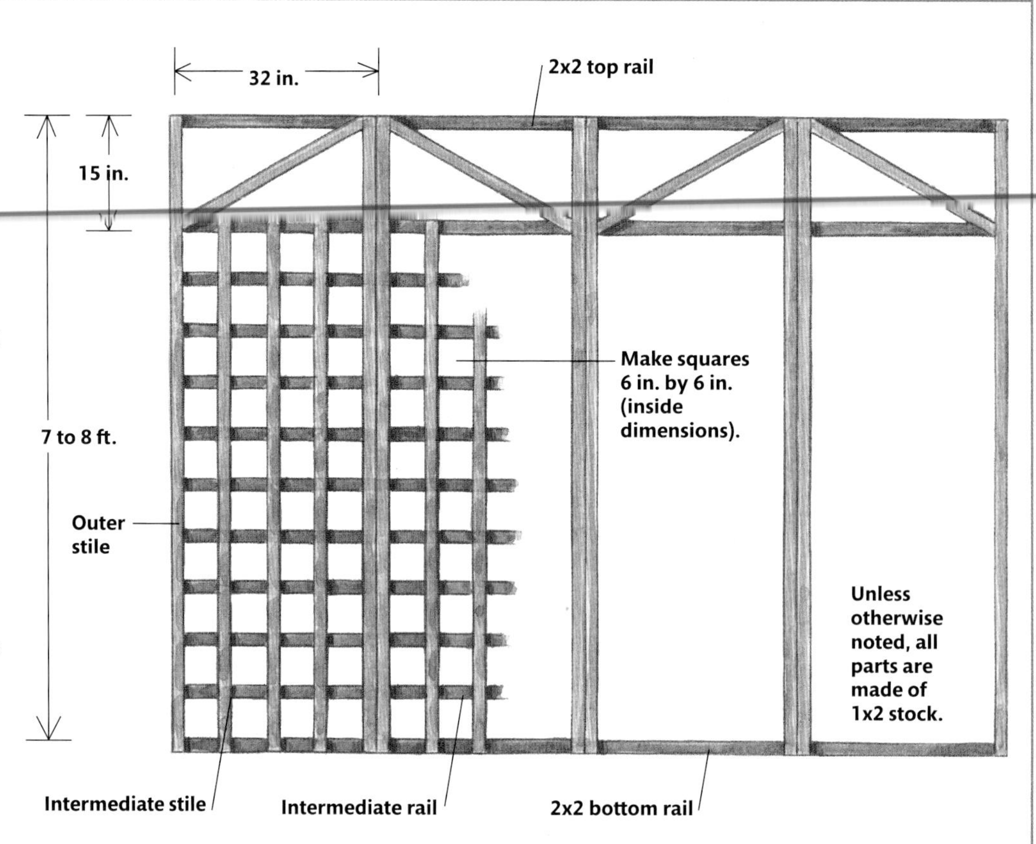

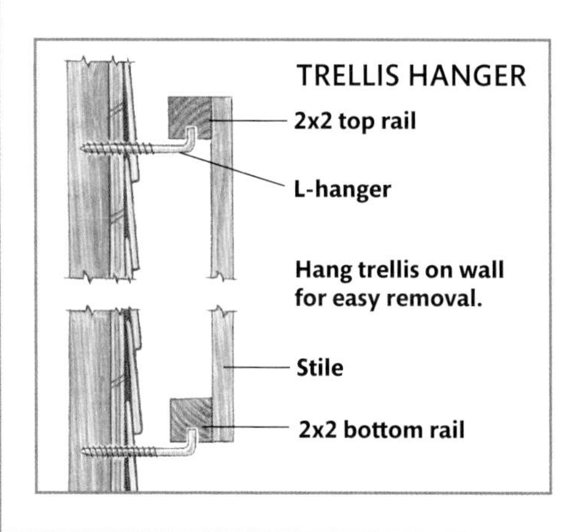

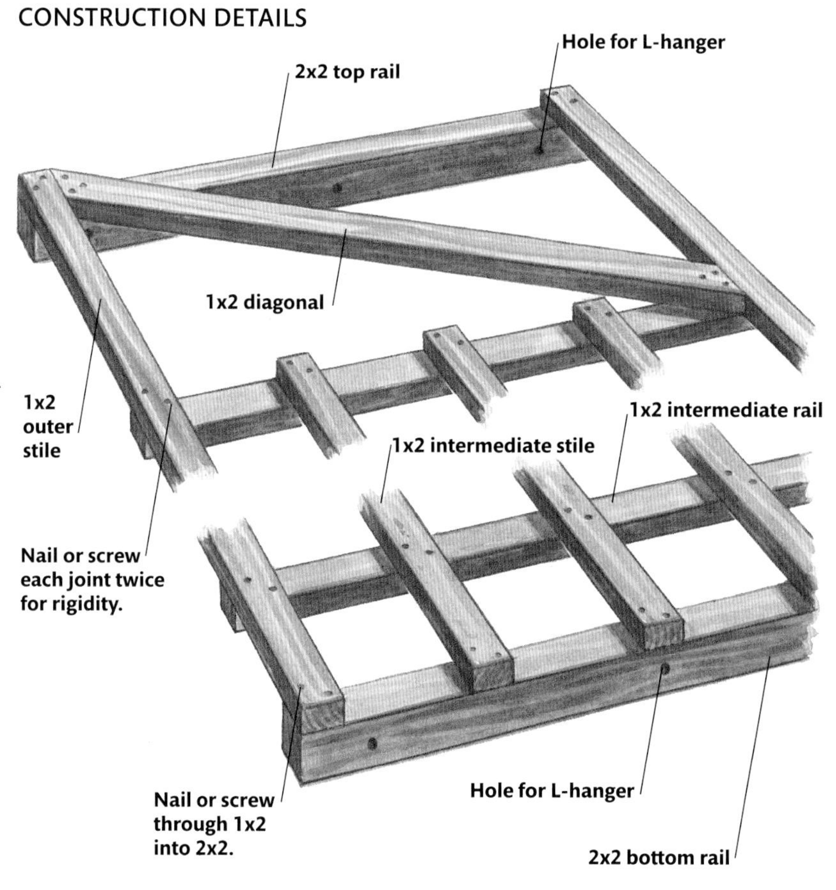

Hideaway arbor (pp. 84–87)

This cozy enclosure shelters a bench and supports vines to shade and soothe the occupants. While 4x4 posts would be sturdy enough to support mature wisteria or kiwi vines, the 6x6 posts shown provide more satisfying proportions to the structure. Build the arbor before setting the flagstone pavement under it.

After the posts are firmly set in their holes (see pp. 177–179), attach the 2x10 joists with carriage bolts. Tack the joists in place with nails; then bore holes for the bolts through post and both joists with a long electrician's auger bit. Use sturdy metal rafter ties to fix the rafters; the weight of the vines might dislodge toenailed rafters.

Sandwich store-bought lattice between 1x3s to make the trellis panels for the vines, and attach them to the posts with metal connectors. Overlap the corner joints or reinforce them with metal brackets, or both, as shown in the drawing.

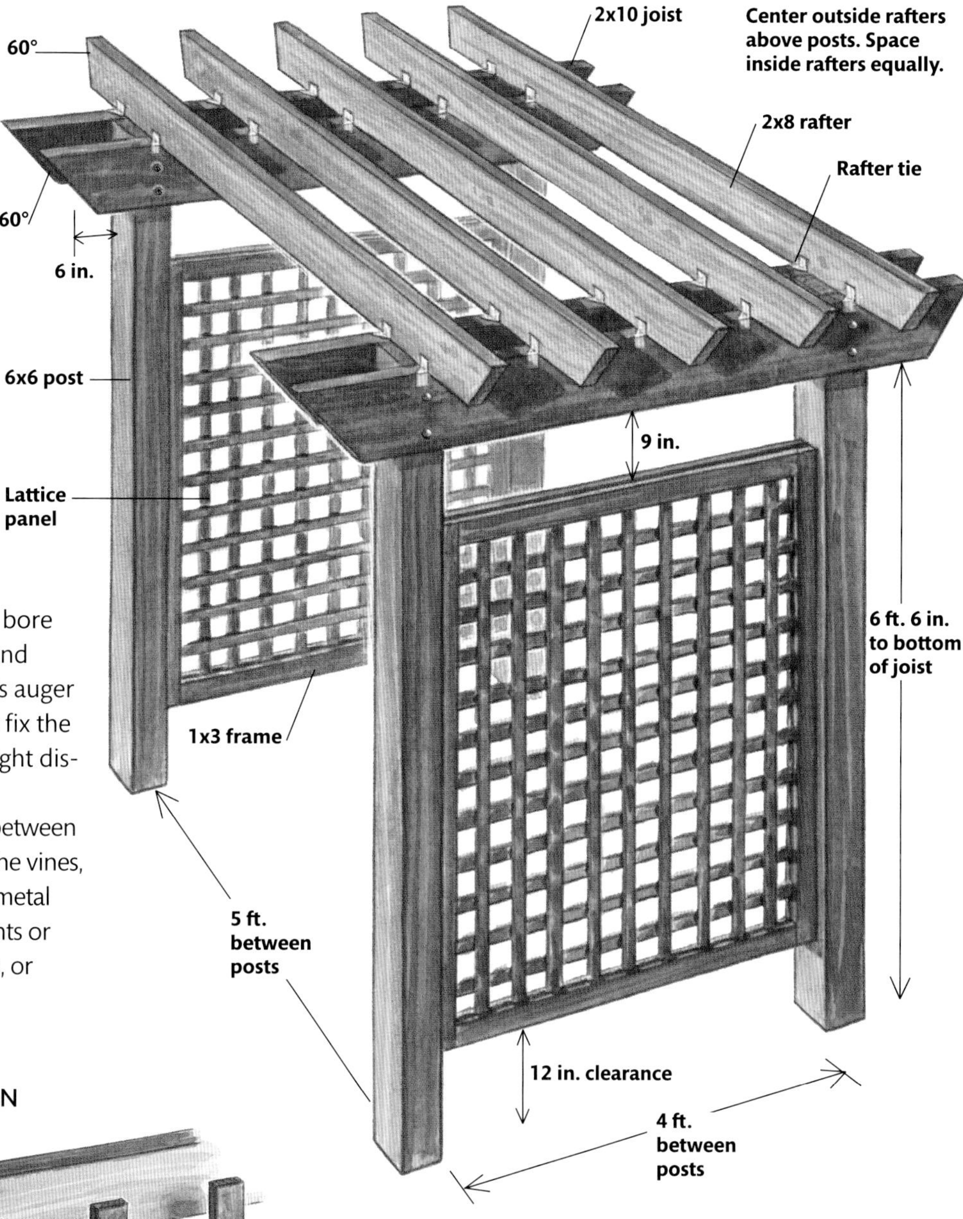

TRELLIS-PANEL CONSTRUCTION

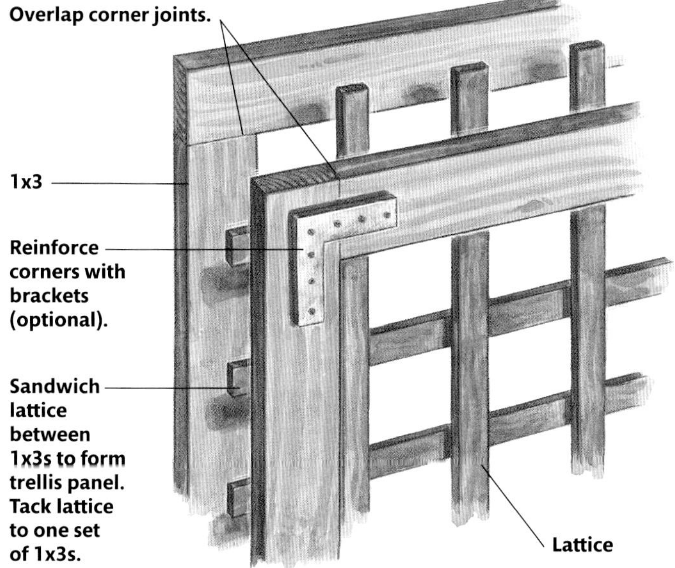

POST-TO-POST DETAIL

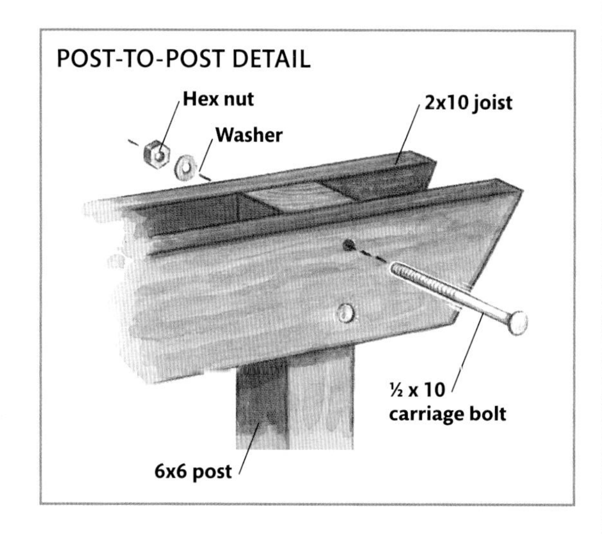

Louvered fence
(pp. 88–89; 92–93)

Made of vertical slats set at an angle, this 6-ft.-tall fence allows air circulation to plants and people near the patio while providing a privacy screen. Be sure to check local codes about height and setback from property lines.

The slats are supported top and bottom by 2x4 rails; a 2x6 beneath the bottom rail stiffens the entire structure, keeps the slat assembly from sagging, and adds visual weight to the design. Set the posts (see pp. 177–179); then cut the rails to fit between them. Toenailed nails or screws or metal connectors are strong enough, but you can add a 2x4 nailer between the rails (as shown in the drawing at bottom right) to make positioning and assembly easier.

Position the 1x6 slats with a spacer block 1½ in. wide and angled 45° at its ends. Nailing or screwing down through the top rail is easy. Nailing up through the bottom rail is more difficult; instead, you could toenail through the edges or faces of the slats into the bottom rail. You may need to cut the final slat narrower to maintain the uniform spacing.

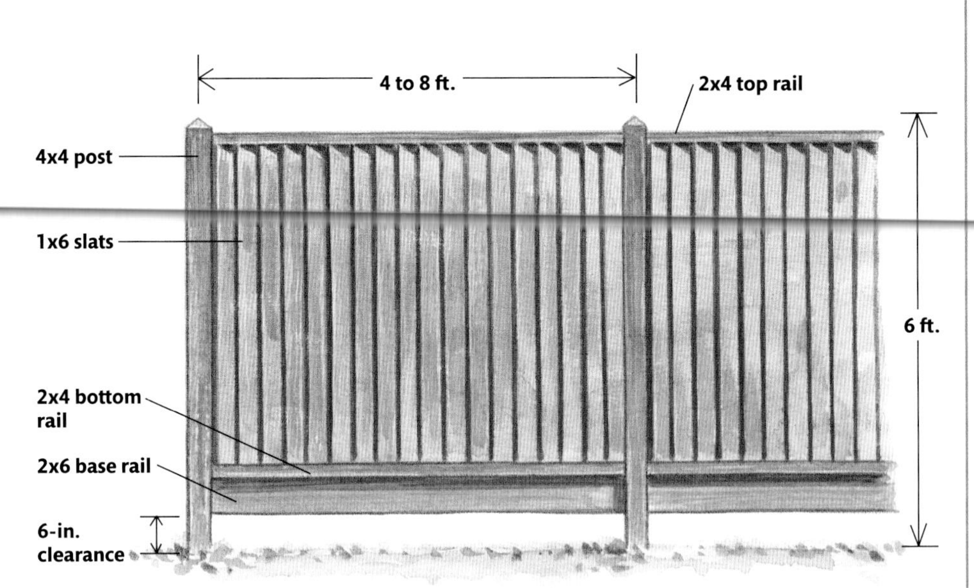

SLAT ASSEMBLY

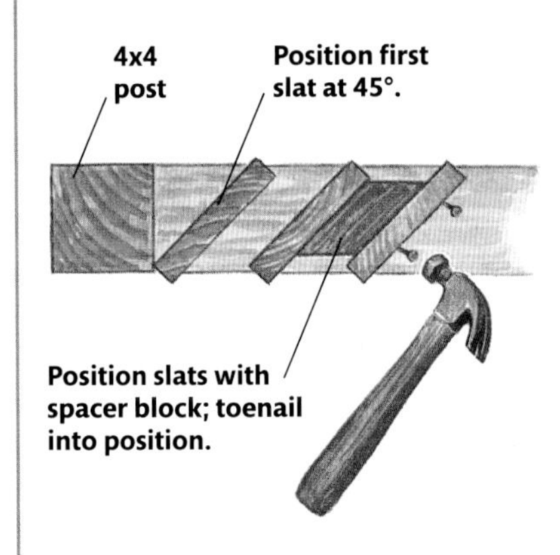

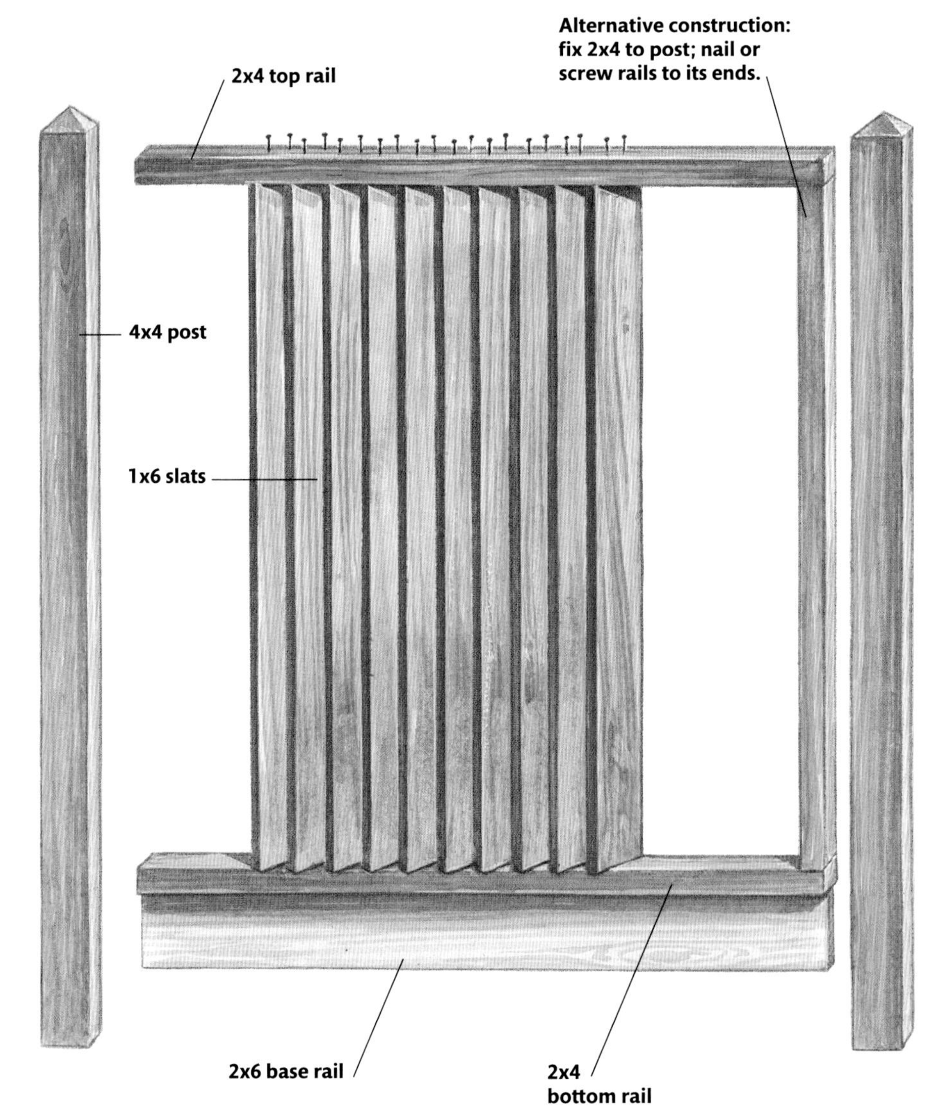

Board-and-lattice fence

(pp. 102–105)

Displayed in front of this tall fence, plants in a traditional border will be the center of attention, catching the eye without distractions in the background. If the fence is near a property line, remember to check local codes for rules about fence height.

This fence looks complicated, but it is easy to build. After you set the posts (see pp. 177–179), install the four horizontal rails, working from the bottom up. The support rail, a 2x6 turned on edge, provides visual weight (makes the fence look better) and keeps the bottom rail and slats from sagging if the distance between posts is 6 ft. or more.

The slats and lattice are sandwiched between two strips of wood (called "stops") nailed to each rail. These can be square or quarter-round in section. Attach one side of each pair of stops before fixing the rails to the posts. Cut lattice and slats to fit between the rails; then add the second stop. You could toenail the slats to the rail before adding the second stop to keep the slats from shifting side to side.

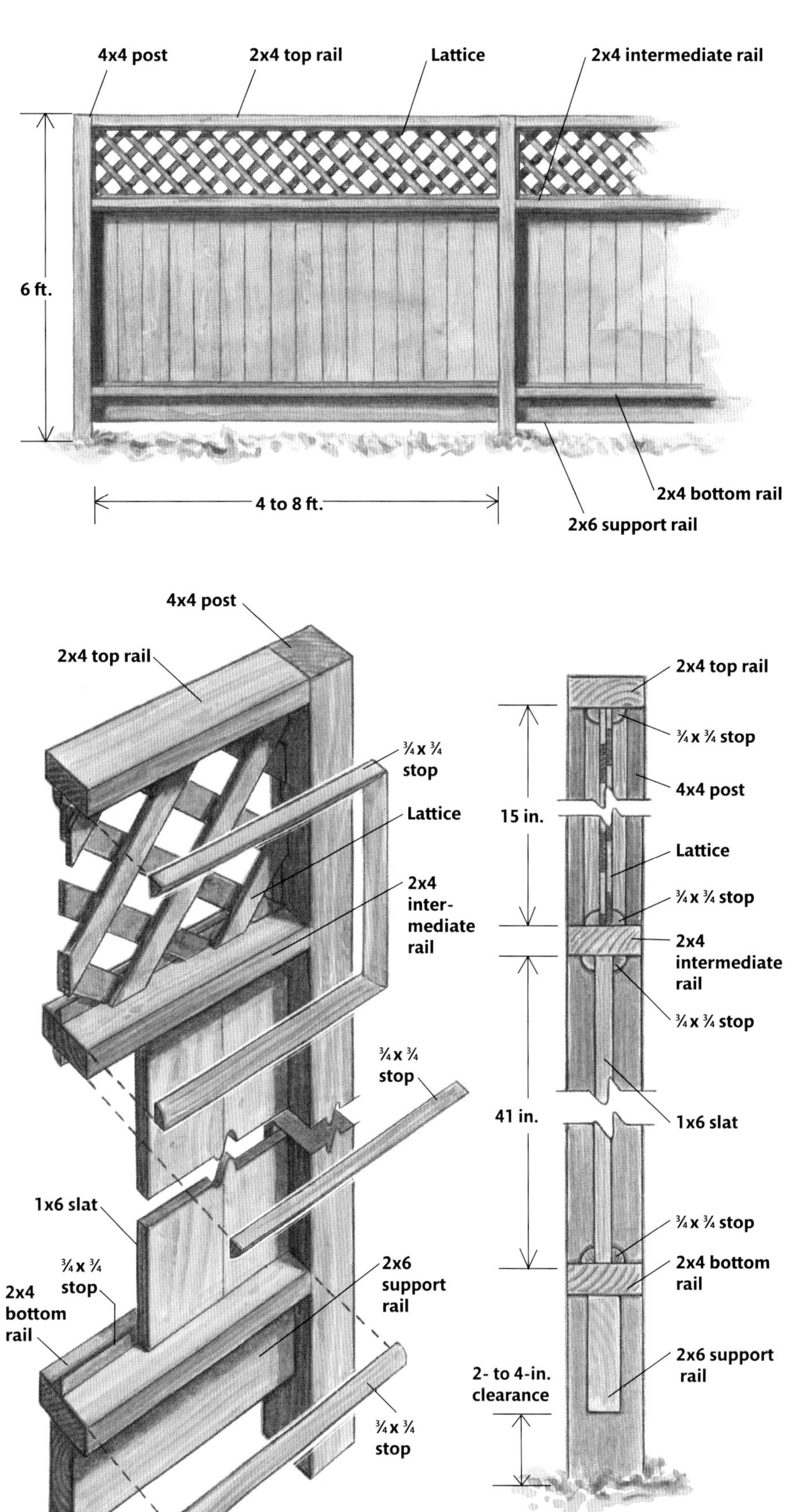

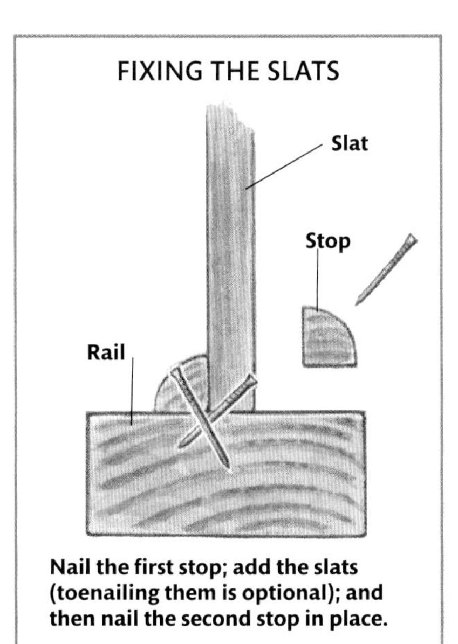

Nail the first stop; add the slats (toenailing them is optional); and then nail the second stop in place.

PLAN VIEW

67½°

112½°

3 ft.

Octagonal bench
(pp. 112–113)

A wrap-around bench offers a comfortable place to enjoy a large shade tree and the surrounding plantings.

Made of eight identical sections, the bench is most easily and efficiently produced if you set up a small production line to cut identical parts at the same time. This is an excellent project for do-it-yourselfers with a radial-arm saw. Set stops on the saw and cut 16 identical legs, then 16 identical top rails, and so on. If you don't have a power saw, and aren't confident of your handsawing, have your local lumberyard cut all the parts to size.

Nail or screw together the eight leg assemblies first. Then attach the seat slats and apron rails to pairs of leg assemblies to make four of the octagon's eight wedges. To do this, tack a straight piece of scrap wood along the centerline of the leg assemblies and position the ends of the slats against the scrap as shown in the boxed drawing. When fastening the front slat, remember that it oversails the apron rail (as shown in the drawing); hold the rail in place to position the slat. You can fix the apron rails in place now or wait until the bench is assembled around the tree.

Place the assembled wedges equidistant around the tree and join them with the remaining seat slats and apron rails. As you work, level the bench if necessary by removing soil or adding gravel fill beneath the legs. Finally, fix the stretchers between the lower rails for added stability.

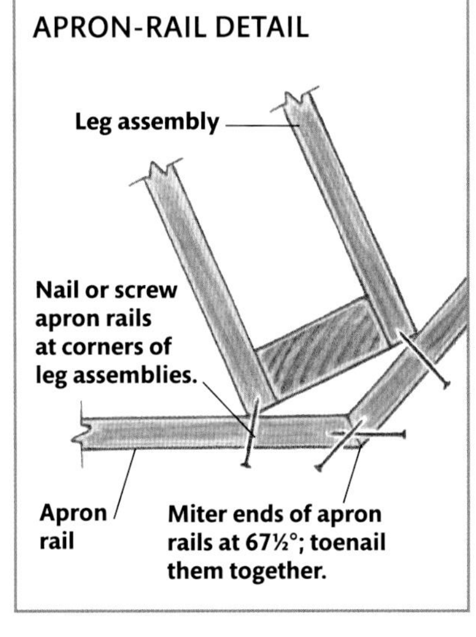

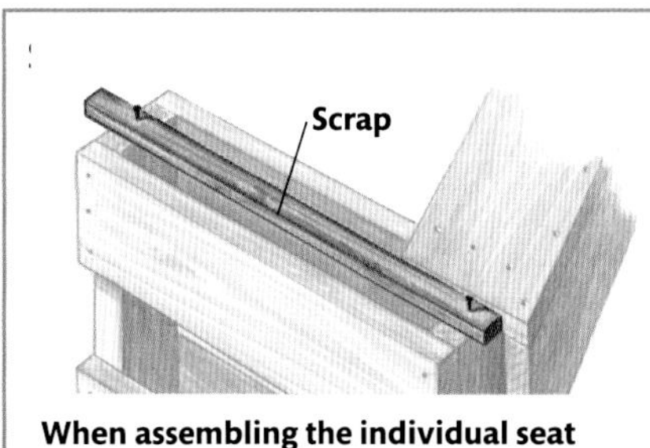

When assembling the individual seat wedges, position the seat slats against scrap wood temporarily nailed along the center of the leg assembly.

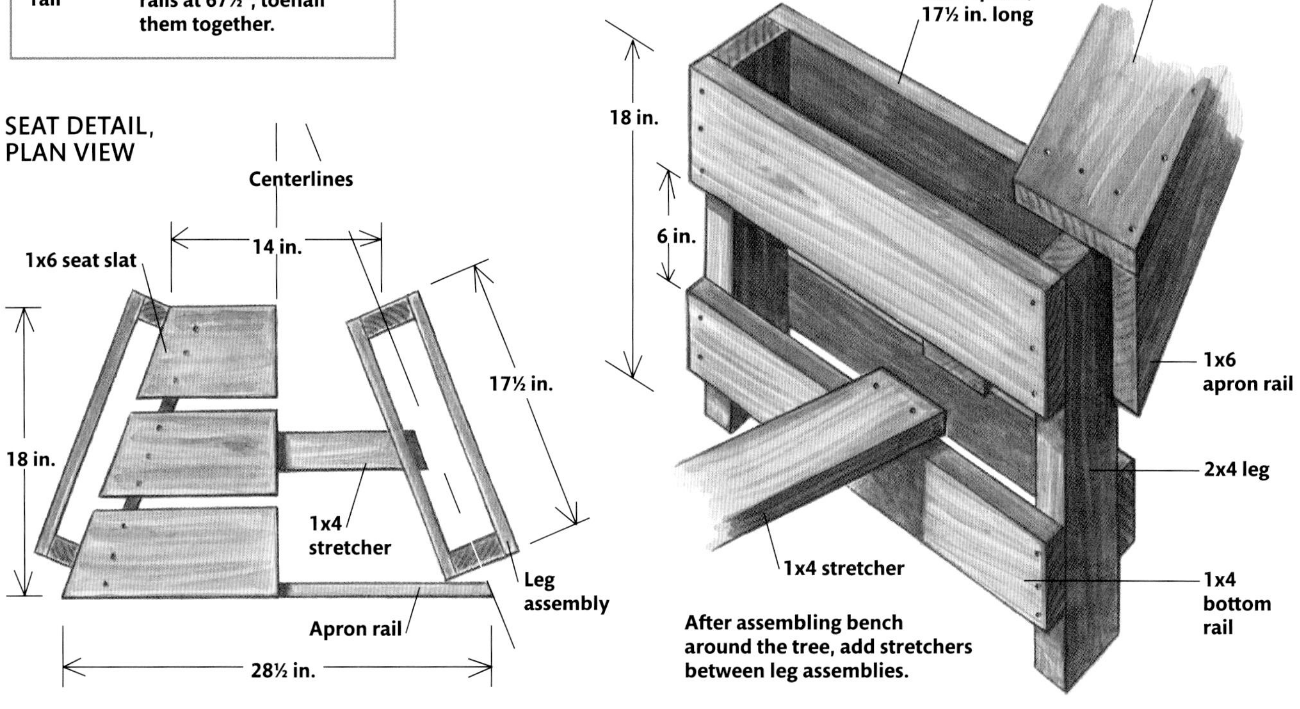

After assembling bench around the tree, add stretchers between leg assemblies.

Dressing up a deck
(pp. 114–115)

Combined with attractive plants, the ladder trellises and simple board partitions shown here effect a remarkable transformation of a nondescript backyard deck.

Attached to 4x4 deck posts and a few additional posts, these are very simple features to install. Attach the partition rails to posts with metal joint hangers, which will be hidden from view by the slats. Nail or screw the partition slats in place; then add the cap piece. Note that the length of the slats depends on the height of the deck above ground and that the additional posts are the same height as the partitions.

The trellises are just simple ladderlike structures made of 2x2s spanning the gap between posts. The end of each 2x2 rests in a 90° notch cut in a bracket nailed to the post. You can nail the 2x2s to the posts or leave them loose in the bracket. Use a bandsaw, saber saw, or handsaw to notch 1x3 brackets, or combine two 1x2s whose ends have been mitered at 45°, as shown in the drawing at bottom right.

Decks built with 4x4 posts often look spindly. To add some visual heft to the posts, nail 1x3s to each face as shown below. This feature can be used on its own or in conjunction with the partitions and ladder trellises.

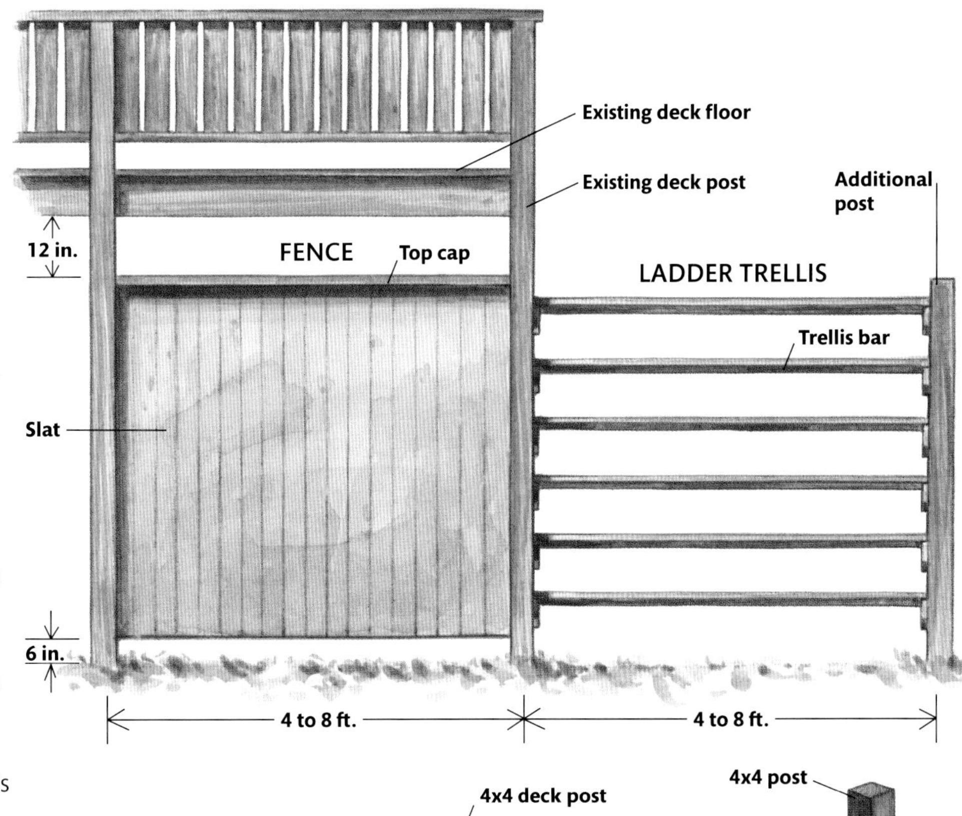

4x4 deck post

4x4 post

Allow 12 in. from cap to deck fascia or joist.

2x2 trellis bar

1x4 cap

2x6 top rail

2x4 midrail

1x4 fence slat (length of slats depends on height of deck)

Joist hanger

6-in. clearance to ground

2x6 bottom rail

TRELLIS BRACKETS (2 styles)

3 in.

6 in.

6 in.

6 in.

OPTION 1: 1x3 support bracket

2x2 trellis bar

45°

OPTION 2. Miter ends of 1x2s at 45°; then combine to form bracket with 90° notch.

BEEFING UP 4x4 POSTS

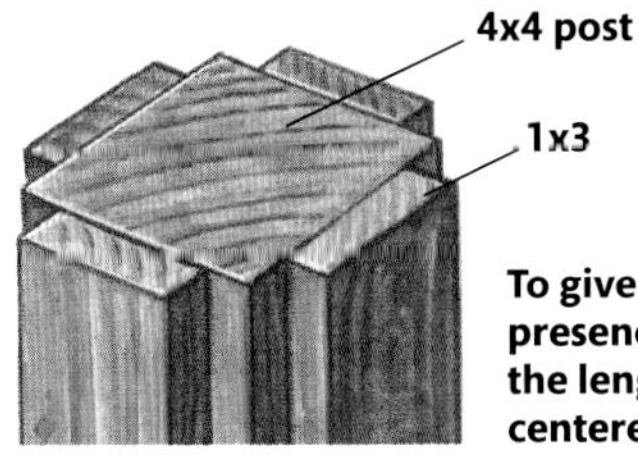

To give 4x4 posts more presence, nail on 1x3 strips the length of the post, centered on each face.

Entry arbor and fence (pp. 62–65)

This arbor makes an event of the passage from sidewalk to front door or from one part of your property to another. Two versions are shown in the Portfolio. One features a stand-alone arbor; the other adds a stylized picket fence. Construction details for both are shown here.

When the arbor stands on its own, a ladderlike trellis on each side gives the clematis something to climb. To provide a bit of visual interest, the spaces between the 1x2 rungs decrease from bottom to top. The drawings show how the fence is incorporated into the design. You can install ladder trellis rungs above the fence as shown. If you want a more open arbor, replace the trellis rungs with heavy wires to support the vines.

Arbor and fence are both simple to make. The fence will go up quickest if you cut rails to length and nail or screw slats to them; then attach these assembled sections to the posts.

DETAIL OF ARBOR PEDIMENT

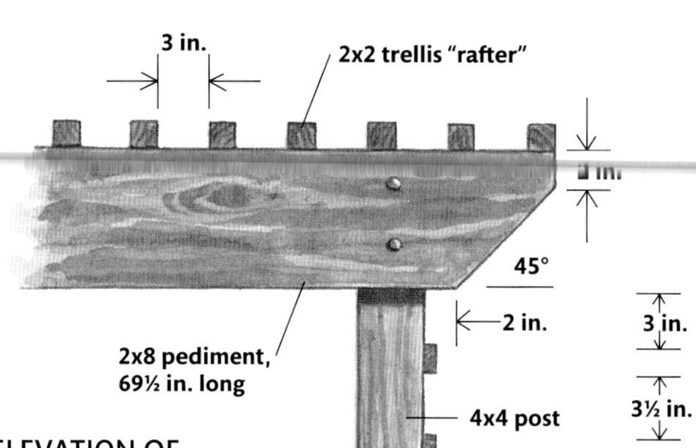

SIDE ELEVATION OF FREESTANDING ARBOR

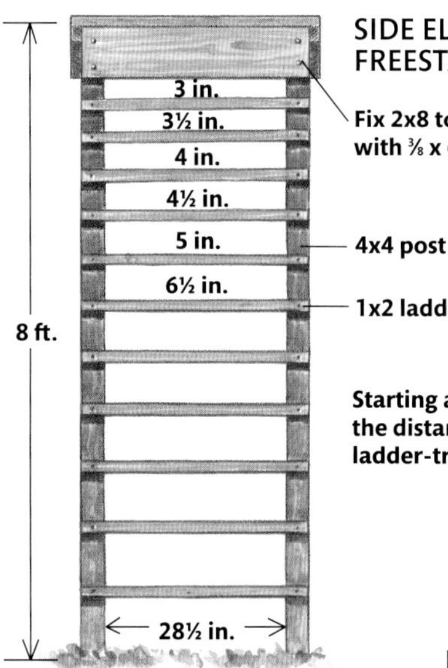

Fix 2x8 top plate to posts with ⅜ x 6 carriage bolts.

4x4 post

1x2 ladder-trellis rung

Starting at the top, increase the distance between each ladder-trellis rung by ½ in.

3 in.
3½ in.
4 in.
4½ in.
5 in.
5½ in.
6 in.

ELEVATION OF FENCE

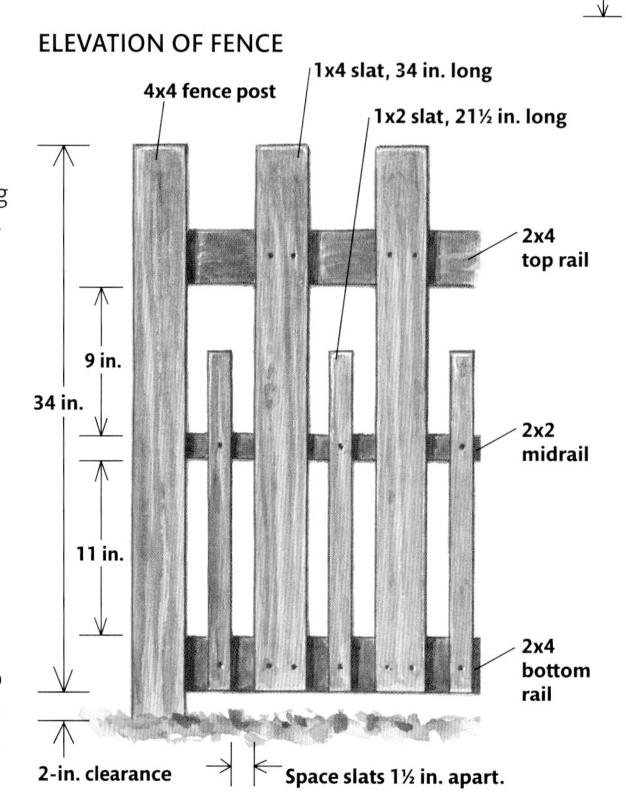

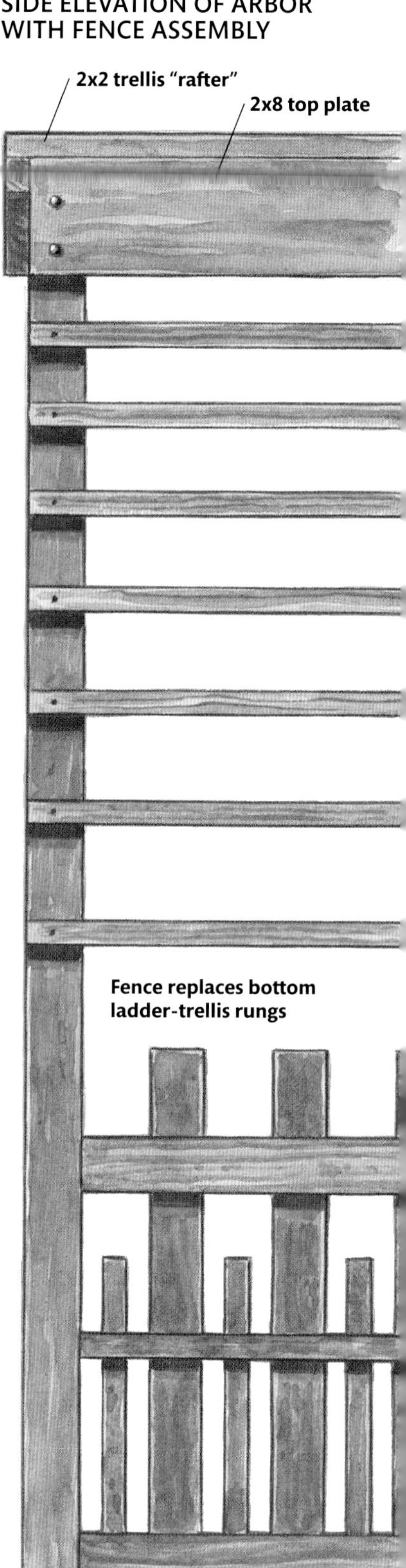

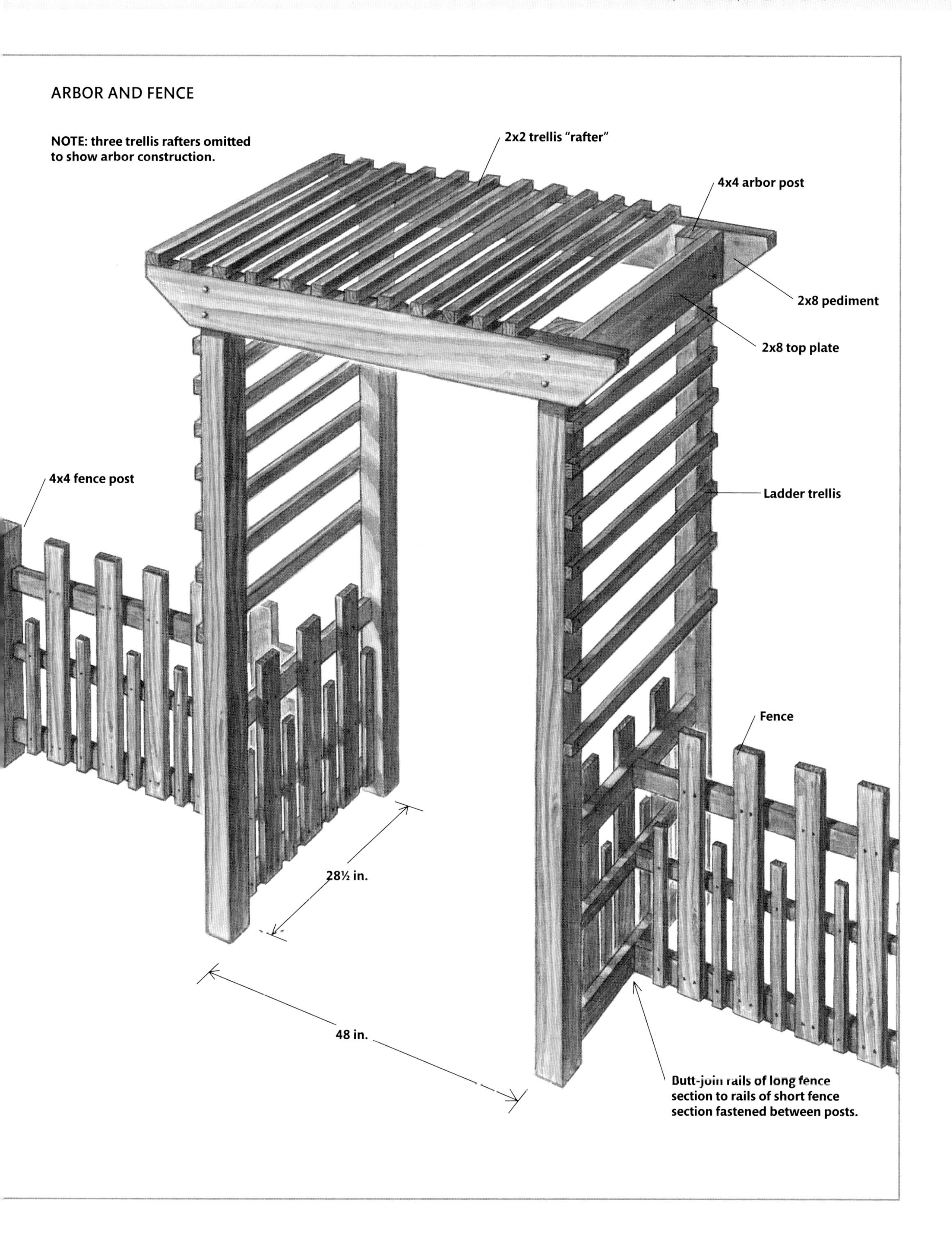
ARBOR AND FENCE
NOTE: three trellis rafters omitted to show arbor construction.
2x2 trellis "rafter"
4x4 arbor post
2x8 pediment
2x8 top plate
4x4 fence post
Ladder trellis
Fence
28½ in.
48 in.
Butt-join rails of long fence section to rails of short fence section fastened between posts.

Preparing the Soil for Planting

The better the soil, the better the plants. Soil quality affects how fast plants grow, how big they get, how good they look, and how long they live. But on many residential lots, the soil is shallow and infertile. Unless you're lucky enough to have a better-than-average site where the soil has been cared for and amended over the years, perhaps for use as a vegetable garden or flower bed, you should plan to improve your soil before planting in it.

If you were planting just a few trees or shrubs, you could prepare individual planting holes for them and leave the surrounding soil undisturbed. However, for nearly all the plantings in this book, digging individual holes is impractical, and it's much better for the plants if you prepare the soil throughout the entire area that will be planted. (The major exception is when you're planting under a tree, which we'll discuss on p. 201.)

For most of the situations shown in this book, you could prepare the soil with hand tools—a spade, digging fork, and rake. The job goes faster, though, if you use a rototiller, and a rototiller is better than hand tools for mixing amendments into the soil. Unless you grow vegetables, you probably won't use a rototiller often enough to justify buying one yourself, but you can easily borrow or rent a rototiller or hire someone with a tiller to come and prepare your site.

Common fertilizers and soil amendments

The following materials serve different purposes. Follow soil-test recommendations or the advice of an experienced gardener in choosing which amendments would be best for your soil. If so recommended, you can apply two or three of these amendments at the same time, using the stated rate for each one.

Material	Description	Amount for 100 sq. ft.
Bagged steer manure	A weak all-purpose fertilizer.	6–8 lb.
Dried poultry manure	A high-nitrogen fertilizer.	2 lb.
5-5-5 all-purpose fertilizer	An inexpensive and popular synthetic fertilizer.	2 lb.
Superphosphate or rock phosphate	Supplies phosphorus. Work into the soil as deep as possible.	2–4 lb.
Greensand	Supplies potassium and many trace elements.	2–4 lb.
Regular or dolomitic limestone	Used primarily to sweeten acid soil.	5 lb.
Gypsum	Helps loosen clay soil. Also helps reduce salt buildup in roadside soil.	2 lb.
Wood ashes	Supplies potassium, phosphorus, and lime.	2–4 lb.

Loosen the soil

After you've removed any sod or other vegetation from the designated area (see pp. 158–159), the first step is digging or tilling to loosen the soil ❶. Do this on a day when the soil is moist—not so wet that it sticks to your tools or so dry that it makes dust. Start at one end of the bed, and work back and forth until you reach the other end. Try to dig down at least 8 in., or deeper if possible. If the ground is very compacted, you'll have to make repeated passes with a tiller to reach 8 in. deep. Toss aside any large rocks, roots, or debris that you encounter. When you're working near a house or other buildings, watch out for buried wires, cables, and pipes. Most town and city governments have a number you can call to request that someone help you locate buried utilities. This is critical.

After this initial digging, the ground will probably be very rough and lumpy. Farmers used to plow in the fall and let frost break the clods apart over the winter. That's still a good system; if you plan ahead and do the initial digging in fall, it's easy to finish preparing the soil in spring. But you can do the whole job in one day, too, if you want. Hit the clods with the back of a digging fork, or make another pass with the tiller. Continue until you've reduced all the clumps to the size of apples.

Loosening the existing soil comes first because that's when you can dig as deep as possible. Then add some topsoil, and rake it around if you want to fill in some low spots, refine the grade, or raise the planting area above the surrounding grade for improved visibility and better drainage. Unless you need just a few bags of it, order screened topsoil by the cubic yard from a reliable landscape contractor.

Add organic matter

Common dirt (and purchased topsoil, too) consists mainly of rock and mineral fragments of various sizes—which are mostly coarse and gritty in sandy soil, and dust-fine in clay soil. One of the best things you can do to improve any kind of soil for garden plants is to add some organic matter. Sold in bags or in bulk at nurseries and garden centers, organic materials include all kinds of composted plant parts and animal manures.

How much organic matter should you use? Spread a layer 2 to 3 in. thick across the entire area you're working on ❷. At this thickness, a cubic yard (about one heaping pickup-truck load) of bulk material, or six bales of peat moss, will cover 100 to 150 sq. ft. If you're working on a large area and need several cubic yards of organic matter, have it delivered. Ask the driver to dump the pile as close to your project area as possible; it's worth allowing the truck to drive across your lawn to get there. You can spread a big truckload of material in just a few hours if you don't have to cart it very far.

Add fertilizers and mineral amendments

Organic matter improves the soil's texture and helps it retain water and nutrients, but it doesn't actually supply many nutrients. To provide the nutrients that plants need, you need to use organic or synthetic fertilizers and powdered minerals. It's most helpful if you mix these materials into the soil before you do any planting, putting them down into the root zone as shown in the drawing ❸, but you can also sprinkle them on top of the soil in subsequent years to maintain a planting.

Getting a sample of soil tested (a service that's usually available free or at low cost through your County Extension Service) is the most accurate way to determine how much of which nutrients is needed. Less precise, but often adequate, is asking the advice of an experienced gardener in your neighborhood. Test results or a gardener's advice will point out any significant deficiencies in your soil, but these are uncommon. Most soil just needs a moderate, balanced dose of nutrients.

Most important is to avoid using too much of any fertilizer or mineral. Don't guess at this; measure and weigh carefully. Calculate your plot's area. Follow your soil-test results, instructions on a commercial product's package, or the general guidelines given in the table opposite, and weigh out the appropriate amount, using a kitchen or bathroom scale. Apply the material evenly across the plot with a spreader or by hand.

PREPARING THE SOIL FOR PLANTING

❶ Use a spade, digging fork, or tiller to dig at least 8 in. deep and break the soil into rough clods. Discard rocks, roots, and debris. Watch out for underground utilities.

❷ Spread a 2- to 3-in. layer of organic matter on top of the soil.

❸ Sprinkle measured amounts of fertilizer and mineral amendments evenly across the entire area, and mix thoroughly into the soil.

Mix and smooth the soil

Finally, use a digging fork or tiller and go back and forth across the bed again until the added materials are mixed thoroughly into the soil and everything is broken into nut-size or smaller lumps ❹. Then use a rake to smooth the surface ❺.

At this point, the soil level may look too high compared with adjacent pavement or lawn, but don't worry. It will settle a few inches over the next several weeks and end up close to its original level.

Working near trees

Plantings under the shade of lovely old trees can be cool, lovely oases, like the ones shown on pp. 110–113. But to establish the plants, you'll need to contend with the tree's roots. Contrary to popular belief, most tree roots are in the top few inches of the soil, and they extend at least as far away from the trunk as the limbs do. If you dig anyplace in that area, you'll probably cut or bruise some of the tree's roots. When preparing for planting beneath a tree, therefore, it is important to disturb as few roots as possible.

It is natural for a tree's trunk to flare out at the bottom, and for the roots near the trunk to be partly aboveground. Don't bury them. However, if the soil has eroded away from roots farther out from the trunk, it's okay to add a layer of soil up to several inches deep and top the new soil with a thinner layer of mulch. Adding some soil this way makes it easier to start ground covers or other plants underneath a tree. (See p. 201 for planting instructions.) Just don't overdo it—covering roots with too much soil can starve them of oxygen, damaging or killing them, and piling soil close to the trunk can rot the bark.

❹ Use a tiller or digging fork to mix everything together, again working as deep as possible.

❺ Finish by smoothing the surface with a rake.

Making neat edges

All but the most informal landscapes look best if you define and maintain neat edges between the lawn and any adjacent plantings. There are several ways to do this, varying in appearance, effectiveness, cost, and convenience. For the Northeast region, some of the best methods are cut edges, dry-laid brick or stone, and wood or timber. Several other prefab edging systems that you may see in catalogs work well only in warmer climates; they tend to frost-heave in cold winters. In any case, the time to install an edging is after you prepare the soil but before you plant the bed.

Cut edge

Lay a hose or rope on the ground to mark the line where you want to cut. Then cut along the line with a sharp spade or edging tool. Lift away any grass that was growing into the bed (or any plants that were running out into the lawn). Use a rake or hoe to smooth out a shallow trench on the bed side of the cut. Keep the trench empty; don't let it fill up with mulch.

Pros and cons: Free. Good for straight or curved edges, level or sloped sites. You have to recut the edge at least twice a year, in spring and late summer, but you can cut 50 to 100 ft. in an hour or so. Don't cut the trench too deep; if a mower wheel slips down into it, you'll scalp the lawn. Crabgrass and other weeds may sprout in the exposed soil.

Brick or stone mowing strip

Dig a trench about 8 in. wide and 4 in. deep around the edge of the bed. Fill it halfway with sand; then lay bricks on top, setting them level with the soil on the lawn side. You'll need three bricks per foot of edging. Sweep extra sand into any cracks between the bricks. You'll probably have to reset a few frost-heaved bricks each spring. You can substitute cut stone blocks or concrete pavers for bricks.

Pros and cons: Good for straight or curved edges on level or gently sloped sites. Looks good in combination with brick walkways or a brick house. Fairly easy to install and maintain.

Wood or timber edging

You can make a sturdy edging quickly by laying pressure-treated 3x4 landscape timbers from the lumberyard around the edge of the bed. For a rustic look, use tree trunks or limbs about 4 to 6 in. in diameter. Sink the timbers partway into the soft soil of the bed so they won't roll out of place. Simply butt ends together to extend the edging's length or to form a corner.

Pros and cons: Keeps mulch from drifting out of the bed but doesn't confine vigorous plants. Works best for straight edges on level sites, unless you choose curved limbs and fit them to the contours of the bed. Liable to frost-heave, but you can easily push timbers back into place in the spring. Natural wood looks pleasingly rustic and is cheap and easy to work with, but it decays after several years and needs replacement. Pressure-treated timbers cost more but look more formal and last longer. You can't mow right up to a wood edging, but you can cut the grass with a string trimmer.

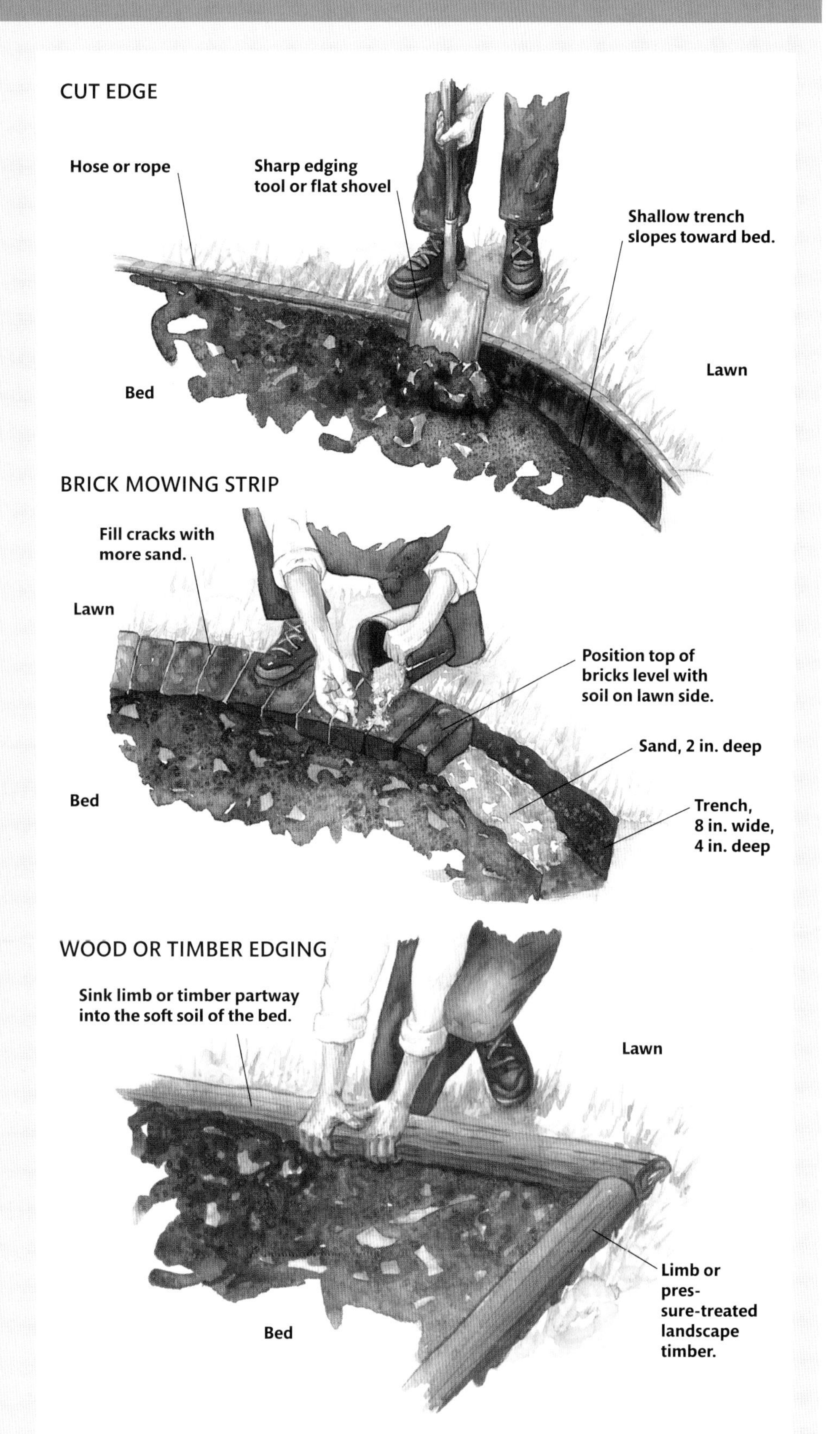

Buying Plants

Once you have chosen and planned a landscape project, make a list of the plants you want and start thinking about where to get them. You'll need to locate the kinds of plants you're looking for, choose good-quality plants, and get enough of the plants to fill your design area.

Where and how to shop

You may already have a favorite place to shop for plants. If not, look online or in the Yellow Pages under Nursery Stock, Nurserymen, Garden Centers, and Landscape Contractors, and choose a few places to visit. Take your shopping list, find a salesperson, and ask for help. The plants in this book are commonly available in the Northeast region, but you may not find everything you want at one place. The salesperson may refer you to another nursery, recommend an online nursery, offer to special-order plants, or recommend similar plants as substitutes.

If you're buying too many plants to carry in your car or truck, ask about delivery—it's usually available and sometimes free. Some nurseries offer to replace plants that fail within a limited guarantee period, so ask about that, too.

The staff at a good nursery or garden center will usually be able to answer most of the questions you have about which plants to buy and how to care for them. If you can, go shopping on a rainy weekday when business is slow, so staff will have time to answer your questions.

Don't be lured by the low prices of plants for sale at supermarkets or discount stores unless you're sure you know exactly what you're looking for and what you're looking at. The salespeople at these stores rarely have the time or knowledge to offer you much help, and the plants are often disorganized, unlabeled, and stressed by poor care.

If you can't find a plant locally or have a retailer order it for you, you can always order it yourself from a mail-order nursery. Most mail-order nurseries produce good plants and pack them well, but if you haven't dealt with a business before, be smart and place a minimum order first. Judge the quality of the plants that arrive; then decide whether or not to order larger quantities from that firm.

Timing

It's a good idea to plan ahead and start shopping for plants before you're ready to put them in the ground. That way, if you can't find everything on your list, you'll have time to keep shopping around, place special orders, or choose substitutes. Most nurseries will let you flag an order for later pickup or delivery, and they'll take care of the plants in the meantime. Or you can bring the plants home; just remember to check the soil in the containers every day and water if needed. Avoid putting them in full sun as they dry out rapidly.

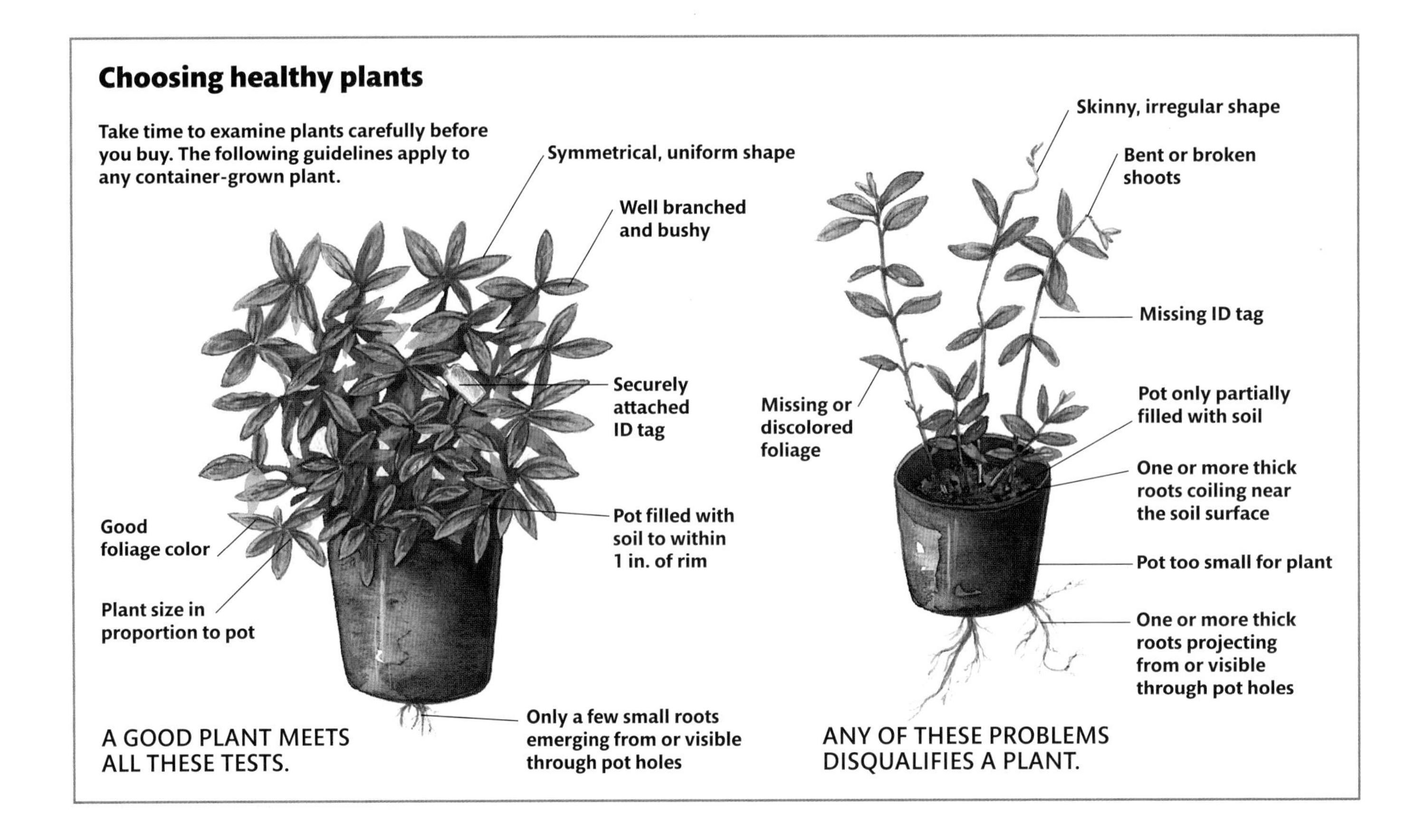

Choosing particular plants

If you need, for example, five mugo pines and the nursery or garden center has a whole block of them, how do you choose which five to buy? The sales staff may be too busy to help you decide; you often have to choose by yourself.

Most plants nowadays are grown in containers, so it's possible to lift them one at a time and examine them from all sides. Following the guidelines shown in the drawings on the opposite page and on page 199, evaluate each plant's shape, size, health and vigor, and root system.

Trees and shrubs are frequently sold "balled-and-burlapped," that is, with a ball of soil and roots wrapped tightly in burlap. For these plants, look for strong limbs with no broken shoots, an attractive profile, and healthy foliage. Then press your hands against the burlap-covered root-ball to make sure that it feels firm, solid, and damp, not loose or dry. (If the ball is buried within a bed of wood chips, pull the chips aside; then push them back after inspecting the plant.)

To make the final cut when you're choosing a group of plants, line them up side by side and select the ones that are most closely matched in height, bushiness, and foliage color. If your design includes a hedge or mass planting where uniformity is very important, it's a good idea to buy a few extra plants as potential replacements in case of damage or loss. It's easier to plan ahead than to find a match later. Plant the extras in a spare corner and you'll have them if you need them.

Sometimes a plant will be available in two or more sizes. Which is better? That depends on how patient you are. The main reason for buying bigger plants is to make a landscape look impressive right away. If you buy smaller plants and set them out at the same spacing, the planting will look sparse at first, but it will soon catch up. A year after planting, you can't tell if a perennial came from a quart- or gallon-size pot: they look the same. For shrubs, the difference between one size pot and the next usually represents one year's growth.

The Planting Process

Throughout the Northeast, spring is the best season for planting. You can start planting as soon as the soil thaws and the nurseries open, and continue through mid-June with good results. Planting in spring gives the plants a whole growing season to send out roots and get established before facing the rigors of winter. The second-best time for planting is from mid-August until the end of September, after the heat of summer but before hard frosts. If you want to plant during the summer, do it on a cloudy day when rain is forecast for the next day or so, or cover them with light fabric.

Compared with preparing the soil, putting plants in the ground goes quite quickly. If you're well prepared, you can plant a whole bed in just an hour or two.

Try to stay off the soil

Throughout the planting process, do all you can by reaching in from outside the bed—don't step on the newly prepared soil if you can help it. Stepping or walking in the bed compacts the soil and makes it harder to dig planting holes. Use short boards or scraps of plywood as temporary stepping-stones if you do need to walk around on the soil. As soon as you can decide where to put them, you might want to lay permanent steppingstones for access to plants that need regular maintenance.

Check placement and spacing

The first step in planting is to mark the position of each plant. The simplest way to do this is to arrange the plants themselves on the bed. Use an empty pot or a stake to represent any plant that's too heavy to move easily. Use a yardstick to check the spacing, and set the plants in place.

Then step back and take a look. Walk around and look from all sides. Go into the house and look out the window. What do you think? Should any of the plants be adjusted a little? Don't worry if the planting looks a little sparse now—it should. Plants almost always grow faster and get bigger than you can imagine when you're first setting them out, and it's almost always better to allow space and wait a few years for them to fill in than to crowd them too close together at first and have to keep pruning and thinning them later.

PLANTING POINTERS

When working on top of prepared soil, kneel on a piece of plywood to distribute your weight.

Use empty pots or stakes to mark positions of plants not yet purchased or too heavy to move frequently.

Moving through the job

When you're satisfied with the arrangement, mark the position of each plant with a stake or stone, and set the plants aside out of the way so you won't knock them over or step on them as you proceed. Start planting in order of size. Do the biggest plants first; then move on to the medium-size and smaller plants. If all the plants are about the same size, start at the back of the bed and work toward the front, or start in the center and work to the edges.

Position trees and shrubs to show their best side

Most trees and shrubs are slightly asymmetric. There's usually enough irregularity in their branching or shape that one side looks a little fuller or more attractive than the other sides do. After you've set a tree or shrub into its hole, step back and take a look. Then turn it partway, or try tilting or tipping it a little to one side or the other. Once you've decided which side and position look best, start filling in the hole with soil. Stop and check again before you firm the soil into place.

The fine points of spacing

When you're planting a group of the same kind of plants, such as perennials or ferns, they normally look best if you space them informally, in slightly curved or zigzag rows, with the plants in one row offset from those of the next row. Don't arrange plants in a straight row unless you want to emphasize a line, such as the edge of a bed. After planting, step back and evaluate the effect. If you want to adjust the placement or position of any plant, now is the time to do so.

Rake, water, and mulch

Use a garden rake to level out any high and low spots that remain after planting. Water enough to settle the soil into place around the roots. Mulch the entire planting area with 1 to 3 in. of composted bark, wood chips, or other organic matter. Mulch is indispensable for controlling weeds and regulating the moisture and temperature of the soil. If you're running out of time, you don't have to spread the mulch right away, but try to get it done within the next week or so.

Using annuals as fillers

The plants in our designs have been spaced so they will not be crowded at maturity. Buying more plants and spacing them closer would fill things out faster, but doing that would mean that in a few years (for perennials; longer for shrubs) you'll need to remove plants or prune them frequently.

If you want something to fill the gaps between newly planted perennials, shrubs, or ground covers for that first year or two, use annuals. The best annual fillers are compact plants that grow only 6 to 10 in. tall. These will hide the soil or mulch and make a colorful carpet. Avoid taller annuals, because they can shade or smother your permanent plantings.

The annuals listed here are all compact, easy to grow, and inexpensive. Seeds of those marked with a symbol (✿) can be sown directly in the garden about the time of last frost. For the others, buy six-packs or flats of plants. Thin seedlings or space plants 8 to 12 in. apart.

China pink ✿: Red, pink, white, or bicolor flowers. Blooms all summer.

Dusty miller: Silvery foliage, often lacy-textured. No flowers.

Edging lobelia: Dark blue, magenta, or white flowers. Likes afternoon shade.

English daisy: Fluffy asterlike flowers in shades of red, pink, and white. Prefers cool weather.

Flossflower: Fluffy blue, lavender, or white flowers. Choose dwarf types.

Garden verbena: Bright red, pink, purple, or white flowers. Good for sunny dry sites.

Globe candytuft ✿: Pink or white flowers. Grows and blooms fast, then goes to seed.

Moss rose: Bright flowers in many colors. Good for sunny dry sites.

Pansy and viola: Multicolored flowers. Grow best in cool weather.

Sweet alyssum ✿: Fragrant white or lilac flowers. Blooms for months. Very easy.

Wax begonia: Rose, pink, or white flowers. Good for shady sites but also takes sun.

Planting Basics

Most of the plants that you buy for a landscaping project today are grown and sold in individual plastic containers, but large shrubs and trees may be balled-and-burlapped. Mail-order plants may come bare-root. And ground covers are sometimes sold in flats. In any case, the basic concern is the same: be careful what you do to a plant's roots. Spread them out; don't fold or coil them or cram them into a tight hole. Keep them covered; don't let the sun or air dry them out. And don't bury them too deep; set the top of the root-ball level with the surrounding soil. Always water well to settle the soil.

Planting container-grown plants

The steps are the same for any plant, no matter what size container it's growing in. Dig a hole that's a little wider than the container but not quite as deep ❶. Check by setting the container into the hole—the top of the soil in the container should be slightly higher than the surrounding soil. Dig several holes at a time at the positions that you've already marked out.

Remove the container ❷. With one hand, grip the plant at the base of its stems or leaves, like pulling a ponytail, while you tug on the pot with the other hand. If the pot doesn't slide off easily, don't pull harder on the stems. Try whacking the pot against a hard surface; if it still doesn't slide off, use a strong knife to cut or pry it off.

Examine the plant's roots ❸. If there are any thick, coiled roots, unwind them and cut them off close to the root-ball, leaving short stubs. If the root-ball is a mass of fine, hairlike roots, use the knife to cut three or four slits from top to bottom, about 1 in. deep. Pry the slits apart and tease the cut roots to loosen them. This cutting or slitting may seem drastic, but it's actually good for the plant because it forces new roots to grow out into the surrounding soil. Work quickly. Once you've taken a plant out of its container, get it in the ground as soon as possible. If you want to prepare several plants at a time, cover them with an old sheet or tarp to keep the roots from drying out.

Set the root-ball into the hole ❹. Make sure that the plant is positioned right, with its best side facing out, and that the top of the root-ball is level with or slightly higher than the surface of the bed. Then add enough soil to fill in the hole, and pat it down firmly.

PLANTING CONTAINER-GROWN PLANTS

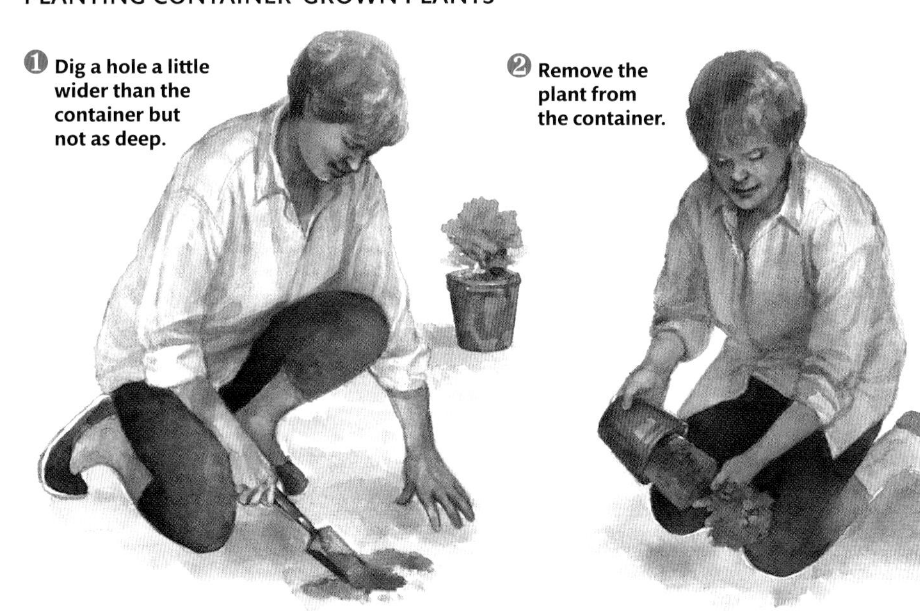

❶ **Dig a hole a little wider than the container but not as deep.**

❷ **Remove the plant from the container.**

❸ **Unwind any large, coiled roots and cut them off short. Cut vertical slits through masses of fine roots.**

❹ **Position the plant in the hole, and fill in around it with soil and firm well.**

Planting a balled-and-burlapped shrub or tree

Nurseries often grow shrubs and trees in fields, and then dig them with a ball of root-filled soil and wrap a layer of burlap snugly around the ball to keep it intact. The problem is that even a small ball of soil is very heavy. A root-ball that is a foot wide is a two-person job. For larger root-balls, ask the nursery to deliver and plant it. Here's how to proceed with plants that are small enough that you can handle them.

Dig a hole several inches wider than the root-ball but not quite as deep as the root-ball is high. Firm the soil so the plant won't sink. Set the plant into the hole, and lay a stick across the top of the root-ball to make sure it's at or a little higher than grade level. Be sure to cut or untie any twine that wraps around the trunk. Fold the burlap down around the sides of the ball. Don't try to pull the burlap out altogether—roots can grow out through it, and it will eventually decompose. Fill soil all around the sides of the ball, and pat it down firmly. Spread only an inch of soil over the top of the ball. Water well.

The top of the ball should be level with the surrounding soil. Cut twine that wraps around the trunk. Fold down the burlap, but don't remove it.

Planting bare-root plants

Mail-order nurseries sometimes dig perennials, roses, and other plants when the plants are dormant, cut back the tops, and wash all the soil off the roots to save space and weight when storing and shipping them. If you receive a plant in bare-root condition, unwrap it, trim away any roots that are broken or damaged, and soak the roots in a pail of water for several hours.

To plant, dig a hole large enough that you can spread the roots across the bottom without folding them. Start covering the roots with soil; then lay a stick across the top of the hole and hold the plant against it to check the planting depth, as shown in the drawing. Raise or lower the plant if needed in order to bury just the roots, not the buds. Add more soil, firming it down around the roots, and continue until the hole is full. Water.

Dig a hole wide enough that you can spread out the roots. A stick helps position the plant at the correct depth as you fill the hole with soil.

Planting ground covers from flats

Sometimes ground covers are sold in flats of 25 or more rooted cuttings. Start at one corner, reach underneath the soil, and lift out a portion of the flat's contents. Working quickly because the roots are exposed, tease the cuttings apart, trying not to break off any roots, and plant them individually. Then lift out the next portion and continue planting. Water thoroughly.

Remove a clump of little plants, tease their roots apart, and plant them quickly.

Planting bulbs

Plant spring-blooming bulbs from September to November. If the soil in the bed was well prepared, you can use a trowel to dig holes for planting individual bulbs; where you have room, you can dig a wider hole or trench for planting a group of bulbs all at once. The perennials, ground covers, shrubs, and trees you planted earlier in the fall or in the spring will still be small enough that you won't disturb their roots. As a rule of thumb, plant small (grape- or cherry-size) bulbs about 2 in. deep and 3 to 5 in. apart, and large (walnut- or egg-size) bulbs 4 to 6 in. deep and 6 to 10 in. apart. Water in well.

Plant bulbs with the pointed end up, at a depth and spacing determined by the size of the bulb.

Basic Landscape Care

The landscape plantings in this book will grow increasingly carefree from year to year as the plants mature, but of course you'll always need to do some regular maintenance. Depending on the design you choose, this ongoing care may require as much as a few hours a week during the season or as little as a few hours a year. No matter what you plant, you'll have to control weeds, use mulch, water as needed, and do spring and fall cleanups. Trees, shrubs, and vines may need staking or training at first and occasional pruning or shearing afterward. Perennials, ground covers, and grasses may need to be cut back, staked, deadheaded, or divided. Performing these tasks, which are explained on the following pages, is sometimes hard work, but for many gardeners it is enjoyable labor, a chance to get outside in the fresh air. Also, spending time each week with your plants helps you identify and address problems before they become serious.

Mulches and fertilizers

Covering the soil in all planted areas with a layer of organic mulch does several jobs at once: it improves the appearance of your garden while you're waiting for the plants to grow, reduces the number of weeds that emerge, reduces water loss from the soil during dry spells, moderates soil temperatures, and adds nutrients to the soil as it decomposes. Inorganic mulches such as clear or black plastic, landscape fabric, and gravel also provide some of these benefits, but their conspicuous appearance and the difficulty of removing them if you ever want to change the landscape are serious drawbacks.

Many materials are used as mulches; the box on p. 202 presents the most common, with comments on their advantages and disadvantages. Consider appearance, availability, cost, and convenience when you're comparing different products. Most garden centers have a few kinds of bagged mulch materials, but for mulching large areas, it's easier and cheaper to have a landscape contractor or other supplier deliver a truckload of bulk mulch. A landscape looks best if you see the same mulch throughout the entire planting area, rather than a patchwork of different mulches. You can achieve a uniform look by spreading a base layer of homemade compost, rotten hay, or other inexpensive material and topping that with a neater-looking material such as bark chips, shredded bark, or cocoa hulls.

It takes at least a 1-in. layer of mulch to suppress weeds, but there's no need to spread it more than 3 in. deep. As you're spreading it, don't put any mulch against the stems of any plants, because that can lead to disease or insect problems. Put most of the mulch *between* plants, not right *around* them. Check the mulch each spring when you do an annual garden inspection and cleanup. Be sure it's pulled back away from the plant stems. Rake the surface of the mulch lightly to loosen it, and top it up with a fresh layer if the old material has decomposed.

Fertilizer

Decomposing mulch frequently supplies enough nutrients to grow healthy plants, but using fertilizer helps if you want to boost the plants—to make them grow faster, get larger, or produce more flowers. There are dozens of fertilizer products on the market—liquid and granular, fast-acting and slow-release, organic and synthetic. Choose whichever you prefer; they all give good results if applied as directed. And observe the following precautions: don't overfertilize, don't fertilize when the soil is dry, and don't fertilize after midsummer, because plants need to slow down and finish the season's growth before cold weather comes.

Planting under a tree

When planting beneath a mature tree, as for the design on pp. 110–113, remember that most tree roots are in the top few inches of the soil, and they extend at least as far away from the trunk as the limbs do the dripline. For areas of ground cover and most container-grown perennials, you can add topsoil and organic amendments up to about 6 in. deep over the entire area; then set the plants out in the new soil. Larger plants need deeper holes. Whether you dig planting holes in existing soil or through a layer of added topsoil, dig carefully, disturbing as few tree roots as possible. If you encounter a large root, move the planting hole rather than sever the root.

Confining perennials

Yarrow, bee balm, artemisia, sweet autumn clematis, and various other perennials, grasses, and ferns are described as invasive because they spread by underground runners. To confine these plants to a limited area, install a barrier when you plant them. Cut the bottom off a 5-gal. or larger plastic pot; bury the pot so its rim is above the soil; and plant the perennial inside. You'll need to lift, divide, and replant part of the perennial every second or third year.

Mulch materials

Bark products

Bark nuggets, chipped bark, shredded bark, and composted bark, usually from conifers, are available in bags or in bulk. All are attractive, long-lasting, medium-priced mulches.

Chipped tree trimmings

The chips from utility companies and tree services are a mixture of wood, bark, twigs, and leaves. These chips cost less than pure bark products. (You may be able to get a load for free.) But they don't look as good, and you have to replace them more often because they decompose fast.

Sawdust and shavings

These are cheap or free at sawmills and woodshops. They make good path coverings, but they aren't ideal mulches, because they tend to pack down into a dense, water-resistant surface.

Hulls and shells

Cocoa hulls, buckwheat hulls, peanut shells, and nut shells are available for pickup at food-processing plants and are sometimes sold in bags or bulk at garden centers. They're all attractive, long-lasting mulches. Price varies from free to quite expensive, depending on where you get them.

Tree leaves

A few big trees may supply all the mulch you need, year after year. You can just rake the leaves onto the bed in fall, but they'll probably blow off it again. It's better to chop them up with the lawn mower, pile them in compost bins for the winter, and spread them on the beds in late spring. If you have the space for two sets of compost bins, give leaves an extra year to decompose before spreading them. Pine needles make good mulch, too, especially for rhododendrons, mountain laurels, and other acid-loving shrubs. You can spread pine needles in fall because they cling together and don't blow around.

Grass clippings

A 1- to 2-in. layer of dried grass clippings makes an acceptable mulch that decomposes within a single growing season. Don't pile clippings too thick, though. If you do, the top surface dries and packs into a water-resistant crust, and the bottom layer turns into nasty slime.

Hay and straw

Farmers sell hay that's moldy, old, or otherwise unsuitable for fodder as "mulch" hay. This hay is cheap, but it's likely to include weed seeds, particularly seeds of weedy grasses such as barnyard grass. Straw—the stems of grain crops such as wheat—is usually seed-free but more expensive. Both hay and straw are more suitable for mulching vegetable gardens than landscape plantings because they have to be renewed each year. They are bulky at first but decompose quickly. They also tend to attract rodents.

Gravel

A mulch of pea gravel or crushed rock, spread 1 to 2 in. thick, helps keep the soil cool and moist, and many plants grow very well with a gravel mulch. However, compared with organic materials such as bark or leaves, it's much more tiring to apply a gravel mulch in the first place; it's harder to remove leaves and litter that accumulate on the gravel or weeds that sprout up through it; it's annoying to dig through the gravel if you want to replace or add plants later; and it's extremely tedious to remove the gravel itself, should you ever change your mind about having it there.

Landscape fabrics

Various types of synthetic fabrics, usually sold in rolls 3 to 4 ft. wide and 20, 50, or 100 ft. long, can be spread over the ground as a weed barrier and topped with a layer of gravel, bark chips, or other mulch. Unlike plastic, these fabrics allow water and air to penetrate into the soil. It's useful to lay fabric under paths, but not in planted areas. In a bed, it's a two-person job to install the fabric in the first place, it's inconvenient trying to install plants through holes cut in the fabric, and it's hard to secure the fabric neatly and invisibly at the edges of the bed. The fabric lasts indefinitely, and removing it—if you change your mind—is a messy job.

Clear or black plastic

Don't even think about using any kind of plastic sheeting as a landscape mulch. The soil underneath a sheet of plastic gets bone-dry, while water accumulates on top. Any loose mulch you spread on plastic slips or floats around and won't stay in an even layer. No matter how you try to secure them, the edges of plastic sheeting always pull loose, appear at the surface, degrade in the sun, and shred into tatters.

Watering

Watering is less of a concern for gardeners in the Northeast region than in other parts of the country, but even here there are dry spells and droughts when plants could use some extra water. New plantings, in particular, almost always need water more often than rain provides it.

Deciding whether water is needed

Usually only experienced gardeners can judge whether plants need water simply by looking at their leaves. Their appearance can be misleading. Moreover, you can't go by your own feelings about the weather.

Fortunately, there are two very reliable ways of deciding whether you should water. One is to check the soil. Get a paint stirrer or similar piece of unfinished, light-colored wood and use it as a dipstick. Push it down through the mulch and a few inches into the soil; leave it there for an hour or so; and pull it out to see whether moisture has discolored the wood. If so, the soil is moist enough for plants. If not, it's time to water. You have to let the stick dry out before you can use it again; it's handy to have several of these sticks around the garden shed.

The other method is to make a habit of monitoring rainfall by having your own rain gauge or listening to the weather reports, and marking a calendar to keep track of rainfall amounts. In the Northeast region, most landscape plants thrive if they get 3 to 4 in. of rain a month. You should make every effort to water new plantings if there's been less than 1 in. of rain in two weeks. In subsequent years, after the plants have had time to put down roots, they can endure three or more weeks with no rain at all; even so, you should water them if you can. In this region, established plants rarely die from drought, but they do show many signs of stress—wilting leaves, premature leaf drop, failure to bloom or to set fruit, and increased susceptibility to insect and disease attacks.

Pay attention to soil moisture or rainfall amounts from April through October, because plants can suffer from dryness throughout that entire period, not just in the heat of summer, and water whenever the soil is dry. As for time of day, you can water whenever the plants need it and you get the chance. Gardening books sometimes warn against watering plants late in the day, saying that plants are more vulnerable to fungal infections if the leaves stay wet at night. That's true, but plants get wet with dew most nights anyway.

How much to water

It's easy to overwater a houseplant but hard to overwater a plant in the ground. Outdoors, you're much more likely to water too little than too much. You could spend an hour with hose in hand, watering the plants in a flower bed, and supply the equivalent of ¼ in. of rain or less. Holding a hose or carrying a bucket is practical for watering new plantings only where the plants are few, small, or relatively widely spaced. To thoroughly water an area that's filled with plants, you need a system that allows you to turn on the water, walk away, and come back later. An oscillating sprinkler on the end of a hose works fine, or you can weave a soaker hose through the bed.

No matter how you water, you should monitor how much water you have applied and how evenly it was distributed. If you're hand-watering or using a soaker hose, the watering pattern may be quite uneven. One way to eliminate this situation is to put several wooden "dipsticks" (you can use a wooden skewer or chopstick) in different parts of the bed to make sure that all areas have received enough water to moisten the sticks. To monitor the output of a sprinkler, set tuna-fish cans around the bed. Check the cans the next time you run the sprinkler to see how much water they catch. (You can use the same technique for measuring rainfall.) Let the sprinkler run until there's about an inch of water in each can.

Drought resistance

There are many plants that have evolved naturally in regions with little natural rainfall, often with porous sandy soil. Common characteristics of such plants include water-storing foliage, such as succulents and cacti, and leaves that appear silvery from a covering of small hairs that reflect light, common in yarrow, lavender, bluebeard, Russian sage, and wormwoods. Plants with large fleshy leaves, often tropicals, lose huge amounts of water through transpiration, but small-leaved plants, such as creeping thymes, creeping Jenny, sweet woodruff, and foamflower, lose little. Deep- and wide-rooted butterfly weed, false indigo, switchgrass, and coneflowers are others that resist drought readily. Amend soil with organic matter and apply mulch to help retain soil moisture.

Controlling weeds

Weeds are not much of a problem in established landscapes. Once the good plants have grown big enough to merge together, they tend to crowd or shade out all but the most persistent weeds. But weeds can be troublesome in a new landscape unless you take steps to prevent and control them.

There are two main types of weeds: those that mostly sprout up as seedlings and those that keep coming back from perennial roots or runners. Try to identify and eliminate any perennial weeds before you start a landscaping project. Then you'll only have to deal with new seedlings later.

Annual and perennial weeds that commonly grow from seeds include crabgrass, chickweed, dandelions, plantain, purslane, ragweed, and violets. Trees and shrubs such as silver maple, wild cherry, cottonwood, willow, black locust, buckthorn, and honeysuckle produce weedy seedlings, too. For any of these weeds that grow from seeds, the strategy is twofold: try to keep the weed seeds from sprouting, and eliminate any seedlings that do sprout as soon as you see them, while they are still small.

Almost any patch of soil includes weed seeds that are ready to sprout whenever that soil is disturbed. You have to disturb the soil to prepare it before planting, and that will probably cause an initial flush of weeds, but you'll never see that many weeds again if you leave the soil undisturbed in subsequent years. You don't have to hoe, rake, or cultivate around perennial plantings. Leave the soil alone, and fewer weeds will appear. Using mulch helps even more; by shading the soil, it prevents weed seeds from sprouting. And if weed seeds blow in and land on top of the mulch, they'll be less likely to germinate there than they would on bare soil.

Pull or cut off any weeds that appear while they're young and small. Don't let them mature and go to seed. Most weed seedlings emerge in late spring and early summer.

Using herbicides

Two kinds of herbicides can be very useful and effective in maintaining home landscapes, but only if used correctly. You have to choose the right product for the job and follow the directions on the label regarding dosage and timing of application exactly.

Preemergent herbicides. Usually sold in granular form, these herbicides are designed to prevent weed seeds, particularly crabgrass and other annual weeds, from sprouting. Typically one application is enough to last through the growing season, but you need to apply the product quite early in spring, at the time forsythias start blooming. If you wait until later, many weeds will already have sprouted, and a preemergent herbicide will not stop them then.

WEEDS THAT SPROUT FROM SEEDS

Simple root systems can be easily pulled while still small.

Plantain **Maple seedling** **Dandelion**

WEEDS THAT SPROUT BACK FROM PERENNIAL ROOTS OR RUNNERS

Connected by underground runners, the shoots of these weeds need to be pulled repeatedly, smothered with a thick mulch, or killed with an herbicide.

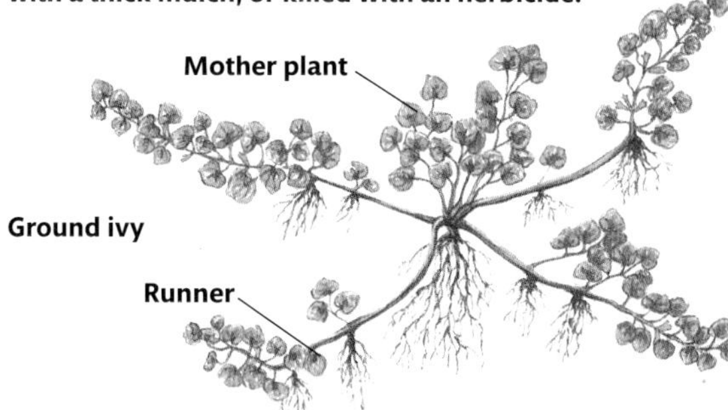

Use a disposable, sponge-type paintbrush to apply the herbicide selectively, painting only the weeds. Prepare the solution as directed for spray application. Use only enough to wet the leaves so that none drips.

USING HERBICIDES ON PERENNIAL WEEDS

Ready-to-use spot-weeder sprays are convenient, but you must aim carefully. Try using a sheet of cardboard as a backdrop to protect desirable plants from herbicide drift.

Read the label carefully, and make sure the herbicide you buy is registered for use around the kinds of ground covers, perennials, shrubs, or other plants you have. Measure the area of your bed; weigh out the appropriate amount of granules; and sprinkle them as evenly as possible across the soil. Wear heavy rubber gloves that are rated for use with farm chemicals, not common household rubber gloves, and follow the safety precautions on the product label.

Postemergent herbicides. These chemicals are used to kill plants. Some kinds kill only the aboveground parts of a plant; other kinds are absorbed into the plant and kill it, roots and all. Postemergent herbicides are typically applied as sprays, which you can buy ready-to-use or prepare by mixing a concentrate with water. Look for those that break down quickly, and read the label carefully for registered applications, specific directions, and safety instructions.

Postemergent herbicides work best if applied when the weeds are growing vigorously. You usually have to apply enough to thoroughly wet the plant's leaves, and do it during a spell of dry weather. Applying an herbicide is an effective way to get rid of a perennial weed that you can't dig or pull up, but it's really better to do this before you plant a bed, as it's hard to spray herbicides in an established planting without getting some on your good plants. Aim carefully, and don't spray on windy days. Brushing or sponging the herbicide on the leaves avoids damaging adjacent plants.

Using postemergent herbicides in an established planting is a painstaking job, but it may be the only way to get rid of a persistent perennial weed. For young weed seedlings, it's usually easier and faster to pull them by hand than to spray them.

Caring for Woody Plants

A well-chosen garden tree, such as the ones recommended in this book, grows naturally into a neat, pleasing shape; won't get too large for its site; is resistant to pests and diseases; and doesn't drop messy pods or other litter. Once established, these trees need very little care from year to year.

Regular watering is the most important concern in getting a tree off to a good start. Don't let it suffer from drought for the first few years. To reduce competition, don't plant ground covers or other plants within 2 ft. of the tree's trunk. Just spread a thin layer of mulch there.

Arborists now dismiss other care ideas that once were common practice. According to current thinking, you don't need to fertilize a tree when you plant it. (In fact, most landscape trees never need fertilizing.) Keep pruning to a minimum at planting time; remove only dead or damaged twigs, not healthy shoots. Finally, if a tree is small enough that one or two people can carry and plant it, it doesn't need staking and the trunk will grow stronger if unstaked. Larger trees that are planted by a nursery may need staking, especially on windy sites, but the stakes should be removed within a year.

Pruning to direct growth

Pruning shapes plants not only by removing stems, branches, and leaves but also by inducing and directing new growth. All plants have a bud at the base of every leaf. New shoots grow from these buds. Cutting off the end of a stem encourages the lower buds to shoot out and produces a bushier plant. This type of pruning makes a hedge fill out and gives an otherwise lanky perennial or shrub a better rounded shape.

The same response to pruning also allows you to steer the growth of a plant. The bud immediately below the cut will produce a shoot that extends in the direction the bud was pointing. To direct a branch or stem, cut it back to a bud pointing in the direction you want to encourage growth. This technique is useful for shaping young trees and shrubs and for keeping their centers open to light and air.

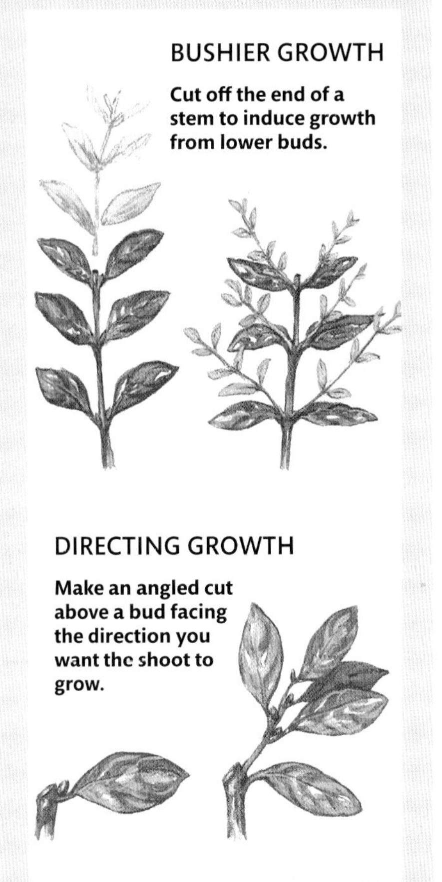

BUSHIER GROWTH

Cut off the end of a stem to induce growth from lower buds.

DIRECTING GROWTH

Make an angled cut above a bud facing the direction you want the shoot to grow.

Pruning roses

Roses are vigorous, fast-growing shrubs that need regular pruning to keep them shapely and attractive. Most of this pruning should be done in early spring, just as the buds start to swell but before the new leaves start to unfold. All roses need similar care at this time. Prune off any shoots frozen or broken during the winter; remove old or weak shoots and crossing or crowded stems; and trim back any asymmetric or unbalanced shoots.

Don't be afraid of cutting back too hard; it's better to leave just a few strong shoots than a lot of weak ones. If you cut off old stems at ground level, new ones will grow to replace them. Cut damaged or asymmetric stems back partway and they will branch out.

Always use sharp pruning shears, and cut back to a healthy, outward-facing bud, leaving no stub. Right after pruning you can add fresh mulch around the plant.

An annual spring pruning is enough to keep shrub roses such as 'Bonica' and 'Frau Dagmar Hartop' fairly neat and compact, but you may want to remove or trim an errant or too-vigorous shoot during the summer. You can do that anytime.

Climbing roses don't need as much spring pruning as shrubs do—just remove weak or damaged shoots—but they need more attention throughout the summer because their stems or canes can grow a foot or more in a month. Check regularly, and tie this new growth to the trellis while it's still supple and manageable. When the canes grow long enough to reach the top of the trellis or arbor, cut off their tips and they will send out side shoots, which are where the flowers form.

It's up to you whether to prune off the flower stalks as the roses fade. If you don't, many kinds of roses will proceed to form small red or orange fruits, called rose hips. These are decorative throughout the late summer and fall, and they sometimes last into the winter. Roses are so vigorous that it doesn't hurt the plant to let it set plenty of fruits. On the other hand, roses often look messy as the petals fade, so you might prefer to remove them. Also, most roses bloom more abundantly and over a longer season if you keep pruning off the flowers to keep the hips from developing. If you decide to remove the flowers, use your pruning shears to cut the stem back to a healthy leaf or bud. If you prefer to let the hips form, prune them off in late winter or early spring by cutting in the same way.

PRUNING A SHRUB ROSE

Cut blackened winter-damaged shoots back to healthy, green tissue.

Old

Weak, crossing

BEFORE

AFTER

Every spring, remove old, weak, or damaged shoots; stems that are crossing or crowded; and stems that stick out too far and look asymmetric. Don't be afraid to cut a lot away.

REMOVING FLOWERS OR HIPS

If you prefer to let the hips develop, leave the flowers alone. Remove the old bunches of hips in winter or spring, cutting back to a healthy bud.

Shaping young trees

As a tree grows, you can direct its shape by pruning once a year, in winter or summer. (See the box on p. 205.) Don't prune just for the sake of pruning. If you don't have a good reason for making a cut, don't do it. Follow these guidelines:

- **Use sharp pruning shears, loppers, or saws,** which make clean cuts without tearing the wood or bark.
- **Cut branches back** to a healthy shoot, leaf, or bud, or cut back to the branch collar at the base of the branch, as shown at right. Don't leave any stubs; they're ugly and prone to decay.
- **Remove any dead or damaged** branches and any twigs or limbs that are very spindly or weak.
- **Where two limbs cross over or rub** against each other, save one limb—usually the thicker, stronger one—and prune off the other one.
- **Prune or widen narrow crotches.** Places where a branch and trunk or two branches form a narrow V are weak spots, liable to split apart as the tree grows. Where the trunk of a young tree exhibits such a crotch or where either of two shoots could continue the growth of a branch, prune off the weaker of the two. Where you wish to keep the branch, insert a piece of wood as a spacer to widen the angle, as shown below. Leave the spacer in place for a year or so.

WHERE TO CUT

When removing the end of a branch, cut back to a healthy leaf, bud, or side shoot. Don't leave a stub. Use sharp pruning shears to make a neat cut that slices the stem rather than tears it.

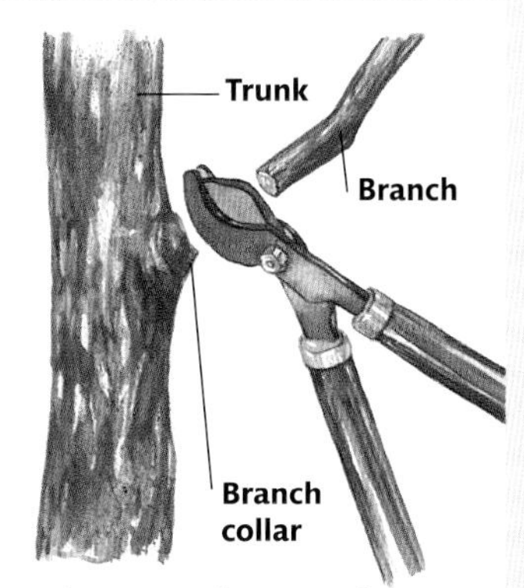

When removing an entire branch, cut just outside the slightly thickened area, called the "branch collar," where the branch grows into the trunk.

One trunk or several?

If you want a young tree to have a single trunk, identify the leader or central shoot and let it grow straight up, unpruned. The trunk will grow thicker faster if you leave the lower limbs in place for the first few years, but if they're in the way, you can remove them. At whatever height you choose—usually about 8 ft. off the ground if you want to walk or see under the tree—select the shoots that will become the main limbs of the tree. Be sure they are evenly spaced around the trunk, pointing outward at wide angles. Remove any lower or weaker shoots. As the tree matures, the only further pruning required will be an annual checkup to remove dead, damaged, or crossing shoots.

Some of the trees in this book, including river birch, 'White Spire' birch, Japanese maple, Japanese tree lilac, star magnolia, redbud, and serviceberry, are often grown with multiple (usually two to four) trunks, for a graceful, clumplike appearance. When buying a multiple-trunk tree, what's most important is that the trunks should diverge at the base. The more space between them, the better. Prune multiple-trunk trees as previously described for single-trunk trees, and remove some of the branches that are growing toward the center of the clump, so it doesn't get too dense and tangled.

AVOIDING NARROW CROTCHES

A tree's limbs should spread wide, like outstretched arms. If limbs angle too close to the trunk or to each other, there isn't room for them to grow properly and they may split apart after a few years, ruining the tree.

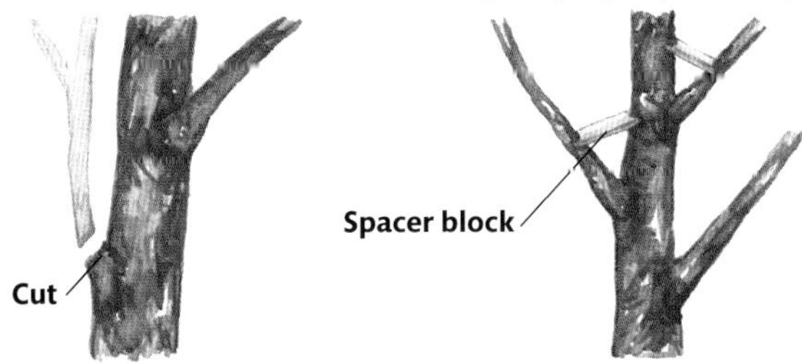

SINGLE-TRUNK TREES: Correct narrow crotches on a young tree by removal or by widening the angle with a wooden spacer block. Choose well-spaced shoots to become the main limbs of a shade tree.

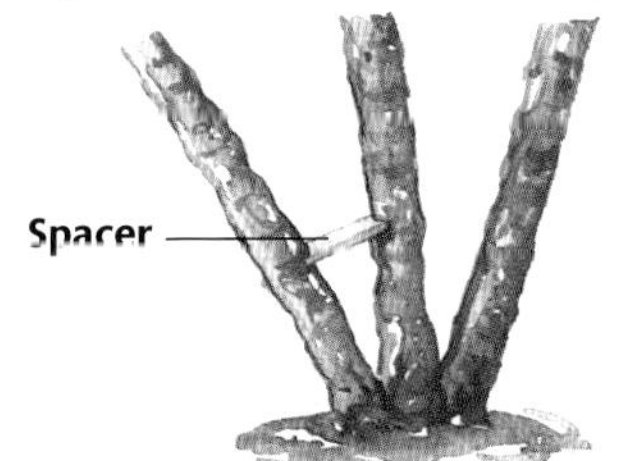

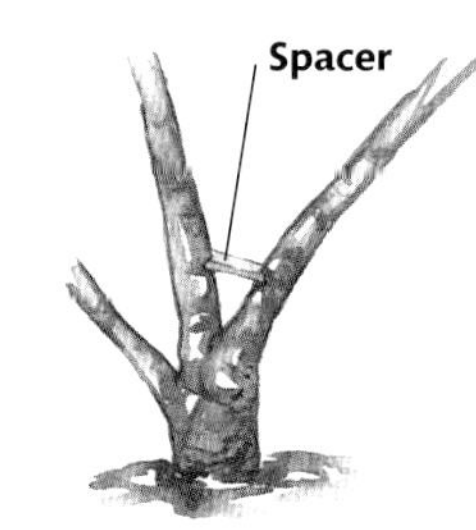

MULTIPLE-TRUNK TREES: Whether the stems of a multiple-trunk tree emerge from the ground or from a single trunk near the ground, widen angles if necessary to keep the trunks from touching.

Pruning shrubs

Shrubs are generally carefree plants, but they almost always look better if you do some pruning at least once a year. As a minimum, remove dead twigs from time to time, and if any branches are broken by storms or accidents, remove them as soon as convenient, cutting back to a healthy bud or to the plant's crown. Also, unless the shrub produces attractive seedpods or berries, it's a good idea to trim off the flowers after they fade.

Beyond this routine pruning, some shrubs require more attention. (The entries in Plant Profiles, pp. 128–153, give more information on when and how to prune particular shrubs.) Basically, shrub pruning falls into three categories: selective pruning, severe pruning, and shearing.

Selective pruning means using pruning shears to remove or cut back individual shoots, in order to refine the shape of the bush and maintain its vigor, as well as limit its size. (See the drawing at right.) This job takes time but produces a very graceful and natural-looking bush. Cut away weak or spindly twigs and any limbs that cross or rub against each other, and cut all the longest shoots back to a healthy, outward-facing bud or to a pair of buds. You can do selective pruning on any shrub, deciduous or evergreen, at any time of year.

Severe pruning means using pruning shears or loppers to cut away most of a shrub's top growth, leaving just short stubs or a gnarly trunk. This kind of cutting back is usually done once a year in late winter or early spring. Although it seems drastic, severe pruning is appropriate in several situations.

It makes certain fast-growing shrubs such as bluebeard and butterfly bush flower more profusely. It keeps others, such as lavender and spirea, compact and bushy, and it stimulates Siberian dogwood to produce canelike stems with bright red bark.

One or two severe prunings done when a shrub is young can make it branch out at the base, producing a bushier specimen or a fuller hedge plant. Nurseries often do this pruning as part of producing a good plant, and if you buy a shrub that's already bushy you don't need to cut it back yourself.

Older shrubs that have gotten tall and straggly sometimes respond to a severe pruning by sprouting out with renewed vigor, sending up lots of new shoots that bear plenty of foliage and flowers. This strategy doesn't work for all shrubs, though—sometimes severe pruning kills a plant. Don't try it unless you know it will work (check with a knowledgeable person at a nursery) or are willing to take a chance.

Shearing means using hedge shears or an electric hedge trimmer to trim the surface of a shrub, hedge, or tree to a neat, uniform profile, producing a solid mass of greenery. Both deciduous and evergreen shrubs and trees can be sheared; those with small, closely spaced leaves and a naturally compact growth habit usually look best. A good time for shearing most shrubs is early summer, after the new shoots have elongated but before the wood has hardened, but you can shear at other times of year, and you may have to shear some plants more than once a year.

If you're planning to shear a plant, start when it is young and establish the shape—cone, pyramid, flat-topped hedge, or whatever. Looking at the profile, always make the shrub wider at the bottom than on top, otherwise the lower limbs will be shaded and won't be as leafy. Shear off as little as needed to maintain the shape as the shrub grows. Once it gets as big as you want it, shear as much as necessary to keep it that size.

SELECTIVE PRUNING. Remove weak, spindly, bent, or broken shoots (red). Where two branches rub on each other, remove the weakest or the one that's pointing inward (orange). Cut back long shoots to a healthy, outward-facing bud (blue).

SEVERE PRUNING. In late winter or early spring, before new growth starts, cut all the stems back close to the ground.

SHEARING. Trim with hedge clippers to a neat profile.

Making a hedge

To make a hedge that's dense enough that you can't see through it, choose shrubs that have many shoots at the base. If you can only find skinny shrubs, prune them severely the first spring after planting to stimulate bushier growth.

Hedge plants are set in the ground as described on p. 200 but are spaced closer together than they would be if planted as individual specimens. We took that into account in creating the designs and plant lists used throughout this book; just follow the spacings recommended in the designs. If you're impatient for the hedge to fill in, you can simply space the plants closer together.

A hedge can be sheared, pruned selectively, or left alone, depending on how you want it to look. Slow-growing, small-leaved plants such as boxwood and Japanese holly make rounded but natural-looking hedges with no pruning at all, or you can shear them into any profile you choose and make them perfectly neat and uniform. (Be sure to keep them narrower at the top.) Choose one style and stick with it. Once a hedge is established, you can neither start nor stop shearing it without an awkward transition that may last a few years before the hedge looks good again.

Getting a vine off to a good start

Nurseries often sell clematis, honeysuckle, and other vines as young plants with a single stem fastened to a bamboo stake. To plant them, remove the stake and cut off the stem right above the lowest pair of healthy leaves, usually about 4 to 6 in. above the soil ❶. This forces the vine to send out new shoots low to the ground. As soon as those new shoots have begun to develop (normally within four to six weeks after planting), cut them back to their first pairs of leaves ❷. After this second pruning, the plant will become bushy at the base. Now, as new shoots form, use sticks or strings to direct them toward the base of the support they are to climb ❸.

Once they're started, both clematis and honeysuckle can scramble up a lattice trellis, although it helps if you tuck in any stray ends from time to time. The plants can't climb a smooth surface, however. For them to cover a fence or post, you have to provide something the vine can wrap around. Fasten a few eyescrews to the top and bottom of such a support, and stretch wire, nylon cord, or polypropylene rope between them. (The wires or cords should be a few inches out from the fence, not flush against it.)

Other vines need different treatments. 'Golden Showers' and other so-called climbing roses don't really climb at all by themselves—you have to fasten them to a support. Twist-ties are handy for this job. Roses grow fast, so you'll have to tie in the new shoots every few weeks from spring to fall. Climbing hydrangea and English ivy are both slow starters, but once under way, they can climb any surface to any height by means of their clinging rootlets and so they need no further assistance or care.

After the first year, the vines in this book don't need pruning on a regular basis, but you can cut them back whenever they get too big, and you should remove any dead or straggly stems from time to time.

Caring for Perennials

Perennials are simply plants that send up new growth year after year. A large group, perennials include flowering plants such as daylilies and astilbes as well as grasses, ferns, and hardy bulbs. Although some perennials need special conditions and care, most of the ones in this book are adaptable and easygoing. Get them off to a good start by planting them in well- prepared soil, adding a 2 in. layer of mulch, watering as often as needed throughout the first year, and keeping weeds away. After that, keeping perennials attractive and healthy typically requires just a few minutes per plant each year.

Routine annual care

Some of the perennials that are used as ground covers, such as lily-of-the-valley, myrtle, pachysandra, sweet woodruff, and sweet violet, need virtually no care. On a suitable site, they'll thrive for decades even if you pay them no attention at all.

Most garden perennials, though, look and grow better if you clean away the old leaves and stems at least once a year. When to do this depends on the plant. Perennials such as aster, daylily, dwarf fountain grass, hosta, interrupted fern, iris, and peony have leaves and stalks that turn tan or brown after they're frosted in fall. Cut these down to the ground in late fall or early spring; either time is okay.

Perennials such as beach wormwood, bigroot geranium, blue oat grass, Christmas fern, dianthus, Lenten rose, lilyturf, and moss phlox have foliage that is more or less evergreen, depending on the severity of the winter. For those plants, wait until early spring; then cut back any leaves or stems that are discolored or shabby-looking. Don't leave cuttings lying on the soil, because they may contain disease spores. Do not compost diseased stems or leaves.

Right after you've cleared away the dead material is a good time to renew the mulch on the bed. Use a fork, rake, or cultivator to loosen the existing mulch, and add some fresh mulch if needed. Also, if you want to sprinkle some granular fertilizer on the bed, do that now, when it's easy to avoid getting any on the plants' leaves. Fertilizing perennials is optional, but it does make them grow bigger and bloom more than they would otherwise.

Remove faded flowers

Removing flowers as they fade (called "deadheading") makes the garden look neater, prevents unwanted self-sown seedlings, and often stimulates a plant to continue blooming longer than it would if you left it alone, or to bloom a second time later in the season. (This is true for shrubs and annuals as well as for perennials.)

Pick large flowers such as daisies, daylilies, lilies, peonies, pincushion flower, and tulips one at a time, snapping them off by hand. Use pruning shears on perennials, such as astilbe, bee balm, bleeding heart, hosta, lady's mantle, phlox, and yarrow, which produce tall stalks crowded with lots of small flowers, cutting the stalks back to the height of the foliage. Use hedge shears on bushy plants that are covered with lots of small flowers on short stalks, such as basket-of-gold, catmint, dianthus, evergreen candytuft, and germander, cutting the stems back by about one-half.

Instead of removing them, you may want to let the flowers remain on coneflower, purple coneflower, false indigo, Siberian iris, 'Autumn Joy' sedum, and the various grasses. These plants all bear conspicuous seedpods or seed heads on stiff stalks that remain standing , provide food for birds, and look interesting throughout the fall and winter.

Pruning and shearing perennials

Some perennials that bloom in summer or fall respond well to being pruned earlier in the growing season. Bee balm, boltonia, garden phlox, New England aster, and 'Autumn Joy' sedum all form tall clumps of stems topped with lots of little flowers. Unfortunately, tall stems are liable to flop over in stormy weather, and even if they don't, too-tall clumps can look leggy or top-heavy. To prevent floppiness, prune these plants when the stems are about 1 ft. tall. Remove the weakest stems from each clump by cutting them off at the ground; then cut all the remaining, strong stems back by about one-third. Pruning in this way keeps these plants shorter, stronger, and bushier, so you don't have to bother with staking them.

'Silver Mound' artemisia and ribbon grass are grown more for their foliage than for their flowers. You can use hedge shears to keep them neat, compact, and bushy, shearing off the tops of the stems once or twice in spring and summer.

Prune to create neater, bushier clumps of some summer- and fall-blooming perennials such as phlox, chrysanthemums, New England aster, and bee balm. When the stalks are about 1 ft. tall, cut them all back by one-third. Remove the weakest stalks at ground level.

Dividing perennials

Most perennials send up more stems each year, forming denser clumps or wider patches. Dividing is the process of cutting or breaking apart these clumps or patches. This is an easy way to make more plants to expand your garden, to control a plant that might otherwise spread out of bounds, or to renew an old specimen that doesn't look good or bloom well anymore.

Most perennials can be divided as often as every year or two if you're in a hurry to make more plants, or they can go for several years if you don't have any reason to disturb them. You can divide them in early spring, just as new growth is starting, or in late summer and fall, up until a month before hard frost.

There are two main approaches to dividing perennials, as shown in the drawings at right. You can leave the plant in the ground and use a sharp shovel to cut it apart, like slicing a pie, and then lift out one chunk at a time. Or you can dig around and underneath the plant and lift it out all at once, shake off the extra soil, and lay the plant on the ground or a tarp where you can work with it.

Some plants, such as boltonia, yarrow, and most ferns, are easy to divide. They almost fall apart when you dig them up. Others, such as astilbe, daylily, and most grasses, have very tough or tangled roots, and you'll have to wrestle with them. Chop them with a sharp butcher knife, pry them apart with a strong screwdriver or garden fork, or even cut through the roots with a hatchet or pruning saw. However you approach the job, before you insert any tool, take a close look at the plant right at ground level, and be careful to divide *between*, not *through*, the biggest and healthiest buds or shoots. Using a hose to wash loose mulch and soil away makes it easier to see what you're doing.

Don't make the divisions too small; they should be the size of a plant that you'd want to buy, not just little scraps. If you have more divisions than you need or want, choose just the best-looking ones to replant and discard or give away the others. Replant new divisions as soon as possible in freshly prepared soil. Water them right away, and water again whenever the soil dries out over the next few weeks or months until the plants are growing again.

Divide hardy bulbs such as daffodils and crocuses every few years by digging up the clumps after they have finished blooming but before the foliage turns yellow. Shake the soil off the roots; pull the bulbs apart; and replant them promptly, setting them as deep as they were buried before.

DIVIDING PERENNIALS

You can divide a clump or patch of perennials by cutting down into the patch with a sharp spade, like slicing a pie or a pan of brownies, then lifting out the separate chunks.

Or you can dig up the whole clump, shake the extra soil off the roots, then pull or pry it apart into separate plantlets.

Problem Solving

Some plants are much more susceptible than others to damage by severe weather, pests, or diseases. In this book, we've recommended plants that are generally trouble free, especially after they have had a few years to get established in your garden. But even these plants are subject to various mishaps and problems. The challenge is learning how to distinguish which problems are really serious and which are just cosmetic, and deciding how to solve—or, better yet, prevent—those problems that are serious.

Pests, large and small

Deer, rabbits, and woodchucks are liable to be a problem if your property is surrounded by or adjacent to fields or woods. You may not see them, but you can't miss the damage they do—they bite the tops off or eat whole plants of hostas, daylilies, and many other perennials. Deer also eat the leaves and stems of maples, azaleas, arborvitae, and many other trees and shrubs. In fall, bucks rub their antlers on the trunks, causing damaged scars. Commercial or homemade repellents that you spray on the foliage may be helpful if the animals aren't too hungry. (See the box below right for plants that deer seem to avoid.) But in the long run, the only solution is to fence out deer and to trap and remove smaller animals.

Chipmunks and squirrels are cute but naughty. They normally don't eat much foliage, but they do eat some kinds of flowers and several kinds of bulbs, they dig up new transplants, and they "plant" nuts in your flower beds and lawns. Voles and field mice can kill trees and shrubs by stripping the bark off the trunk, usually in the winter when the ground is covered with snow, and they eat away at many perennials, too. Moles don't eat plants, but their digging makes a mess of a lawn or flower bed. Persistent trapping is the most effective way to control all of these little critters.

Insects and related pests can cause minor or devastating damage. Most plants can afford to lose part of their foliage or sap without suffering much of a setback, so don't panic if you see a few holes chewed in a leaf. However, when-

Identify, then treat

Don't jump to conclusions and start spraying chemicals on a supposedly sick plant before you know what (if anything) is actually wrong with it. That's wasteful and irresponsible, and you're likely to do the plant as much harm as good. Pinpointing the exact cause of a problem is difficult even for experienced gardeners, so save yourself frustration and seek out expert help from the beginning.

If it seems that there's something wrong with one of your plants—for example, if the leaves are discolored, have holes in them, or have spots or marks on them—cut off a sample branch; wrap it in damp paper towels; and put it in a plastic bag (so it won't wilt). Take the sample to the nursery or garden center where you bought the plant, and ask for help. If the nursery can't help, contact the nearest office of your state's Cooperative Extension Service or a public garden in your area and ask if they have a staff member who can diagnose plant problems.

Meanwhile, look around your property and around the neighborhood, too, to see whether any other plants (of the same or different kinds) show similar symptoms. If a problem is widespread, you shouldn't have much trouble finding someone who can identify it and tell you what, if anything, to do. If only one plant is affected, it's often harder to diagnose the problem, and you may just have to wait and see what happens to it. Keep an eye on the plant; continue with watering and other regular maintenance; and see whether the problem gets worse or goes away. If nothing more has happened after a few weeks, stop worrying. If the problem continues, intensify your search for expert advice.

Plant problems stem from a number of causes: insect and animal pests, diseases, and poor care, particularly in winter. Remember that plant problems are often caused by a combination of these; all the more reason to consult with experts about their diagnosis and treatment.

Deer-resistant plants

Deer may nibble these plants, but they're unlikely to strip them bare. If you live in an area where deer populations are high, consider substituting some of these plants for others that are specified in a design.

Trees and Shrubs

Andromeda	Dogwood	Magnolia
Barberry	Forsythia	Pine
Boxwood	Holly	Spirea
Daphne	Lilac	Spruce

Perennials

Astilbe	Geranium	Lenten rose
Bee balm	Grasses	Peony
Blazing star	Heuchera	Russian sage
Bluebeard	Iris	Sage
Daffodil	Lamb's ears	Veronica
Ferns	Lavender	Yarrow

ever you suspect that insects are attacking one of your plants, try to catch one of them in a glass jar and get it identified, so you can decide what to do.

There are several new kinds of insecticides that are quite effective but much safer to use than the older products. You must read the fine print on the label to determine whether an insecticide will control your particular pest. Follow the directions for how to apply the product carefully, or it may not work.

Coping with deer

Deer have become a serious problem in many gardens year-round. When food is scarce in the winter, they will eat almost anything that is growing. Spring, when the new fawns are born, is another difficult time in gardens as the lush soft growth of plants, such as hostas, tulips, and daylilies, are just appearing. Fawns often behave like human toddlers and put everything in their mouths. For instance, the soft young sprouts of boxwoods are often nipped off; when the stems toughen up and become woody, they are mostly ignored as deer food. During dry summer spells, deer and other creatures become thirsty. Avoid watering after midday so foliage dries off before dusk. Watering late in the day almost guarantees a visit from the local herd. As temperatures drop in fall, the bucks prepare for the mating season. They feast on fallen acorns, beechnuts, crab apples, and other tasty morsels; always remove dropped fruits. More permanent damage is inflicted by the bucks rubbing their antlers on tree trunks. This removes the soft velvet covering from the antlers but results in scraping or scratching the bark, especially on young or thin-barked specimens.

To protect your garden, install physical barriers of wire or netting around susceptible plants. If you can install a surrounding fence, it should be at least 6 to 8 ft. high as deer are fine jumpers. Always alert the deer and people by attaching attention-getting flags at intervals on the fence. Changing heights

Winter protection

More plants are damaged or killed in the winter than in any other season. They may freeze during a severe cold spell, get broken by snow or ice, dry out, or be drowned. There are a few steps you can take to prevent winter damage.

Plant shrubs far enough away from a street, driveway, or building that they won't get crushed by the extra snow that accumulates from shoveling or slides off a roof. (Where designs in this book call for plantings in these kinds of areas, we've selected plants that hold up well.) Use stakes to mark the edge or corners of any planting that's adjacent to a walk or driveway, so you can avoid hitting the plants with a snowblower or shovel.

Spray evergreen shrubs with an anti-transpirant in late fall to keep their leaves from dehydrating in the cold winter winds. Or you can erect burlap tents around young shrubs to protect them from November until April. Drive four stakes in the ground and staple burlap to the sides. Leave the top open.

Any small or medium-size perennial or shrub that is planted in the fall is liable to be pushed up out of the ground, or frost-heaved, if the soil repeatedly freezes and thaws, and that means its roots get dried out. To prevent this, cover the ground around these plants with a loose mulch such as evergreen (limbs from discarded Christmas trees) as soon as the soil has frozen hard, and don't remove the covering until midspring.

Many more plants die from being too wet in winter than from getting too cold. Any plants growing where water collects and the ground stays saturated in winter are liable to rot. If you're thinking about planting in a low spot, prevent this kind of loss by preparing the site before you plant. Dig deep to loosen compacted subsoil, and add more topsoil to raise the surface of the bed so that water will drain both down and away from the root zone.

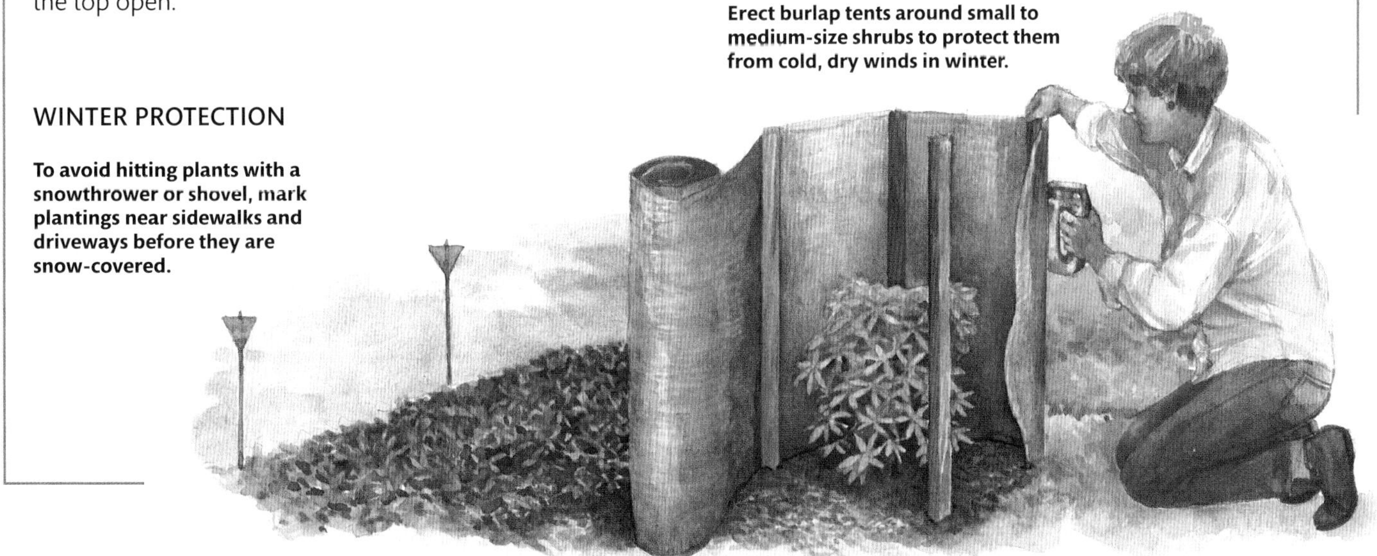

WINTER PROTECTION

To avoid hitting plants with a snowthrower or shovel, mark plantings near sidewalks and driveways before they are snow-covered.

Erect burlap tents around small to medium-size shrubs to protect them from cold, dry winds in winter.

within your property deters deer as they appear scared of negotiating different levels. Plenty of chemical or herbal sprays, liquid and granular, are available to deter deer. These must be applied regularly, often every 2 to 3 weeks, and especially after rain. Hanging smelly soap is popular, but seldom very effective.

Not all plants are palatable to deer. They usually avoid poisonous plants, such as daffodils, Lenten roses, fuzzy-leaved lambs ears, and Lady's mantle. Their superb sense of smell deters them from browsing plants with aromatic foliage, including many culinary herbs: mints, garlic, ornamental onions, rosemary, yarrow, and wormwood. Plants with highly fragrant flowers, like lilac, lavender, lily-of-the-valley, and summersweet, also irritate sensitive noses. Some plant families, including the poppy and milkweed families, are not palatable due to their milky saps. Another is the odorous-leaved mint family that includes beebalms, hummingbird mints, and lamiums. Grasses, sedges, and ferns are usually ignored also, along with tough-leaved plants like Japanese pachysandra, peonies, many irises, and yuccas.

Diseases

Several types of fungal, bacterial, and viral diseases can attack garden plants, causing a wide range of symptoms such as disfigured or discolored leaves or petals, powdery or moldy-looking films or spots, mushy or rotten stems or roots, and overall wilting. As with insect problems, if you suspect that a plant is infected with a disease, gather a sample of the plant and show it to someone who can identify the problem before you do any spraying.

In general, plant diseases are hard to treat, so it's important to take steps to prevent problems. These steps include choosing plants adapted to your area, choosing disease-resistant plants, spacing plants far enough apart so that air can circulate between them, and removing dead stems and litter from the garden.

Some perennials that would otherwise be healthy are prone to fungal infections during spells of hot humid weather, especially if the plants are crowded together or if they have flopped over and are lying on top of each other or on the ground. Look closely for moldy foliage, and if you find any, prune it off and discard it. (Don't compost it.) It's better to cut the plants back severely than to let the disease spread. Plan to avoid repeated problems by dividing the perennials, replanting them farther apart, and pruning them early in the season so they don't grow so tall and floppy again. Crowded shrubs are also subject to fungal problems in the summer and should be pruned so that air can flow around them.

Glossary

Amendments. Organic or mineral materials such as peat moss, perlite, or compost that are used to improve the soil.

Annual. A plant that germinates, grows, flowers, produces seeds, and dies in the course of a single growing season; a plant that is treated like an annual and grown for a single season's display.

Antitranspirant. A substance sprayed on the stems and leaves of evergreen plants to protect them from water loss caused by winter winds.

Balled-and-burlapped. Describes a tree or shrub dug out of the ground with a ball of soil intact around the roots, the ball then wrapped in burlap or other material and tied for transport.

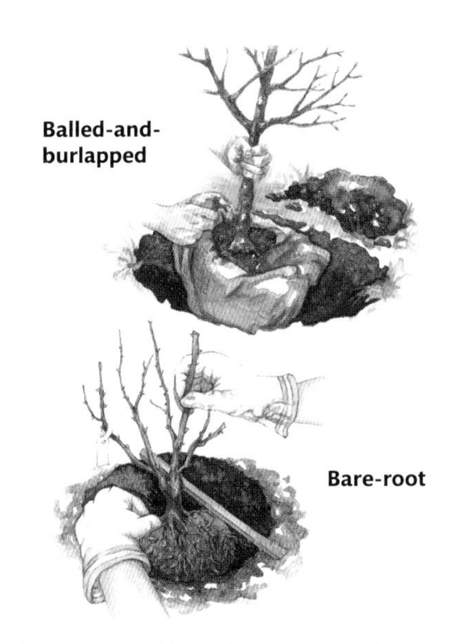

Bare-root. Describes a plant dug out of the ground and then shaken or washed to remove the soil from the roots.

Compound leaf. A leaf with two or more leaflets branching off a single stalk.

Container-grown. Describes a plant raised in a pot that is removed before planting.

Crown. That part of a plant where the roots and stem meet, usually at soil level.

Cultivar. A cultivated variety of a plant, often bred or selected for some special trait such as double flowers, compact growth, cold hardiness, or disease resistance.

Deadheading. Removing old flowers during the growing season to prevent seed formation and to encourage the development of new flowers.

Deciduous. Describes a tree, shrub, or vine that drops its leaves in winter.

Division. Propagation of a plant by separating it into two or more pieces, each of which has at least one bud and some roots. Used mostly for perennials, grasses, ferns, and bulbs.

Drainage. The movement of water down through the soil. With good drainage, water disappears from a planting hole in just a few hours. If water remains standing overnight, the drainage is poor.

Drip line. An imaginary line on the soil around a tree that mirrors the circumference of the canopy above. Many of the tree's roots are found in this area.

Dry-laid. Describes a masonry path or wall that is installed without mortar.

Edging. A shallow trench or physical barrier of steel, plastic, brick, or boards used to define the border between a flower bed and adjacent turf or path.

Espalier. The training of a plant to grow flat along wires, often against a wall or framework. A plant so trained may be called an "espalier."

Exposure. The intensity, duration, and variation in sun, wind, and temperature that characterize any particular site.

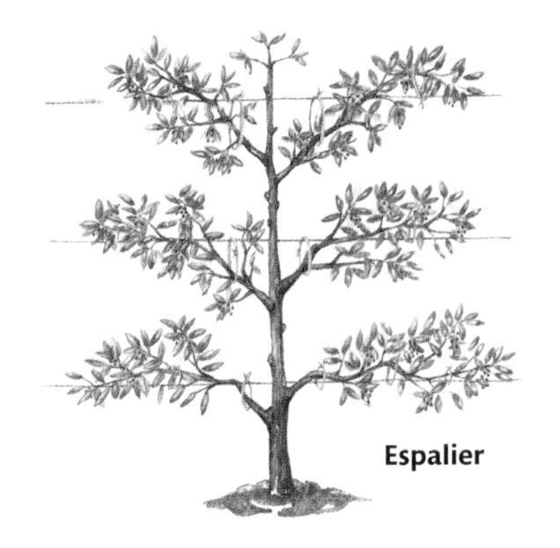

Feeder roots. Slender branching roots that spread close to the soil surface and absorb most of the nutrients for a tree or shrub.

Formal. Describes a style of landscaping that features symmetrical layouts, with beds and walks related to adjacent buildings, and often with plants sheared to geometric or other shapes.

Foundation planting. Traditionally, a narrow border of evergreen shrubs planted around the foundation of a house. Contemporary foundation plantings often include deciduous shrubs, grasses, perennials, and other plants as well.

Frost heaving. A disturbance or uplifting of soil, pavement, or plants caused when moisture in the soil freezes and expands.

Full shade. Describes a site that receives no direct sun during the growing season.

Full sun. Describes a site that receives at least eight hours of direct sun each day during the growing season.

Garden soil. Soil specially prepared for planting to make it loose enough for roots and water to penetrate easily. Usually requires digging or tilling and the addition of some organic matter.

Grade. The degree and direction of slope on a piece of ground.

Ground cover. A plant such as ivy, liriope, or juniper used to cover the soil and form a continuous low mass of foliage. Often used as a durable substitute for turfgrass.

Habit. The characteristic shape or form of a plant, such as upright, spreading, or rounded.

Hardiness. A plant's ability to survive the winter without protection from the cold.

Hardiness zone. A geographic region where the coldest temperature in an average winter falls within a certain range, such as between 0° and -10°F.

Hardscape. Parts of a landscape constructed from materials other than plants, such as walks, walls, and trellises made of wood, stone, or other materials.

Herbaceous. Describes plants that have soft stems like a herb that die back to the ground during winter. They start into new growth the following spring. They may be perennial or grow well for several years.

Herbicide. A chemical used to kill plants. Preemergent herbicides are used to kill weed seeds as they sprout, and thus to prevent weed growth. Postemergent herbicides kill plants that are already growing.

Hybrid. A plant resulting from a cross between two parents that belong to different varieties, species, or genera.

Interplant. To combine plants with different bloom times or growth habits, making it possible to fit more plants in a bed, thus prolonging the bed's appeal.

Invasive. Describes a plant that spreads quickly, usually by runners, or self-seeding, and mixes with or dominates adjacent plantings.

Landscape fabric. A synthetic fabric, sometimes water-permeable, spread under paths or mulch to serve as a weed barrier.

Lime, limestone. White mineral compounds used to combat soil acidity and to supply calcium for plant growth.

Loam. An ideal soil for gardening, containing plenty of organic matter and a balanced range of small to large mineral particles.

Microclimate. Local conditions of shade, exposure, wind, drainage, and other factors that affect plant growth at any particular site.

Mowing strip. A row of bricks or paving stones set flush with the soil around the edge of a bed, and wide enough to support one wheel of the lawnmower.

Mulch. A layer of bark, peat moss, compost, shredded leaves, hay or straw, lawn clippings, gravel, paper, plastic, or other material, spread over the soil around the base of plants. During the growing season, a mulch can help retard evaporation, inhibit weeds, and moderate soil temperature. In the winter, a mulch of evergreen boughs, coarse hay, or leaves is used to protect plants from freezing and heaving.

Native. Describes a plant that occurs naturally in a particular region and was not introduced from some other area.

Nutrients. Nitrogen, phosphorus, potassium, calcium, magnesium, sulfur, iron, and other elements needed by growing plants. Nutrients are supplied by the minerals and organic matter in the soil and by fertilizers.

Organic matter. Plant and animal residues such as leaves, trimmings, and manure in various stages of decomposition.

Peat moss. Partially decomposed mosses and sedges, mined from boggy areas and used to improve garden soil or to prepare potting soil.

Perennial. A plant that lives for a number of years, generally flowering each year. By "perennial," gardeners usually mean "herbaceous perennial," although woody plants such as vines, shrubs, and trees are also perennial.

pH. Indicates the acidity or alkalinity of a soil sample. Acid soil has a pH of less than 7; alkaline or sweet soil has a pH of more than 7. Neutral soil has a pH of about 7.

Pressure-treated lumber. Softwood lumber treated with chemicals that protect it from decay.

Propagate. To produce new plants by sowing seeds, rooting cuttings, dividing plant parts, layering, grafting, or other means.

Retaining wall. A wall built to stabilize a slope and keep soil from sliding or eroding downhill.

Rhizome. A horizontal underground stem, often swollen into a storage organ. Both roots and shoots emerge from rhizomes. Rhizomes generally branch as they creep along and can be divided to make new plants.

Root-ball. The mass of soil and roots dug with a plant when it is removed from the ground; the soil and roots of a plant grown in a container.

Rosette. A low, flat cluster of leaves resembling the petals of a rose.

Selective pruning. Using pruning shears to remove or cut back individual shoots, in order to refine the shape of a shrub, maintain its vigor, or limit its size.

Severe pruning. Using pruning shears or loppers to cut away most of a shrub's top growth, leaving short stubs or a gnarly trunk.

Shearing. Using hedge shears or an electric hedge trimmer to shape the surface of a shrub, hedge, or tree and produce a smooth, solid mass of greenery.

Specimen plant. A plant displayed alone in a prominent position.

Spike. An elongated flower cluster, with individual flowers borne on very short stalks or attached directly to the main stem.

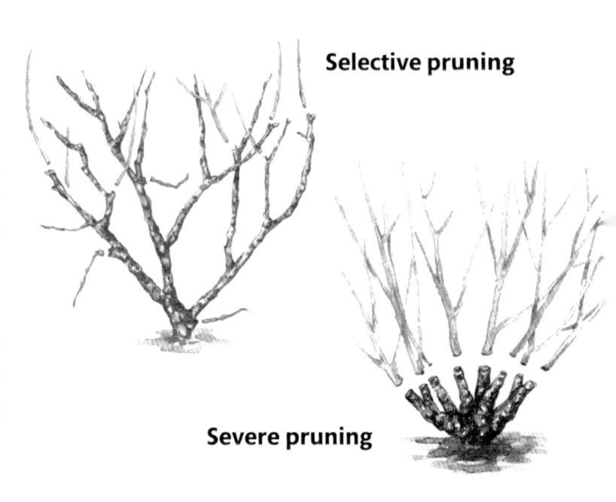

Standard. A plant trained to grow a round bushy head of branches atop a single upright stem.

Taproot. A main root; usually long, plump, and roundish with lateral roots growing from the sides. It provides stability for the plant and takes in water. Dandelions are the best-known example.

Transpiration. Plants lose water through openings on the leaf cell surfaces called stomata. Water evaporates off the plants as part of the complete water system of a plant, encouraging moisture to be drawn up from the roots.

Tender. Describes a plant that is damaged by cold weather.

Underplanting. Growing short plants, such as ground covers, under a taller plant, such as a shrub.

Variegated. Describes foliage that is marked, striped, or blotched with color other than green.

Index

NOTE: Page numbers in ***bold italic*** *refer to photos.*

C

D

E

I

J

K

L

M

S

T

Photo Credits

Front Cover: *main image* Onepony/Dreams-time.com; *top left* Dency Kane; *top right* Jerry Pavia

Back Cover: *left* Richard Gunion/Dreamstime.com; *right* Onepony/Dreamstime.com

page 1: Saxon Holt

page 7: Charles Mann

pages 18–19: Richard Gunion/Dreamstime.com

page 23: *top right* Saxon Holt; *middle right* Charles Mann; *bottom right* Rita Buchanan; *bottom left* Ollga P/Shutterstock.com; *top left* Dency Kane

page 29: *top both* Galen Gates; *middle left* Charles Mann; *middle & bottom right* Lauren Springer Ogden; *bottom left* Saxon Holt

page 32: *top right* Charles Mann; *middle right* Saxon Holt; *bottom right* Galen Gates; *bottom left* Rita Buchanan; *middle left* Jerry Pavia

page 39: *top left* Charles Mann; *top right & middle right* Rita Buchanan; *bottom right,* center & *middle left both* Galen Gates; *bottom left* Karen Bussolini

page 42: *top left* Karen Bussolini; *top right & middle right* Charles Mann; *bottom both* Jerry Pavia

page 46: *top left* Lauren Springer Ogden; *top right* Charles Mann; *middle right & bottom left* Rick Mastelli; *bottom right* Jerry Pavia; *center* Saxon Holt; *middle left* Rita Buchanan

page 51: *top, middle left & bottom left* Charles Mann; *middle right* Lauren Springer Ogden; *bottom right* Rita Buchanan

page 55: *top & bottom right* Karen Bussolini; *middle right* Carole Ottesen; *bottom left* Galen Gates; *middle left* Jerry Pavia; *center* Charles Mann

page 58: *top right* Carole Ottesen; *middle right & top left* Charles Mann; *bottom right* Lauren Springer Ogden; *bottom left* Galen Gates; *middle left* Jerry Pavia

page 64: *top both* Galen Gates; *middle right & middle left* Jerry Pavia; *bottom right* Rita Buchanan; *bottom left* Charles Mann; *center* Saxon Holt

page 69: *top left & bottom both* Galen Gates; *top right, middle left & center* Saxon Holt; *middle right* Rita Buchanan

page 73: *top middle & top right* Charles Mann; *bottom right* Galen Gates; *top & bottom left* Rita Buchanan

page 77: *top right* Saxon Holt; *middle right* Galen Gates; *bottom both* Lauren Springer Ogden; *middle left* Charles Mann; *top left* Carole Ottesen

page 83: *top all & bottom right* Saxon Holt; *middle right & bottom left* Jerry Pavia; *center* Galen Gates

page 87: *top right* Saxon Holt; *top middle right* Rick Mastelli; *bottom middle right* Galen Gates; *bottom right* Charles Mann; *bottom left* Jerry Pavia; *top left* Carole Ottesen

page 90: *top right & middle right* Saxon Holt; *bottom both* Rita Buchanan; *middle left* Galen Gates; *top left* Charles Mann

page 97: *top right* Ruth Rogers Clausen; *bottom right* Jerry Pavia; *bottom left* Galen Gates; *middle left & center* Charles Mann; *top left* Saxon Holt

page 101: *top right, bottom middle* Charles Mann; *middle right* Jerry Pavia; *bottom right, bottom* left, *top left* Rita Buchanan; *top middle* Galen Gates

page 105: *top & bottom right* Charles Mann; *middle right & bottom left* Jerry Pavia; *top left* Lauren Springer Ogden

page 109: *top right & middle left* Karen Bussolini; *middle right* Charles Mann; *bottom right & top left* Jerry Pavia; *bottom left* Carole Ottesen

page 113: *top right & bottom left* Jerry Pavia; *middle right* Galen Gates; *bottom right* Karen Bussolini; *top left* Rita Buchanan

page 117: *top right* Rita Buchanan; *bottom right* Saxon Holt; *bottom middle* Carole Ottesen; *bottom left* Jerry Pavia; *middle left* Elena Blokhina/Shutterstock.com; *top left* Karen Bussolini; *center* Charles Mann

page 122: *top* Jerry Pavia; *top middle right* Charles Mann; *bottom middle right & bottom both* Galen Gates; *top left* Michael Dirr

page 127: *top, bottom middle right & bottom left* Galen Gates; *top middle right* Lilihu/Dreams-time.com; *middle left & bottom right* Jerry Pavia

pages 128–129: Onepony/Dreamstime.com

page 131: Galen Gates

page 132: *top* Rita Buchanan; *bottom* Galen Gates

page 133: Galen Gates

page 134: *top* Rita Buchanan; *bottom* Galen Gates

page 135: *top left* Elena Blokhina/Shutterstock.com; *top right* Charles Mann; *middle right* Galen Gates; *bottom* Rita Buchanan

page 137: *top* Jerry Pavia; *bottom* Galen Gates

page 138: Charles Mann

page 140: Rick Mastelli

page 141: *top right* Jerry Pavia; *bottom both* Rita Buchanan

page 142: Jill Lang/Dreamstime.com

page 143: Rita Buchanan

page 144: *top* Charles Mann; *bottom* Galen Gates

page 145: Galen Gates

page 146: *top* Saxon Holt; *bottom* both Jerry Pavia

page 148: *left* Karen Bussolini; *right* Galen Gates

page 149: *left* Jerry Pavia; *middle* Saxon Holt; *right* Dency Kane

page 150: Saxon Holt

pages 151–152: *both* Jerry Pavia

page 153: Rick Mastelli

pages 154–155: Onepony/Dreamstime.com